THE HANDBOOK OF STOCK INDEX FUTURES AND OPTIONS

THE HANDBOOK OF STOCK INDEX FUTURES AND OPTIONS

Edited by

Frank J. Fabozzi

and

Gregory M. Kipnis

DOW JONES-IRWIN
Homewood, Illinois 60430

© RICHARD D. IRWIN, INC., 1989

Dow Jones-Irwin is a trademark of Dow Jones & Company, Inc.

This publication is designed to provide accurate and
authoritative information in regard to the subject matter
covered. It is sold with the understanding that neither the
author nor the publisher is engaged in rendering legal, accounting,
or other professional service. If legal advice or other expert
assistance is required, the services of a competent
professional person should be sought.

From a Declaration of Principles jointly adopted by a Committee
of the American Bar Association and a Committee of Publishers.

Project editor: Karen Smith
Production manager: Carma W. Fazio
Compositor: Weimer Typesetting Co., Inc.
Typeface: 11/13 Times Roman
Printer: Arcata Graphics/Kingsport

LIBRARY OF CONGRESS
Library of Congress Cataloging-in-Publication Data

The Handbook of stock index futures and options / edited by Frank J.
Fabozzi and Gregory M. Kipnis.
    p. cm.
    Includes index.
    ISBN 1-556-23104-0
    1. Stock index futures. 2. Options (Finance) I. Fabozzi, Frank
J. II. Kipnis, Gregory M.
HG6043.H36 1989
332.63'222–dc19   88–17784
                                                   CIP

Printed in the United States of America
1 2 3 4 5 6 7 8 9 0 K 5 4 3 2 1 0 9 8

FJF's corner
    To my sister, Lucy

GMK's corner
    To my tolerant wife, Claire,
    and my patient children,
    Christine and Pascale

CONTRIBUTORS

Robert D. Arnott, President and Chief Investment Officer, *First Quadrant Corporation*

W. Gordon Binns, Jr., Chairman of the Committee on Investment of Employee Benefit Assets (CIEBA), *Financial Executives Institute*

Keith C. Brown, Ph.D., Assistant Professor of Finance, Graduate School of Business, *University of Texas at Austin*

B. Thomas Byrne, Jr., J.D., Vice President, *Shearson Lehman Hutton Inc.*

Don M. Chance, Ph.D., C.F.A., Associate Professor of Finance, *Virginia Polytechnic Institute and State University*

Roger G. Clarke, Ph.D., Managing Partner and Chief Investment Officer, *TSA Capital Management*

Bruce M. Collins, Ph.D., Vice President, Equity Arbitrage Group, Index Products Research, *Shearson Lehman Hutton Inc.*

Ravi E. Dattatreya, Ph.D., Director, Financial Strategies Group, *Prudential Bache Capital Funding*

Frank J. Fabozzi, Ph.D., C.F.A., Visiting Professor of Finance, Sloan School of Management, *Massachusetts Institute of Technology*

T. Dessa Fabozzi, Ph.D., Senior Security Analyst, Financial Strategies Group, *Merrill Lynch Capital Markets*

Bruce D. Fielitz, Ph.D. Research Professor of Finance, *Georgia State University*

Crisostomo B. Garcia, Ph.D., Professor of Management Science, Graduate School of Business, *University of Chicago*

Gary L. Gastineau, Vice President, *Salomon Brother Inc*

Gerald D. Gay, Ph.D., Associate Professor of Finance, *Georgia State University*

Floyd J. Gould, Ph.D., Hobart W. Williams Professor of Applied Mathematics and Management Science, Graduate School of Business, *University of Chicago*

H. Nicholas Hanson, Ph.D., Vice President, *Salomon Brothers Inc*

Joanne M. Hill, Ph.D., Vice President, *PaineWebber*

Jonathan C. Jankus, Vice President, *Kidder, Peabody & Co., Inc.*

Donald B. Keim, Ph.D., Associate Professor, Wharton School, *University of Pennsylvania*

Gregory M. Kipnis, Principal, *Morgan Stanley & Co., Inc.*

Stanley J. Kon, Ph.D., Professor of Finance, Graduate School of Business Administration, *University of Michigan*

Robert W. Kopprasch, Ph.D., C.F.A., Vice President, *Goldman Sachs & Company*

Hayne Leland, Ph.D. Professor of Finance, *University of California, Berkeley;* and Director, *Leland, O'Brien and Rubinstein Associates*

Donald L. Luskin, Senior Vice President, *Wells Fargo Investment Advisors*

Albert Madansky, Ph.D., Professor of Business Administration, *University of Chicago*

Benjamin S. Neuhausen, C.P.A., Partner, *Arthur Andersen & Co.*

Edgar E. Peters, Portfolio Manager, Structured Investment Products Division, *The Boston Company, Inc.*

David T. Posen, First Vice President, Equity Arbitrage Group, *Shearson Lehman Hutton Inc.*

James A. Schmidt, Vice President, Equity Arbitrage Group, *Shearson Lehman Hutton Inc.*

Michael Smirlock, Ph.D., Vice President, *Franklin Savings Bank*; and Associate Professor, Wharton School, *University of Pennsylvania*

Meir Statman, Ph.D., Associate Professor of Finance and Chairman, Department of Finance, Leavey School of Business and Administration, *Santa Clara University*

Steve Tsang, Ph.D., Vice President, *Prudential Bache*

Benjamin Wolkowitz, Ph.D., Principal, *Morgan Stanley & Co., Inc.*

Mark A. Zurack, C.F.A., Vice President, *Goldman Sachs & Company*

CONTENTS

CHAPTER 1

INTRODUCTION

Frank J. Fabozzi, Ph.D., C.F.A.
Visiting Professor of Finance
Sloan School of Management
Massachusetts Institute of Technology

Gregory M. Kipnis
Principal
Morgan Stanley & Co. Inc.

Stock index futures and options have constructively and dramatically changed the equity investment process and the way capital markets work. The events leading up to and including the October 19, 1987, market break and the still evolving regulatory and market responses underscore the respect for and the importance of the new derivative market instruments. The speed with which investors could now assert their will had been greatly underestimated—but no more so than the capacity for the existing market structure to stand up under such a load was *over*estimated.

This book was written for the most part before the events of October 19, 1987. Nonetheless, the ideas, strategies and insights are still relevant for the individual and the institutional investor—perhaps even more so as the playing field is levelled and broadened for all market participants. More about that later.

Since the inception of stock index futures contracts in February 1982, trading activity has grown rapidly. Stock index futures have been a success, and the rapid climb in trading volume relative to the New York Stock Exchange has been especially impressive. Futures trading in the three major stock index futures contracts (Standard & Poor's 500 Composite Index, New York Stock Exchange Composite Index, and Value Line Average Index), expressed on a dollar value basis, had surpassed the volume of trading on the NYSE by March 1983. Since then, trading of stock index futures (the three major contracts and other contracts added in the interim, most notably the Major Market Index) has exceeded NYSE volume on a regular basis—by 1987 it was frequently double the value of the NYSE trading.

The activity in the cash-settled options on stock indexes has even surpassed the success of stock index futures. Since the first cash-settled options on the S&P 100 (OEX) stock index commenced in March 1983, trading volume exploded, reaching about 20 percent of all options' daily volume within one year. Currently, the total put-and-call volume for all cash-settled broad- and narrow-based index options routinely accounts for better than 50 percent of the total volume traded on all option exchanges.

The great popularity of index options and futures contracts may be explained by many factors. First, there is enormous interest in the equity markets. Furthermore, investors perceive themselves as having a correct opinion on the probable direction of the market more often than they are certain about which stocks to buy or sell. The stock index options and index futures contracts have become a viable alternative means to taking positions based on the direction of market moves. Second, the economic, financial and political information which tends to affect stock market prices is widely disseminated by the news media daily, and the general public normally feels in a good position to evaluate general market conditions. Third, institutions and individuals holding large stock portfolios can use the index products as a timing device to either protect their cash values, accelerate market entry, or enhance returns. Fourth, professional arbitrageurs often use the stock index options and index futures contracts to create synthetic stock and money-market positions, depending on relative price levels, to profit from market inefficiencies. Fifth, options and futures contracts are leveraged investments, which involve high financial risks; however, the potential profitability, to a correct futures or options position, could be very rewarding on a leveraged basis.

STOCK INDEX OPTIONS AND FUTURES CONTRACTS DEFINED

Stock index options and futures contracts are highly leveraged investment instruments. A "call" option conveys to the buyer the right to purchase a specific stock index, at a specific strike price, during a specific period of time. A "put" option conveys to the buyer the right to sell a specific stock index, at a specific strike price, during a specific period of time. In both cases, the seller (writer) of an option assumes the contract obligations to the buyer, and for this receives a fee, i.e., the option premium. Thus, the potential loss to the option buyer is limited to the entire premium paid, while the potential gain is not limited. This limited liability feature of the option contract offers the buyer the great benefit of staying power.

On the other hand, the potential profit for the option writer is limited only to the premium received, while the potential loss is unlimited. Since the option contract represents the right to buy and sell, the holder may exercise the right prior to contract maturity whenever market conditions warrant such an action, such as getting out of a thinly traded market.

A futures contract is an agreement to buy or to sell a specific stock index at a market-determined price at the end of a specific period of time. Thus, unlike an option contract, the potential gains and losses for both a futures buyer and a seller are unlimited. Because a futures contract represents only an agreement to buy or to sell, neither the buyer nor the seller has the right to exercise the contract prior to the time specified in the contract, but he can offset his position anytime through trading. A further difference is that futures are marked-to-the market daily and the gains, or losses, are settled up in cash each day. Thus, the buyer or seller of futures must have short-term liquidity to retain his position.

BATTLE OF TITANS—THE CASH VERSUS THE FUTURES MARKETS

The introduction of stock index futures and options was destined to ultimately bring about a collision between the stock market and the derivatives markets as they fought for primacy in the setting of prices. In the long history of the futures markets, a derivative instrument has never been introduced in the presence of another efficient, continuously traded, central auction market. The only close comparisons in recent history are the gold, bonds, foreign exchange, and fixed income markets. Though very large, each is basically an "upstairs" dealer market and one never knew precisely where the market was. The futures markets offered a centralized, competitive marketplace that led to greater overall efficiency in price setting. Thus, during normal trading hours the futures markets essentially became the "tape," or reference point, for determining cash market prices in each case.

The regulatory environment may be changed in the aftermath of the market collapse of October 19, 1987, and the outcome is not known, but it was essentially a mismatch from the beginning. The index futures market had three clear advantages in becoming the dominant price setter: (1) macro efficiency in adjusting exposure and prices swiftly without need to address the micro price structure of underlying stock prices; (2) greater leverage—a 5–10 percent good faith deposit for index futures versus 25–50 percent margin rates for straight equities; and (3) lower overall transactions costs, by roughly one tenth, of futures over equities (the comparison includes commissions and bid/ask slippage).

LOOKING AHEAD AND ABROAD
BY LOOKING BACKWARD

Risk, opportunities, and innovative responses never cease, and the interplay of these forces dominates our daily lives and institutions. The futures industry has a long and successful history of placing itself at the intersection of risk and opportunity and generating an innovative response. A case can readily be made that collectively, the futures exchanges have been one of the major agents of positive change in every sector of the U.S. economy where they have innovated. For the first 125 years, futures exchanges concerned themselves with inventing capital market instruments to make what economists call the "real sector" of the economy more price efficient—especially in the agricultural and industrial sectors. Farmers could plan better and get more credit because they could hedge, thus "fixing" the selling price of their crop. In a number of economic sectors, the terms for inventory loans were a lot easier if the commodity was well hedged. The advent of futures contracts was often instrumental in converting monopolistic and oligopolistic markets into competitive markets. This was true in the case of grain, gold, and copper. In the past 15 years, the creative burst extended itself into the financial sectors, including currency, fixed income, the money market, and the equities markets. In 1987 alone, new equity index products have been proposed and introduced such as the Russell and Institutional Investor indexes.

The positive benefits have gone beyond U.S. borders. For many world-traded commodities, the world price has become transparent and competitively set on U.S. exchanges. Tropical commodities, such as sugar, coffee, and cocoa—as well as petroleum prices—come to mind.

The same trend is now emerging for financial futures as international stock index futures are being innovated here and in such countries as Japan, United Kingdom, the Netherlands, Canada, and Singapore. Index futures have an even greater economic advantage internationally, particularly with respect to transactions costs and macro-price efficiency. United States investors can invest internationally without worrying about stock selection; exchange risk management; and execution, clearance, and settlement costs. Hence, the proposed EAFE (Europe, Australia, and Far East) Index and other international indexes, to be traded in the United States, hold great appeal.

GROWING INTEGRATION

As the cross impacts between futures and underlying markets reveal previously invisible structural flaws, the need for greater coupling between exchanges and regulatory bodies increases to ensure mutually profitable survival and stability. Index futures propagated the more rapid growth in index and extended index funds, which in turn induced new trading accommodations at block desks to facilitate whole programs simultaneously rather than as piecemeal stock transactions. Portfolio insurance and arbitrage trading lead to further innovations in trading tactics and technology, such as "sunshine" trading and the New York Stock Exchange's SuperDot system. Unavoidably, this would lead to closer coordination between the more forward-looking exchanges and service vendors to head off problems and create new trading technologies. The NYSE and CME worked closely to minimize expiration volatility. The CME and Reuters are working on an after-hours automated futures execution system, and Instinet and Posit are developing an alternative mechanism for crossing portfolios and stocks at closing prices (but after the NYSE close) or other negotiated prices to further reduce the market impact of sizable trades.

Ultimately, the regulatory bodies, including the Fed, SEC, CFTC, and Congress, will harmonize rules and regulations to level the playing field for traders and investors with regard to leverage and trading practices and to protect investors and the financial system from undue risk.

REGULATION AND BLACK MONDAY

This book is a testament, by a broad cross section of the investment and academic community, to the view that derivative equity index instruments have great logic and value in the marketplace. The very existence of these instruments is a clear expression of legitimate need by legitimate marketplace participants. The contributed analyses to this book predate the market crisis of October 19–20, 1987; thus the individual authors make no attempt to respond to any of the issues raised by these market events and the recommendations of the recent Katzenbach report[1] and the Brady Commission report[2] in particular.

It is the view of the editors of this book that the problems that were exposed by selected market events in recent years, especially the crisis of October 19–20, 1987, are more problems of "engineering" than of moral philosophy. To illustrate our point we have in

---

[1] Nicholas deB. Katzenbach, *An Overview of Program Trading and Its Impact on Current Market Practices,* a study commissioned by the New York Stock Exchange (New York: NYSE, December 21, 1987).

[2] Nicholas F. Brady et. al., *Report of the Presidential Task Force on Market Mechanisms* (Washington, D.C.: U.S. Government Printing Office, January 1988).

mind a metaphor that, although not exactly analogous, at least sorts out the basic issues into compact form. This metaphor likens the current problems (and their solutions) of the organized exchanges to the problems of the New Jersey Turnpike.

The New Jersey Turnpike is a key transportation link between the greater metropolitan area of the New York City and the Baltimore–Washington region. One would never dream of permanently closing down the highway because of engineering deficiencies or because some of the drivers violated the law. Such engineering questions as the width of the lanes, grades, and safety details were resolved at inception, based on projections of likely traffic loads, speeds, and vehicle sizes. With the passage of time, advances in technology, regulatory changes, and mother nature, many of the original assumptions are now inappropriate. If an accident occurs on a fog-bound night, it would be unconscionable not to temporarily shut down the highway, detour traffic, and lower speeds, else hundreds of cars would pile up. That is an obvious engineering fix to a structural problem. But what about the problem caused by larger trucks and faster driving? The original lane widths may not be sufficient to provide a large enough safety zone buffer between lanes, given the larger, faster-moving trailer trucks. Some engineering solutions could be lowered speeds, widened lanes, more lanes, or restricted-use lanes. What if speeders, cigarette smugglers, or drug dealers routinely use the N.J. Turnpike? Here again, a well-researched solution might include radar traps, spot inspections, or more computer-assisted surveillance.

Of all of the solutions which could be proposed, one which never logically would surface is the idea of terminating the highway itself as a way of ending accidents, improving safety, or reducing crime! Engineering-based thinking, not moral philosophy, would be the logical way to put things right.

The problems that currently beset the equity and futures exchanges were not caused by immoral or unethical behavior (though it is quite possible some is present) but by structural defects in exchange mechanisms and regulations which were revealed by a major change in fundamentals. The motivations behind transactions should not be the basis for formulating new rules and regulations. Changes should be promulgated to fix defects and imbalances, not to impair or shut down exchanges.

SECTION 1

BACKGROUND INFORMATION

CHAPTER 2

RISK-RETURN CHARACTERISTICS OF STOCK INDEX FUTURES AND OPTIONS

Don M. Chance, Ph.D., C.F.A.
Associate Professor of Finance
Virginia Polytechnic Institute and State University

In this chapter we will explore the risk-return characteristics of stock index futures and options. Our discussion encompasses three instruments: stock index options, stock index futures, and options on stock index futures. These instruments were created to manage the risk of equity portfolios. It is important to understand not only how to use them but to also understand their economic purpose in our financial market system. Therefore this chapter examines the concept of risk in our economy and financial system, then discusses some basic concepts germane to each instrument. We will be careful to identify the similarities and differences of the instruments, particularly the two types of options. We will then examine relationships that exist between the instrument price and the underlying index, followed by a look at the basic strategies used in stock index futures and options trading. The chapter concludes with a discussion of some special considerations faced in trading these instruments.

THE CONCEPT OF RISK

The capitalist economic system is characterized by a growing quantity of tangible and intangible assets. These assets are typically organized into business firms that combine the assets to produce goods and services. These business units are formed by pooling the capital of those wanting to participate in the profitability of the economy. The uncertainty of the performance of the business in generating marketable goods and services produces risk which is assumed by the owners. Shareholders are the risk-takers that accept the basic risk of the assets in the economy.

If the firm is large enough, its shares may trade in a financial market, which is an organized system designed for the inexpensive transfer of ownership from one party to another. The price of a share reflects the value and risk of the assets owned by the firm. Thus, the stock market reflects the basic risk of the economy. In our rapidly expanding economy, the assumption of risk creates frequent opportunities for increasing the wealth of the owners of the shares; however, wealth can be lost by the mismanagement of the underlying assets. That is the nature of risk.

Financial markets offer numerous opportunities for the efficient management of risk. For example, the returns on securities are not perfectly correlated; therefore, they can be combined and diversified into portfolios to reduce risk. Securities differ in their degrees of risk, and a low-risk security (such as a Treasury bill) can be combined with a high-risk security (such as a speculative stock) to bring the average risk to a more desirable level. For those with a need to increase risk, short selling and margin trading offer such opportunities.

Exchange-traded options on individual stocks were created in 1973 and provided the first step toward increasing the equity risk management opportunities. Prior to this there were no contractual instruments to help manage risk (except the old over-the-counter options and a limited forward market in a few types of securities). About 10 years later, index options and futures products were introduced, and they opened up a panorama of means for equity investors to modify risk.

Stock index futures and options are devices for the efficient management and transfer of risk. The markets themselves are not a source of risk. All of the gains earned by any single participant are losses incurred by some other participant. Thus, unlike the stock and bond markets, these markets do not create and destroy wealth. Instead, they inexpensively transfer risk from those who do not want it to those who do want it.

Consider an equity portfolio manager facing an unusually volatile market. The manager might want to temporarily lower the risk of the portfolio until the outlook is more stable, but stock and bond markets are not set up to easily modify risk levels. It may be necessary to execute a large number of transactions which, depending on the size of the portfolio, could have a significant market impact, and incur substantial transaction costs. It would be a better alternative to sell either call options or futures contracts or buy put options. A specific number of contracts can be identified as the optimum and the transaction is likely to be easily absorbed by the market with no price impact. When the manager decides that the risk needs to be increased, the contracts can be closed out in the market. The cost of such trading will be negligible relative to the size of the portfolio.

In this type of transaction, the portfolio manager is executing a hedge. A hedge begins with someone holding a risky position. Those who assume risk expect to earn a risk premium—an additional expected return commensurate with the level of risk. When the hedge is placed, the risk premium is transferred to someone taking the opposite position in the options or futures market. For example, say the portfolio manager hedges by selling a futures contract to a futures trader (a speculator who expects to make an additional return commensurate with the risk). The risk premium then passes from the portfolio manager to the futures trader.

Futures and options markets serve our economy by assuming risk that is not wanted by holders of stock and bond portfolios. Formerly limited to agricultural markets, the creation of stock index futures and options has brought the futures and options markets of Chicago closer to the stock markets of New York. It's no wonder that these instruments have been called "pin-striped pork bellies."

SOME BASIC CONCEPTS OF STOCK INDEX FUTURES AND OPTIONS

In this section we will introduce some fundamentals necessary for the study of stock index futures and options. We will take each of the three instruments separately. The following notation will facilitate the discussion:

I = Value of the index today
I^* = Value of the index at expiration
F = Price of the futures contract today
F^* = Price of the futures contract at expiration
C = Price today of a call option on the index
P = Price today of a put option on the index
c = Price today of a call option on the futures
p = Price today of a put option on the futures
E = Exercise price of an option
r = Risk-free rate
T = Time to expiration

Note that because the futures contract is settled in cash, $F^* = I^*$. Let us begin with options on stock indexes.

Options on Stock Indexes

Premium. The premium is the price of the option—the amount of money paid up front by the buyer for the granting of the option privilege. The money goes to the writer, but during the life of the contract, the clearinghouse holds the premium and an additional sum of money, the margin, posted by the writer. The premium is negotiated by the buyer and seller of the option on the floor of the exchange.

Intrinsic Value. The intrinsic value is the minimum value of the option. To understand intrinsic value, first consider the terms *in-the-money* and *out-of-the-money*. For a call option, in-the-money means that the index exceeds the exercise price. For a put option, in-the-money means that the exercise price exceeds the index. Out-of-the-money means that the exercise price exceeds the index for a call and the index exceeds the exercise price for a put.

Out-of-the-money options would never be exercised. The exercise of an in-the-money call results in the holder receiving $I - E$ and the exercise of an in-the-money put pays the holder $E - I$. The intrinsic value is defined as

$$\text{Intrinsic value of a call} = \text{Max}\ (0,\ I - E)$$
$$\text{Intrinsic value of a put} = \text{Max}\ (0,\ E - I)$$

The term *Max* means to take the maximum of the two expressions in parentheses, zero for out-of-the-money options or $I - E$ for an in-the-money call and $E - I$ for an in-the-money put. Thus, the intrinsic value defines a floor or minimum value of the option.

Time Value.   The actual price of an index option will probably exceed its intrinsic value because buyers of the option are willing to pay an additional amount for the likelihood that the index will move further. This additional amount is called the "time value." To be precise, time value is defined as

$$\text{Time value of a call} = C - \text{Max}\ (0, I - E)$$
$$\text{Time value of a put} = P - \text{Max}\ (0, E - I)$$

The time value will reflect the speculative attraction of the option and will be greater the longer the time to expiration. As expiration approaches, the time value will decrease—this is the *time value decay*. At expiration there will be no time value, and the option will sell for its intrinsic value. Volatility is another factor that greatly affects the time value.

Volatility.   One of the most important considerations in determining the price of the option is the volatility of the return on the underlying index. Greater volatility makes the option more valuable. For example, the holder of a call on an index wants the market to be volatile because this increases the chance that it will expire in-the-money. It also increases the chance that it will expire out-of-the-money, but if it expires out-of-the-money, the holder of the call will not care how far out-of-the-money it is. The loss incurred by the holder of an out-of-the-money call will be the same regardless of how low the index is. Similar arguments can be made for a put.

For options on individual stocks, volatility can vary from high volatility speculative stocks to low volatility blue-chips. Because the market as a whole is diversified, the volatility of an index will be lower than the average volatility of its component stocks. Nonetheless, the index volatility can be highly unstable.

Exercise.   Index options are exercised by cash settlement. The holder of the call is paid the amount $I - E$; the holder of the put is paid $E - I$, with the money coming from the writer. Most index options have American-style exercise—they can be exercised any day up through the expiration day. However, the S&P 500 index option has a European-style exercise—it can only be exercised on the expiration day.

Sometimes it is optimal to exercise American-style index options prior to expiration, but we will discuss this point later.

Dividends.   Options do not pay dividends, and the holders of options are not entitled to receive dividends unless the option is exercised before the stock goes ex-dividend. However, dividends on the stocks in the index will be a factor in pricing the option. Quarterly stock dividends are not necessarily paid on the same quarterly dates. This gives the stock indexes a fairly continuous stream of dividend payments with occasional large dividends every three months. This can affect the decision of whether to exercise the option early.

Stock Index Futures

The Futures Price.   The futures price is unlike the price of any other instrument. A stock price is the present value of what the owner expects to receive—specifically the dividends. An option price reflects what the owner expects to earn off of the option. A futures price is neither of these. A futures contract is a contractual agreement to trade at a future date at the futures price. One does not "buy" the contract by paying the "futures price"; the parties promise to transact at that price in the future. The amount actually paid for the futures contract is the margin deposit—a very small percentage of the price of the contract.

A controversy exists over the interpretation of the futures price: is it the expected future price of the underlying instrument, in our case, the stock index? We will not explore that issue here, but it is correct to say that expectations play a major role in the formation of futures prices.

Marking-to-Market. When a buyer has found a seller, both parties post a small margin deposit which is held by the clearinghouse. At the end of each trading day, the clearinghouse determines the settlement price, an average of the prices of the last few trades of the day. If the settlement price is higher than the previous day's settlement price, the difference is credited to the margin accounts of those holding long positions and charged to the margin accounts of those holding short positions. If the settlement price is lower than that of the previous day, the difference is credited to those holding short positions and charged to those holding long positions.

This is called the daily settlement or marking-to-market. Each account must maintain a minimum margin. If the daily settlement results in a deficiency in the margin account, additional funds must be deposited or the broker must close out the contract by selling (or for short positions, buying) it back in the market. Excess margin can be withdrawn or left in to meet future margin calls.

Marking-to-market can be a significant factor in futures trading; however, its effect on futures prices is rather small.

The Cost of Carry. One of the most important concepts in futures markets is the cost of carry—the cost incurred when the spot commodity is purchased and stored. In the case of stock index futures this would refer to the purchase and holding of the securities underlying the index. The direct cost of storing the securities is minimal; however, the interest forgone on the money—the financing cost—can be substantial. On the other hand, the securities generate dividend income which in some cases can completely offset the financing cost.

The cost of carry determines the relationship between futures prices and spot prices. The net cost of carry is the financing cost minus the dividend. When the financing cost exceeds the dividend, carry is negative and the futures price is greater than the index by the net cost of carry. When the dividend exceeds the financing cost, carry is positive and the index exceeds the futures price by the net cost of carry.

Options on Stock Index Futures

Many of the concepts that were discussed in the section on options on stock indexes apply to options on stock index futures. There are a few important differences, however.

Premium. The option premium on stock index futures is exactly like the premium on an option on a stock index. It is the price paid by the buyer to the seller for granting the option. The premium on an option on the index is not necessarily equal to the premium on an option on the futures.

Intrinsic Value. The concept of intrinsic value of an option on a futures is the same as an option on the index, but the underlying instrument is a futures contract so this changes the measure slightly. Specifically,

$$\text{Intrinsic value of a call} = \text{Max}\,(0,\, F - E)$$
$$\text{Intrinsic value of a put} = \text{Max}\,(0,\, E - F)$$

Here the futures price, not the index, is used to compute the intrinsic value. When an in-the-money option is exercised, it is the futures price, not the index level, that determines the payoff. Of course at expiration, the futures price equals the index and the intrinsic value of an option on the index will equal the intrinsic value of an option on the futures, provided that the options and futures expire simultaneously.

Time Value. Prior to expiration, the option on a futures will typically sell for more than its intrinsic value. This is because the buyer of the option is willing to pay an additional amount for the possibility that the price of the futures contract will move. The excess of the option's premium over its intrinsic value is the time value. Thus,

$$\text{Time value of a call} = c - \text{Max}\,(0,\, F - E)$$
$$\text{Time value of a put} = p - \text{Max}\,(0,\, E - F)$$

Volatility. The volatility of the underlying futures contract influences the price of an option on a futures. However, the volatility of the futures contract is not necessarily equal to the volatility of the stock index. It may be more or less, but more importantly the volatility is likely to increase as the futures contract approaches its expiration date. This makes valuing the option on the futures somewhat more difficult. Greater volatility leads to a higher option premium because it increases the chance of the option expiring in-the-money.

Exercise. Exercise of an option on a futures contract establishes a position in the futures contract. For example, suppose the holder of a call exercises when the futures price is F. Then a long futures contract is established at a price of E. The writer of the call is credited with a short futures position at a price of E. If the holder of a put exercises when the futures price is F, a short futures position at a price of E is established. The writer of the put is credited with a long futures position at a price of E. Both parties are required to post margin and the account is marked-to-market on a daily basis as described earlier.

If the holder of an option on a futures wishes to avoid taking the long position in the futures contract, it is necessary to establish an offsetting contract. That is, the holder of the call credited with a long futures contract can immediately sell the futures for a price of F and thereby release cash in the amount of $F - E$ from the margin account.

Dividends. Dividends affect the option on the futures contract by their role in the cost of carry on the underlying futures. The higher the dividend, the lower the cost of carry which leads to a lower futures price. Dividends also influence the decision of whether to exercise the option early.

Now that we have examined some of the basic concepts of the instruments, we can proceed to a discussion of some important relationships in the pricing of these instruments.

PRICING RELATIONSHIPS AMONG
THE INSTRUMENTS

In order to intelligently use the various strategies involving these instruments, it is important to understand how the prices of the six instruments are related. Accordingly let us examine what are called the *parity models* that relate the price of the put and call on the index, the put and call on the futures, the futures, and the index itself.

Let us introduce one additional variable, the dividend. Let D be the dividend paid on the stocks contained in the index. To keep things simple, let the index stocks pay only a single, known dividend on the expiration day. An alternative and equally correct interpretation of D is the compound future value of a stream of known dividends paid over the life of the contract. In either case the variable will play an important role in pricing these instruments.

We will assume that the options are European, since the valuation of American options is more complex. (We will discuss how American option prices would differ from European option prices later in this chapter.)

We are going to form a series of riskless portfolios. We will show that these portfolios will produce the same payoff regardless of the index value at expiration. Since they are riskless, the current value of the portfolio should equal the present value of the future value of the portfolio. The present value is found by discounting the future value at the risk-free rate r over the period of time T.

Table 2–1 constructs a portfolio consisting of the index stocks held in the same proportions as the index, hereafter called the index portfolio, plus a put on the index and a short position in a call on the index. At expiration, the index will be worth I^* plus the dividend, while the options will be worth their intrinsic values. Since we are short the call, the value of the call is negative its intrinsic value.

As the table indicates, the overall portfolio of stocks and options is worth $E + D$ regardless of the value of I^*. The current value of the portfolio is the value of the index portfolio plus the value of the put minus the value of the short call or $I + P - C$. This must equal the present value of $E + D;$ thus,

TABLE 2–1
Put-Call Parity—Options on Stock Indexes

Construct the following portfolio: Buy the index stocks in the same proportions as in the index, sell a call on the index, and buy a put on the index.

	Value of the Portfolio at Expiration	
	$I^* < E$	$I^* > E$
Index portfolio	$I^* + D$	$I^* + D$
Short call	0	$-(I^* - E)$
Long put	$E - I^*$	0
Total	$E + D$	$E + D$

Outcome: The portfolio value at expiration is $E + D$ in either case. Thus, the value of the portfolio today must equal the present value of $E + D$. The value of the portfolio today is the value of the index portfolio, plus the value of the put, minus the value of the short call or $I + P - C$. Thus,

$$I + P - C = (E + D)e^{-rT}$$

$$I + P - C = (E + D)e^{-rT}$$

This expression is commonly known as put-call parity. It is usually rewritten as

$$P = C - (I - De^{-rT}) + Ee^{-rT}$$

The put price is expressed as a function of the call price, the value of the index, the present value of the dividends, and the present value of the exercise price.

Table 2–2 illustrates the concept of put-call-futures parity. Our portfolio contains a long position in the futures contract instead of the index. At expiration the futures contract pays off $F^* - F$, the change in the price of the futures contract; however, at expiration $F^* = I^*$.

As the table shows, the portfolio value at expiration is $E - F$. The current value of the portfolio is, however, only $P - C$ because the value of the futures contract at the initiation of the contract is zero. This is because the futures contract requires no initial payment to purchase it.

The resulting equation is

$$P - C = (E - F)e^{-rT}$$

TABLE 2–2
Put-Call-Futures Parity—Options on Stock Indexes

Construct the following portfolio: Buy the futures, sell a call on the index, and buy a put on the index.

	Value of the Portfolio at Expiration	
	$I^* < E$	$I^* > E$
Long futures	$I^* - F$	$I^* - F$
Short call	0	$-(I^* - E)$
Long put	$E - I^*$	0
Total	$E - F$	$E - F$

Outcome: The portfolio value at expiration is $E - F$ in either case. Thus, the value of the portfolio today must equal the present value of $E - F$. The value of the portfolio today is the value of the put minus the value of the call. Since no outlay is required to buy the futures, the value of the futures contract is zero. Thus, the value of the portfolio today is $P - C$. Therefore,

$$P - C = (E - F)e^{-rT}$$

which is sometimes written as

$$C - P = (F - E)e^{-rT}.$$

This expression defines the relationship between the put and call on the index and the futures on the index. Combining this result with our first put-call parity equation reveals that

$$F = Ie^{rT} - D.$$

Here we see that the futures price equals the compound future value of the index minus the dividend. This is the cost-of-carry relationship discussed earlier. The compound future value of the index reflects the current value of the index and the interest incurred in financing the purchase of the index portfolio. If the cost of carry exceeds the dividend, as it usually does, the futures price will exceed the index value.

Table 2–3 illustrates the put-call-futures parity equation when the options are on the futures. Note that Table 2–3 is essentially identical to Table 2–2. The resulting parity equation,

$$p - c = (E - F)e^{-rT}$$

TABLE 2–3
Put-Call-Futures Parity—Options on Stock Index Futures

Construct the following portfolio: Buy the futures, sell a call on the futures, and buy a put on the futures.

	Value of the Portfolio at Expiration	
	$F^* < E$	$F^* > E$
Long futures	$F^* - F$	$F^* - F$
Short call	0	$-(F^* - E)$
Long put	$E - F^*$	0
Total	$E - F$	$E - F$

Outcome: The portfolio value at expiration is $E - F$ in either case. Thus, the value of the portfolio today must equal the present value of $E - F$. The value of the portfolio today is the value of the put minus the value of the call since as in Table 2–2, the value of the futures contract is zero. Thus, the value of the portfolio today is $p - c$. Therefore,

$$p - c = (E - F)e^{-rT}$$

implies that

$$p - c = P - C.$$

A call on the futures produces the same payoff at expiration as a call on the index, and a put on the futures produces the same payoff as a put on the index. Thus, $c = C$, and $p = P$.

Therefore, options on futures and options on the index are identical. This statement is only true because we have assumed that these are European options. The possibility of early exercise means that options on futures will not be identical to options on the index.

In the absence of dividends, American call options on the index will not be exercised early; however, American call options on the futures do have a possibility of early exercise. In the presence of dividends both types of options may be exercised early. Let us initially assume that the cost of carry exceeds the dividend. Then the futures price exceeds the index value. An option on the futures should, therefore, be worth more than an option on the index; however, the futures price only exceeds the index price prior to expiration. Thus, it is only the possibility of early exercise that makes the option on the futures have a greater value. The result is just the opposite for puts. Put options on the index have a lower price than put options on the futures; this is also because it may be exercised early. The results are reversed if the dividend exceeds the cost of carry which causes the futures price to be less than the index value.

Violations of the parity equations lead to potential profit opportunities. For example, if the call on the index is overpriced and the put on the index is underpriced, the investor should sell the call on the index, buy the index portfolio, and buy the put on the index. This is a *conversion* and creates a position which will be worth E dollars at expiration. The cash paid up front will be less than the present value of E. If the call is underpriced and the put overpriced, an investor should buy the call, sell short the stock, and sell the put. This is a *reverse conversion* or *reversal* and is a portfolio that will require the investor to pay out E dollars at expiration. However, if put-call parity is violated, the cash received up front can be invested to earn sufficient interest so that there will be more than E dollars accumulated by the expiration date.

Similar concepts apply to options on futures. Instead of selling short the index portfolio, a long or short position is established in the futures. Since it is difficult and expensive to replicate the index portfolio, conversions and reversals using options on futures are much easier to execute. Moreover, unlike the options on the index, options on the futures and the underlying instrument, the futures, trade side by side. For floor traders this makes conversions and reversals even more practical.

BASIC INDEX OPTIONS AND FUTURES STRATEGIES

In this section we examine the characteristics of some basic strategies using index options, futures, and options on futures. We will present a graph showing the value of the position at the expiration of the contract plotted against the value of the index at expiration. We then discuss the risk and return of the strategy. Because of the very small deposit required on futures contracts, we assume that the margin is zero.

The examples used here are taken from the S&P 500 futures, options, and options on futures on November 5, 1986. The options expire December 19. Their prices are:

Dec 245 call on the index: 6.375
Dec 250 call on the index: 4
Dec 245 call on the futures: 6.80
Dec 250 call on the futures: 4.25
Dec 245 put on the index: 4.75
Dec 250 put on the index: 7.50
Dec 245 put on the futures: 4.60
Dec 250 put on the futures: 7
December futures: 247.20
Index: 246.58

In actual trading each of the contracts has a specific size. For example, the futures contract has a multiplier of 500, so if the futures are bought at 247.20, the actual price is 247.20(500) = 123,600. In the examples below, we simply assume one unit of each instrument is traded and that the option on the futures is an American option which can be exercised early. The option on the index is a European option and cannot be exercised early.

Futures.   We start by examining the payoff from a strategy of simply trading the futures contract. Remember that we are examining the value of the contract at expiration given the value of the index at expiration. The futures price at expiration is the value of the index at expiration. Since we are assuming a zero margin requirement, the value of a long futures contract at expiration is the index value at expiration minus the original futures price. The value of a short futures contract is minus the value of the long futures contract. The graph is shown in Figure 2–1.

The graph indicates that the futures transaction is quite risky. The long position has the potential for unlimited gains. The potential loss is quite large, but limited. For example, if the contract is bought at 247.20, the lowest price it can go to is zero for

FIGURE 2–1
Value of Futures at Expiration

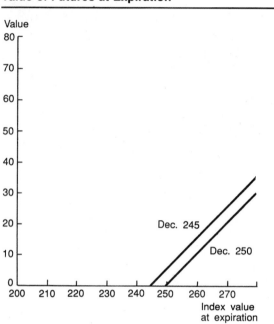

a loss of 247.20. For short positions, the maximum gain occurs if the contract price goes to zero; therefore, the maximum gain is 247.20. The maximum loss is infinite since there is no upper limit on the value of the index.

Calls.   Because the futures price at expiration equals the index value at expiration, the value of a call option on the futures at expiration is the same as the value of a call option on the index at expiration. Both options will, of course, be worth their intrinsic values. The graph is presented in Figure 2–2.

It is clear that buying a call option is a bullish strategy. In the case of index options or index options on futures, the strategy is one of being bullish on the market as a whole. The graph indicates that the call with exercise price of 245 has a greater value at expiration than the call with exercise price of 250 provided that the index value is greater than 245. Thus, the 245 call is a more

FIGURE 2–2
Value of Call at Expiration

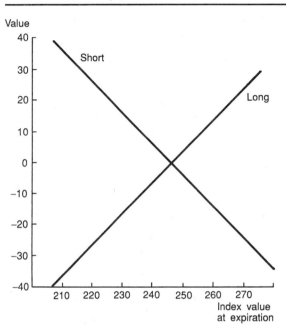

bullish strategy. However, because of its higher potential payoff, the 245 call will cost more than the 250 call. This will be true for options on the index or options on the futures. The option is worthless, however, if the index value is less than the respective exercise price.

Note that while both the option on the index and the option on the futures have the same payoffs, they do not have the same premiums. The option on the futures has a higher premium because it has a possibility of early exercise. If exercised early, the holder of the call will capture the difference between the futures price and the exercise price. If the cost of carry exceeds the dividend, as it apparently does in this example, the futures price exceeds the index level and the option on the futures is worth more.

The graph shows the value of the position at expiration. The transaction will not be profitable if the value of the position does not exceed the premium paid up front. Therefore, the index value at expiration must exceed the exercise price by the amount of the premium. The interest forgone on the money paid for the option should also be taken into account.

We have not shown or discussed the writing of uncovered calls. The value of the position would be the reverse of the value of the long position and would have the potential for unlimited losses.

Puts.   The value at expiration of a put option on the index is the same as the value at expiration of a put option on the futures. The value at expiration of a put is shown in Figure 2–3.

The index put option is a bearish strategy, taken in anticipation of an expected drop in the market. The graph indicates that the 250 put has a greater value at expiration than the 245 put provided the index value is less than 250. Therefore, the price of the 250 put will exceed the price of the 245 put.

FIGURE 2–3
Value of Put at Expiration

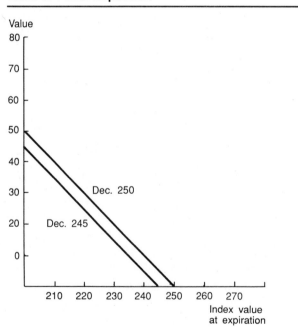

As described earlier, the price of the put on the index exceeds the price of the put on the futures due to the early exercise feature. The position will not be profitable unless the index value at expiration is less than the exercise price by more than the premium paid for the put.

We have not discussed the writing of puts. The results of a put-writing strategy are simply a reversal of the results of a put-buying strategy. This is a high-risk strategy that has the potential for large losses.

The Covered Call and the Protective Put.   Now let us look at two option strategies designed to protect positions in the index portfolio or the futures contract—*covered calls* and *protective puts*.

The covered call involves the purchase of either the index or the futures and writing a call against whichever instrument is purchased. For example, one could purchase a portfolio of stocks that replicates the index and write a call on the index. If the index moves down, the portfolio loses value, but the option is unlikely to be exercised and the writer will keep the premium. This cushions the loss on the stocks. If the index moves up, the portfolio will increase in value and the option will probably end up in-the-money and exercised. This will force the investor to liquidate the portfolio to generate the cash necessary to meet the cash settlement on the option.

Another strategy to protect a position in the index portfolio is a protective put. The holder of the index portfolio buys a put on the index. If the index goes down and the put expires in-the-money, the put is exercised. This amounts to selling the portfolio at a fixed price—the exercise price of the put. If the index goes up and the put expires out-of-the-money, the put is not exercised. Because the premium was paid regardless of what happens to the put, this cuts into the profit on the upside.

The protective put serves as an insurance policy on the portfolio by establishing a floor on the value at which a portfolio can be liquidated. The price of the put is like an insurance premium— paid regardless of whether a claim is filed. The exercise price is like a deductible. The higher the exercise price, the higher the assured value at which the portfolio can be liquidated in a bear market. This is like taking a small deductible which in an insurance policy leads to a higher premium. In the case of a put, the higher the exercise price, the higher the premium. It is tempting to think that when an option such as a protective put is purchased, the buyer should hope that the option will be exercised. That is equivalent to buying fire insurance in the hope that the house will burn down!

Figure 2–4 illustrates the covered call and protective put. Note how the protective put using the December 245 establishes 245 as the minimum value at which the portfolio can be liquidated. In a bull market the portfolio value is directly related to the index value at expiration. The covered call establishes a maximum value of the portfolio at expiration. In a bear market the loss on the portfolio is directly related to the index value at expiration, but is less than if the index were held without the call.

Why isn't the protective put preferred over the covered call since it establishes a minimum liquidation value of the portfolio

FIGURE 2–4
Value of Covered Call and Protective Put at Expiration (Index Options)

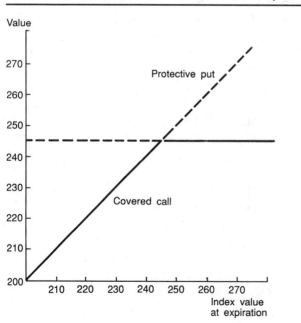

while the covered call establishes a maximum liquidation value? Both the call and the put are priced correctly in the market to reflect their economic worth. The protective put costs money up front while the covered call results in the receipt of money up front. Interest is forgone on the money paid for the put while interest is earned on the money received for the call. Neither strategy is dominant over the other. The protective put is preferred in a strong bull or bear market while the covered call is preferred in a more neutral market.

Covered calls and protective puts can also be done using options on futures to protect long positions on futures contracts. This is illustrated in Figure 2–5. The concepts and most of the important points discussed for options on the index are applicable to options on futures. For a covered call the holder of a long futures contract simply writes a call on the futures. If the index goes down, the futures will go down, but the call will probably

FIGURE 2–5
Value of Covered Call and Protective Put at Expiration
(Index Options on Futures)

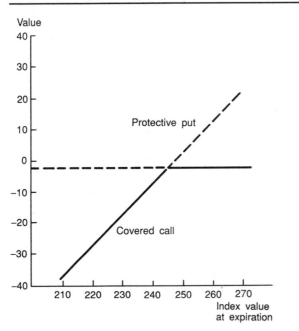

expire out-of-the-money so the writer keeps the premium. This cushions the loss on the futures position. On the upside the option will probably be exercised which establishes for the writer a short futures position. This completely offsets the long futures position.

A put on a futures contract can also be used to protect a long futures position—similar again to insurance. If the market moves down, the loss on the futures contract is completely offset by the exercise of the put. The put effectively establishes a minimum sale price for the futures. On the upside, the put will not be needed and can be viewed as insurance that expired without a claim.

We have not looked at how short positions in the index portfolio or futures contracts can be protected. It should be clear that either long calls or short puts can be used to protect short positions in either the index or the futures contract. The graphs from such strategies would be Figures 2–4 and 2–5 in reverse.

Straddles and Spreads.   One of the attractive features of options is that they can be combined in many ways to take advantage of market forecasts. For example, sometimes the market is expected to move substantially without the forecaster knowing in which direction. A straddle can be used in such a situation so that the investor will profit from either an upward or a downward move.

A straddle is a long position in a put and a call with the same exercise price. If the market moves up and at expiration the index value exceeds the exercise price, the call is exercised. If the market moves down so that the index value is less than the exercise price, the put is exercised. Figure 2–6 illustrates the value of a straddle using the December 245 options.

The straddle is a symmetric strategy—a given move on either side of the exercise price results in the same value of the position. The worst possible outcome is if the index value ends up equal to the exercise price. Since that is not likely, the straddle will probably have some value at expiration. However, that does not necessarily mean that the value will exceed the price originally paid for it. It is tempting to think that the straddle is a strategy that rewards you regardless of what the market does, but the market

FIGURE 2–6
Straddle

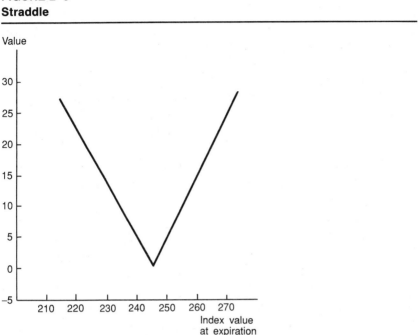

does not move as much as many people think it will. The investor who trades straddles will probably make an occasional large profit and a large number of small losses.

If the investor believes the market will not move much, a short straddle—sell a put and a call—is a possibility. However, the holder of the short straddle can lose a great deal if the market does move substantially. If the market moves up, the loss is potentially infinite.

Another useful option strategy is the money spread. This involves the purchase of an option with one exercise price and the sale of an identical option with a different exercise price. Money spreads can be bull spreads or bear spreads and can be executed with either calls or puts.

A bull call spread consists of the purchase of the call with the lower exercise price and the sale of the call with the higher exercise price. A bear call spread is the purchase of the call with the higher exercise price and the sale of the call with the lower exercise price. A bear put spread consists of the purchase of the put with the higher exercise price and the sale of the put with the lower exercise price. A bull put spread is the purchase of the put with the lower exercise price and the sale of the put with the higher exercise price. For illustrative purpose we will use the call bull spread and the put bear spread.

The purpose of a money spread is to take a position, either bullish or bearish, but to keep the risk below what it would be if one had simply bought a single call or put. For example, suppose one were bullish on the market. The purchase of a call would be profitable if the market did rise sufficiently; however, if the market went down, the call holder would lose. By selling a call at a higher exercise price, a loss on the long call would be somewhat offset by a gain on the short call. That is, if the long call expires out-of-the-money, so will the short call. The premium on the short call cushions the loss on the long call. If the market goes up and the long call expires in-the-money, the short call may or may not be exercised, depending on how high the market goes. In the worst case, however, the exercise of the long call and the short call will result in the spread being worth the difference in the exercise prices. Similar arguments apply to the put bear spread with, of course, the direction of the effects being opposite. The value of the spread at expiration is shown in Figure 2–7.

The bull spread is only profitable if the market moves up and the spread value at expiration exceeds the premium. The bear spread is only profitable if the market moves down and the spread value at expiration exceeds the premium. In addition the option purchased results in the loss of interest on the money paid and the option sold generates interest income on the premium received. The net interest should also be considered in determining whether the position is profitable.

Most option traders on the floor of the exchanges make liberal use of spreads. Successful traders are fairly conservative (or at least conservative at the appropriate times). One conservative strategy is the covered call. For index options the expense and difficulty of constructing an index portfolio make the covered call a fairly impractical strategy for floor traders to use. Thus, they frequently resort to spreads to keep their risk to a manageable level. Some other types of spreads used are time spreads, butter-

FIGURE 2–7
Value of Bull Spread with Calls and Bear Spread with Puts

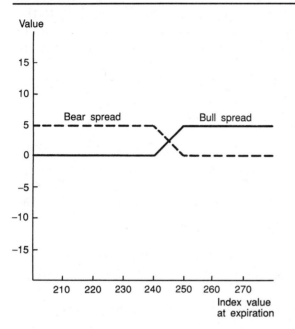

flies, and condors. Interested readers can learn about these strategies from any of a number of excellent books on option strategies.

SOME SPECIAL CONSIDERATIONS
OF INDEX OPTIONS

Trading index options and futures is not much different from trading options and futures on other securities and commodities, but a few important distinctions should be remembered.

Early Exercise. Call options on indexes should only be exercised early if there is a dividend. At the instant a stock goes ex-dividend, the value of the index will fall. If the amount of this fall is less than the time value, the option should be exercised. A put option on the index might be exercised early regardless of whether there is a dividend. If the put is sufficiently deep in-the-money, the put will have a zero time value and at that point should be exercised. This happens for a put and not for a call because there is an upper limit on the price of the put. Since the stock price can go no lower than zero, the put price can go no higher than the exercise price. For a call, however, there is no upper limit on the value of the stock or the call.

A call option on the futures may be exercised early regardless of whether there is a dividend on any stock in the index. The call option on the futures should be exercised early when the option has a zero time value. This is also true of the put option on the futures. The payment of dividends on the underlying stocks will slightly change the time when this occurs.

Tracking Error. Holders of an index portfolio who trade options on the portfolio should be aware that the portfolio will not precisely replicate the index. This problem, called *tracking error,* is nearly always present where index funds or portfolios are being managed. It is not a result of trading options on the portfolio. Nonetheless, when options are being used, the consequences of tracking error can be substantial.

When the index is constructed, the securities must be weighted in the correct proportions. This is not an easy task since it requires the simultaneous purchase of all of the securities and the futures contract. In many cases the updating of the index value, which is used by the futures market to determine the futures price, lags the actual market prices of the component stocks in the index. Thus, the futures price obtained may not be contemporaneous with the prices of the stocks in the index. Let us assume, however, that the trades are simultaneously executed. For a value-weighted index like the S&P 500, the weights are proportional to the relative market values of the securities. The weights will automatically adjust so no further trading is necessary to track the index. For a price-weighted portfolio like the Major Market Index, stock splits alter the original weightings so that adjustments must be made.

In reality, it is nearly impossible to simultaneously execute the trades in the futures and in the correct market weightings in the stocks. Most portfolio managers use a subset of the stocks in the index, reasoning that a highly correlated proxy for the index will serve adequately. This leads to one of several problems associated with the cash settlement at expiration.

At expiration the futures price is settled at the index value and the options are exercised accordingly. If the portfolio chosen to replicate the index contains tracking error, the exercise of the option or cash settlement of the futures will not produce the values indicated in the previous section on strategies. The error may or may not go in one's favor. It is important to minimize the tracking error and this requires periodic trades in some of the underlying stocks. The benefits must be weighed against the additional transaction costs.

Program Trading and the Expiration Day Effect. There is a substantial amount of trading in which large institutions attempt to buy or sell short a portfolio which replicates the index while taking an opposite position in options or futures. The purpose of this trading is to take advantage of any discrepancies in the theoretical relationship between the instruments suggested by the parity models discussed earlier. Because computers continuously monitor the market and flash immediate buy and sell signals, this arbitrage trading is often called *program trading*.

Suppose futures are overpriced relative to the index portfolio. The computers at these institutions flash a signal to buy the index portfolio and sell the futures. If futures are underpriced, the computers signal an order to buy the futures and sell short the index portfolio. These positions are held until the futures expire. If stocks were originally sold short, they will be bought at expiration. If stocks were originally bought, they will be sold at expiration. With so many institutions playing this game, it has caused some substantial price movements on expiration days, particularly in the last hour of trading.

Options on stock indexes expire every month; futures and options on stock index futures expire in March, June, September, and December. On the third Friday in March, June, September, and December, three different types of instruments expire and the substantial price movements observed in the last hour of trading on those four days of the year have caused it to be known as the "triple witching hour."

The volatility of the market at the expiration dates, poses a major risk for holders of stocks, options, and futures. Many a skilled trader has been wiped out because of these effects. It is important to be aware of the extreme volatility expected on these expiration days; one should either be prepared for it or be out of the market completely.

SUMMARY

Stock index futures and options play an important role in our economy by providing a simple and efficient means of managing the risk of aggregate market movements. It is necessary to obtain a basic understanding of the risk and return properties of these products to fully appreciate their many advantages.

In this chapter we (1) presented a general overview of risk and return characteristics of stock index futures and options products; (2) learned about factors that influence the prices of these instruments and observed how those factors interact to create unique opportunities for investors; (3) looked at some basic parity relationships and examined a number of trading strategies, and (4) looked at some special risks faced when trading the instruments.

CHAPTER 3

A COMPARATIVE GUIDE TO STOCK INDEX FUTURES CONTRACTS

Bruce M. Collins, Ph.D.
Vice President
Equity Arbitrage Group
Index Products Research
Shearson Lehman Hutton Inc.

This chapter compares six important and currently traded stock index futures contracts, four domestic and two foreign. The contracts are based on the S&P 500 Composite Index, the New York Stock Exchange Composite Index, the Major Market Index, and the Value Line Index. The Financial Times Stock Exchange 100 Index, and the Nikkei 225 Index (the foreign futures contracts) are also included because global investment strategies are increasingly more important and many investment strategies, such as dynamic asset allocation (portfolio insurance) require the use of futures contracts.[1] All stock index futures contracts are standardized agreements traded on a commodity exchange. Each contract is unique because contract specifications vary from exchange to exchange. The common features of a contract include contract size and value, margin requirements, information related to trading issues (such as daily price change limits and minimum price change limits), and delivery and settlement specifications.

---

[1]See Chapter 12 for a discussion of this strategy.

A futures contract is a firm legal agreement between two parties: a buyer or a seller and an established exchange or clearinghouse. In this contract the parties agree to take or make delivery of a commodity at a specific price and at a specified time and place. Stock index futures contracts are the latest of the financial futures contracts. A stock index futures contract is an agreement to pay or receive some dollar amount ($500 for New York Futures Exchange (NYFE) contract and the S&P 500 contract, $250 for the Major Market Index (XMI)) times the difference between the purchase price and the sale price. They differ from traditional commodity futures contracts (such as agricultural futures or interest rate futures contracts) in that there is no claim on an underlying deliverable asset. The claim is on the value of the contract and settlement is in cash. All futures contract positions are adjusted on a daily basis (that is, they are marked-to-the-market) and a payment is made. At the end of each trading day, the current futures price is compared to the previous day's closing price, and if the futures price has risen (fallen), the long (short) investor receives from the short (long) investor the amount of the increase (decrease). Although this procedure is accomplished through an exchange, the investor's account is adjusted daily.[2] Settlement is made by an exchange of money determined by the difference between the value of the contract at the final settlement and the previous day's closing price. Stock index futures (SIF) contracts are similar to the more traditional futures contracts, as they provide equity managers with the tools they need to hedge market-related portfolio risks and allow them to quickly change market strategy without altering their equity portfolio.

The contract specifications for each of the six contracts are included in Table 3–1.

CONTRACT VALUE

The value of a single stock index futures contract is the product of a multiple and the current futures prices. The value of the multiple has influenced the success or failure of a futures contract.

---

[2]The mechanics of trading stock index futures contracts are described in Chapter 5.

TABLE 3–1
Stock Index Contract Specifications

Contract	S&P 500	NYSE Composite	XMI	Value Line	FT-SE	Nikkei
Ticker	SPX	NYA	XMI	XYL	FT	NK
Exchange	CME	NYFE	CBT	KCBT	LIFFE	SIMEX
Trading hours*	9:30 AM–4:15 PM	9:30 AM–4:15 PM	9:15 AM–4:15 PM	9:30 AM–4:15 PM	9:05 AM–4:05 PM	8:00 AM–2:15 PM
Contract size (multiple)	500	500	250	500	25	500
Trading months	Mar., June Sept., Dec.	Same	Same plus nearest 3 months	Same	Same	Same plus Jan.
Minimum fluctuation in price (tick size)	.05	.05	.05	.05	.05	5 pts.
Dollar value of tick	$25	$25	$12.50	$25	12.50†	Yen 2,500
Daily price limit	15§	None	20	15	100‡	15%‖
Settlement	3rd Friday of contract month—opening	3rd Friday of contract month—close	Same	Same	First business day following last business day of trading month	3rd Wed. of contract month

*All trading hours are Eastern time except the FT-SE 100 and Nikkei contracts, which refer to local time.
†In pound sterling.
‡Price limit is in ticks and does not apply to the last hour of trading.
§15% price limit after first 30 minutes of trading. First 30 minutes, 10% above or below previous day's settlement price.
‖5-point limit for first 10 minutes.

The current Major Market Index futures contract (the Big Contract) is a revised version of an earlier contract (Missile or MX). A larger multiple effectively reduces transactions costs for investors using the contract because an inverse relationship exists between the size of the multiple and the number of futures contracts required to satisfy a specific dollar level. For example, with the Major Market Index trading at 400 and a multiple of 250, the value of one futures contact is:

$$\$250 \times 400 = \$100,000$$

Based on the old contract (with a smaller multiple of 100), this is equivalent to two and a half contracts and since transaction costs are assessed by contract, the cost differential is considerable. Also, a larger multiple contributes to the liquidity of the contract. If held until expiration, the final settlement value of the futures contract is the multiple times the closing price of the underlying cash index on that day.

REGULATION OF FUTURES PRICE MOVEMENT

A commodities exchange can use two methods to control stock index futures price movements. First, each contract is subject to a minimum price change or "tick." Second, an exchange may impose daily price limits. For all but the Nikkei futures contract, a minimum price move is .05 points. The dollar equivalent of a tick is the product of the multiple and a tick. For example, for the S&P 500 futures contract, the minimum dollar change is .05 × 500 or $25. The value of a tick for the Nikkei futures contract is 5(points) times the multiple or yen 2,500.

Most futures exchanges impose daily price limits for futures contracts on hard commodities and some financial futures. Stock index futures, historically, with the exception of the Financial Times Stock Exchange 100 Index futures contract, have had no daily price limits. Commodity exchanges also reserve the right to increase daily price limits or impose new price limits after two successive days of limit moves. Although the exchanges do not usually impose price limits on futures contracts which currently are not subject to such limits, after the market debacle of October 19, 1987, domestic commodity exchanges imposed daily price limits on stock index futures contracts (see Table 3–1). This is a response to continued concern expressed by legislators and regulators regarding increased intraday market volatility caused by program trading and the role it may have played on October 19th.[3]

---

[3]Program trading is explained in Chapter 15.

MARGIN

There are two concepts of margin that relate to futures contracts. The first is the traditional margin requirements regulated by the exchanges. A second concept of margin refers to variation margin and is defined as the daily gains or losses that result from the daily settlement feature of futures contracts and essentially represents the daily adjustment to changes in contract value. This section focuses on traditional margin requirements and the leverage it provides for investors in stock index futures. Chapter 5 elaborates on the concept of variation margin and Chapter 8 will discuss the implications of variation margin for futures pricing models.

Margin requirements for futures contracts are similar in concept to stock margin requirements—both serve to provide brokers with protection from trading losses and foster investor confidence in the financial markets. Margin requirements for futures contracts, however, differ from stock margin in significant ways. Stock margin is essentially a down payment toward the purchase of a property where ownership changes hands on its receipt. In contrast, futures margin is a performance bond or good-faith payment that acknowledges that the contractual obligations will be honored.

Margin requirements include initial margin and maintenance margin. Initial margin is the minimum amount that a customer must provide before a transaction can be executed. Maintenance margin represents the minimum level of equity that must be preserved in an account to maintain a position. Table 3–2 lists the margin requirements for each stock index futures contract.

The size of the initial and maintenance margin for futures contracts is regulated by the commodity exchange where the contract trades. Stock margin is regulated by the Federal Reserve Board, the Securities and Exchange Commission, and the exchange where the stock is traded. In addition, brokerage firms have the discretion to set their own margin requirements but must satisfy the minimum margin requirements set by the exchanges.

The Federal Reserve sets margin requirements in percent, and therefore the dollar value of stock margin changes with stock price changes. initial and maintenance margin requirements con-

TABLE 3–2
Stock Index Futures Margin Requirements

Contract	S&P 500	NYSE Composite	XMI	Value Line	FT-SE	Nikkei
Hedger:						
Initial	$10,000	$4,000	$10,000	$5,000	£3,000	yen 1mm
Maintenance	10,000	4,000	10,000	5,000	3,000	yen 850K
Speculator:						
Initial	19,000	–0–	7,500	7,500	–0–	1 mm
Maintenance	10,000	4,000	7,500	7,500	–0–	850 K
Spreader (calendar):						
Initial	400	200	Market*	400	250	150 K
Maintenance	200	100	Market	200	250	75 K

*Margin is determined by the value of the spread.

stitute 50 percent and 25 percent of the value of the underlying stock position. Futures margin, on the other hand, is a fixed dollar amount. Periodically, this amount may be adjusted to reflect the appreciation of the index. The speculative margin for the S&P 500 futures contract prior to October 1987 was $10,000 initial and $5,000 maintenance. As of June 1, 1988, the initial and maintenance margin requirement is $20,000 and $10,000, respectively. Despite an increase in the fixed dollar amount in initial margin for stock index futures contracts, on a percentage basis, futures provide over six times the leverage of stocks bought on margin (Table 3–3).

TABLE 3–3
Stock Index Futures Leverage*

Contract	Leverage Factor	
	Hedgers	Speculators
S&P 500	12.07	6.67
NYFE	7.18	3.78
XMI	9.49	6.33
Value Line	22.26	14.84
FT-SE 100	11.92	5.95
Nikkei futures	13.64	13.64

*Based on price levels as of May 27, 1988.

The daily settlement feature of futures contracts yields daily changes in the customer account balance. The daily cash flows, or variation margin, are debited or credited to the account. A reduction in the account balance from adverse price movements may require that the customer post additional margin. Unlike futures contracts, the gains or losses from stock price movements are not realized until the stock is sold. In addition, when the futures account balance falls below the required maintenance margin level, enough additional margin must be posted to satisfy the initial margin requirement, which is not true for stock. After a stock is purchased and the initial margin has been posted, only the maintenance margin requirement must then be satisfied.

Margin requirements are specified differently for speculators, hedgers, and spreaders (Table 3–2). The differential is intended to reflect the risk associated with the intent of the investor. Naturally, a hedged position assumes less risk than a speculative position. In fact, a fully hedged position is expected to yield a risk-free rate of return. In order to qualify as a hedger, an investor must assume a dollar equivalent position in stock index futures that offsets a position in the underlying cash index. A legitimate hedge holds a diversified portfolio that exactly replicates the underlying index (zero tracking error) and shorts the dollar equivalent of futures contracts.[4] In two situations it is difficult to ascertain the legitimacy of a hedging strategy. The first is an "anticipatory hedge," where the purchase of futures contracts serves as a substitute for a subsequent purchase of a replicating portfolio. The second situation involves determining when the amount of tracking error between the replicating portfolio and the underlying index is large enough to regard the strategy as speculative.

Futures markets facilitate the economic transfer of risk among investors interested in reducing risk exposure (hedgers) and those willing to assume additional risk (speculators). The absence of either player threatens the success of the futures contract. Therefore, to assure the efficient operation of a futures

---

[4]Tracking error refers to the expected performance differential between a replicating portfolio and its benchmark. It can be estimated by the standard deviation of the difference in returns measured over time.

market, hedgers must be able to adjust their risk exposure at a reasonable cost and speculators need the ability to assume a large enough position to satisfy hedgers. These objectives are met through leverage. Table 3–3 contains the leverage factor for each of the futures contracts. The leverage factor is the reciprocal of the margin requirement as a percent of the contract value. Investors can carry large positions in stock index futures value for a rather modest amount of capital outlay. The potential loss for an investor, however, is not limited to the initial capital outlay. Under extreme adverse conditions, losses may accumulate in excess of the original capital outlay. For example, if the initial margin requirement for a speculative position is 7.14 percent of the total futures contract value, the index value is 280 and the multiple is 500, a market move of -10 percent (from 280 to 252) will result in a loss of $14,000, which exceeds the capital outlay (initial margin) of $10,000. Although leverage is a necessary ingredient for a successful futures market, the risk of losses is as great as a dollar equivalent unleveraged position.

CASH SETTLEMENT

There is no underlying deliverable asset in stock index futures contracts: settlement is in cash. Historically, commodity futures prices and prices on the underlying cash commodity were kept in line because commodity futures contracts require delivery of the cash commodity at expiration. Although few positions are held for delivery, the prospect of delivery forces the futures price and cash price to converge at expiration. When the differential of futures prices and cash prices, known as the basis, fail to converge, arbitrage activity will emerge to realign the prices.

Arbitrage opportunities arise when market sentiment causes a divergence of the futures price from its fair value implied by the cost of carry. The cost of carry is the net cost of owning an asset for a period of time. For traditional commodities, the cost of carry includes storage, insurance, transactions, and interest costs. The cost of carry for financial instruments includes the net interest differential between the yield on the cash investment and the cost of borrowing the money to purchase the asset. Those participating in futures-related arbitrage must be capable, financially and physically, of taking delivery of the underlying cash commodity. Speculators, on the other hand, usually are not capable of taking delivery and, therefore, close out their positions prior to expiration.

These physical restrictions do not apply to stock index futures because they are settled in cash; the convergence of the futures price and cash price at expiration is assured by definition. The closing futures price equals the closing value of the index on expiration regardless of the number of bid and asks in the pit. Furthermore, because the fear of delivery is absent, unlike traditional futures contracts, all investors, including speculators, may hold positions through expiration. At expiration, the difference—in cash—between the final settlement price and the previous day's close is transferred in or out of the customer's account in the same manner as all prior daily settlements. The only difference is, after final settlement, the position is no longer held. The cash settlement feature also pre-empts a "short-squeeze" so familiar to investors in traditional commodity futures. A short squeeze occurs when investors who are short the futures contract must go out into the cash market to purchase the commodity for delivery.

TRADING HOURS

The stock index futures market closes at 4:15 P.M. Eastern time while New York Stock Exchange closes at 4:00 P.M. The original intent of the discrepancy was to capture new information from money supply announcements by the Federal Reserve Board at 4:10 PM on Fridays, but the Fed has since modified this practice.

The different closing times for futures and cash (spot) markets introduces a measurement error or bias into a fair valuation process that uses closing prices. In addition, some traders use this bias as a leading or contrarian sentiment indicator for moves in the cash market the following day.

CHAPTER 4

A COMPARATIVE GUIDE TO STOCK INDEX OPTIONS

Bruce M. Collins, Ph.D.
Vice President
Equity Arbitrage Group
Index Products Research
Shearson Lehman Hutton Inc.

James A. Schmidt
Vice President
Equity Arbitrage Group
Shearson Lehman Hutton Inc.

This chapter is a comparative guide to several index option contracts, on either a cash index or a futures contract, and will summarize the contract specifications and margin requirements of the following underlying indexes or futures contract: the S&P 100 Composite Index (OEX), the S&P 500 Composite Index (SPX), the New York Stock Exchange (NYSE) Composite Index (NYA), the Major Market Index (MMI), the Institutional Index (XII), the Value Line Index (XVL), the S&P 500 futures contract, and the New York Stock Exchange Composite Index futures contract.

Exchange-listed options on common stock were first listed on the Chicago Board Options Exchange (CBOE) in 1973. Subsequently, listed options began trading on the American Stock Exchange in January of 1975 and on several regional exchanges. In February of 1982, the Kansas City Board of Trade introduced the first stock index futures contract, followed in April 1982 by the S&P 500 futures contract. Early in 1983, the Chicago Mercantile Exchange (CME) began trading options on the S&P 500 futures contract, and the New York Futures Exchange (NYFE) began trading options on the New York Stock Exchange Composite Index futures contract. Since that time options on several cash indexes have been created. The most successful to date is the CBOE 100 or OEX option.

DEFINITIONS AND CONTRACT SPECIFICATIONS

An option is a negotiable contract which gives its owner the right and not the obligation to purchase or sell a fixed amount of a designated underlying security at a specified price within a specified period of time. The seller of an option is the *option writer*. The price at which the security can be bought or sold under the terms of the agreement is referred to as the exercise or strike price, and the date when the terms of the option ends is known as the expiration date. A contract giving the owner the right to purchase (sell) the underlying security is a call (put) option. Options that can only be exercised at the expiration date are known as European options. American options can be exercised anytime on or before expiration date. An option on a stock index futures contract gives the owner of the option the right to assume a position in the underlying stock index futures contract at a specified price anytime during the life of the option.

Tables 4–1 and 4–2 compare the contract specifications of options on cash indexes and options on index futures, respectively. Further information on the contract specifications of index futures is found in the previous chapter.

CONTRACT VALUE AND PRICE QUOTATIONS

The value of a single option on a cash index is equivalent to the index value times $100.

Dollar value of one contract = Index value × $100

TABLE 4–1

Contract Specifications for Options on Cash Indexes

Contract	Institutional Index	NYSE Composite Index	Major Market Index	S&P 100 Index	S&P 500 Index	Value Line Index
Exchange	AMEX	NYFE	AMEX	CBOE	CBOE	KCBT
Trading symbol	XII	NYA	XMI	OEX	SPX	XVL
Contract size	Index × $100	Index × $100	Index × $100	Index × $100	Index × $100	Index × $100
Minimum price change	1/16, or, $6.25, when less than three or 1/8, $12.50	Same	Same	Same	.05 or $5	Same
Contract months	Three near term plus up to two months in succession from March-June-Sept.-Dec. cycle	Three near term expiration months	Three near term expiration months	Four near term expiration months	Two near term months plus up to three mos. in succession from March-June-Sept.-Dec. cycle	Three near term months plus up to two mos. from March-June-Sept.-Dec. cycle
Exercise provision	European	American	American	American	European	American
Strike prices	5 point intervals	2 1/2 or 5 point intervals	5 point intervals	5 point intervals	5 point intervals	5 point intervals
Position	15,000 contracts on either side of the market— 25,000 total	Contracts with total value not exceeding $300 million.	10,000 contracts on either side of the market— 17,000 total	15,000 contracts on either side of the market— 17,000 total	15,000 contracts on either side of the market— 25,000 total	$300MM on either side of the market
Daily price limit	None	None	None	None	None	None
Settlement	Cash	Cash	Cash	Cash	Cash	Cash
Trading hours	9:30 AM to 4:15 PM Eastern time	Same	Same	Same	Same	Same

For an OEX option with the index at 277, the value of one contract is 277 × $100 or $27,700. The value of a single option of an index futures contract is the futures value times $500. An option on the S&P 500 futures with the futures trading at 282 is valued at 282 × $500 = $141,000. The greater leverage of the index futures options is derived from the higher multiple. The price of an index option or option premium is quoted in index points. Each point on a cash

TABLE 4–2
Contract Specifications for Options on Stock Index Futures

Contract	S&P 500 Index Futures	NYSE Composite Index Futures
Exchange	CME	NYFE
Trading symbol	CS(Calls) PS(Puts)	YX
Contract size	Futures × $500	Futures × $500
Minimum price	.05 or $25.00	.05 or $25.00
Contract months	March-June-Sept.-Dec. cycle	March-June-Sept.-Dec. cycle
Exercise provision	American	American
Strike prices	Five point intervals	Integers which are evenly divisible by two
Position limit	5,000 combined futures and options positions, on one side of the market, with futures and options calculated on a net basis	10,000 combined futures and options on same side of the market, with futures calculated on a net basis and options calculated on a gross basis
Daily price limit	Closes when futures closes	None
Settlement	Delivery of long or short position in the underlying future	Same
Trading hours	9:30 AM to 4:15 PM Eastern Time	Same

index option is worth $100 while each point on an index futures option is $500. Thus, a cash index option trading two and a half points will cost the option buyer 2.5 × $100 or $250. A stock index futures option trading two and a half will cost 2.5 × $500 or $1,250.

Contract value is important to the determination of appropriate position size given a desired market exposure. The number of contracts in a position has a secondary impact on transaction costs which influences strategy implementation. As an example, let's consider a $100 million portfolio indexed to the S&P 500.

On May 17, 1982, the S&P 500 cash index was 118.01. To completely hedge a $100 million indexed portfolio, a manager needed to sell 1,695 contracts against his/her position.

On May 25, 1988, the S&P 500 cash index was 253.76. A $100 million portfolio hedge on this date would translate into only 788 contracts, or 53 percent fewer than the number required in May 1982. This difference arises from the tremendous intervening stock market rally, but in terms of transaction costs, the same dollar hedging decision can be made more easily and with lower market impact.

EXERCISE PROVISIONS

There are two general exercise provisions for index options, European and American. The American provision allows for exercise on any business day prior to expiration via notice to the clearing corporation. In the case of cash index options, exercise will result in a cash settlement as determined by the index closing price on the date of exercise. The primary difference between index options and common stock options or stock index futures options is in the cash settlement feature of exercise. The exercise of a common stock option requires the delivery of the underlying security. The exercise of long stock index futures put and call options will result in the assignment of an actual short position (puts) or long position (calls) in the underlying future, and not cash settlement. Index options are settled with the payment of cash and the amount of cash exchanged is determined by the difference between the option's strike price and the value of the underlying index when the option is exercised. For example, a June 270 option on an S&P 500 futures contract assigned (exercised) by the holder of a call option when the futures is trading at 280 results in the delivery of a futures contract on the next trading day by the option writer. The holder of the call option is now long an S&P 500 futures contract. By contrast, if the holder of a June 275 OEX call option exercises the option when the OEX closed at 285, the writer who is assigned is obligated to pay $1,000 ([285 − 275] × $100) in cash to the holder.

The European provision only allows for exercise on the last trading day prior to expiration. Therefore, option writers may carry hedged positions throughout the contract life without fear of early assignment.

EXERCISE PRICE

There are several different exercise or strike prices for all put and call cash index options and stock index futures options. Exercise prices are set at five point intervals for most index options. The two exceptions to this rule are the NYSE Composite Index option which trades at exercise price intervals of two and one half or five points and the NYSE Composite Index futures option which trades at exercise prices that are evenly divisible by two. As a general rule, a minimum of seven exercise prices are set at all times which reflect three in-the-money, one at-the-money, and three out-of-the-money options.[1] In 1986 and 1987, the fast pace of market advances resulted in a number of exercise prices far in excess of the minimum.

MINIMUM PRICE CHANGE

The minimum price change for an option is specified by the exchange. Currently, all index futures options have a minimum price change, or tick, of .05 index points which is valued at $25 (.05 × $500). The minimum price change is the same for all but one cash index option; 1/16 for option series trading below $3 and 1/8 for all others. A 1/16 change is equivalent to $6.25 (1/16 × $100) and a 1/8
change is equivalent to $12.50 (1/8 × $100). An exception to this rule is the S&P 500 cash index option which has a minimum price change of .05 index points or $5 (.05 × $100). There are currently no price limits on any index option.

---

[1]This is a general rule of the CBOE. As a practical matter, the exchange confers with the crowd and responds to market movements when considering exercise prices.

MARGIN REQUIREMENTS

There are no margin requirements for the buyer of an index option once the premium has been paid in full since the maximum amount that an investor can lose is restricted to the option premium.

The option writer, on the other hand, has agreed to accept all of the risk of the underlying security. The writer therefore must satisfy margin requirements issued by the Federal Reserve Board and each individual exchange. In addition, an adverse price movement may require the writer to post additional margin on the increased premium. All index options are marked-to-the-market. The margin requirements for cash and stock index futures options are presented in Tables 4–3 and 4–4.

Margin requirements for out-of-the-money index futures options are adjusted for the amount the option is out-of-the-money. For options on the S&P 500 futures contract the margin is reduced by one half the out-of-the-money amount while the margin requirement is reduced by the entire out-of-the-money amount for options on the NYSE Composite Index futures contract.

The required initial margin for an option writer is illustrated in the following examples. On May 27, 1988, the S&P 500 futures settled at 253.50 and the S&P 500 Index settled at 253.42. Suppose an option writer could have sold the following call options at the indicated prices:

	Exercise Price	Option Premium
S&P 500 futures	245	12.40
June contract	260	3.70
S&P 500 Index	245	11.25
June contract	260	2.25

The margin requirement for the option on the S&P 500 futures is the initial margin requirement on the futures plus the option premium less one half the amount the option is out-of-the-money or a minimum of the option settlement premium plus the minimum set by the Exchange, or $10,000. The initial margin on an S&P 500 futures contract is $19,000. The June 245 option has a premium of $6,200 (12.40 × $500) and is in the money. Therefore,

TABLE 4–3
Cash Index Option Margin Requirements

Contract	Major Market Index	S&P 100 Index	S&P 500 Index	Institutional Index	NYFE Composite Index	Value Line
Long call	Pay for call or put premium in full	Same	Same	Same	Same	Same
Short call or put	Full option proceeds plus 15 percent of the underlying index value less out-of-the money amount or minimum of options proceeds plus 10 percent of underlying index value or, index option escrow receipt for calls. Cash or equivalents equal to aggregate excess price for puts.	Same	Same	Same	Same	Same
Maintenance	Marked-to-market	Same	Same	Same	Same	Same
Spread (in which short side expires before or concurrent with long side)	The amount by which short call/ long put aggregate exercise price is below long call/short put aggregate exercise price. Pay for long option in full	Same	Same	Same	Same	Same
Maintenance	Initial spread requirement	Same	Same	Same	Same	Same

the initial margin requirement is $19,000 plus $6,200, or $25,200. The premium for the June 260 contract is $1,850. The amount out-of-the-money is $3,250 (6.50 × $500). The amount of initial margin required for the option writer is reduced by one half this amount ($1,625) and is $19,000 plus $1,850 minus $1,625, or $19,225.

The initial margin on the S&P 500 Index option is the full option premium plus 15 percent of the underlying instrument, minus any out-of-the-money amount to a minimum of 10 percent of the underlying plus the option premium. The option premium for

TABLE 4–4
Stock Index Futures Option Margin Requirements

Contract	NYSE Composite Index Futures	S&P 500 Index Futures
Long call or put	Pay for call or put premium in full.	Same
Short call or put uncovered	Option settlement premium plus margin on futures less out-of-the-money amount, or a minimum of $750 per option.	Option settlement premium plus margin on futures minus one half of the amount the option is out-of-the-money or a minimum of option settlement premium plus $10,000
Maintenance.	Marked-to-market.	Same
Covered out-of-the-money	Option settlement premium plus the hedge margin on futures.	Option settlement premium plus underlying futures hedge margin minus one half the amount the option is in-the-money, if any, or a minimum of option settlement premium plus $10,000
At or in-the-money	Option settlement premium plus the greater of hedge margin on futures less in-the-money amount, if any, or underlying futures spread margin.	Same as above
Maintenance	Marked-to market.	Same
Spread (in which short side expires before or concurrent with long side)	The amount by which short settlement premium exceeds long plus difference between strikes but not greater than futures margin or less than spread margin where long call/short put strike is greater than short call/long put.	For bull call spreads and bear put spreads, no margin. For bear call and bull put spreads, lesser of the difference in option exercise prices or futures hedge margin plus excess of short premium over long premium

the June 245 contract is $1,125 (11.25 × $100). Also, 15 percent of the value of the underlying is $3,801.30 (.15 × 100 × 253.42). Since the contract is in-the-money, the required margin is $4,926.30. Because the June 260 contract is out-of-the-money, the initial margin required is reduced by $658 (6.58 × $100), and the initial margin requirement is $225 plus $3,801.30 minus $658, or $3,368.30.

EXPIRATION OF TRADING/FINAL EXERCISE

The termination of trading for cash index options occurs on the third Friday of the contract month. Options expire on the Saturday following the third Friday of the contract month. Once again, settlement of final exercise is in cash based on the closing index level on expiration Friday. The expiration of trading for index options on futures is the same as the underlying future. The difference here is in settlement which occurs in cash rather than in the delivery of a futures position due to the fact that the deliverable future is expiring and also is cash settled.

CHAPTER 5

MECHANICS OF TRADING STOCK INDEX FUTURES

Bruce M. Collins, Ph.D.
Vice President
Equity Arbitrage Group
Index Products Research
Shearson Lehman Hutton Inc.

Frank J. Fabozzi, Ph.D., C.F.A.
Visiting Professor of Finance
Sloan School of Management
Massachusetts Institute of Technology

This chapter will discuss the mechanics of stock index futures trading, including a brief discussion of "sunshine trading." It is absolutely essential to understand these mechanics if one intends to employ these contracts in an investment strategy.

SELECTING A BROKERAGE FIRM AND A BROKER

The first step after deciding to use stock index futures contracts is to select the organization that will execute the transactions. All brokers executing futures transactions for the public, known as *futures commission merchants,* must register with the Commodity Futures Exchange Commission (CFTC). A commodity futures merchant need not be a member of a futures exchange. Some organizations deal exclusively in futures transactions; other organizations handle securities transactions as well as futures transactions.

The selection of a broker depends on what the investor wants from the relationship. Some organizations provide research information and supporting services as well as execution, while others, called *discount brokers,* provide only the execution function. Discount brokers offer no frills, and generally charge lower commissions.

The investor who wants research information and other assistance should examine the line of services provided by the organization under consideration. The quality of the services rendered varies and is often difficult to measure. One brokerage firm may excel in providing a particular service, but fall short in different types of service.

The margin requirements established by the organization must also be considered. Although the exchange establishes the minimum initial and maintenance margin requirements, brokerage firms are free to set their own minimum as long as it is not less than that set by the exchange. Although competition keeps the minimum margin requirements from varying substantially from firm to firm, the investor should compare the margin requirements established by the brokerage firms that are under consideration.

The selection of an account representative at the brokerage firm is important if the investor intends to rely on the account representative's recommendations. The account representative should have successfully completed the National Commodity Representatives Examination and should be registered with the CFTC. Inquiry into the background and performance of the account representative should be undertaken. The account representative should fully understand the investor's trading philosophy.

TYPES OF ORDERS

When an investor wishes to buy or sell a futures contract, the price and conditions under which the order is to be executed must be communicated to the account representative.

The simplest type of order, yet the most dangerous from the investor's perspective, is the *market order*. When a market order is placed, it is executed at the best price available as soon as it reaches the trading pit.[1] Market orders are fine for security trades involving long-term strategies since security prices do not fluctuate as much as futures prices between the decision to trade and the time the order reaches the trading floor. Nevertheless, although 75 percent of stock transactions are placed as market orders, market impact (measured as the difference in price from the time the decision is made to trade and the time of execution) can represent a substantial cost to a trading strategy and must be acknowledged when considering a market order. Stock index futures prices jump around a great deal during short intervals of time. Coupled with the higher leverage associated with the stock index futures, an adverse movement of just a few ticks between the time the investor decides to transact based on prevailing market prices and the time the order reaches the trading pit could make the difference between a successful strategy and a disastrous one. Market orders are useful for trading strategies that are relatively insensitive to price. Portfolio insurance strategies, for example, are primarily concerned with the replication of target positions in cash and equity.[2] For the strategy to be successful, it is essential to meet these targets. This type of strategy has only a general sensitivity to the absolute purchase or sale price for futures and, thus, market orders make sense. In fact, one practice among portfolio insurance vendors, known as "sunshine" or "blimp" trading, is to announce their intention to buy or sell stock index futures prior to placing the order.[3]

Another order related to market orders is a *market not held order*. A not held order has the same characteristics as a market order, but is more flexible with respect to the time of execution. The broker has some discretions to obtain a better price. This type of order is beneficial when a large number of futures con-

---

[1]The trading pit is the trading area on the floor of a futures exchange where all transactions for a specific contract are made.

[2]Portfolio insurance is covered in Chapter 12.

[3]This is discussed later in this chapter.

tracts must be bought or sold relative to the number offered or bid at the time of entry.

A *market on close (MOC) order* is a market order executed on the day it was entered at the official closing of the market. MOC orders are often used in program trading to guarantee a price.

To avoid the dangers associated with market orders, the investor can place a *limit order* that designates a price limit for the execution of the transaction. A *buy limit order* indicates that the futures contract may be purchased only at the price designated or at a lower price. A *sell limit order* indicates that the futures contract may be sold at the price designated or at a higher price. Strategies that are sensitive to absolute execution price would use this type of order. In the case of stock index futures arbitrage, the sale price of futures contracts is important to the profitability of the position.[4] Thus, only if futures can be executed at a particular price and relation to the index will the trade be initiated.

One variation of a limit order is a *contingent order* which transfers some risk of simultaneous execution to the trading crowd. An order to buy or sell futures is entered with instructions to execute only if the futures bear a specific relationship to the cash index. The absolute price level of the futures is not important. The arbitrageur may use this order in lieu of a limit order in instances where futures markets are volatile and lead last sale information on the trading screen. A contingency order involving the simultaneous purchase and sale of futures is a *spread order*. This order is used by traders to take advantage of mispricing between futures of different expiration.

The danger with a limit order is that there is no assurance that it will be executed. The designated price may not be reached. Even if it is reached at a later time, the order may not be fulfilled because there is no one on a futures exchange to assure the role of the specialist on a stock exchange, who keeps a book on unfilled limit orders and executes them when the designated price is reached. Nevertheless, the dangers of a limit

---

[4]Arbitrage is discussed in Chapters 14 and 15.

order are far less than the dangers of a market order. The investor has more control with a limit order since the price designated in the limit order can be revised based on prevailing market prices.

The limit order is a conditional order: it is executed only if the limit price or a better price can be obtained. Another type of conditional order is the *stop order,* which specifies that the order is not to be executed until the market reaches a designated price at which time it becomes a market order. A *buy stop order* specifies that the order is not to be executed until the market rises to a designated price. A sell stop order specifies that the order is not to be executed until the market price falls below a designated price. A stop order is useful when a futures trader cannot watch the market constantly. Profits can be preserved or losses minimized on positions by allowing market movements to trigger a strategy.

To understand how a stop order can be used and how it differs from a limit order, consider the following examples. Suppose that an investor purchased an S&P 500 futures contract for 268 and futures price is 279. The investor wants to protect the paper profit. The investor could place a sell stop order at 275. This means that when the futures price falls to 275 or lower, the futures contract is sold at the best price possible. To see how an investor can use a sell stop order to limit a loss, suppose that the investor purchased a NYSE Composite Index futures contract for 159 and that the position was taken in the expectation that the futures prices would increase. To limit the loss should the futures price decline instead, the investor could place a sell stop order at 155. The two examples of a sell stop order show how it can be used by an investor in a long position. An investor in a short position can utilize a buy stop order to protect a paper profit or limit a loss.

Notice that in a sell stop order the designated price is less than the current market price of the futures contract. In a sell limit order, however, the designated price is above the market price of the futures contract. In a buy stop order the designated price is above the market price. In a buy limit order it is below the market price.

There are two dangers associated with stop orders. Since the stock index futures market exhibits abrupt price changes, the direction of the change in the futures price may be only temporary, resulting in the premature closing of a position. Also, once the designated price is reached, the stop order becomes a market order and is subject to the uncertainty of the execution price noted earlier for market orders.

A stop-limit order, a hybrid of a stop order and a limit order, is a stop order that designates a price limit. The order can be used to cushion the market impact of a stop order. Futures traders may limit the possible execution price after the activation of a stop. Sometimes the activation of a stop market order can cause brief but violent price movements followed by a retracement to previous levels. The stop-limit order may help take advantage of this phenomenon. The risk is, however, that prices do not retrace and additional losses are incurred. For example, in our illustration of the S&P 500 futures contract that was purchased at 268 and is now priced at 279, the investor can place a sell stop-limit order that goes into effect at a futures price of 275 and has a limit price of 272. As with a limit order, the limit price may never be reached and therefore the order will not be executed. This defeats the purpose of the stop order which is to protect a paper profit or limit a loss.

Conditional orders such as the limit order or the buy order must designate the time period for which the order is effective—a day, week, or month. An open order is good until the order is cancelled.

TAKING AND LIQUIDATING A POSITION

Once an account has been opened, the trader may take a position in the market. If the trader does this by buying a futures contract, the trader is said to be in a *long position*. If the trader's opening position is the sale of a futures contract the trader is said to be in a *short position*.

The trader can liquidate a position prior to the final settlement date by taking an offsetting position. For a long position, this means selling an identical number of contracts; for a short position, it means buying an identical number of contracts. Or the trader can wait until the final settlement day and liquidate his or her position by cash settlement.

The broker is required to provide confirmation of the execution of an order as soon as possible. The confirmation form that is filled out when a position is taken indicates all the essential information about the trade. When the order involves the liquidation of a position, the confirmation form shows the profit or loss on the position and the commission costs.

It is not uncommon to purchase a security through one brokerage firm and sell it through another. However, this is usually not done with futures contracts. The brokerage firm that executes the order to establish the initial position also executes the order to liquidate the position.

When a trader takes a position in the market, another party is taking the opposite position and agreeing to satisfy the commitment set forth in the contract. What if the party defaults on the obligation? Is the trader's only recourse to sue the defaulting party? Does that mean a trader must be concerned with who the other party is before taking a position in the futures market? Moreover, if the trader wants to liquidate a position before the final settlement date, must the trader do so only with that party?

The trader need not worry about the financial strength and integrity of the other party to the contract. Once the order is executed, the direct relationship between the two parties is severed. A clearing corporation associated with each exchange interposes itself as the buy to every sale and the seller to every purchase. Thus, each of the parties to the contract is free to liquidate his position without being concerned about the other party.

MARGIN REQUIREMENTS

In the previous chapter the various margin requirements for trading stock index futures contracts were explained. These margin requirements can be illustrated through a stock replacement strategy used by some institutional index funds indifferent between holding the stocks or holding futures. An index fund will sell its stocks, replace them with a dollar equivalent of futures contracts and place the proceeds in Treasury bills.[5] This strategy was available in the third week of April 1988, using the June 1988 S&P 500 futures contract.

Suppose that an index fund invested $25,052,888 in S&P June 1988 futures contracts to replace an equivalent amount of stock on April 14, 1988.[6] The closing futures price that day was 259.0 and the closing cash index was 259.75. The number of contracts required to satisfy the dollar value of the portfolio is 193 ($25,052,088/500 ÷ 259.75). The futures position is viewed as a hedge against cash, and therefore, the initial margin requirement is $10,000 times 193 or $1,930,000. The investor's cash position can be used to satisfy the initial margin. The maintenance margin for this transaction is the same as the initial margin.

Table 5–1 presents the closing settlement price of the S&P 500 June 1988 futures contract for nine days following April 14, 1988. The variation margin from the account is examined on a day-to-day basis below and is summarized in Table 5–2. We assume that daily variation margin is reflected by the equity in the account. In practice, institutional investors post the initial margin in Treasury bills while satisfying the negative variation margin with cash (which is required). They withdraw positive variation margin and maintain only the minimum required. In our example, we relax this assumption.

Day 2.   The futures price declined from 259.00 to 258.60 or .40 index points. The decrease in the contract value is subtracted from the investor's account. This is what is meant by marked-to-the-market. The equity in the investor's account is the initial

---

[5]The example applies to an institutional account where the stock position is replaced with a futures position and Treasury bills. The Treasury bill account usually is not touched and variation margin is satisfied each day in cash. Index funds are discussed in Chapter 16.

[6]The correct calculation to determine the number of futures contracts to be sold is dollar value/500 × cash index. This number, as a rule of thumb, should come within .10 of a round number of futures contracts which is equivalent to $9,650 on 193 contracts, or .1 × 500 × 193. This represents an approximate $25 million position adjusted to account for the necessity of using a round number of futures contracts.

TABLE 5–1

Assumed Futures Position and Value of Contracts for Margin Requirement Illustration

Day	Trade Price	Value of 193 Contracts (dollars)*
1	$259.00	$259.00 × 500 × 193 = $24,993,500

Trading Days 2 through 10:

Day	Settlement Price	Value of 193 Contracts
2	$258.60	$24,954,900
3	259.25	25,017,625
4	257.30	24,829,450
5	257.90	24,887,350
6	256.20	24,723,300
7	261.85	25,268,525
8	263.85	25,461,525
9	264.80	25,553,200
10	264.00	25,476,000

*The contract value is $500 times the futures price. Since there are 193 contracts, the per contract value is multiplied by 193.

margin less $38,600. The investor must now transfer the entire amount, $38,600, into the account to satisfy the maintenance margin. If the maintenance margin is below the initial margin, as is the case with speculators, no additional margin would be required. The initial margin for speculators is $3,667,000 (193 × $19,000). In this case, $1,737,000 would have to be lost before the maintenance margin requirement is violated. In practice, when the equity in the account is near the maintenance margin level, additional cash may be added to the account in anticipation of a decline in futures prices. The additional amount provides a cushion and may prevent a margin call. This is particularly important when there is a differential between initial margin and maintenance margin.

Day 3. The futures price increased from 258.60 to 259.25 or .65 index points. The contract value of the position is increased by $62,725. Notice that the equity in the account is $62,725 above

TABLE 5–2
Margin Requirements and Account Equity for the Purchase of 193 S&P 500 Contracts

Initial margin per S&P 500 contract = $10,000
Initial margin for 193 S&P 500 contracts = $1,930,000 (193 × $10,000)
Maintenance margin per S&P 500 contract = $10,000
Maintenance margin for 193 S&P 500 contracts = $1,930,000

Day	Settlement Price	Value for 193 Contracts*	Equity in Account*	Variation Margin*
1	$259.00	$24,993,500	$1,930,000	——
2	258.60	24,954,900	1,891,400	$ (38,600)
3	259.25	25,017,625	1,992,725†	62,725
4	257.30	24,829,450	1,804,550	(188,175)
5	257.90	24,887,350	1,987,900	57,900
6	256.20	24,723,300	1,823,850	(164,050)
7	261.85	25,268,525	2,475,225	545,225
8	263.85	25,461,525	2,668,225	193,000
9	264.80	24,553,200	2,759,900	91,675
10	264.00	25,476,000	2,682,700	(77,200)

*Amounts are in dollars.
†Accounts have 24 hours to satisfy negative variation margin. Margin calls are satisfied the next day. Thus, $1,992,725 = $1,930,000 + $62,725.

the margin requirements because the account had previously been restored to the maintenance margin level.

Day 4.   The futures price declined by 1.95 index points settling at 257.30. This reduces the equity in the account by $188,175. The loss pushes the equity in the account below the required maintenance margin and the investor must raise additional cash to satisfy the margin.

Day 5.   A .60 index point increase in the futures price to 257.90 increases the equity in the account by $57,900. Because the equity in the account was restored on the previous day to the maintenance margin level, the account balance is $1,987,900.

Day 6.   A significant decline of 1.7 index points in the futures price yields a $164,050 reduction to the equity in the account. The investor has 24 hours to satisfy the maintenance margin requirement.

Day 7. A dramatic increase in the futures price to 261.85 adds $545,225 to the equity in the account. The value of the account now amounts to $2,475,225. Thus, the futures price can fall by 4.16 index points or 1.59 percent before the margin requirements are violated.

Day 8. An increase in the futures price to 263.85 increases the equity in the account by $193,000. This adds to the surplus in the account. The investor may choose to withdraw the cash for alternative investments, which is often the practice of institutional investors.

Day 9. A .95 index point rise in the futures price increases the equity in the account by $91,675. If we assume the investor does not withdraw cash from the account, there is sufficient equity in the account to satisfy margin requirements should the futures price fall 6.27 points at some time in the future.

Day 10. On the final day of our analysis the futures price has fallen to 264.00. There is a $77,200 reduction to the equity in the account. Because there is a surplus of equity in the account, no margin call is required.

The foregoing illustrated the purchase of stock index futures contracts by an institutional investor. Table 5–3 shows what would happen if 193 S&P 500 contracts were sold rather than purchased. Notice that the excess equity in the account is the opposite of that shown in Table 5–2.

In our illustration we have assumed that the index fund deposited cash to meet the initial and variation margins. As an alternative, Treasury bills or letters of credit may be used for initial margin. Variation margin *must* be satisfied with cash.

COMMISSIONS

Like the commissions on common stock transactions, the commissions on executions of stock index futures contracts are fully negotiable. The commissions charged on stock index futures contracts are based on a round trip. For individual investors, these commissions range from $40 to $100 per contract at full service

TABLE 5–3
Margin Requirements and Account Equity for the Sale of 193 S&P 500 Contracts

Initial margin per S&P 500 contract = $10,000
Initial margin for 193 S&P 500 contracts = $1,930,000 (193 × $10,000)
Maintenance margin per S&P 500 contract = $10,000
Maintenance margin for 193 S&P 500 contracts = $1,930,000

Day	Settlement Price	Value for 193 Contracts*	Equity in Account*	Variation Margin*
1	$259.00	$24,993,500	$1,930,000	——
2	258.60	24,954,900	1,968,600	$ 38,600
3	259.25	25,017,625	1,905,875	(62,725)
4	257.30	24,829,450	2,118,175†	188,175
5	257.90	24,887,350	2,060,275	(57,900)
6	256.20	24,723,300	2,224,325	164,050
7	261.85	25,268,525	1,679,100	(545,225)
8	263.85	25,461,525	1,737,000‡	(193,000)
9	264.80	25,553,200	1,838,325	(91,675)
10	264.00	25,476,000	2,007,200	77,200

*Amounts are in dollars.
†$2,118,175 = $1,930,000 + $188,175.
‡$1,737,000 = $1,930,000 − $193,000.

brokerage firms. For institutional investors, the typical commission per contract is under $15. Assuming a round-trip commission of $50 per contract, the cost of transacting is typically less than 0.1 percent (0.001) of the contract value. A round-trip commission for a portfolio consisting of the underlying stocks would be roughly 1 percent of the value of the stocks.

SUNSHINE TRADING

The intent of sunshine or blimp trading[7] is to secure the best futures price with least market impact for a sizable trade under adverse conditions. In contrast to volatility trading strategies,

---

[7]Sunshine trading was pioneered by Leland, O'Brien and Rubinstein as part of a portfolio insurance investment strategy. The authors are grateful to Larry Edwards of LOR for his comments regarding sunshine trading.

sunshine trades are designed to dampen volatility. The central idea is to create an auction environment where all potential participants are provided with information regarding what will be traded and when it will be traded. Furthermore, a sunshine trade is a large "informationless" trade. The motivation behind the trade contains no market forecast information (i.e., new information) unlike other sizable trades with unknown motivation.

Key to the success of a sunshine trade is the ability to predisclose the trade. Currently, predisclosure takes place informally outside the brokerage industry because of regulatory requirements. A recent disclosure proposal by the New York Futures Exchange attempted to address this issue, but was withdrawn from consideration because it did not satisfy the CFTC requirement that disclosure be broad enough. Consequently, the ability to predisclose continues to be inhibited by regulation. An investor must put out the information through the wire services and in the trading pit arena without the assistance of a broker. Should the information set be incomplete prior to the time of execution, front running is more likely and the trade more costly.

In February of 1986, Leland, O'Brien and Rubinstein (LOR) sold 1,200 S&P 500 futures contracts using a sunshine trade. It was the first known application of the concept. Essentially, the LOR version of a sunshine trade works as follows. Information about the trade is disseminated in advance of an 11:00 AM EST designated trading time. At that time, a limit order is shown for the entire trade within the existing bid-ask spread for one minute. After such time, the order is withdrawn if not completed and is shown again 15 minutes later for another minute. This process is repeated until the order is complete.

Sunshine trading improves market liquidity, and market impact is reduced. Predisclosure dispels the uncertainty of the trade and allows the market time to adjust. The disadvantage of sunshine trading is that it is implemented only under adverse market conditions. Furthermore, incomplete dissemination of information can lead to front-running where the locals rally the market into the merchandise.

CHAPTER 6

MECHANICS OF TRADING STOCK INDEX OPTIONS

Bruce M. Collins, Ph.D.
Vice President
Equity Arbitrage Group
Index Products Research
Shearson Lehman Hutton Inc.

James A. Schmidt
Vice President
Equity Arbitrage Group
Shearson Lehman Hutton Inc.

The volume of stock index options trading continues to grow as more professional money managers understand how options can be used to develop strategies that contribute to attaining their investment objectives. The use of stock index options enables the investor to modify the risk-return profile of equity portfolios quickly and effectively. This chapter will discuss the mechanics of trading stock index options.

SELECTING A BROKERAGE FIRM AND A BROKER

The selection of a broker and the firm for the execution of stock index options involves three levels of decision. The first level requires that the broker meet the qualifications of stock index option trading. That is, the general securities examination and registration requirements in the case of cash index options; and further, the commodities futures examination and CFTC registration for options on index futures.

Another decision is based on the investor's expectations of the broker and the firm. Investors who do not require significant advisory or educational input may be more sensitive to commission level and have more definitive execution requirements. These investors make their own investment/trading decisions and may find discount brokers best suit their needs. On the other hand, an investor who wants traditional account support, recordkeeping, research, education, and advice will need to evaluate the potential firms' expertise in these particular services.

Finally, there is the decision regarding the individual representative within the firm selected. Background and track record are easily checked, but personality fit is equally important. Apart from instinctive feel, perhaps the best way to find a compatible representative is to ask about the objectives of their own personal accounts. This may indicate the likelihood that the broker's trading philosophy and concern will match those of the investor.

TAKING AND PROCESSING A POSITION

Once an account has been opened the trader can buy or sell options on behalf of a customer. The customer decides with the trader what action to take. A customer, for example, who is bullish on the market yet wants to minimize downside risk may decide to purchase a call option. The trader phones directly to the floor of the appropriate exchange (CBOE or AMEX as the most active option exchanges), and places an order with a floor broker. The floor broker executes the order on the floor, and phones a report back to the trader, where the order ticket is written and the customer account number is reported to the floor. The wire operator books the trade to the customer's account and sends a hard copy confirm to the firm's branch where the customer is located.

On a nightly basis the option operation area of the brokerage firm will match all trade tickets to the hard copy confirms to verify the contract. The buy/sell, price, quantity, account number, open/close will be checked for accuracy and commissions calculated for each ticket. In addition, the operations area will send details of all the trades done by the firm to the Options Clearing Corporation (OCC). The OCC then matches the buy and sell orders across brokerage house inventories and, in the event of discrepancies, adjusts contracts and dollars where necessary. The call option purchased by the customer will be matched by the OCC with a written option by a second party. As with index futures, the clearing corporation acts as intermediary of all trades and thus each of the parties to be contracted is free to liquidate the position without being concerned about the other party.

Prior to sending the customer a confirm, a trading desk clerk will match trade tickets and reports with the hard copy customer confirms to verify the account. On properly matched trades the confirm is sent to the customer. If a correction is necessary, the clerk will adjust the trade and again verify all trade information on the confirms the next morning.

Finally, the firm's margin department will settle all contracts. A check is issued on a sell to the customer, or on a buy the customer will deliver an escrow receipt from his bank. In addition, the margin department will assign operating requirements for any opening short positions and issue any margin call that may be necessary for new or existing positions.

MECHANICS OF INDEX OPTIONS TRADES

In Chapter 4, the margin requirements for index options were listed and examples of initial margins were provided. In this section, we illustrate the daily cash flows associated with marginable option positions. Option writers, having agreed to assume the risk of the underlying security, must post initial margin. Index option positions are marked-to-the-market and therefore cash flows in and out of the customer's account on a daily basis. To illustrate how this works, suppose an investor initiates a covered call strategy which involves writing an option against a long position in the underlying security. A popular application of this strategy among institutional investors is an index buy/write. The introduction of options on the Major Market Index (XMI) has provided institutional investors with an alternative for traditional covered call strategies. The purchase of stock and sale of calls against the shares held are intended to yield incremental return with a degree of downside protection.

Suppose the investor is long 3,000 shares of each XMI stock (an approximate $3.5 million position). This requires the sale of 86 XMI call options.[1] The initial margin requirement on a covered XMI call option can be satisfied with an Index Option Escrow Receipt.[2] Subsequently, the position is marked-to-the-market, with the XMI at 395 and 3,000 shares of each stock held. The value of the portfolio that must be indicated on the escrow receipt is the sum of the value of the component stocks or 3,000 × 395 × 2.85813 = $3,386,884. Also, July 405 calls priced at $7¾ on the bid side generate 86 × 100 × $7¾ = $66,650 in option premium. Thus, the investor purchases $3,386,884 in stock value while receiving $66,650 in option premium. The option premium can be placed in an interest-bearing asset. By contrast, an uncovered short call option requires an initial margin payment of $66,650 + 15 percent × 100 × 395 × 86, or $576,200, less the out-of-the-money amount of $86,000 ($10 × 86 × 100), which equals $490,200. The initial margin can be satisfied with cash or cash equivalents. If Treasury bills are used, 95 percent of the loan value can be applied to the margin requirements.

Because index options are settled in cash there is no underlying deliverable security. Consequently, covered call writing in the traditional sense is not possible. Therefore, a call writer with a long position in a portfolio of stocks that replicates the index is not considered covered for margin purposes. Consistent with this interpretation, the illustration which follows assumes the option is uncovered.

---

[1]The value of any number of index call options is:

Number of options × Multiple × Option premium

[2]The escrow receipt is the result of the pilot index option escrow receipt program approved by the SEC. The escrow receipt is issued by the customer's bank and essentially acts as collateral. Cash, cash equivalents, or one or more marginable equity securities can be used. In addition, a "Letter of Guarantee" issued by the customer's bank can also act as collateral.

TABLE 6–1
Index Valuation XMI Market Scenarios

Day	Closing Price	Index Value of 86 Call Options*	15 Percent of Index Value
1	395	$3,397,000	$509,550
2	400	3,440,000	516,000
3	392	3,371,200	505,680
4	387	3,328,200	499,230
5	377	3,242,200	486,330
6	397	3,414,200	512,130

*The value of the index is the multiplier × index. This applies to each option position.

Table 6–1 presents closing price scenarios for the XMI index and the value of 3,000 equal shares held in each of the 20 stocks that make up the index for six successive trading days. The maintenance margin requirements for uncovered calls are examined day to day and summarized in Table 6–2.

Day 2. The XMI index rose five points from 395 to 400. The value for the call option increased from 7¾ to 9⅞. Applying the marked-to-the-market margin requirement forces the customer to post additional margin by the amount of the change in the call's value per contract. Since in this illustration 86 call options were written, the amount of additional margin is (9⅞ − 7¾) × $100

TABLE 6–2
Margin Requirements for Uncovered XMI Index Call Options Positions

Day	Closing Index Price	Last Call Price	Uncovered Call
1*	395	7¾	$490,200
2	400	9⅞	557,925
3	392	6⅜	448,705
4	387	4½	383,130
5	377	2	324,220†
6	397	7½	507,830

*Represents initial margin requirements at the time the trade is entered.
†Reflects minimum maintenance margin, or 10 percent of the index value.

× 86, or $18,275. In addition, 15 percent of the difference in the value of the index is added to the account (.15 × $100 × 86) or $6,450. Since the option is less out-of-the money, additional margin is necessary, $5 × 100 × 86, or $43,000. The total additional margin, then, is $43,000 + $6,450 + $18,275, or $67,725.

Day 3. The XMI index declined eight points to 392 while the option value fell to 6⅜. The total margin requirement is reduced by $3.5 × 100 × 86, or $30,100. The amount of cash or cash equivalents held in the customer's account may be reduced by this amount. The margin account housing the uncovered call position is further reduced because of the 15 percent of index value requirement (.15 × 100 × 8 × 86), or $10,320. The current total dollar value of the margin account that must be maintained for the uncovered call position is $505,680 plus $54,825 less $111,800, or $448,705. This compares with an initial margin requirement on day one of $490,200.

Day 4. The market continued to decline with the XMI closing at 387. The call option remains out-of-the-money and thus the margin adjustment is straightforward. A 1⅞ point decline in the option value reduces the margin requirement by $1.875 × 100 × 86, or $16,125. The margin requirement is reduced by an additional $6,440 plus $43,000 because the index declined and the option is further out-of-the-money.

Day 5. A 2.58 percent decline in the XMI index to 377 leaves the call option further out-of-the-money with a time premium valued at $2.00. The margin requirement then becomes $2 × $100 × 86, or $17,200, less the out-of-the-money amount of (387 − 377) × $100 × 86, or $86,000. Since this amount falls below the minimum margin requirement of 10 percent of the underlying index (.10 × $100 × 86 × 377, or $324,220), this amount must be held in the account. Thus, the margin requirement for the uncovered call position is $324,220.

Day 6. The XMI index rose dramatically to 397. The call option closed at 7½. The option is still, however, out-of-the-money. The margin requirement is increased an additional $183,610. If, on any day, the option writer is assigned, the index

TABLE 6–3
Margin Requirements Comparing Short XMI Index Call and Put Options Positions

Day	Last Call	Last Put	Margin Requirements Call	Put	Short/Short Call/Put
1	7¾	15¼	$490,200	$640,700	$1,130,900
2	9⅞	12⅜	557,925	622,425	1,180,350
3	6⅜	17	448,705	651,880	1,100,585
4	4½	20½	383,130	675,530	1,058,660
5	2	28½	324,220	731,430	1,055,650
6	7½	13½	507,830	628,230	1,136,060

options are settled in the payment of cash. In the case where the index closes above the strike price, the option holder is entitled to receive the difference between the option's aggregate exercise price and the closing index price. Settlement takes place on the following business day. If the covered call is a buy/write strategy the customer is left long the stock position while the customer with a naked call position is flat. The choice of what outstanding options are assigned is a decision made by the OCC through a random drawing process and may or may not include all options held.

The daily marked-to-the-market of short index option positions was illustrated using uncovered call option positions. Table 6–3 presents the daily margin requirements for the same market scenarios for a short put option position and a combination of a short put and a short call. Day 1 represents the initial margin requirement for each position. The same margin requirement rule applies to the short put position. In addition, the margin requirement for a combination of short put and short call on the same index with the same multiplier is the sum of the short put and short call requirement.

COMMISSIONS

The commissions on the execution of the index option contracts, like the commissions on common stock transactions on executions of stock index futures, are fully negotiable. Individual traders will think of commission rates as a percent off the original fixed-rate commission schedule for institutions. Actual commission levels are quoted on a one-way basis and may vary widely as a function of size and frequency of trading for a particular customer. Using the buy/write illustration in the previous section, a one-way commission of $4.50 is equivalent to .045 XMI index points. For 86 contracts this amounts to 86 × 4.50, or $387. This is significantly lower than the commissions incurred on the stock which at $.05/per share adds up to (.05 × 20) × 3,000, or $3,000.

SECTION TWO

PRICING AND PERFORMANCE CHARACTERISTICS

CHAPTER 7

STOCK MARKET INDICATORS

Joanne M. Hill, Ph.D.
Vice President
Paine Webber

Frank J. Fabozzi, Ph.D., C.F.A
Visiting Professor of Finance
Sloan School of Management
Massachusetts Institute of Technology

Jonathan C. Jankus
Vice President
Kidder, Peabody & Co., Inc.

Stock market averages and indexes peform a variety of functions, from serving as benchmarks for performance analyses to answering the question, "How did the market do today?" Thus the averages and indexes have become a part of everyday life for the investment practitioner. Even though many of the stock market indicators are used interchangeably, each measures a different facet of the market. Understanding the differences is essential for investors who contemplate the use of futures and options contracts based on these indicators.

The success of hedging strategies that employ stock index futures and options contracts depends to some extent on the nature of the average or index. Therefore, we will explain the nature of the various averages and indexes on which major futures contracts are currently traded—the New York Stock Exchange (NYSE) Composite Index, the Standard & Poor's (S&P) 500

Composite Index, the Major Market Index (MMI or XMI), the Value Line Average Composite (VLA), the Russell 2000 and the Russell 3000. The Russell 3000 is a broad-based equity index that represents some 98 percent of the investable U.S. equities. The Russell 2000 represents the 2,000 smallest capitalization stocks in the Russell 3000, about 9 percent of the total U.S. equity market. Other widely followed indexes which do not have associated futures contracts such as the Dow Jones Industrial Average, the S&P 100, the American Stock Exchange Market Value Index and Institutional Index, the NASDAQ Composite Index, and the Wilshire 5000 Equity Index are also reviewed.

WHY DO STOCK MARKET INDICATORS EXIST?

Indexes serve many purposes, probably the most important of which is a mechanism for summarizing value and changes in value within the segment of the equity market covered by that index. In this sense an index serves as a proxy for a set of securities much like the Consumer Price Index serves as a measure of the general level of prices of consumer goods in the U.S. economy. Just as consumers have an interest in measuring changes over time in the aggregate level of prices of goods and services, so are investors concerned with monitoring the aggregate level of equity prices.

By keeping track of an index, an investor can measure how well specific stock selections are performing relative to a general market barometer. The return of an index often serves as a performance benchmark against which an actively managed stock portfolio can be judged. Investment in stocks according to their weights in a stock market index is often referred to as passive management. Basically, an investor passively selects, buys, and holds the included issues without concern for relative values, earnings prospects, or technical indicators. Many investors invest in equities by purchasing so-called *index funds* which are specifically constructed and managed to track the performance of a specific market index. Since some critical mass of funds is required to purchase all of the stocks in an index at a reasonable transaction cost, passive management is usually done indirectly by the purchase of a mutual fund that follows such a strategy or by hiring an investment manager who specializes in index fund management.

CONSTRUCTION OF STOCK MARKET AVERAGES AND INDEXES

In general, the various stock market indicators rise and fall together. There are, however, important differences in the magnitude of these moves. To understand the reasons for these differences, it is necessary to understand how indicators are constructed.

Three factors differentiate stock market averages and indexes:

1. The universe of stocks represented by the indicator.
2. The relative weights given to the stocks.
3. The method of averaging used.

The Universe of Stocks Represented

An index of averages can be designed from all publicly traded stocks or from a sample of publicly traded stocks. The Russell 3000 and Wilshire 5000 cover over 95 percent of all publicly traded issues; however, no index or average currently traded is based on all publicly traded stocks. For the indexes on which futures contracts are currently traded, the NYSE Composite Index consists of just under 1,600 stocks, the S&P 500 consists of 500 stocks, the MMI consists of 20 stocks and the VLA consists of about 1,700 stocks. The breadth of coverage differs among these market indicators. The NYSE Composite Index, first computed in 1966, reflects the market value of all issues traded on the NYSE. The indicator series computed by Standard & Poor's represents selected samples of stocks chosen from the major exchanges—NYSE and the American Stock Exchange(AMEX)–and the over-the-counter market. The universe represented at any point in time is determined by a committee of Standard & Poor's Corporation, which may occasionally add or delete individual stocks or entire industry groups. The aim of the committee is to capture present overall stock market conditions representing a very broad range of economic indicators. The VLA, produced by Arnold Bernhard & Co., covers a broad range of widely held and actively traded issues selected by Value Line.

The most commonly quoted indicator, the Dow Jones Industrial Average (DJIA), monitors 30 of the largest blue-chip companies traded on the NYSE. These companies change over time as companies are dropped due to mergers, bankruptcy, or because of a very low level of trading activity. When a company is replaced by another company, the average is readjusted in such a way as to provide comparability with earlier values. The Major Market Index has a great deal of similarity with the Dow Jones Industrial Average, as shown in Table 7–1. Seventeen of the 20 stocks in the MMI are also in the DJIA.

The American Stock Exchange Market Value Index, introduced in September 1973, reflects the market value of all issues traded on that exchange. This index generally includes companies with smaller capitalization than the companies traded on the NYSE and has a proportionally greater foreign and energy-related orientation. The NASDAQ Composite Index, introduced in February 1971, reflects changes in the market value of the over-the-counter stocks traded by the National Association of Securities Dealers (NASD). The NASDAQ Composite Index represents companies with much smaller capitalization than that of the companies represented by the two exchange indexes and has proportionally greater representation of banks and insurance companies.

The Wilshire 5000 Equity Index, created in 1974 and published by Wilshire Associates of Santa Monica, California, is a comprehensive index that represents all actively traded companies. It is, therefore, very broad in its coverage and serves as the basis of many so-called extended index funds. These funds would appeal to investors that wish a wider representation in their passive equity holdings than could be achieved by the S&P 500 which is the most widely used index for passive management purposes.

The Russell Indexes are maintained by the Frank Russell Company, a leading consultant firm with a client base consisting of pension funds and institutional investors. The Russell Indexes are market-capitalization weighted portfolios of the largest 1,000,

TABLE 7–1
Composition of Dow Jones Industrial Average and Major Market Index

Stocks	Stocks in DJIA	Stocks in MMI
Allied Signal	X	
Alcoa	X	
American Express	X	X
AT&T	X	X
Bethlehem Steel	X	
Boeing	X	
Chevron	X	X
Coca-Cola	X	X
Dow Chemical		X
DuPont	X	X
Eastman Kodak	X	X
Exxon	X	X
General Electric	X	X
General Motors	X	X
Goodyear	X	
IBM	X	X
International Paper	X	X
Johnson & Johnson		X
McDonalds	X	
Merck & Co	X	X
MMM	X	X
Mobil		X
Navistar	X	
Phillip Morris	X	X
Primerica	X	
Procter & Gamble	X	X
Sears Roebuck	X	X
Texaco	X	
Union Carbide	X	
USX	X	X
United Technology	X	
Westinghouse	X	
Woolworth	X	

2,000, and 3,000 stocks traded in the U.S. equity market. The Russell 1000 firms have a market value of approximately $350 million or more; the Russell 2000 firms, representative of the second tier of the equity market, have market values between $20 million and $350 million; and the Russell 3000 tracks almost 97 percent of the stocks held by institutional investors. Like the Wilshire 5000, it is the benchmark index for certain extended index fund products. Futures trading is presently limited to the Russell 2000 and Russell 3000 indexes.

The S&P 100 index consists of 100 actively traded blue-chip stocks, which are widely held in institutional portfolios and which also happen to have related equity options traded. This index, originally constructed by the Chicago Board Options Exchange (CBOE), is the index on which the most actively traded stock index option is based.

Table 7–2 shows the average capitalization of stocks in several of the market indexes discussed above. The MMI consists of very large capitalization issues averaging $27.7 billion in size as compared to the NYSE and S&P 500 indexes which are also heavily weighted in large capitalization stocks but have much lower average capitalizations of $13.1 and $15.4 billion, respectively. The Russell 2000, which represents the smallest capitalization segment of the equity market, has an average capitalization of $200 million.

Relative Weights

The stocks included in a stock market indicator must be combined in certain proportions to construct the index or average. Each stock, therefore, must be assigned some relative weight. There are several ways in which weights may be assigned. The three used in the indexes of interest here are (1) weighting by the market value of the company; (2) weighting by the price of the company's stock; and (3) weighting each company equally, regardless of its price or value.

TABLE 7–2
Average Capitalization of Stock Market Indexes ($ billions)*

Major Market Index	$27.7
S&P 500	15.4
NYSE	13.1
Russell 3000	11.5
Russell 1000	11.3
Russell 2000	.2

*Source: Chicago Board of Trade and Frank Russell Company, July 1987.

With the exception of the VLA and the MMI, the market indicators on which futures are currently traded are market value-weighted. The S&P 100 Index, American Stock Exchange Market Value Index, the NASDAQ Composite Index, and the Wilshire 5000 Equity Index are also market value-weighted. The VLA, however, is an equally-weighted index, while the DJIA and MMI are price-weighted indicators. Each of these relative weighting schemes will be illustrated later in this chapter.

Method of Averaging

Given the stocks that will be used to create the sample and the relative weights to be assigned to each stock, it is then necessary to average the individual components. Two methods of averaging are possible—arithmetic and geometric. With the exception of the VLA, all of the market indicators discussed in this chapter are based on an arithmetic mean.

An arithmetic mean is basically a simple average of the component stocks, calculated by summing the components and dividing by the number included.

A geometric average involves multiplication of the components, after which the product is raised to a power of 1 divided by the number of components.

The arithmetic mean of multiple returns will always be greater than their geometric mean. Consequently, as long as there is any variability of returns among the stocks comprised by the index, an index constructed by using geometric averaging will always grow more slowly, or decline less rapidly, than an index constructed by using arithmetic averaging. This implies that a geometric mean index will be less volatile than an arithmetic mean index constructed from the same equity issues.

Selecting the Base Year Value for the Indicator

To gauge the movements in the stocks comprised by the indicator, some time period must be designated as the base period and a value assigned to the indicator at that time. For example, the base period for the Consumer Price Index is 1967 and the value of the index assigned for the base period is 100. The CPI in March 1983 was 293, indicating that the CPI was 193 percent greater in March 1983 than it was in the base period, 1967. However, the value assigned to the base year of an index need not be 100. For the NYSE Composite Index, the base year is 1965 and the value assigned to the index for that year is 50. The base selected for the S&P 500 is the period 1941–1943. The average prices over that period are assigned an index value of 10.

Although an arbitrary value can be assigned to the base year of a value-weighted and equally weighted index, this cannot be done with a price-weighted market indicator such as the DJIA. This is so because price-weighted indicators are not really indexes. A price-weighted market indicator is an average of the prices included in the indicator after making adjustments for stock splits.

Table 7–3 summarizes for the S&P 500, NYSE Composite, MMI, VLA, and Russell indexes the coverage, type of relative weighting scheme, method of averaging, base year, and value of index or average in the base year. Some specifications of the futures contracts which are traded on these indexes are also detailed in this table.

Illustration of Index Construction and the Effects of Computational Differences

To illustrate the construction of an index based on the three relative weighting schemes and the two methods of averaging, we use a hypothetical example. Assume that the various indexes reflect the same population of stocks, so that we may focus on the biases produced by computational differences, as opposed to differences in the stocks comprising the index.

We begin with three stocks, A, B, and C, whose prices in the base or initial period (0) and some future time period (t) are given in Table 7–4. The value assigned to the index in the base year is 100 for all but the price-weighted index.

Market Value-Weighted Index

The total market value of each stock in the index is computed by multiplying the price of each by the corresponding number of shares outstanding. The market value-weighted index is then

TABLE 7–3
Summary Information on Stock Indexes and Stock Index Futures

	S&P 500	NYSE	MMI	Value Line	Russell 3000	Russell 2000
Coverage	500 major companies	NYSE-listed companies	20 blue-chip companies (17 in the DJIA)	1700 selected companies	3000 companies (representing 98 percent of U.S. equities)	The smallest (capitalization) 2,000 companies in the Russell 3000.
Weighting scheme	Market value	Market value	Price	Equal	Market value	Market value
Method of averaging	Arithmetic	Arithmetic	Arithmetic	Arithmetic	Arithmetic	Arithmetic
Base year	1941–43	1965	1975	1961	1978	1978
Futures exchange*	CME	NYFE	CBT	KCBT	NYFE	NYFE
Trading months†‡	End of quarter	End of quarter	Each month	End of quarter	End of quarter	End of quarter
Minimum price change	.05 or $25	.05 or $25	1/8 or $12.50	.05 or $25	.05 or $25	.05 or $25
Multiplier	500	500	250	500	500	500

*CME = Chicago Mercantile Exchange; NYFE = New York Futures Exchange; CBT = Chicago Board of Trade; KCBT = Kansas City Board of Trade.
†Settlement is based on opening (S&P 500) or closing index value (MMI) on the third Friday of the contract month.
‡Settlement is in cash based on the settlement price multiplied by the index multiplier.

TABLE 7-4
The Effect of Various Computational Techniques on Index Values

Stock	Base Year Price (0)	Number of Shares	Market Value	Price at Time t	Price Change (percent)	New Market Value	Percent Change in Market Value
A	$100	50	$ 5,000	$110.00	10	$ 5,500	10
B	20	400	8,000	21.00	5	8,400	5
C	50	200	10,000	50.00	0	10,000	0
Total			$23,000			$23,900	

	Base Year Index (0)			Value of Index at Time t		Change in Index (percent)	
Market value-weighted index	100.00			103.91		3.91	
Price-weighted index	56.67			60.33		6.47	
Equally-weighted arithmetic index	100.00			105.00		5.00	
Equally-weighted geometric index	100.00			104.92		4.92	

computed by dividing the current total market value of all the stocks used to construct the index by the total market value of all these stocks in the initial or base period. The quotient is then multiplied by the value assigned to the index in the base period. Mathematically, this is expressed as follows:

$$\text{Market value-weighted index} = \frac{\text{Total market value in period } t}{\text{Total market value in base period}} \times \text{Index value in base period}$$

Using the data for the hypothetical three-stock index given in Table 7–4, the initial total market value is set at 100, then the market value-weighted index in time period t is 103.91, as shown below:

$$\frac{\$23,900}{\$23,000} \times 100 = 103.91$$

Had the value of the index in the base period been set at 40 instead of 100, the market value-weighted index in period t would be 41.57. Regardless of the value assigned to the index in the base period, the percentage change is 3.91 percent, which reflects an increase from \$23,000 to \$23,900 in the aggregate wealth in this hypothetical market portfolio. In the preceding computation, the arithmetic mean was used to construct the index.

Price-Weighted Index

A price-weighted index reflects changes in the average price of the stocks used to construct the index, adjusting for stock splits. Assuming no stock splits between the base period and period t for any of the three stocks in Table 7–4, the average price of the three stocks changed from \$56.67 ([100 + 20 + 50]/3) to \$60.33 ([110 + 21 + 50]/3), or an increase of 6.47 percent.

Relative to the market value-weighted index, the price-weighted index considerably overstates the overall market portfolio change in this illustration. The reason is that the price-weighted index overweights the movement of Stock A, simply because stock A had the highest price. Aggregate market value is not considered.

In this illustration the method of averaging is the arithmetic average. This is the method used to compute the MMI and DJIA, which are price-weighted indexes. Alternatively, a price-weighted average based on the geometric mean of the prices could be computed.

Let us now drop the assumption that all three stocks in Table 7–4 did not have a stock split between the base period and time period t. Instead, assume that in time period t stock A split two for one and the market price of stock A fell from $110 per share, the price it would have had in the absence of the stock split, to $55 per share. As a result of the stock split, the average price in time period t is now $42 ([55 + 21 + 50]/3). This is less than the base period average price of $56.67 and implies that the average stock price has declined. Of course, this is ridiculous. An adjustment is required so that the indicator will not be misleading as a result of the stock split.

The adjustment is made by changing the divisor that is used to compute the average. In the absence of the stock split, the sum of the three prices in time period t (181) is divided by three, the number of stocks in our hypothetical index, resulting in the average price of $60.33. The sum of the three prices in time period t after the stock split is $126. If the divisor now becomes 2.089 (126 divided by 60.33), the average price would be $60.33 and the index in time period t would be 106.47, just as before the stock split.

Revising the divisor is the procedure currently employed by Dow Jones to adjust for stock splits. Consequently, the computation of the DJIA can be expressed mathematically using the following formula:

$$\text{DJIA} = \frac{\text{Sum of the price of the 30 stocks}}{\text{Divisor}}$$

The divisor takes into consideration not only stock splits but also changes in the composition of the stocks used to compute the DJIA. As noted earlier, occasionally companies are dropped from the DJIA and replaced by other companies. Notice that an adjustment for stock splits is not necessary for a market value-weighted index. The market value-weighted index would still be 103.91 after the two for one split of stock A.

It seems that the adjustment factor can provide comparability with previous years after a stock split. This, however, would not be a proper conclusion. Recall that the adjustment factor is computed by looking for the value that will preserve the average price after the stock split. An alternative approach is to reweight the price after the stock split. For example, in our illustration of a two for one split for stock A, the weight for stock A would be doubled in determining the numerator of the price-weighted index, leaving the numerator unchanged before and after the stock split. This approach was in fact used for the DJIA prior to 1928.

Equally-Weighted Arithmetic Index

In an equally-weighted arithmetic index, an equal dollar amount is assumed to be invested in each stock comprised by the index. Suppose that in the base year $1,000 is invested in each of the three stocks in Table 7–4. Given the same prices in the base year as used in the example above (i.e., 100, 20, and 50), the number of shares of stocks A, B, and C that could be purchased for $1,000 each is 10, 50, and 20, respectively. Thus the investment in the base year is $3,000. In time period t, as prices changed to 110, 21, and 50, respectively, the portfolio value of those shares would be equal to $3,150 ([110 × 10] + [21 × 50] + [50 × 20]). The value of the portfolio therefore increases by 5 percent ([3,150/3,000] − 1). If the base year index was 100, the index at time period t would be 105(100 × 1.05).

An alternative way of viewing the construction of this index is to note that the index percentage change equals the arithmetic average of the percentage changes in the prices of each of the three stocks, which is also 5 percent ([10 percent + 5 percent + 0 percent]/3). This property will always be true when the current period is compared to the base period, but not for subsequent period-to-period comparisons.

Equally-Weighted Geometric Index

As just noted, the equally-weighted arithmetic index reflects the arithmetic average percentage change in the stocks comprising the index calculated between the current period and the base period. The equally-weighted geometric index has a similar interpretation. The difference is that the geometric mean is used to compute the average percentage change in the stocks in the index.

The following steps are used to compute the geometric mean of the percentage change in the price of N stocks in an index.

Step 1. Compute the ratio of the price in period t to the base period price for each of the N stocks comprising the index. (Prices must be adjusted for stock splits and dividends. Notice that the ratio represents 1 plus the percentage price change).

Step 2. Multiply the ratios obtained from Step 1.

Step 3. Find the Nth root of the product computed in Step 2. (The Nth root is the value that produces the value computed in Step 2 if multiplied by itself N times.)

Step 4. Subtract 1 from the value found in Step 3.

Using the three stocks in Table 7–4, the geometric mean return is found as follows:

Step 1. The ratio for each stock is:

$$A = 110/100 = 1.10$$
$$B = 21/20 = 1.05$$
$$C = 50/50 = 1.00$$

Step 2. Multiply the three ratios:

$$1.10 \times 1.05 \times 1.00 = 1.155$$

Step 3. Find the third root of 1.155, that is, $(1.155)^{1/3}$. The value we seek is 1.0492 since

$$1.0492 \times 1.0492 \times 1.0492 = 1.155$$

Step 4. Subtract 1 from the value found in Step 3:

$$1.0492 - 1 = .0492, \text{ or } 4.92 \text{ percent}$$

Notice that the geometric mean return is less than the arithmetic mean return of 5 percent. This is consistent with the mathematical property of the geometric mean discussed earlier in this chapter. The small difference between the geometric mean and the arithmetic mean in this illustration is due to the relatively small variation in the individual returns. The equally-weighted geometric index is found by multiplying one plus the geometric mean return by the value of the index in the base period. Assuming the value of the index in the base period to be 100, then the equally-weighted geometric index for our hypothetical three-stock index would be 105(1.05 × 100).

A property of the geometric index is that both the period-to-period and the current period-to-base period percentage changes will be the same for the index and the individual stocks. The VLA is the only index discussed in this chapter that is an equally-weighted geometric index.

IMPLICATIONS FOR ASSET ALLOCATION STRATEGIES

An important consideration for the hedger is the asset allocation strategy that corresponds to each of the computational methods discussed in this chapter. A value-weighted index is an appropriate benchmark for an index fund that attempts to invest in "the market." Certainly, all investors in aggregate define the market. With commissions ignored, a value-weighted index represents the performance achievable by investing in the stocks in the subset in proportion to their market value.

A price-weighted index is an appropriate benchmark for an investor who apportions his or her wealth among stocks in ratios that correspond to their current prices. For the example in Table 7–4, the investor would invest five times as much in stock A as in stock B, simply because the price of stock A is five times that of stock B. Equivalently, this strategy implies that the investor invests in an equal number of shares of each stock, regardless of the price.

The equally-weighted arithmetic index is an appropriate benchmark for an investor who apportions his or her wealth in equal dollar amounts among all stocks selected. These examples cannot be extended to a comparable asset allocation strategy for the equally-weighted geometric index. Proponents of this type of index claim that arithmetic averages overstate attainable results. However, it is important to understand that the results described by a geometric index are simply unattainable by means of any portfolio strategy. That is, an investor could not (*ex ante*) construct a portfolio of stocks whose total appreciation would equal the geometric mean of the percentage appreciation of all.

RETURN, ABSOLUTE, AND RELATIVE RISK OF STOCK MARKET INDICATORS

Table 7–5 shows the performance and volatility of selected indexes during 1980–1987. (Volatility is measured as the annualized volatility of the standard deviation of daily percentage changes in

TABLE 7–5

A. Performance of Stock Indexes
(Based on Percentage Change in Value—No Compounding)

	1987 (in percent)	1986 (in percent)
S&P 500	2.03	14.62
S&P 100	3.10	12.17
NYSE	− 0.60	13.98
DJIA	2.26	22.58
MMI	7.60	23.91
Value Line	−10.58	5.01
Russell 1000	0.02	-
Russell 2000	−10.80	4.04
Russell 3000	− 0.95	13.16

B. Volatility of Stock Indexes
(Based on Daily Percentage Changes over Entire Period)

	1987 (in percent)	1986 (in percent)	1980–85 (in percent)
S&P 500	31.5	14.4	14.0
S&P 100	33.1	15.2	15.6
NYSE	29.7	13.3	13.4
MMI	34.4	16.0	15.0
Value Line	26.2	11.2	11.9
Russell 1000*	29.4	-	13.1
Russell 2000*	25.4	-	11.9
Russell 3000*	28.5	-	12.8

*Data for Russell indexes through December 1987 and for 1979–86.

index values.) As the performance data for 1986 indicate, it is not unusual to have very different returns among indexes, particularly those representing specific subsets of the stock market. The DJIA and MMI indexes appreciated by 22.6 percent and 23.9 percent respectively in 1986, while the VLA index gained only 5 percent in value. On the other hand, the market-value weighted, broad-based indexes, such as the Russell 3000, NYSE, and S&P 500, all had capital returns in the 13–14 percent range over the same year. The underperformance of small-capitalization issues in 1986 is evidenced by the low relative return of 4.0 percent for the Russell 2000 index.

Volatility can be measured either in absolute terms or relative to some other index. Part B of Table 7–5 shows some absolute volatility measures for the indexes for the 1980s. Interestingly, the MMI index and S&P 100, both representing the largest capitalized segment of the equity market and both being the least diversified indexes of those shown in the table have the highest volatility. The Value Line index has low volatility in part because of the geometric weighting used in its construction and also because of the large number of issues it contains.

CO-MOVEMENTS OF STOCK MARKET INDICATORS

Table 7–6 presents the correlation coefficients among various indexes based on daily percentage price changes for selected periods in the 1980s. Overall, the correlations are quite high—it is surprising that the interrelationship among indexes should be so strong, in light of the sizable computation and coverage differences. A moment's reflection on the universe biases involved gives some explanation. Prices of the movements in the largest stocks have a strong influence on all indexes especially those weighted by market value. Price-weighted indexes like the DJIA and MMI have few issues, but those included are the same stocks that tend to dominate the market-value weighted indexes which are broader in composition.

It is also important to understand that correlation statistics simply measure the extent to which variables move in the same

TABLE 7-6
Correlation of Stock Indexes
(Based on Daily Percentage Changes over Entire Period)

		S&P 100	NYSE	MMI	Value Line	Russell 1000	Russell 2000	Russell 3000
S&P 500	1987	.991	.997	.985	.876	.991	.746	.989
	1986	.968	.974	.942	.875	.992	.795	.988
	1980–85	.973	.990	.938	.872	—	—	—
S&P 100	1987	-	.983	.986	.834	.977	.691	.970
	1986		.937	.951	.815	.952	.724	.946
	1980–85		.995	.953	.807	—	—	—
NYSE	1987	-	-	.977	.906	.995	.789	.996
	1986			.912	.889	.998	.836	.997
	1980–85			.918	.894	—	—	—
MMI	1987	-	-	-	.828	.972	.685	.965
	1986				.776	.927	.685	.919
	1980–85				.773	—	—	—
Value Line	1987	-	-	-	-	.904	.956	.923
	1986					.906	.942	.919
Russell 1000	1987	-		-	-	-	.794	.995
	1986						.842	.999
Russell 2000	1987	-	-	-	-	-	-	.825
	1986							.863

direction. These statistics say nothing about the relative magnitude of the co-movement of the variables, indexes in this case. Also correlations essentially represent an average over many data points; even with a high correlation, it is still possible to have significantly different performance between one index and another on occasion. This makes it easier to understand why these indicators should follow each other so closely.

Note that the indexes that have the lowest correlation with the rest of the group and highest correlation with one another are the Value Line and Russell 2000. Both of these indexes as noted above give a much larger weight to small capitalization issues than the other indexes; in addition, the Value Line has its own unique basis for weighting stocks.

A matter of great interest to the potential hedger or speculator using stock index futures contracts should certainly be the relative volatility of the various indexes. To examine that relative volatility, a simple linear regression was run between the monthly percentage changes in the values of each pair of indexes. The simple linear regression estimated can be expressed as follows:

$$Y_t = A + BX_t$$

where

Y_t = Percentage change in the value of index Y in month t

X_t = Percentage change in the value of index X in month t

and A and B are the values estimated by using least squares regression analysis.

The estimate of B is a measure of the relative volatility of index Y with respect to the monthly percentage changes in the value of index X and is commonly referred to as the *beta coefficient,* or simply *beta*. Table 7–7 presents the beta between each pair of indexes, along with the intercept term, or *alpha*. There are, of course, ranges of uncertainty in these statistical data, and the betas and alphas computed in the table are subject to sampling error over the period of the study. Nevertheless, some obvious differences do appear.

If we use the S&P 500 Composite Index as a benchmark portfolio (index X in the regression), for example, we can see that the index with the highest beta relative to this portfolio would be

TABLE 7-7
Beta and Alpha Estimates for Selected Indexes*

Beta

Index Used as Benchmark	S&P 500	S&P 100	NYSE	MMI	DJIA	VLA	Russell 1000	Russell 2000	Russell 3000
S&P 500	1.000	0.997	0.997	0.991	0.987	0.860	0.981	0.694	0.966
S&P 100	0.963	1.000	0.954	1.002	0.982	0.819	0.940	0.659	0.923
NYSE	0.996	0.987	1.000	0.975	0.980	0.876	0.983	0.713	0.970
MMI	0.873	0.914	0.860	1.000	0.949	0.727	0.844	0.569	0.828
DJIA	0.925	0.945	0.915	0.993	1.000	0.804	0.899	0.637	0.886
VLA	0.994	0.980	1.012	0.954	0.996	1.000	0.996	0.840	1.001
Russell 1000	1.008	0.999	1.010	0.984	0.990	0.886	1.000	0.723	0.984
Russell 2000	1.083	1.065	1.113	1.008	1.061	1.134	1.099	1.000	1.115
Russell 3000	1.018	1.008	1.023	0.991	1.000	0.913	1.010	0.723	1.000

Alpha

Index Used as Benchmark	S&P 500	S&P 100	NYSE	MMI	DJIA	VLA	Russell 1000	Russell 2000	Russell 3000
S&P 500	0.00	0.06	.03	-0.10	-0.04	0.41	0.09	0.34	0.09
S&P 100	-0.01	0.00	0.02	-0.17	-0.08	0.39	0.08	0.33	0.09
NYSE	-0.02	0.05	0.00	-0.10	-0.05	0.36	0.06	0.29	0.06
MMI	0.27	0.27	0.31	0.00	0.17	0.65	0.37	0.62	0.37
DJIA	0.15	0.17	0.18	0.09	0.00	0.51	0.24	0.46	0.24
VLA	-0.25	-0.18	-0.25	-0.31	-0.31	0.00	-0.19	-0.13	-0.21
Russell 1000	-0.07	0.00	-0.05	-0.15	-0.10	0.32	0.00	0.23	0.01
Russell 2000	-0.02	0.06	-0.03	-0.04	-0.07	0.21	0.03	0.00	-0.01
Russell 3000	-0.08	0.00	-0.06	-0.15	-0.11	0.30	0.00	0.20	0.00

*Based on monthly percentage changes in index values over the period 1980 through July 1987.

the Russell 2000 with a beta of 1.08. The index with the lowest relative beta to the S&P 500 is the MMI index with a beta of .873. This contrasts with the fact that the MMI had the highest absolute volatilities over a comparable time period.

Because of the differences among the indexes discussed earlier in this chapter, betas vary depending on the benchmark used. For example, the beta of the NYSE index relative to the S&P 500 is .996, very close to 1, meaning these two indexes tend to move in equal direction and magnitude. In contrast when the Value Line becomes the benchmark index, the NYSE beta drops to .876.

As the betas for the Russell 2000 make clear, small capitalization stocks tend to have higher relative risk than large capitalization issues. However, as shown in the Value Line betas, the method of index construction can temper the expected higher relative volatility measures for this index.

It is apparent from the results reported in these tables, that despite the fact that all stock market indicators attempt to measure relatively the same phenomena, significant differences in relative performance and volatility do occur over periods of time. These differences are small compared to the differences we observe in the return and risk of specific stocks in the marketplace, but they can be critical to the determination of how well an index fulfills its function of serving as a stock market proxy or benchmark.

SUMMARY

The successful use of stock index futures and options contracts by both hedgers and speculators requires an understanding of how stock indicators are constructed and what they represent. In this chapter we discussed the various factors that differentiate stock indexes and the role that each plays in the construction of indexes on which futures are based. We also provided some empirical evidence on the co-movements of the various major stock indexes.

CHAPTER 8

PRICING OF STOCK INDEX FUTURES

H. Nicholas Hanson, Ph.D.
Vice President
Salomon Brothers Inc

Robert W. Kopprasch, Ph.D., C.F.A.
Vice President
Goldman Sachs & Company

When stock index futures first began trading, in February 1982, professional market participants began to transfer the pricing knowledge accumulated (sometimes the hard way) in earlier financial futures. Investors found that the basic *logic* used in pricing Treasury bond futures, for example, was equally applicable to stock index futures. But just as debt *options* players found that they could not directly transfer the equity option experience because of structural differences in the markets, so too did equity players find that certain peculiarities of their market required adjustments to the standard pricing "rules" of interest rate futures. In this chapter we will examine the pricing logic of futures (and other forward commitments) and then discuss the specific unique features of equity index contracts that require some alteration of previously developed debt futures pricing. Recognizing that some readers may already be familiar with interest rate futures, some sections will be followed by comparisons with Treasury bond futures.

We will first develop an arbitrage pricing model by example. Next we will present a more formal derivation using an "equivalent portfolio" approach. Happily, both lead to the same pricing equation. Technically, the equations developed are for forward contracts as opposed to futures contracts. We will later show that there is little theoretical difference between forwards and futures *in terms of pricing*, despite the margin flows inherent in futures.

THE ARBITRAGE APPROACH

Cost of Carry

Most forward commitments are priced on the basis of net "cost of financing." The cost of financing refers to the rate that would have to be paid to borrow funds to buy the asset, or the rate that could be earned on the funds if the asset were sold. "Net" financing adjusts the cost for any monetary benefits received as a result of holding the asset. Holders of Treasury bonds receive coupon income; holders of gold find that they can "lend" their gold and receive a fee, say 2 percent; and holders of stock portfolios receive dividends. In any model of pricing, these "yields" must be considered.

The term *cost of carry* (or "carry" for short) is used to refer to the net financing cost after consideration of the yield on the asset. Thus, while financing cost is always referred to as negative because it represents a cash outflow to the asset holder, carry can be positive or negative. Positive carry implies that the cash yield on the asset is greater than the financing cost, while negative carry implies the opposite.

Arbitrage Pricing

Let us develop the valuation methodology of forward commitments by example. Consider an asset that has a market value of $100 and that offers a yield of 5 percent (earned evenly throughout the year but paid at the end of the period). If the financing rate is 8 percent (also accumulating evenly throughout the year), what should the forward price be? Any investor can buy the asset for $100 (which he borrows) and knows that by the end of the year he will have accumulated a yield of $5 (i.e., 5 percent × $100) and a financing cost of $8. This results in a net carry of negative $3 (a cost). Thus he must receive at least $103 in order to break even. If the forward price is any higher, say $105, an arbitrageur will engage in this transaction and will risklessly earn $2 on every unit asset in the trade.[1] He would buy for 100 (borrowed), sell forward at 105. At the end of the period, he would collect his "yield" of $5, deliver the asset to the forward buyer at 105, and simultaneously repay his loan of $100 plus $8 interest (5 + 105 − 108 = $2). Note that the profit (at the *end* of the period) equals the excess of the forward price of $105 over the theoretical price of $103.

This example is one of negative carry, and the theoretical forward price (103) is above the current or spot price (100). If the example had involved positive carry, the theoretical forward price would have been lower than the spot price. Note that the "expected" future price never enters into the forward price. The reason for this is arbitrage, which will bring the prices back into line until no further arbitrage profits are available. In order to demonstrate this, let us assume that short selling is permitted and that the short seller has use of the funds raised. If bearish forward sellers drove the one-year forward price down to 101, here is how arbitrage would enter into the market. Arbitrageurs would buy forward at 101 and sell the asset short at today's spot price of 100. They would earn 8 percent on the $100 raised and would have to pay the $5 yield to the lender of the asset. This would leave them with $103, only $101 of which is required to take delivery of the asset on the forward settlement date. The asset thus purchased is used to settle the short positions. This would result in a profit of $2, the difference between the theoretical forward price ($103) and the actual forward price ($101). As expected, when the forward price is too low, the arbitrageur buys the contract because it is too cheap.

---

[1]The arbitrage is riskless only if the credit of the contra party in the trade (the forward buyer) is impeccable. The clearing organizations in futures and the mark-to-market margin mechanism combine to reduce the credit problem to a minor consideration.

In symbolic form, we can write the arbitrage pricing equation as follows:

$$F_0 = S_0 + rS_0 - S_0 y \qquad (8\text{–}1)$$

where

F_i = Forward price at time i

S_i = Spot price at time i (i.e., price of asset)

r = Cost of financing (expressed in decimal form)

y = Current yield on asset (expressed in decimal form)

The forward price, as discussed above and as shown in Equation (8–1), should equal the spot price today plus the financing cost minus the cash yield on the asset. Note that r and y represent periodic rates, not annualized rates. Note also that $S_0 y$ represents the dollar dividend paid at the end of the forward period. Using D to represent this dividend, we can rewrite Equation (8–1) as

$$F_0 = S_0 + rS_0 - D \qquad (8\text{–}2)$$

We can also rearrange Equation (8–1) to

$$\begin{matrix} F_0 & = & S_0 & + & S_0(r - y) \\ \text{Forward} & = & \text{Spot} & + & \text{Net carry} \\ \text{price} & & \text{price} & & \text{adjustment} \end{matrix} \qquad (8\text{–}3)$$

When r is greater than y, the futures price should be above the spot price, or "trade at a premium to cash." When r is less than y, the futures price should be below spot, that is, it should "trade at a discount."

Several assumptions were made in the simple model described above. We will mention them here only because many of them are also required for the "equivalent portfolio" derivation. Following that derivation, we will examine the conformance of the real world to the assumptions.

1. The nature of the asset at delivery is identical to its current form. This assumption is necessary to allow the arbitrageur to use the asset purchased forward to cover his short sale, or, in the opposite transaction, to allow him to deliver the asset purchased today to satisfy his forward sale.

2. The asset price is known (we need the asset price to derive the theoretical forward price).

3. The asset can be sold short at any time.

4. The proceeds from the short sale are either available to the investor or "invested" for him to provide a return.

5. The yield on the security is known, and paid at the end of the forward period.

6. The term financing rate is known, and paid at the end of the forward period (5 and 6 together determine carry).

7. There are no transaction costs.

THE EQUIVALENT PORTFOLIO APPROACH

Let us now look at a more formal derivation of the valuation equation. Until now, we have referred to "the asset," "the yield," and so on, without limiting the discussion to equities. At this point we will assume that we are pricing a forward on *one stock* rather than a portfolio. Then we will expand the discussion to include consideration of a portfolio as "the asset."

Consider the following two investment strategies.

Strategy 1.   Buy one share of stock XYZ for S_0 dollars. The return (in dollars) over a holding period ending at time T will be

$$\tilde{R}_1 = \tilde{S}_T - S_0 + D \qquad (8\text{--}4)$$

where $\tilde{R}_1$ = dollar return at time T and the other notation is as defined earlier. The tilde ($\sim$) over a variable indicates that it is a random variable and cannot be known in advance. $\tilde{R}_1$ is a random variable because it depends on the value of XYZ at the end of the period, $\tilde{S}_T$.

Strategy 2.   Invest S_0 dollars in the risk-free asset (e.g., Treasury bills) and enter into a forward commitment to take delivery of one share of stock XYZ at time T in the future for a dollar amount F_0, the current forward price. In this case the dollar return will be

$$\tilde{R}_2 = \tilde{F}_T - F_0 + rS_0 \qquad (8\text{--}5)$$

Since $\tilde{F}_T = \tilde{S}_T$ (that is, the forward price when there is no time left before delivery equals the spot price)

$$\tilde{R}_2 = \tilde{S}_T - F_0 + rS_0 \qquad (8\text{--}6)$$

Under our assumptions, the two strategies are equivalent in risk and therefore, in equilibrium, should provide the same return. Hence

$$R_1 = \tilde{R}_2$$

Setting the right-hand sides of Equations (8–4) and (8–6) equal we have

$$S_T - S_0 + D = \tilde{S}_T - F_0 + rS_0,$$

and

$$F_0 = S_0 + rS_0 - D \qquad (8\text{--}7)$$

This is the same result as Equation (8–2).

Since S could represent the market value of a portfolio of stocks, the same result holds for the price of a forward contract on a portfolio. For example, S could be the price of a share of an open-end mutual fund. In a frictionless world (one without transaction costs) a stock market index can in most cases be duplicated by a portfolio, so that Equation (8–4) is also the correct pricing formula for a forward contract on a stock index. Indexes such as the Standard & Poor's 500 Composite, the New York Stock Exchange Composite, and the Dow Jones Industrial Average can be duplicated by a portfolio. Until recently the Value Line Average Composite, because of its computational procedure, could not be, so that Equation (8–4) would not give the correct pricing for a forward contract on it.[2]

To this point we have referred to *forward* contracts instead of futures contracts. Although we have not yet established that future prices should be the same as those derived for forwards, further reference to forwards in the sections that follow would

---

[2]Because of the geometric averaging procedure used, the Value Line Average Composite used to always have a lower return than an equally weighted portfolio of its component stocks. Beginning with the June 1988 futures contract expiration, all future contract months will be based on a new arithmetic averaging procedure, hence removing this bias. See Chapter 7.

appear artificial because generally such contracts do *not* exist. We will discuss theoretical futures prices as if they were interchangeable with forward prices. The final section of this chapter will discuss the relationship between theoretical forward and futures prices.

The two approaches used to obtain the pricing model above suggest that two different actions (similar in effect) will take place whenever there is a discrepancy between the market price of the futures contract and the theoretical price. For example, if the actual futures price is *lower* than the theoretical price, the equivalent portfolio approach holds that investors who are not constrained should sell their portfolios and replace them with Treasury bills and futures contracts.[3] The selling activity should result in lower equity prices, which would lower the theoretical futures price toward the actual futures price. The buying of the futures should drive the futures price higher, so that the gap between actual and theoretical will be further narrowed or eliminated.

The arbitrage model goes even further. The potential participants are not limited to those with equity portfolios. Pure arbitrageurs, having no equity position to begin with, engage in the same transactions (with the same directional effects) by buying futures and selling stock short. Thus the magnitude of trading could conceivably exceed the size of the portfolios of those following the equivalent portfolio logic. These powerful forces should combine to drive the actual and theoretical prices together if the assumptions of the model are not overly simplified or restrictive.

EXAMINING THE ASSUMPTIONS

Let us return to the list of assumptions given earlier. For convenience, we will examine them in the order shown, although no ranking of importance is meant to be implied.

---

[3]Constraints such as statutory prohibition, loss recognition, tax effects, and imperfect information would prevent some investors from engaging in the strategy.

The Nature of the Asset at Delivery

There are several aspects of reality that conflict with this assumption. First, stock index futures do not have a simple asset underlying the contract. The stock index is a concept more than an asset, though it can be approximated by a diversified portfolio. Due to the large number of securities needed, it is difficult to buy (or short) an exact duplicate of the asset.[4] In addition, changes in the index to reflect stock splits, stock dividends, or changes in the securities that the index comprises further complicate the matching process. This is not to say that the approximation cannot be close, but the holder (or seller) will have a small amount of uncertainty introduced by this mismatch.

Of potentially greater importance is the contract specification that calls for cash settlement of the contract instead of delivery of the asset by the seller and payment by the purchaser. Even if the investor is able to match the index exactly, the underlying portfolio cannot be delivered, resulting in transactions costs that may be significant, especially since the entire portfolio would have to be liquidated (or repurchased if short) simultaneously if the investor did not want any unhedged long or short position.[5]

The Price of the Underlying Asset

In order to evaluate the potential arbitrage transactions, the value of the stock index must be available during the trading hours of the futures contracts. The values of the S&P 500, the NYSE Composite, and the Value Line Average Composite are available during trading hours, but they may lag market movements. This is because they are based on the last sale of the component stocks and not on the current bid/ask. As such, the last trade may be somewhat lower (or higher) than where the stock would trade at the time the arbitrage is being evaluated. Thus, while a trade may look attractive—perhaps the index looks "cheap" relative to

---

[4]Enhancements in program trading (the ability to trade portfolios as if they were a single entity), as well as electronic order routing, has greatly reduced these difficulties, thereby increasing the efficiency with which futures are priced.

[5]See footnote 4.

the futures—the arbitrageur might find that his surrogate portfolio would be more expensive than the index indicated. This may not seem like a large factor, but it may explain in part why there is much greater intraday volatility of the futures than of the indexes.

Short Sales of the Asset

Because the index is difficult to duplicate, and because its price may not reflect the current market, it is difficult to short, even in theory, the exact asset underlying the contract. Market practitioners do not need to be told of the difficulty of shorting an entire portfolio. The requirement that stocks (but not futures) be shorted only on an uptick also complicates the potential arbitrage.[6]

As an example of how the uptick rule affects arbitrage, consider the following example. Suppose we have two stocks, A and B, that make up an index. Initially, A and B are each priced at $50 a share, so that the index, which comprises one share of each, is $100. An arbitrageur, detecting cheap futures, wishes to sell A and B short and buy the futures. Suppose that A then trades at 50⅛ and B at 49⅞, the index remaining at 100. The arbitrageur can short A (at 50⅛) but not B (at 49⅞), because of the uptick rule. What does he do? Does he go ahead and short A, hoping for an uptick on B? This could be very risky, since the market may drift downward and the uptick on B may not come until B is much lower, and by then he may have a loss on the futures. The "pure arbitrage" is thus very difficult, and certainly not riskless.

However, the marginal pricer in this case need not be the pure arbitrageur. Suppose a portfolio manager already owns A and B. He may sell them out of his portfolio (sell long) and buy the cheap futures, capturing the mispricing in this manner. This type of arbitrage is much easier to do because long sales are not subject to the uptick rule, so that it is much easier to get the trades off simultaneously, or nearly simultaneously.

---

[6]An uptick occurs when a stock trades at a price higher than the previous transaction. A short sale is also permitted on a zero uptick, that is, when the last price change was up but the current trade is at the same price as that of the previous trade.

Proceeds of the Short Sale

When the proceeds of the short sale are available to the investor, he can invest these proceeds to earn the short-term rate until he "unwinds" the trade. In reality, there are varying degrees of availability of these proceeds to different classes of investors. Retail investors will find that not only are the proceeds not available but that Regulation T requires an additional deposit of at least 50 percent of the value at the time of the short sale.[7] Thus the model described earlier does not accurately reflect the constraints of the retail investor and his theoretical price would vary from the theoretical price determined by less constrained investors.

Broker-dealers find that the proceeds are basically available to them when selling short. The shares are borrowed in any one of three basic methods described below.

Borrow versus Cash. The shares are borrowed from a customer who has a long position, and the cash proceeds are given to the customer as collateral for the loan. Because the customer continues to earn the yield on the equity, he must offer a return on the cash, usually 75 percent of the broker call rate. Because the customer can earn more than this on the cash, he is being compensated for the extra credit risk and the service of lending securities.

Borrow versus Collateral. The borrower of the shares places other collateral (securities) with the lender to eliminate the credit risk and pays a fee of 1 to 2 percent (annual rate) of the value of the shares to the lender for the service.

Borrow versus Letter of Credit. In this case the letter of credit eliminates the credit risk and the lender receives a 1 to 2 percent (annual) fee for the service of lending the shares.

The net effect of these implicit and explicit fees is to reduce the price at which the futures become an attractive substitute for

---

[7]Under Regulation T, the Federal Reserve Board controls credit in the securities industry. At the time this book went to press, Regulation T required a minimum deposit of 50 percent, but this *initial margin requirement is subject to change*.

the shares; that is, the break-even theoretical bid price is lowered because of the fees, though the asked price is not similarly lowered. Thus there is frequently a range of prices that offers no arbitrage. When the price exceeds that range, one would sell the futures; and when the price is lower than that range, one would buy the futures.

Dividend Known and Paid at End of Period

One of the assumptions made in the derivation of Equation (8–7) was that the dividend pay date coincided with the settlement date of the contract. This assumption is not necessary and was included only for mathematical simplicity, so that D could be the actual dividend. However, the dividend can be adjusted for the time value of money between the pay date and the settlement date. That is, if the dividend were to be received before settlement, it could be reinvested at the risk-free rate until settlement, in which case D would be larger than the actual dividend received. If the dividend were to be received after settlement, it should be discounted at the risk-free rate. In mathematical terms,

$$F_0 = S_0 + rS_0 - D'$$

where,

$D' = D (1 + r)^n$ (pay date n days before settlement)
$D' = D/(1 + r)^n$ (pay date n days after settlement)

and D is the actual dividend paid. Unless n and/or r is large, the error made by assuming that D' and D are equal is negligible. For example, with a 10 percent annual risk-free rate and a dividend of $1.75 that is received 91 days before or after settlement, D' and D differ only by about four cents. Thus we will continue to use the approximation that $D' = D$. The reader, however, should be aware of this effect and check its size, particularly in the case of futures with a long time until settlement.

A much more important effect when valuing futures contracts on stock indexes is the seasonality in the dividends. Even though an index may contain several hundred stocks, the dividend yield until settlement may vary in a nonlinear way with time. This is illustrated in Figure 8–1, which depicts this nonlinearity for the S&P 500 for the 91-day period ending March 20, the last day of trading of the S&P 500 March 1987 futures contract. From Figure 8–1 it is apparent that during the first half of the "settlement quarter," stocks accounting for only about 25 percent of the total dollar dividends for the quarter have gone ex-dividend. Thus the holder of the S&P 500 over the second half of the settlement quarter will receive about 75 percent of the quarter's dividends. Naturally, this makes the effective annual dividend considerably larger, as shown in Figure 8–2. An interesting result of this is that a properly priced futures contract can sell at a discount to the index if the dividend yield until settlement exceeds the risk-free rate until settlement. This becomes immediately obvious if Equation (8–7) is rearranged so that

$$\frac{F_0 - S_0}{S_0} = r - y$$

where the dividend yield is $y = D/S_0$. If y is greater than r, then the basis, $(F_0 - S_0)/S_0$, is negative.

In the case of Treasury bond futures, the underlying bonds accrue coupon income evenly within each semiannual period. This results in a constant "effective semiannual coupon" that does not depend on the calculation date. (If the coupon date falls before the settlement date for the futures contract the actual/actual date arithmetic used for Treasury bonds causes a slight change in the "effective semiannual coupon," but the impact is small.)

THE RELATIONSHIP BETWEEN FORWARDS AND FUTURES

The major difference between a futures contract and a forward contract results from variation margin, the daily mark-to-the-market of an open futures position.[8] If an investor is long a futures contract and its settlement price on a given day is below

---

[8]See Chapter 5.

FIGURE 8–1
Percent of Quarterly Dividend Remaining
(until March 1987 futures settlement)

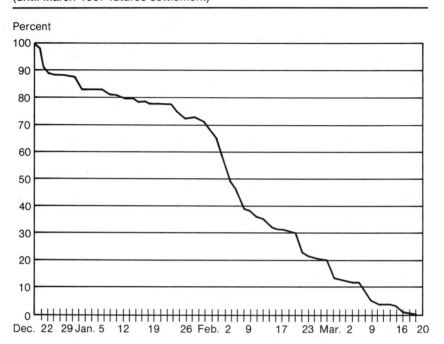

that of the previous day, he is required to post the price difference in cash. If the price rises, he will receive the price difference, again in cash. With forward contracts, only paper profits or losses occur daily. No cash changes hands until expiration of the contracts. Thus an investor who purchases Treasury bills and fairly valued *forward* contracts on the S&P 500 (such that his beta is 1) will realize exactly the same return as an investor who purchases the S&P 500 if the position is held until expiration of the contracts. In fact, the requirement that these two returns be identical led to the pricing equations for the forward contract, Equations (8–2) and (8–7).

Now consider the investor who has purchased Treasury bills and *futures* contracts. If the futures price drops, he will have to meet the variation margin by liquidating some of his Treasury bills. He thus loses the interest on these funds. Of course, if the futures price rises, cash will flow into his account and he will gain

FIGURE 8–2
Effective Annualized Dividend
(until March 1987 futures settlement)

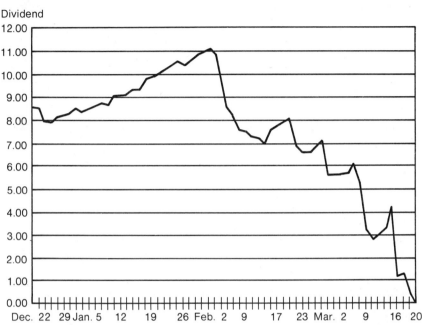

interest by investing these funds in Treasury bills. The net effect of these daily cash flows is to alter the return on his position by the net interest gained or lost. Summarizing in mathematical terms,

a. T-bills and forward contracts: $R_A = R_{500}$

b. T-bills and futures contracts: $R_B = R_{500} + i_M$

where i_M is the net interest gained or lost from variation margin.

If the overnight rate of interest, *r*, remains constant, there exists an adjustment to the number of futures contracts purchased that will make the term i_M equal to zero. To illustrate this, suppose that three days are left until expiration of the futures, as depicted below.

Day	0	1	2	3
Settlement price	F_0	F_1	F_2	F_3

F_3 is the value at expiration of the futures on Day 3. Since the futures contract is marked to the index at expiration, $F_3 = I_3$.

Suppose we buy a futures contract at some time during Day 0 for price F. At the close of Day 0, we will have a dollar return equal to $(F_0 - F)$. If F_0 is greater than F, we can invest this money at the overnight rate of interest for three days. At the end of Day 3, we will have $(F_0 - F)(1 + r)^3$ dollars. If F_0 is less than F, we will liquidate $(F - F_0)$ T-bills, thus losing an amount of interest equal to $(F - F_0)(1 + r)^3$. Each day we repeat this procedure, which is illustrated in Table 8–1. The dollar total return to the holder of the *futures* contract is the sum of the terms in column 4 of Table 8–1.

$$R_{fut} = (F_0 - F)(1 + r)^3 + (F_1 - F_0)(1 + r)^2$$
$$+ (F_2 - F_1)(1 + r) + (I_3 - F_2) \qquad (8\text{--}8)$$

which depends on the daily settlement prices. The total return to the holder of a *forward* contract is given by the sum of the terms in the third column of Table 8–1.

$$R_{fwd} = (F_0 - F) + (F_1 - F_0) + (F_2 - F_1)$$
$$+ (I_3 - F_2) = I_3 - F \qquad (8\text{--}9)$$

Thus the return depends only on the initial and final prices and is independent of the intermediate daily settlement prices.

Suppose that rather than holding one futures contract for the three-day period, the investor holds n_i contracts on Day i. Equation (8–8) may then be rewritten

$$R_{fut} = n_0(F_0 - F)(1 + r)^3 + n_1 (F_1 - F_0)(1 + r)^2$$
$$+ n_2(F_2 - F_1)(1 + r) + n_3(I_3 - F_2) \qquad (8\text{--}10)$$

TABLE 8–1

Day	Settlement Price	Variation Margin	Variation Margin plus Interest at Expiration
0	F_0	$F_0 - F$	$(F_0 - F)(1 + r)^3$
1	F_1	$F_1 - F_0$	$(F_1 - F_0)(1 + r)^2$
2	F_2	$F_2 - F_1$	$(F_2 - F_1)(1 + r)$
3	I_3	$I_3 - F_2$	$I_3 - F_2$

By inspection, we see that if

$$n_0 = \frac{1}{(1 + r)^3} , n_1 = \frac{1}{(1 + r)^2} , n_2 = \frac{1}{(1 + r)} , \text{and } n_3 = 1,$$

Equation (8–10) reduces to

$$R_{fut} = I_3 - F = R_{fwd}$$

Thus the return on the futures position is identical to that on the forward position. There is no net interest gained or lost due to the variation margin. Embodied in Equation (8–10) is the assumption that the daily adjustment to the number of contracts, n_i, is implemented by buying futures at the opening the next day at a price equal to the previous day's settlement price. Note that this procedure does not eliminate the daily cash flows. It just assures that no net interest will be gained or lost due to meeting them. We have created a "forward equivalent." In general, if there are N days left until expiration of the futures, the appropriate number of futures contracts to purchase is

$$n = \frac{1}{(1 + r)^N} \qquad (8\text{–}11)$$

and

$$\text{One forward equivalent} = \frac{1}{(1 + r)^N} \text{ futures contract} \qquad (8\text{–}12)$$

Note that as the number of days until expiration decreases, n increases, approaching unity as N approaches zero. Table 8–2 gives the number of futures contracts required to be in the equivalent

TABLE 8–2

Time until Expiration	Number of Forwards	Number of Futures
1 year	1,000	909
6 months	1,000	953
3 months	1,000	976
2 months	1,000	984
1 month	1,000	992
1 week	1,000	998
1 day	1,000	1,000

position of 1,000 forward contracts, assuming an annual interest rate of 10 percent.[9]

Even if this position is closed out before expiration of the futures, the return is still the same as that which would be obtained with a forward. For example, suppose n_0 contracts were purchased initially during Day 0 at Price F and sold at the close at Price F_0. The return would be

$$n_0(F_0 - F) = \frac{F_0 - F}{(1 + r)^3} \qquad (8\text{--}13)$$

Had this been a forward contract, in order to close out the position, the investor would have to sell a forward at F_0. Since no money would change hands until delivery, his return today would be the present value of the difference in the two prices, or $(F_0 - F)/(1 + r)^3$, identical to that in Equation (8–13).

While this procedure is applicable to futures contracts on any commodity, in the real world it will only allow a futures position to approximate a forward position. Varying interest rates intraday, correlation between spot price changes and interest rate changes, the inability to purchase futures contracts in the morning at the previous day's settlement price, and the inability to purchase fractions of a contract introduce frictions that prevent creation of a perfect "forward equivalent." Nevertheless, for stock index futures this procedure is quite effective in reducing i_M to an essentially negligible amount.

The bottom line on this forward-futures equivalence argument is that if short-term rates are stable or reasonably so, the prices of futures contracts and forward contracts with identical delivery dates should be nearly equivalent. Note that this does not mean that futures and forwards are equivalent in terms of actual dollar volatility *per contract*. For contracts of identical size, futures are more volatile than forwards because of the immediate mark-to-market on the futures. As shown above, the profit on a forward position is the present value of the difference

---

[9]One thousand forward contracts at an S&P 500 price of 250 represents a $125 million ($500 × 250 × 1,000) position in the index.

in purchase and sale prices, while the profit on a futures contract is the undiscounted difference between the prices. Thus, if a strategy is conceived in terms of forwards, and then implemented with futures, the number of contracts must be adjusted to reflect the difference in volatility.[10] When futures positions and forward positions are weighted this way, there is no difference in economic profit between them.

As an example, consider spot silver at $4 per ounce and one-year futures (and forwards) trading at $5 per ounce. If one buys spot and sells it forward (using either futures or forwards), the position established is like a one-year fixed-income instrument with a 25 percent yield. If that *yield* remains constant, the investor should be indifferent to the actual price of silver. Let us look at a scenario in which silver explodes overnight to $40, but the 25 percent market doesn't change, leaving forwards and futures at $50. Assume the investor desires to liquidate his position.

If the investor had used forwards, he would have sold forward an amount equal to his spot holdings. The change in the spot price from $4 to $40 would give him a cash profit of $36. A new forward can now be bought at 50, and when the long and short forward positions settle one year hence, the investor will lose $45 (buy at 50, sell at 5). But $45 one year hence in a 25 percent market is worth $36 today. Thus the investor has no profit or loss despite the large change in price. (And, if his position were held to delivery, the investor would earn the original 25 percent.)

If the trade were done with futures, one would sell $1/(1 + r)^N$ futures contracts. In this case, $1/(1 + 0.25)^1 = 1/1.25 = 0.8$. Thus, when the contract moved from $5 to $50, each contract would provide a $45 loss and 0.8 contracts would lose $36, iden-

---

[10]One might also think of the futures contract as having the volatility of a forward contract of greater size than the futures. This greater size is simply the compounded value of the nominal amount, found by multiplying the nominal amount by $(1 + r)^n$, where r and n are as defined earlier. Thus, if one buys 1,000 units of the underlying instruments, one might sell futures contracts on 900 units if the 900 units have the volatility of 1,000 forward units. As this position moved through time, the futures position would be increased because $(1 + r)^n$ (the volatility factor) declines as n declines.

tical to the gain on the spot silver. This quick example should highlight the price change similarity but volatility differences between forwards and futures.[11]

---

[11]Readers interested in more advanced treatments of this subject are referred to the following articles:

B. Cornell and M. R. Reinganum, "Forward and Futures Prices: Evidence from the Foreign Exchange Markets," *Journal of Finance* 36 (1981), pp. 1035–45.

J. C. Cox, J. E. Ingersoll, and S. A. Ross, "The Relation between Forward and Futures Prices," *Journal of Financial Economics* 9 (1981), pp. 321–46.

E. Elton, M. Gruber, and J. Rentzler, "Intra-day Tests of the Efficiency of the Treasury Bill Futures Market," working paper, New York University, 1982.

K. R. French, "The Pricing of Futures and Forward Contracts," Ph.D. dissertation, University of Rochester, 1982.

K. R. French, "A Comparison of Futures and Forward Prices," working paper, UCLA, 1982.

R. A. Jarrow and G. S. Oldfield, "Forward Contracts and Futures Contracts," *Journal of Financial Economics* 9 (1981), pp. 373–82.

R. J. Rendleman and C. E. Carabini, "The Efficiency of the Treasury Bill Futures Market," *Journal of Finance* 34 (1979), pp. 895–914.

S. F. Richard and M. Sundaresan, "A Continuous Time Equilibrium Model of Forward Prices and Futures Prices in a Multigood Economy," *Journal of Financial Economics* 9 (1981), pp. 347–72.

CHAPTER 9

CLASSICAL THEORY, DIVIDEND DYNAMICS, AND STOCK INDEX FUTURES PRICING

Gregory M. Kipnis
Principal
Morgan Stanley & Co., Inc.

Steve Tsang, Ph.D.
Vice President
Prudential Bache

The investor, hedger, arbitrageur, spread trader, or speculator should have a clear understanding of the determinants of the spreads between futures contracts and stock index prices. Only when rational futures prices are defined can the risks and opportunities of using futures be identified.

In this chapter we define the determinants of expected return for a stock index futures portfolio and how this differs from expected returns to a stock portfolio. A stock portfolio realizes price appreciation plus dividends and reinvestment. The stock index futures contract portfolio, on the other hand, will realize an interest rate of return (Treasury bill rate) plus price appreciation. Since like things should yield like returns, then in equilibrium, assuming no leverage, futures will price themselves in such a way that the two returns will be equal. For example, when interest rates exceed dividend yields, the futures contract's appreciation will be less than the stock price gain by the difference between the interest rate and the dividend yield. The theoretically correct futures price cannot be known exactly. However, to obtain the most nearly correct estimate, one must not confuse futures prices with forward or expected prices. To make these points clearly, numerical examples are given where appropriate.

In this chapter we also discuss several important issues related to the correct measurement of dividend yields. This seemingly simple concept must be looked at entirely differently when evaluating a maturing asset such as a futures contract. Utilizing yield-to-maturity calculations and incorporating the unique features of the seasonal dividend distribution lead to important discoveries about how different futures maturities and different stock index futures markets should behave in relation to their underlying market index.

We end by showing an actual example of the calculations for the theoretical price for an S&P 500 futures contract.

RELATIONSHIP BETWEEN EXPECTED, FORWARD, FUTURES, AND SPOT STOCK PRICES

Classical Theory of Expected Prices

According to classical stock valuation theory, the *expected price of stocks should always be higher than the current price level* unless the market discount rate is lower than the expected dividend yield. This pricing relationship simply implies that the current stock price is the equilibrium price of the collective market assessment, which always reflects the expected dividend flows and stock appreciation in relation to the investment risk over a holding period. If the collective assessment lowered the expected price and dividend flows, the present value stock price would have to be adjusted downward accordingly. Spot market price movements, therefore, continuously reflect the market assessment process. Since equity markets are liquid and efficient, any short-term shocks will be discounted quickly by the market.

The classical stock pricing theory is sound because no rational investor would buy equity securities at the current price if the expected return, that is, price appreciation plus dividends yield, were less than the cost of equity capital for a specific holding period. Based on this formulation, the link between the current (spot) market price and the expected price, for a fixed holding period, would be as follows:

$$P_0 = \frac{D}{(1 + k)} + \frac{P_t}{(1 + k)} \qquad (9\text{--}1)$$

The two prices should relate as follows:

$$P_t = (1 + k - d)P_0 = (1 + i + e - d)P_0 \qquad (9\text{--}2)$$

where:

P_0 = Present (spot) price of the stock

P_t = Expected price of the stock at the end of holding period t

D = Expected dividend at the end of holding period

k = Market discount rate for the stock = $i + e$

i = Risk-free *i*nterest

e = *E*quity risk premium

d = Expected *d*ividend yield, i.e., D/P_0.

If the dividend yield (d) is 6 percent for a selected stock and the relevant market discount rate (k) is 21 percent per year, then the expected stock price (P_t) should be 15 percent higher than the present price (P_0) one year from now to justify the investment.

The Expected Price Is Not a Forward Price

It is essential to understand that the expected price differs significantly from the forward price for the same time horizon. They differ because the actual price in the future is unknown; it can only be forecast. The expected price for a future date only represents the most likely market expectation at the moment in time. A forward price, on the other hand, is a carrying cost concept; that is, it is a cost accounting calculation for holding the asset.

As indicated in Equation (9–2), the expected price (P_t) is dependent on the difference between the market discount rate (k) and the dividend yield (d) for the holding period. The market discount rate has two major components: the riskless interest rate (i) and the equity risk premium (e). The risk premium is compensation for the investment risk (uncertainty) of holding equities.

The forward price for a storable asset, such as gold, silver, or stocks, on the other hand, is theoretically bounded by the net cost of carry for a predetermined holding period. Cost of carry normally includes net capital costs, insurance, storage, commissions, and so forth. In other words, the forward price is an accounting estimate of the cost of inventorying the item. Therefore, the equity risk premium is not a factor in estimating the forward price.[1] By dropping out the risk premium (e) component from the market discount rate in Equation (9–2), the link between the present (spot) price and the forward price for a stock would be as follows:[2]

$$FP_t = (1 + i - d)P_0 \qquad (9\text{--}3)$$

where

FP_t = Forward price for holding period t
i = Riskless interest rate, i.e., the market discount rate less the equity risk premium ($k - e$).

Equation (9–3) indicates that the forward price of a stock is dependent on the difference between the riskless interest rate and the dividend yield. If the dividend yield is 6 percent and the riskless rate is 12 percent per annum, then the one-year forward price should be 6 percent higher than the present stock price to prevent arbitrage opportunities. This result is quite different from that of the previous example, where the premium for the expected price is 15 percent because of the inclusion of the equity risk premium (e).

Another implication of Equations (9–2) and (9–3) is that the expected price is always higher than the forward price, because the expected risk premium must be positive. Furthermore, al-

---

[1]For nonstorable assets, the forward price is not bounded by the cost of carry. Thus the difference between the expected price and the forward price diminishes.

[2]This equation holds if borrowing and lending rates are equal to the riskless interest rate.

though the forward price premium can be negative, the expected price premium for all practical cases must be positive as long as earnings growth is anticipated.

A Futures Contract Is Not a Forward Contract

One might think that Equation (9–3) is an appropriate pricing formula for stock index futures contracts. This formula was in fact the general consensus of the futures industry in early 1982, before the Standard & Poor's 500 Composite Index futures started trading.[3] This view, though seemingly close to being correct, fails to give proper consideration to the potentially large risk differences between a futures contract and a forward contract.[4,5]

While both a futures contract and a forward contract represent an agreement to exchange a commodity at a specific future date, the futures contract is different from a forward contract in two important ways that relate to risk, both of which are associated with the daily mark-to-the-market rule for the futures contract. According to this rule, the daily trading gains and losses are settled up as adjustments to the equity positions of both parties, that is, long and shorts (see Chapter 5). Since the gains and losses to equity can be invested or must be financed at the short-term rate of interest, the actual changes in the equity positions of both parties are not identical to the difference between contract initiation and settlement prices. This difference is generally referred to as the *margin variation risk*.

Margin variation risk does not exist in a forward contract because such a contract generally does not involve payments until the maturity date. At that date the short delivers the commodity and receives the agreed-on price from the long. Therefore, the forward price can be viewed as a "riskless" expected price.

The second difference between futures and forwards, associated with the mark-to-the-market rule, is referred to as *capital*

---

[3]G. M. Kipnis and S. Tsang, "Stock Index Futures—From Contango to Backwardation," *ACS Futures Research,* ACLI International, March 1982.

[4]G. M. Kipnis and S. Tsang, "Determinants of Stock Index Futures Prices and Spreads," *ACS Futures Research,* ACLI International, April 1982.

[5]G. M. Kipnis and S. Tsang, "A Conceptual Trap in the Stock Index Pricing Model," *ACS Futures Research,* ACLI International, August 1982.

exposure risk. Since a futures position is marked-to-the-market daily, the contract value is always treated at its full market value, not the cash value of the spot price.

For example, if the spot price of a commodity, say silver, trades at $40 per ounce and a deferred futures contract at $50 (a 25 percent carry cost), using $40 to buy the deferred futures contract could result in a loss larger than the investment capital. This would be the case if the spot price for silver tumbled suddenly to, say, $4 per ounce and futures to $5 (maintaining the same 25 percent carry). Futures would fall by $45, or $5 more than the original equity. This example clearly illustrates that the capital exposure risk in a futures contract is equivalent to the full market value of the futures contract. This consequence is not found in a forward contract because losses associated with sharp swings are not debited to the buyer.

However, the mark-to-the-market risk can be attenuated through a number of trading techniques. Also, the daily margin variation effects may be random at times; thus the net effect over time could be offsetting. In any case, the price for a futures contract is not a true "expected" price as defined in Equation (9–1), because the risk associated with such a contract is not the same as the equity risk premium in the dividend discount model.

Failure to recognize the margin variation risk may be beneficial if futures prices move favorably. Failure to recognize the capital exposure risk can mislead traders into overlooking the need to weight their trade properly and into believing that Equation (9–3) is the correct pricing formula for stock index futures contracts.

In the following sections we develop a formal price model for stock index futures contracts based on an equivalent portfolio approach; that is, the investment capital must carry an identical risk for both portfolios.

Stock Portfolio Return Must Equal Futures Portfolio Return

The components of the investment returns for a stock index futures portfolio differ significantly from a stock portfolio because the futures contract is trading against the stock index rather than a stock portfolio. The stock portfolio return includes stock price appreciation and dividend yield plus reinvestment returns, whereas the stock index only tracks the price appreciation. The difference between investment returns for a stock portfolio and a futures index contract is illustrated in Equations (9–4) and (9–5). The total expected holding period return for an S&P 500 indexed stock portfolio (TRS) would be as follows and must equal the implied market discount rate.

$$\text{TRS} = a + d + r = k \qquad (9\text{–}4)$$

where

a = Stock price *a*ppreciation
d = Stock *d*ividend yield
r = Stock dividend *r*einvestment return
$k = \dfrac{P_t}{P_0} - 1 + d,$ from Equation (9–2), which is the same as appreciation plus dividend yield (and reinvestment) for a continuous investment

However, the stock index futures contract can be bought by posting interest earning assets, such as T bills, for the margin requirement. Thus the total expected return for a futures/bills portfolio (TRF) would be as follows:

$$\text{TRF} = f + i \qquad (9\text{–}5)$$

where:

i = T bill yield
f = Expected return on the stock index futures contract $(F_t - F_0)/P_0$, where F = futures price and P = stock index price

The rate of return of a futures/bills portfolio can be related to a market portfolio return through the capital asset pricing model (CAPM) as follows:

$$f = \text{beta}\,(a + d + r - i) \qquad (9\text{–}6)$$

where beta is the sensitivity (risk) of futures relative to the market and the term in the right-hand bracket is the equity risk premium, that is, the market return less the T bill rate. The equilibrium equation, based on CAPM, simply states that the risk level associated with a futures/bills portfolio determines whether the TRF is greater or smaller than the TRS.

Since the S&P 500 futures contract is designed to track the Standard & Poor's 500 Composite Index, it is reasonable to expect that the risk level of this contract, on a 100 percent equity basis, should approximately equal that of the S&P 500 index, and its beta value, therefore, should approach unity in the long run. Also, the beta value for the S&P 500 index is approximately equal to unity, relative to the market portfolio, due to significantly more stable dividend yields. Therefore, the beta value for the futures/ bills portfolio in Equation (9–6) can be reasonably expected to approximate unity.

If we assume that the beta is exactly equal to one, then Equation (9–6) would be reduced to the following:

$$\begin{aligned} f &= a + d + r - i \\ &= k - i \\ &= e \text{ [see Equations (9–3) and (9–4)]} \end{aligned} \qquad (9\text{–}7)$$

Simply stated, this result means that the price appreciation of a futures position should be equal to the equity risk premium. Rearranging terms, Equation (9–7) can be written as follows:

$$a - f = i - (d + r) \qquad (9\text{–}8)$$

Equation (9–8) simply states that the expected return on a stock index futures contract must be less than the stock index appreciation by the difference between riskless interest income and dividend return. In other words, the futures price appreciation is equal to the risk premium of the market portfolio (e).

The price relationship between the current stock index value and the stock index futures price is graphically shown in Figure 9–1. The expected price (P_t) and the expected futures price converge at time t. The futures price line indicates the theoretical path that futures will travel from F_0 to P_t. The vertical difference between P_t and F_0 represents the expected return to a stock index futures contract (f). Since f equals the risk premium (e), and thus must be positive, the spot futures price (at time 0) must be at a discount to the expected stock price (P_t) and the expected futures price (F_t) at time t.

FIGURE 9–1
Relationship between Futures, Expected, and Spot Stock Index Prices

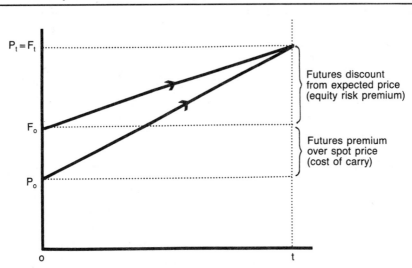

In addition, from Equation (9–8), Figure 9–1 shows that futures price and the cash index can be linked as follows:[6]

$$F_0 = (1 + i - d - r)P_0 \tag{9–9}$$

It is clear that this result is identical to the pricing formula derived for a forward contract in Equation (9–3). Since there are risk differences between futures and forward contracts, the beta for the futures/bills portfolio in Equation (9–6) may not equal one. It has been demonstrated that this difference associated with variation margin flows cannot be hedged away if future interest rates are not deterministic. Also, it can be shown that the expected gains associated with variation margin flows on a futures contract tend to be negative if interest rates are negatively correlated with

---

[6]This result follows from an equilibrium model that sets the total cash flows from each portfolio equal to one another without regard for the implied leverage in the futures portfolio. Thus:

$$P_0 + (P_t - P_0) + (d + r)P_0 = P_0 + (F_t - F_0) + iP_0$$

where P_0 equals both the initial capital and the cash price of the stock index.
Solving this equation for F_0 leads to:

$$F_0 = P_0 + iP_0 - (d + r)P_0$$
$$= (1 + i - d - r)P_0.$$

stock prices. Since this negative relationship generally holds in the case of stocks, it is reasonable to expect that the futures price should trade at a discount to the forward price.[7] Thus we conclude that the theoretical futures value can be best approximated by the following formula:

$$F_0 = \frac{(1 + i)}{(1 + d)} \times P_0 \qquad (9\text{--}10)$$

Five Important Cash/Futures Price Relationships

Equations (9–7) and (9–8) reveal several important relationships between the stock index values and the stock index futures values.

1. If the T bill yield is higher than the expected dividend yield (plus the reinvestment return), the stock index futures value will be higher than the current stock index value. This is called a premium, or positive carrying-cost market.

2. If the T bill yield is less than the dividend yield (plus the reinvestment return), the futures price would trade below the spot index. This is called a discount, or negative carrying-cost market.

3. If the T bill yield is higher than the dividend yield (plus the reinvestment return), the implied equity risk premium would be less than the expected stock price appreciation.

4. If the T bill yield is less than the dividend yield (plus the reinvestment return), the implied equity risk premium would be higher than the expected stock price appreciation.

5. The price of a futures contract is always lower than the expected future price because the equity risk premium is always positive.

**DIVIDEND DYNAMICS OF STOCK INDEX
FUTURES PRICES**

Earlier in this chapter we established the theoretical determinants of stock index futures prices under simplified conditions. In this section we deal with several real-world issues related to the

---

[7]The negative effects of variation margin flows may not hold for the shorter term.

correct measurement of dividend yields. Critical to this measurement issue is an understanding of the differences between the yield-to-maturity concepts for fixed-income instruments and the constant holding period concepts generally used in equity analysis.

In effect, a stock index futures/T bill portfolio is a fixed-income-type instrument. When comparing its return to that of a stock portfolio, the dividend yield for the portfolio should be recalculated to a yield-to-maturity basis, that is, for a fixed-maturity holding period rather than the usually reported annual yield.

Proper recognition of this distinction, and other factors, leads to some important conclusions about how different futures maturities and different stock index contracts should behave in relation to their underlying market index. At certain times it is perfectly rational for some contracts to trade at a discount while others are at a premium to the market. It also would be rational in the same contract month for the S&P and NYSE futures to trade at significantly different spreads to their underlying indexes, at times.

Fixed-Maturity versus Constant Holding Period Yields

In an earlier section we demonstrated that a stock market portfolio and a stock index futures/T bill portfolio will provide equal total returns when the futures price is at a full carry premium to the cash index value. Full carry is roughly equal to the ratio difference between the riskless interest rate (T bill rate) and the dividend yield for a fixed holding period. The fixed-maturity holding period used for the computation *must* correspond to the maturity date of a futures contract because only on that date will the futures price necessarily converge to the underlying stock index value.

It is essential that the importance of the concept of a fixed-maturity holding period be fully understood. For example, in most cases dividend yields for a fixed-maturity holding period will differ significantly, not only for each of the corresponding futures contracts, but also from the conventionally calculated dividend yields for constant holding periods, such as quarterly or annual yields. A fixed-maturity holding period means that the maturity date is fixed; thus each passing day shortens the duration of the next fixed holding period calculation. By contrast, a constant holding period means that the length of the holding interval does not change over time. Virtually all statistical services report dividend yields based on the constant holding period concept.

To graphically demonstrate the differences in dividend yield calculations for a fixed-maturity holding period and a constant holding period, we first analyze the dividend distribution pattern for the Dow Jones 30 stocks for the period from January 1, 1981, to December 31, 1981. We then look at the dynamic effect on yields that comes from shifting the maturity date from December 31 to December 16 (a shift of only 15 days). Finally, we illustrate the dynamic dividend yield pattern corresponding to the maturity date of each of the four S&P 500 Composite Index futures contracts. Since the record date is used as the basis for dividend disbursements, the actual timing of dividend flows is largely irrelevant in determining a fixed-maturity holding period dividend yield. (The payment date normally lags the ex-dividend date by about three to four weeks.) In present value terms this lag is of little importance to the yield calculation and is therefore ignored.

Dividend Yield Dynamics

Figure 9–2 illustrates the quarterly dividend distribution for the 30 Dow Jones Industrials. It is clear that most of the ex-dividend dates tend to concentrate in February, May, August, and November. Except for a few dividend changes, the pattern of quarterly distribution is quite consistent over the year.

Figure 9–3 illustrates the declining balance of the total 1981 dividends a DJ stock portfolio holder would have received during the fixed holding period, with December 31, 1981, as the maturity date. For example, if the DJ stock portfolio were initiated on December 31, 1980, the investor would have received $72.22 by the end of 1981. Note that there are subperiods when the remaining balance holds constant because no dividends are paid out during that period. For example, if the stock portfolio were initiated on any date between June 4 and June 29, the investor would have received the same dividend amount of $37.53 through the end of the year. After the last ex-dividend date, on December 1, 1981,

FIGURE 9–2
Dividend Distribution, Dow Jones 30 Industrials

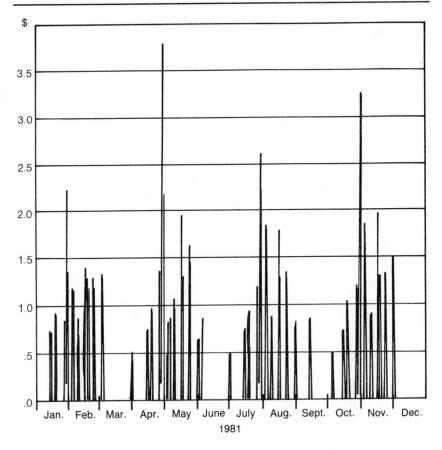

the investor would not receive any dividends for the remainder of the holding period.

A comparison of the dividend yield calculations for both a
fixed-maturity holding period and a constant holding period are
shown in Figure 9–4. The solid line in the chart indicates the annualized yield for the declining balance for the dividends to be
received over the remainder of the fixed-maturity holding period.
The dotted line represents the dividend yield for a constant, one-
year holding period. It is clear from the chart that the fixed-maturity holding period dividend yield is much more volatile than the

FIGURE 9–3
Declining Balance of 1981 Dividends, DJ 30 Stock Industrials

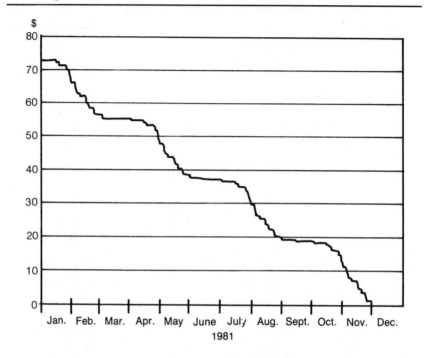

constant holding period yield. The divergence is even more pronounced during the third and fourth quarters of the dividend cycle.

Figure 9–5 illustrates the annualized fixed-maturity dividend yield with the maturity date shifted from December 31 to December 16. This shift is made to conform with the expiration date of the December S&P stock index futures contract (which by formula is the third Thursday of the expiry month). The shift of maturity date of the holding period, however, does not change the dollar amount of dividend distribution to be received. As a result, the fixed-maturity yield differs significantly from the December 31 maturity yield, particularly in the later part of the year. For example, the December 31 dividend yield peaks at 8.5 percent in late October (see Figure 9–4), compared with more than 11 percent (see Figure 9–5) for the December 16 maturity. The shift in

FIGURE 9–4
Fixed Maturity and Constant (One-Year) Holding Period Dividend Yields, at Annual Rates, January 1 to December 31, 1981

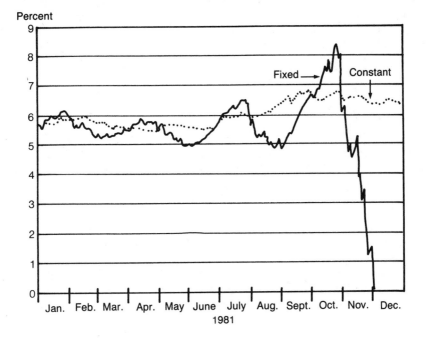

the maturity date, however, does not change the timing of quarterly highs and lows in the yield.

Dividend distributions for the S&P 500 Composite Index generally follow the same pattern as that of the 30 DJ Industrials. Based on a historical dividend distribution pattern for S&P 500 stocks, we calculated the fixed-maturity dividend yields corresponding exactly to the maturity dates of each of the four futures contracts—March, June, September, and December. As shown in Figure 9–6, the differences in the fixed-maturity dividend yields for the different futures contract maturities will be considerably different at certain times of the year. Note the tiering of yields in late July and early August. At the widest point the September maturity yield was about 3 percentage points higher than the June maturity yield. Dividend yields always peak at about six weeks prior to the contract expiration. For example, the fixed-maturity

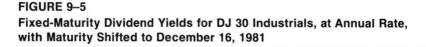

FIGURE 9–5
Fixed-Maturity Dividend Yields for DJ 30 Industrials, at Annual Rate, with Maturity Shifted to December 16, 1981

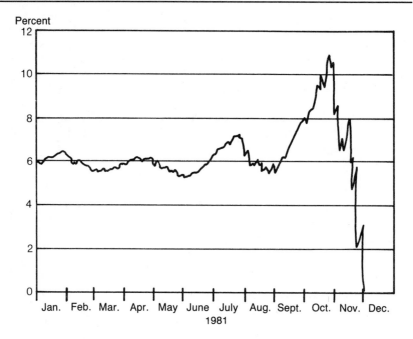

dividend yield for the December contract maturity date peaked in early November at about 10.5 percent. At that time the yield for the March maturity was about 7 percent. By early February the yield for a March maturity reached its high of about 9 percent.

Major Conclusions

The existence of both tiering and seasonality for the fixed-maturity portfolio dividend yield, for the different futures contract maturity dates, leads to interesting and important conclusions about how futures prices should trade in relation to the market index. It is entirely rational for the two following situations to occur:

   1. The nearby futures contracts could sell at discounts to the market index whenever the fixed-maturity yield exceeds the T bill rate, while the other contracts still sell at a premium.

FIGURE 9–6
Fixed-Maturity Dividend Yield for S&P 500 at Annual Rates

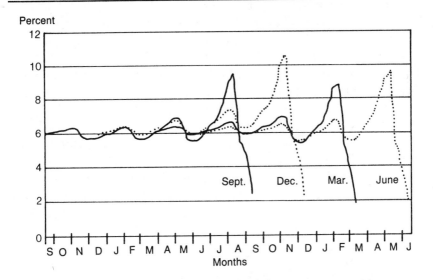

2. The futures contract premiums, or discounts, will vary both between contracts and over time even if the T bill rate does not change over time.

It should be pointed out that the fixed-maturity dividend yield curves portrayed in Figure 9–6 were based on an assumed 6 percent dividend yield for the year ahead (note that each yield curve begins at the 6 percent line). In the real world, however, expected dividend yields change over time. Therefore:

3. Changes and differences in expected dividend yields will cause the magnitude and variability of futures prices to be different for each contract.

Another factor that can alter the expected dividend yields to maturity would be major shifts in the ex-dividend dates. We have noted that the ex date has changed for several securities by one to two weeks from time to time.

4. It is important to know the exact schedule of record dates for dividend disbursements before one can correctly calculate dividend yields to maturity.

Finally, when comparing futures spreads for different stock index futures contracts, one should adjust for the different contract expiration dates. Although currently the quarterly expiration dates are identical for all the index futures, this was not the case in earlier years. Prior to 1984, the NYSE contract for the New York Stock Exchange Composite Index expired on the next to last business day of the contract month, whereas the IMM contract for the S&P 500 Composite Index expired on the third Thursday of the contract month. This difference in contract specification could result in a difference of up to 14 days in the maturity dates. As a result, the fixed-maturity dividend yield could differ between the S&P and NYSE contract by as much as 3 percentage points, at annual rates, during the months prior to contract expiration.

5. Given the difference in the S&P and NYSE contract expiration dates, it was possible for the expiring S&P contract to trade at a discount to its market index while the expiring NYSE contract was at a premium to its market index.

PUTTING IT ALL TOGETHER: EXAMPLE OF THEORETICAL PRICES FOR A FUTURES CONTRACT

As demonstrated earlier, a stock portfolio and a stock index futures/T bill portfolio will provide equal returns when the futures prices are at a full carry to the cash index value. Full carry is roughly equal to the ratio difference between the riskless interest rate and the dividend yield, measured on a yield-to-maturity basis. In Figure 9–7 we show the estimates for the dividend yield to maturity and the T bill interest rate for valuing the S&P 500 December 82 futures contract, which had an expiration date of December 16.

The chart has a number of noteworthy features. For example, the estimate of the dividend yield to maturity for late October and early November was greater than the T bill yield. This would indicate that the December contract should have been trading at a discount at that time. It is also worthy of note that the dividend yield did not reach the high level projected earlier and as shown in Figure 9–6. The market rally that started in mid-August was so strong that it offset the seasonal increase in dividends, so that the

FIGURE 9–7
Dividend Dynamics: T Bill Yield (solid line) versus December Maturity
Dividend Yield (dotted line)

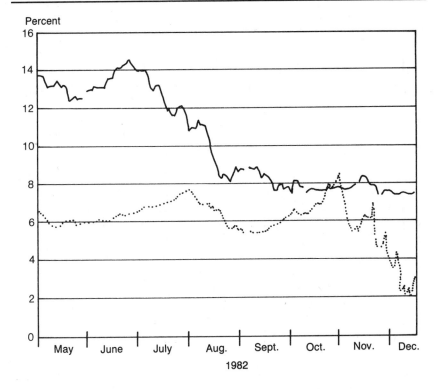

dividend yield to maturity was held down. Even on a constant (one-year) maturity basis, dividend yields were held to below 5 percent.

Based on these two series, the theoretical futures prices are calculated and contrasted with the actual S&P December 82 futures prices in Figure 9–8. Whenever the futures price (solid line) was below the theoretical price (dotted line), the futures contract was undervalued. Conversely, whenever the futures price was above the theoretical price, the futures contract was overvalued.

Figure 9–9 magnifies the relationship between theoretical and actual December futures prices by showing both of them relative to the actual index values. For example, on June 18, 1982, the S&P 500 index closed at 107.28 and the S&P December futures

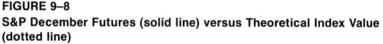

FIGURE 9–8
S&P December Futures (solid line) versus Theoretical Index Value
(dotted line)

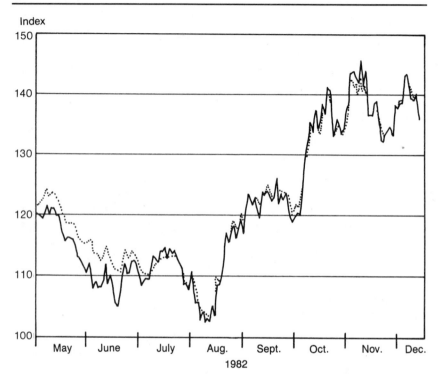

closed at 104.90, or at a 2.38-point discount from the spot index. On the same date the theoretical price for the futures contract was 111.03, or 3.75 points above the actual index. It was possible on that date for an investor to establish a futures position that would outperform the S&P 500 stock index by about 11.8 percent, at an annual rate, for the six-month period June 18–December 16, 1982. This was an unusual day; opportunities of this magnitude rarely occur. But this example does underscore the fact that stock index futures can provide an alternative market for developing strategies to outperform the market.

From Figure 9–9, it can be seen clearly that the market was not very efficient in pricing the new futures contract during the first two months of trading—May and June 1982. Since early July,

FIGURE 9–9

The Spreads: Theoretical (line) versus Actual (dot) —Theoretical Futures less S&P 500 Index (solid line), December 82 Futures less S&P 500 Index (dotted line)

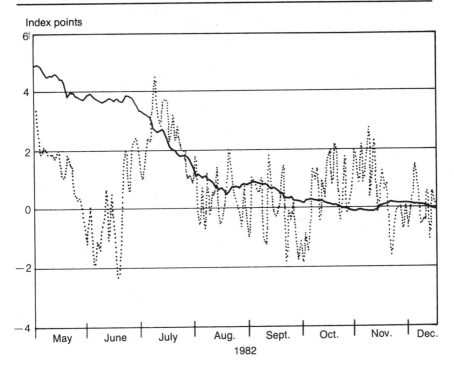

however, the futures contract has traded within a reasonably close range of the theoretical prices. This strongly suggests that the external efficiency of the futures market improved very rapidly. However, there is still room for improvement in the internal efficiency of the market. The trading range will not narrow until the transaction costs and arbitrage risks are reduced further. Most of the time futures trade well within a rational band defined by transaction costs.

CHAPTER 10

PRICING PATTERNS IN STOCK INDEX FUTURES*

Donald B. Keim, Ph.D.
Associate Professor
Wharton School
University of Pennsylvania

Michael Smirlock, Ph.D.
Vice President
Franklin Savings Bank
and
Associate Professor
Wharton School
University of Pennsylvania

There is an increasing use of and interest in stock index futures as speculative, hedging, and arbitrage instruments. They also provide a low-cost management tool for index funds. A potentially important consideration in using stock index futures for these purposes is their temporal price patterns. If pricing patterns can be identified, they can be used to enhance the portfolio performance of stock index futures and possibly provide profitable trading strategies.

Many recent studies have documented regularities in stock index price movements and it is likely that pricing patterns also exist in the stock index futures market. The exploitation of such

*The research assistance of Richard Tinsley is gratefully acknowledged.

index price movements in the cash market requires a substantial amount of trading, incurring brokerage fees and bid/ask spread losses with every trade in each stock. Stock index futures, however, allow investors to participate in market index movements at relatively low costs and provide a vehicle to exploit these pricing regularities.

This chapter investigates temporal pricing patterns in stock index futures markets.[1] We describe three pricing regularities in the cash market and how these pricing patterns translate to the futures market. Using both the S&P 500 stock index and the Kansas City Value Line Composite futures prices, we examine the extent that each cash market pricing regularity is observed in the futures market. We find that for the S&P 500 and Value Line futures contracts, pricing patterns found in the underlying stock market index are observed only erratically in the index futures markets. There is, however, a consistent temporal pricing pattern in a spread position characterized by long one Value Line futures contract and short one S&P futures contract. This position is similar to being long in a portfolio of small capitalization stocks and short in a portfolio of large capitalization stocks.

Before our analysis, an important caveat is in order. Whether an observed pricing pattern is sufficient to justify a temporal-based trading strategy cannot be determined by the results we present. Such a decision is based on numerous investor-specific factors such as risk-return preferences—an "on average" profitable trading strategy can incur large losses for numerous consecutive trades. As important, our results are based on closing prices and do not include the costs of executing or monitoring the futures position. Nonetheless, reliable pricing patterns we identify can provide the impetus and direction for development of profit-

---

[1]Previous research in this area has been done by Edward Dyl and Donald Maberly, "The Weekly Pattern in Stock Index Futures: A Further Note," *Journal of Finance,* July 1986, pp. 1149–52; Dyl and Maberly, "The Daily Distribution of Changes in the Price of Stock Index Futures," *Journal of Futures Markets,* April 1986, pp. 513–21; and Bradford Cornell, "The Weekly Pattern in Stock Returns: A Note," *Journal of Finance,* September 1985, pp. 583–88. This chapter itself draws heavily on our paper, Donald Keim and Michael Smirlock, "The Behavior of Intraday Stock Index Futures Prices," *Advances in Futures and Options Research,* Vol. 2, 1987, pp. 143–66.

able temporal trading strategies. Even if no such strategies exist, knowledge of the temporal pricing pattern can be a useful guide to portfolio managers in timing trades to enhance portfolio returns and improve portfolio performance.

COMMON STOCK INDEX PRICING PATTERNS

Recent analyses by academics and practitioners have uncovered at least three temporal pricing patterns in common stocks.[2] The *day-of-the-week* effect in common stock returns, which dates back at least to the 1920s, is characterized by (on average) negative stock returns on Monday and larger than average returns on Friday. If this return pattern is also observed in the index futures prices, futures market participants can take advantage of this temporal pattern by, for example, selling at the close on Friday and buying at the close on Monday. The *January* or *turn-of-the-year* effect is characterized by significantly larger than average returns in January than in other months. More precisely, a significant portion of the turn-of-the-year return accrues during the short period including the last trading day of December and the first four trading days of the new year. Other research has followed this lead and explored a third pricing pattern, the *turn-of-the-month* effect. The evidence suggests that the turn-of-the-year effect repeats itself, although to a much smaller degree, in nearly every month. That is, there is a turn-of-the-month effect whereby stock returns are larger in the first few days of the month and the last day of the previous month relative to the rest of the days. If these latter two patterns are observed in index futures prices, index futures traders can exploit them by timing purchases to occur at the end of a month and sales to occur after the first trading week.

One additional fact interrelates these three observed pricing patterns. They are all related to some degree to the firm's market

---

[2]For a more complete review of temporal pricing patterns in the stock market, see Donald Keim, "The CAPM and Equity Return Regularities," *Financial Analysts Journal*, May/June 1986, pp. 19–34.

capitalization or, equivalently, firm size. Portfolios of small firms outperform portfolios of large firms over long periods. This difference in performance is especially apparent in the three effects described above. The Friday effect is most extreme for small firms and most of the small firm premium observed over time can be found in the turn-of-the-year effect, although the increased return in small firms is also present at the turn of other months as well.

While these effects and their firm size relationships are statistically significant, they are also of relatively small magnitude. For example, when New York and American Stock Exchange firms are grouped by size into deciles, the smallest decile average daily return exceeds that of the largest decile by only about $1\frac{3}{4}$ percent from 1963–1981, even though the largest decile firms average over \$1 billion in market capital to less than \$5 million for the smallest firms. To take profitable advantage of these pricing patterns requires very low transaction costs and ideally, substantial leverage. The futures markets provide such an opportunity.

THE FUTURES PRICE DATA

We use the S&P 500 stock index and the Kansas City Value Line Composite (hereafter VL) futures contract prices to examine pricing patterns in the stock index futures markets. We can also examine the importance of firm size on futures market prices by using these two contracts. The S&P 500 stock index represents a value-weighted portfolio of common stocks listed mostly on the NYSE, although several are listed on the AMEX and OTC market. The Value Line Composite Index is an equally-weighted geometric index of stocks from the NYSE, AMEX, the OTC, and Canadian exchanges. Thus, the S&P 500 and the Value Line Composite can be viewed as proxies for portfolios of large and small firms, respectively. Further, if an investor were long a VL futures contract and short an S&P 500 futures contract, his position in small firms would be intensified. This intermarket spread position allows the investor to offset to a large degree the long position in large firms in the VL futures contract, by taking a short position in the same firms (although different dollar amounts) in the S&P

500 futures contract, leaving a long position in the smaller firms in the VL index.

We utilize daily price changes based on settle prices of our two futures contracts.[3] Our sample period begins with the commencement of trading of the S&P 500 futures contract on April 21, 1982 (the VL had been trading since February of that year) and ends on December 31, 1986. We focus exclusively on the daily price changes of the nearest contract. We define the nearest contract as being the contract closest to expiration *except* in the month of expiration, when we switch to the contract with the next to closest expiration. For example, on the last trading day in February 1986, the nearest contract is the 1986 March. On the first trading day of March, however, the nearest contract is the 1986 June.

Figure 10–1 shows the time series of closing prices on the nearest futures contracts for both indexes. Since the 1982–1986 period was generally a bull market, it is not surprising that both series trend upward. Although the S&P futures price was higher than the Value Line futures price through much of 1986, the VL–S&P spread was positive throughout the remainder of the period. Given the data in Figure 10–1, we turn to evaluating temporal pricing patterns in the stock index futures markets.

PRICE CHANGES AND DAY-OF-THE-WEEK EFFECTS

Table 10–1 contains average price changes over the sample period for the S&P 500, VL futures contract, and a spread position characterized by long one VL futures contract and short one S&P 500 futures contract. Under each average price change in parentheses is the associated standard error of the price change. A high standard error is indicative of substantial variability in daily price

---

[3]In our paper, Keim and Smirlock, "The Behavior of Intraday Stock Index Futures Prices," we divide daily returns into trading (open-to-close) and nontrading (close-to-open) intervals. The findings reported there suggest substantial difference in price changes in trading and nontrading periods and the interested reader is referred there for a more detailed analysis.

FIGURE 10–1
Stock Index Futures Prices (S&P 500 and VL, 4/82–12/86)

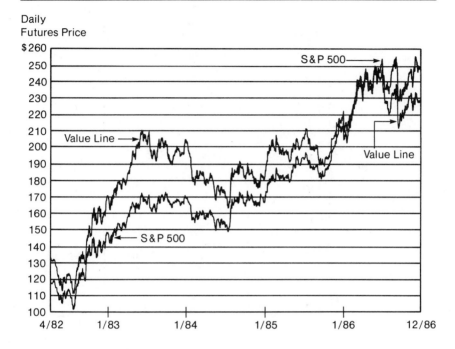

changes that may make it difficult to exploit pricing patterns in a reliable fashion. Below this number is the percentage of days the positions showed an increase or decrease (i.e., a profit or loss). We first discuss the temporal pricing patterns for the separate contracts and then turn our attention to the spread position.

The Separate Contracts

The average price changes across all days for the S&P 500 and VL futures contract are reported in the first column of Table 10–1. The average price change for the S&P 500 futures was 7.42 basis points over the period compared to the 4.70 basis point average increase for the VL futures contract. Since the contracts are designed so that each basis point change is worth five dollars, the daily dollar change in a one contract S&P 500 and VL position is approximately $35 and $20, respectively. The high standard

TABLE 10–1
Daily Price Changes in Basis Points for Stock Index Futures by Day of the Week, 4/82–12/86

	All Days	Monday	Tuesday	Wednesday	Thursday	Friday
S&P 500						
Average	7.42	12.41	5.46	6.28	17.46	−4.15
Standard error	(5.28)	(12.49)	(12.56)	(11.34)	(12.34)	(10.26)
Percentage increase/decrease	51.6/48.4	56.3/43.7	48.9/51.1	47.7/52.3	58.8/41.2	46.8/53.2
K. C. Value Line						
Average	4.70	3.28	−8.37	0.04	28.04	0.85
Standard error	(5.70)	(13.84)	(13.35)	(12.21)	(13.24)	(10.96)
Percentage increase/decrease	49.8/50.2	52.4/47.6	46.9/53.1	48.1/51.9	57.9/42.1	43.9/56.1
Spread position						
Average	−2.71	−9.12	−13.84	−6.24	10.58	5.01
Standard error	(1.89)	(4.44)	(4.25)	(4.00)	(4.24)	(4.11)
Percentage increase/decrease	46.3/53.7	43.1/56.9	38.2/61.8	45.6/54.4	55.8/44.2	48.5/51.5
Number of Observations	1189	227	243	242	238	239

errors associated with the average basis point change indicates a wide variability in daily price changes. Accordingly, buying and selling an S&P 500 contract on a Thursday may have resulted in an average profit of 17.46 basis points $\times$ $5 = $87.30, but could also result in substantial losses. There were several days where this position recorded losses of over $600. This gain also excludes transactions costs, which would further decrease profits and increase losses.

The same risk is involved in holding a contract for several days. For example, buying an S&P 500 contract Monday morning and selling on the close of Thursday yielded an average profit of $208.15, but at times lost more than $1,500 and was profitable less than 55 percent of the time (excluding transactions costs). In fact, despite the differences in average price changes across days of the week, the means are equal in a statistical sense across all days. That is, there is *no* day-of-the-week effect in either contract in a statistical sense.

These daily pricing patterns must persist over time to be the basis of a reliable trading strategy. We may decide that buying a VL contract on Thursday with its expected profit of $140 may be worth the risk if, year after year, the $140 is a reasonable profit to expect. We examine this by presenting, in Table 10–2, price changes by day of the week for each year. As can be seen, the average profits from this Thursday strategy range from 6 basis points to 48 basis points—at the low end barely enough to cover transaction costs much less risk considerations. The same year-to-year variability is observed for other days of the week for both contracts and the spread position. Profitable trading in either contract based on the day of week, particularly when risk is considered, is very unlikely, although a portfolio manager may want to consider these average day-of-the-week price changes in timing trades.

The day-of-the-week effect observed in the cash market is not replicated in the futures market. Indeed, average futures price changes are the opposite of that observed in the cash market. For the S&P 500 contract, Friday price changes are on average negative; for both the S&P 500 and VL contract Monday price changes are on average positive. The high variability associated with these daily price changes and transaction costs, particularly

TABLE 10–2
Daily Price Change in Basis Points for Stock Index Futures by Day of the Week by Year, 1982–1986

	Monday	Tuesday	Wednesday	Thursday	Friday
S&P 500					
1982	40.21	24.45	2.55	4.16	−3.83
	(42.43)	(37.42)	(37.10)	(27.2)	(30.81)
	57.5/42.5	44.4/55.6	40.5/59.5	50.0/50.0	47.2/52.8
1983	19.36	−35.96	34.23	24.90	−2.05
	(20.19)	(25.30)	(21.89)	(22.34)	(17.76)
	59.5/40.5	40.3/59.7	59.6/40.4	62.7/37.3	52.9/47.1
1984	−7.75	10.19	−41.07	35.49	−10.88
	(15.91)	(19.28)	(18.82)	(22.95)	(21.63)
	46.9/53.1	56.8/43.2	27.4/72.6	60.7/39.3	45.1/55.9
1985	15.20	13.36	−1.66	20.30	12.54
	(21.73)	(19.50)	(19.34)	(15.91)	(16.58)
	55.1/44.9	51.9/48.1	50.9/49.1	56.0/44.0	47.0/53.0
1986	4.38	21.15	35.19	−1.80	−16.70
	(38.38)	(37.56)	(30.31)	(42.29)	(29.08)
	63.2/36.8	50.0/50.0	57.6/42.4	62.0/38.0	42.0/58.0
K. C. Value Line					
1982	44.24	14.16	10.17	11.38	−3.83
	(43.19)	(39.94)	(38.69)	(29.49)	(30.83)
	63.6/36.2	38.8/61.2	43.2/56.8	50.0/50.0	47.2/52.8
1983	19.36	−45.38	32.88	40.98	12.15
	(20.19)	(30.33)	(25.58)	(27.01)	(20.26)
	59.5/40.5	42.3/57.7	61.5/38.5	60.8/39.2	43.7/56.3
1984	−25.91	−5.29	−56.86	48.62	−8.61
	(21.87)	(22.81)	(23.26)	(28.65)	(28.46)
	42.8/57.1	47.0/53.0	33.3/66.7	56.8/43.2	41.1/58.9
1985	2.75	3.36	−7.15	27.90	11.76
	(25.81)	(22.96)	(23.25)	(19.11)	(18.75)
	46.9/53.1	51.9/48.1	49.0/51.0	58.0/42.0	50.9/40.1
1986	−7.75	−1.73	22.50	6.00	−12.40
	(38.74)	(34.82)	(27.86)	(39.80)	(24.83)
	57.1/42.9	51.9/48.1	51.9/48.1	62.0/38.0	42.0/58.0
Spread position					
1982	4.03	−10.38	8.41	7.22	5.08
	(9.85)	(9.33)	(9.17)	(8.73)	(11.08)
	57.5/42.5	36.1/63.1	48.6/51.4	55.5/44.5	41.6/58.4
1983	−2.03	−9.42	−1.34	16.07	14.21
	(10.24)	(10.33)	(8.36)	(8.71)	(7.55)
	42.5/57.5	40.3/59.7	50.0/50.0	56.8/43.2	49.0/51.0
1984	−18.16	−15.49	−15.78	13.13	2.25
	(9.71)	(7.97)	(8.48)	(8.33)	(8.98)
	38.7/61.3	39.2/60.8	39.2/60.8	60.8/39.2	52.9/47.1
1985	−12.44	−10.00	−5.49	7.60	−0.78
	(10.31)	(7.55)	(8.17)	(8.39)	(8.40)
	42.8/57.2	40.3/59.7	49.0/51.0	52.0/48.0	41.6/58.4
1986	−12.14	−22.88	−12.69	7.80	4.30
	(9.20)	(11.49)	(10.16)	(12.37)	(10.54)
	38.7/61.3	34.6/65.4	42.3/57.7	54.0/46.0	56.0/44.0

those associated with the cash market portfolio, is likely to render any cash-futures trading strategy based on day-of-the-week effects unprofitable.

In contrast to the results for the individual contracts, the spread position has historically been characterized by a very distinct daily pricing pattern. In particular, Thursday and Friday are on average positive while Monday, Tuesday, and Wednesday are on average negative. Further, the variability of these daily price changes is considerably less in both absolute and relative terms than for an open position in either contract. The negative returns on Monday and Tuesday appear to be particularly stable and consistent. The positive Friday/negative Monday price change pattern is consistent with cash market price movements.

In evaluating the reliability of the pricing pattern, the two-day negative return from shorting the spread at the close on Friday was almost 23 basis points or $105 per single contract spread position. This return was positive almost 60 percent of the time. Any losses incurred were considerably smaller than those achieved by, for example, an open Value Line position for Thursday.

To see if this pricing pattern is stable over time, we report the spread position by day of the week for each year 1982–1986 in Table 10–2. Excluding 1982, the negative Monday-Tuesday return is quite clear and consistent in each year. This two-day trading strategy would have earned an average of almost $125 per trade and made profits three times in five. This profit figure is a gross number—execution and monitoring costs as well as the uncertainty of being able to execute at closing prices has not been netted out.

In sum, there does not appear to be a day-of-the-week effect in an open position in stock index futures and daily pricing patterns identified in these contracts are *opposite* to those observed in the cash market. The spread position has a very distinct and consistent day-of-the-week pattern that exceeds that reported for small firms in the cash market. While a profitable temporal trading strategy may or may not be identifiable, the observed pricing patterns indicate portfolio managers can improve performance by timing trades to take advantage of these temporal patterns.

MONTH-BY-MONTH PRICE CHANGE COMPARISONS

We now turn to the issue of monthly pricing patterns in stock index futures. If we compare average daily price changes by month we expect January's average to exceed other months; this difference should be higher for the VL and spread position. At least, this should be the case if the futures market pricing pattern is consistent with that of the cash market.

Table 10–3 reports the monthly averages of daily price changes for the three futures positions. While the January S&P 500 average exceeds the average across all months, higher daily averages are observed in August, October, and November and a roughly equal average daily price change in March. The VL daily

TABLE 10–3
Daily Price Changes for Stock Index Futures by Month of the Year, 4/82–12/86

	S&P 500	Value Line	Spread Position
January	16.80	25.05	8.25
	(20.33)	(22.36)	(8.17)
February	10.32	2.01	−8.31
	(20.05)	(23.04)	(7.26)
March	14.65	14.12	−0.05
	(17.07)	(19.18)	(7.33)
April	4.50	−3.55	−8.05
	(20.30)	(20.54)	(5.30)
May	2.26	2.35	0.09
	(13.57)	(15.09)	(6.02)
June	10.56	5.56	−5.00
	(16.64)	(18.01)	(6.02)
July	−30.00	−40.14	−10.14
	(17.22)	(19.85)	(6.91)
August	37.07	32.70	−4.36
	(16.95)	(19.35)	(7.17)
September	−28.18	−27.05	1.12
	(22.18)	(23.80)	(6.54)
October	28.33	18.64	−9.68
	(17.74)	(18.53)	(5.18)
November	18.43	22.99	4.55
	(19.70)	(19.96)	(6.06)
December	4.52	4.95	0.42
	(16.43)	(17.32)	(6.40)

average in January also exceeds the average across all months and any individual month except August. Finally, the spread position, which most captures the small firm-large firm differential stock price movement, is highest in January. This pricing pattern in the futures market, unlike that observed for day-of-the-week effects, is very similar to that observed in the cash market. However, none of the futures positions for any month have an average price change statistically different from zero. That is, the average return is characterized by substantial variability. Further, statistical tests confirm that equality of average price changes across months cannot be rejected. Thus, a buy and hold futures strategy designed to buy at the beginning of the month and sell at the end is a highly volatile strategy. What has historically been profitable may well, given the associated variability, be a random occurrence and unreliable in developing explicit trading rules. As before, knowledge of this pricing pattern may be useful to portfolio managers in timing trades.

FUTURES PRICE BEHAVIOR AT THE TURN OF THE YEAR

Perhaps the strongest cash market pricing pattern is the positive and large return at the turn of the year for stocks in general and small stocks in particular. Table 10–4 reports the price movements for the S&P 500, VL futures contracts, and spread futures position for the five-day turn of the year for 1983–1986. The most interesting result involves the spread. Had an investor purchased a spread position at the close on the penultimate trading day in each year and held it for the first four trading days of the year, he would have incurred losses on only 4 of the 20 trading days. Further, his average daily trading gain was 42 basis points or $210. His average profit per spread position was $1,050 over the turn of the year! For each year, as the spread results suggest, the VL contract outperforms the S&P 500, even in the 1985 down market. The average daily gain from holding an open VL futures position at the turn of the year was $425, and losses were incurred only 6 of the 20 trading days. The historical data suggest a possible successful trading strategy by buying a VL contract and/or a

TABLE 10–4
Turn-of-the-Year Effect, by Year, 1983–1986

	Last Trading Day, Previous Year	Trading Day Current Year				Total Basis Point Change
		First	Second	Third	Fourth	
S&P 500						
1983	.65	−2.80	3.50	.40	4.05	5.80
1984	.15	−1.50	3.10	1.20	.60	3.55
1985	−.20	−1.80	−1.35	−.65	.65	−3.35
1986	−1.00	−.90	1.40	.30	2.80	2.60
K. C. Value Line						
1983	1.40	−2.40	3.20	.50	4.65	7.35
1984	.90	−.55	3.80	2.30	1.15	7.60
1985	.00	−1.85	−1.15	.05	1.25	−1.70
1986	−.25	.05	1.80	.10	2.05	3.75
Spread position						
1983	.75	.40	−.30	.10	.60	1.55
1984	.75	.95	.70	1.10	.55	4.05
1985	.20	−.05	.20	.70	.60	1.65
1986	.75	.95	.40	−.20	−.75	1.15

spread position at the turn of the year. Obviously, the small amount of observations must be taken into account. It is worth noting, however, that if one had followed this strategy at the beginning of 1987, an investor would have made $7,825 from an open VL position and $1,425 from the spread position. This pricing pattern is consistent with that observed for much longer periods in the cash market.

FUTURES PRICE BEHAVIOR AT THE TURN OF THE MONTH

Table 10–5 provides evidence on the turn-of-the-month effect in futures markets. This table reports average daily price change for each month around the turn of the month and the rest of the month for the S&P 500 and VL futures contracts and a spread position. Excluding January, there is no obvious pattern across time of the month for either futures contract or the spread position. While the average price change is greater around the turn of the month, especially for the VL contract and spread position, variability of the price changes makes a turn-of-the-month trading rule an obviously risky strategy.

To show this, we report in Table 10–6 the average price gain and the number of months profits and losses were made following this rule (excluding January). The most promising trading results involve the VL futures and spread position. While average profit was $90 and $60 for the VL and spread position respectively, profits were made in only about half of the 52 trading months evaluated. Various stop-loss trading strategies did not significantly improve profit performance to any degree. As with the monthly results described earlier, there is some mild consistency between cash and futures market pricing patterns.

SUMMARY

This chapter has examined temporal pricing patterns with an eye toward (1) their consistency with cash market pricing patterns, and (2) development of trading strategies or trade timing to en-

TABLE 10–5
Daily Price Changes for Turn-of-the-Month Effect, 4/82–12/86

	S&P 500		Value Line		Spread Position	
	Turn of Month	Rest of Month	Turn of Month	Rest of Month	Turn of Month	Rest of Month
January	43.00 (41.26)	1.06 (22.99)	85.00 (40.18)	2.87 (25.66)	42.00 (10.61)	1.81 (9.92)
February	8.50 (43.85)	23.24 (22.71)	2.50 (51.60)	13.42 (26.10)	-6.00 (12.59)	-9.82 (8.76)
March	2.50 (33.69)	18.71 (19.78)	21.00 (47.03)	11.59 (20.58)	18.50 (19.33)	-7.12 (7.61)
April	-78.17 (38.83)	36.10 (22.02)	-85.21 (36.44)	27.65 (23.30)	-7.04 (12.36)	-8.45 (5.78)
May	-7.88 (31.78)	5.33 (15.79)	5.40 (32.68)	3.39 (17.46)	13.28 (11.67)	-1.93 (6.80)
June	0.40 (30.36)	6.14 (20.11)	0.80 (32.49)	-4.19 (21.34)	0.40 (11.71)	-10.34 (6.67)
July	-42.12 (42.38)	-19.87 (18.34)	-20.80 (46.53)	-35.49 (22.12)	-21.32 (13.96)	-15.61 (8.81)
August	8.20 (47.41)	40.75 (17.34)	6.20 (57.39)	32.15 (19.34)	-2.00 (21.91)	-8.60 (6.91)
September	8.40 (44.88)	-36.29 (26.59)	22.00 (49.11)	-35.38 (27.31)	13.60 (13.74)	0.90 (7.41)
October	33.40 (36.74)	24.41 (20.50)	15.20 (39.50)	16.45 (21.19)	-18.20 (10.28)	-7.96 (6.02)
November	68.00 (28.15)	1.23 (22.87)	77.60 (29.85)	5.77 (23.23)	9.60 (8.63)	4.54 (8.24)
December	54.60 (40.33)	-9.32 (18.77)	39.60 (41.83)	-9.32 (19.69)	-15.00 (10.29)	0.00 (7.59)

TABLE 10–6
**Average Price Gain for Turn-of-the-Month Trading Strategy, 4/82–12/86,
excluding January**

	S&P 500	Value Line	Spread Position
Average gain (in basis points)	1.38	3.61	2.23
Months made profit	23	30	29
Months incurred loss	29	26	27

hance portfolio performance. At least five findings should be noted. First, the day-of-the-week effect observed in the cash market is generally not observed in the futures market. To the extent it is, it is the *opposite* of that observed in the cash market. On the other hand, a strong and reliable day-of-the-week effect was observed for the spread position. Second, the January effect, while present in the futures market, is much weaker than in the cash market. The turn-of-the-year effect, however, is quite pronounced and has provided profits in each of the five years that futures contracts have been available. Third, there is a mild turn-of-the-month effect and, to the extent it can be documented, it is more pronounced in the Value Line futures contract and spread position. Fourth, all these effects, except perhaps the spread position that exploits day-of-the-week and turn-of-the-year pricing patterns, are characterized by relatively large amounts of variability, and to rely on them as the basis for trading strategies is probably unwise. The patterns and profits observed for the spread position price movements deserve further investigation and, in particular, evaluation under more realistic trading conditions incorporating execution costs and timing uncertainty. Finally, as guidelines for timing trades involving general portfolio management, the temporal pricing patterns, regardless of use as a trading strategy, can be valuable. As time passes and more data become available, we will better understand temporal pricing patterns in the futures market and their use in portfolio management.

CHAPTER 11

PRICING DETERMINANTS, ROLE IN RISK MANAGEMENT, AND OPTION EVALUATION FOR OPTIONS ON STOCK INDEXES AND STOCK INDEX FUTURES

Frank J. Fabozzi, Ph.D., C.F.A.
Visiting Professor of Finance
Sloan School of Management
Massachusetts Institute of Technology

Gary L. Gastineau
Vice President
Salomon Brothers Inc

Albert Madansky, Ph.D.
Professor of Business Administration
University of Chicago

In this chapter we will discuss (1) the factors that affect the price of an option; (2) the role of options in risk management; and (3) option evaluation. These concepts are equally applicable to options on both stock indexes and stock index futures. Any differences will be highlighted.

FACTORS THAT AFFECT THE OPTION PRICE

The five major factors affecting the option premium (price) are (1) the current price of the futures contract (or the index) relative to the exercise price; (2) the time remaining until the expiration of the option; (3) the anticipated volatility of the price of the underlying futures contract or index; (4) the level of interest rates; and (5) cumulative dividends before expiration or settlement.

1. Current Price of the Futures Contract Relative to the Exercise Price.   The current price of the futures contract relative to the exercise price determines whether the option has intrinsic value. The relationship is also important for the premium over intrinsic value component of the option premium.

All other factors equal, an at-the-money option generally has the greatest premium over intrinsic value. For an in-the-money option in which the current price of the futures contract differs substantially from the exercise price, the premium over intrinsic value is usually small. One of the reasons is the reduced leverage provided by purchasing the option compared to directly acquiring a futures position. For a substantially out-of-the-money option, the premium over intrinsic value is generally small in spite of the substantial leverage afforded by purchasing the option. This is because there is a lower probability that it will be profitable to exercise the option.

2. Time Remaining to the Expiration of the Option.   An option is a "wasting asset"—after the expiration date the option has no value. The longer the time to expiration of the option, the greater the option premium because as the time to expiration decreases, less time remains for the value of the index to change so as to compensate the option buyer for any premium over intrinsic value that he has paid. Consequently, as the time remaining until expiration decreases, the option price approaches its intrinsic value.

3. Anticipated Volatility of the Underlying Stock Index or Stock Index Futures Contract.   The greater the anticipated volatility of the underlying stock index or stock index futures contract, the more an investor would be willing to pay for the option and the more an option writer would demand for it. This is because as the volatility increases, the probability also increases that the price of the underlying trading unit will move in favor of the option buyer before expiration.

4. Level of Interest Rates. To illustrate how the level of interest rates and the cumulative dividends before expiration-settlement affect the option premium, we will use an option on one share of common stock instead of a stock index futures contract or a stock index.

Consider the following two investment strategies.

Strategy 1: Purchase a share of XYZ stock for S dollars.

Strategy 2: (a) Purchase a call option on XYZ stock for P dollars with an exercise price of E dollars and with T months to expiration; and *(b)* place funds in a bank account sufficient to exercise the option at expiration and to pay all dividends that would be paid on XYZ stock prior to expiration of the option.

Assume (1) that the interest that could be earned on the funds placed in the bank account for T months is r percent, and (2) that XYZ stock will pay only one dividend one day prior to expiration of the option in the amount of D dollars. Then the amount to be placed in the bank account, A, is simply the present value of the exercise price plus the present value of the dividends to be paid. That is,

$$\text{Investment under Strategy 2} = A = \frac{E}{1 + r} + \frac{D}{1 + r}$$

Let us investigate Strategy 2. This strategy will produce the same outcome as Strategy 1 at the end of the expiration date if it is beneficial for the investor to exercise the call option (i.e., if the price of XYZ is greater than the exercise price). There will be just enough funds to reproduce the dividends paid on XYZ stock and to pay the exercise price. Hence, if it is beneficial to exercise the call option at expiration, then S at most should be equal to the option premium plus the present value of the dividends plus the strike price, or:[1]

$$S = P + \frac{E}{1 + r} + \frac{D}{1 + r}$$

---

[1]Note that if it is not beneficial to exercise the call option because the price of XYZ is less than the exercise price, Strategy 2 would be better than Strategy 1. Consequently, whether or not it pays to exercise the call option, we know that the value of

Solving for the option premium, P, we have

$$P = S - \frac{E}{1 + r} - \frac{D}{1 + r}$$

As can be seen from the above relationship, as the level of interest rates increases, the present value of the exercise price and dividends decreases and the option premium for a call increases. The opposite occurs for a put. That is, the higher the level of interest rates, the lower the option premium for a put.

5. Cumulative Dividends before Expiration or Settlement. The relationship developed above clearly indicates that as the cumulative dividends before expiration-settlement increase, then, other factors equal, the option premium for a call decreases.

For an option on stock index futures, there are no dividends received by holding the stock index futures contract. For a cash index option, however, cumulative dividends are a factor to be considered in determining the option premium. This factor is discussed later in the chapter.

THE USE OF OPTIONS IN RISK MANAGEMENT

The principles behind the use of options in risk management are well established as a result of academic work on option theory and a decade of experience with listed stock options. Every option contract, whether the option is an index or index futures op-

---

Strategy 2 must be greater than or equal to the value of the price of XYZ stock (Strategy 1) at expiration . Thus,

$$P + \frac{E}{1 + r} + \frac{D}{1 + r} \geq S$$

Solving for the option premium, P, we have

$$P \geq S - \frac{E}{1 + r} - \frac{D}{1 + r}$$

The above relationship places a lower bound on the option premium for a call. Although the foregoing relationship has been developed for the two strategies at expiration, which would be true for a European call option, since an American call option is at least as valuable as a European call option, the relationship still holds for an American call option.

tion, a stock option, or a bond option, has what is variously called an *equivalence ratio,* a *neutral hedge ratio,* a *delta factor,* or an *elasticity.* Whatever the designation, the number represents the fractional change in the price of the option in response to a one-point change in the price of the underlying instrument subject to the option. This number, which we will call here the *hedge ratio,* is used to translate any option into its risk equivalent in the underlying instrument.

We will illustrate the hedge ratio in terms of a simple stock option. If an option changes in price by one-half point when the underlying stock changes in price by one point, that half-point price change on an option on 100 shares of stock is a change in the option's value of $50. The $50 equals the exact change in value that a holder of 50 shares of stock would experience if the stock price changed by $1. Therefore, the option is the risk equivalent of 50 shares of stock. In constructing a portfolio, we use the option as if it were actually 50 shares. If another option changed in price by one-quarter point in response to a one-point move in the stock price, that option would be the equivalent of 25 shares of stock. Every option—stock, bond, or index; in-the-money or out-of-the-money; put or call—can be translated into a fractional equivalent of the underlying instrument. If the fractional price change is one-half point on the option for a one-point change on the underlying instrument, it is simply a matter of multiplying that fraction by the number of units covered by the option contract, be it 100, 500, or some other number selected for the contract. The hedge ratio can be calculated for puts as well as calls and can be used to evaluate and control the degree of risk taken on or laid off in the options market.

Obviously, a certain amount of care must be taken in using this number because the hedge ratio will change as the market moves up and down. An option moving in-the-money or out-of-the-money will have a different hedge ratio than an option that is at-the-money. In a properly constructed stock option portfolio, the net stock-equivalent exposure of the portfolio may change relatively slowly because the risks of long and short option positions usually change in offsetting directions. In a portfolio using index options to control risk, the hedge ratio may change relatively quickly in periods of high market volatility because the portfolio will usually be long or short one type of index options, rarely on both sides of the option contract. A position that seems to provide an appropriate degree of risk may turn out to have too much or too little risk in the aftermath of a significant market move. Frequent adjustments of the index equivalence of an option position may be necessary.

Once the technique of using the hedge ratio is thoroughly understood, most investors find this approach more useful than the traditional option diagrams used in Chapter 2 to show the profit or loss of an option relative to a position in the underlying instrument. The hedge ratio provides a dynamic risk analysis in contrast to the static analysis of the profit-loss lines.

The concept of beta is useful in analyzing differences in portfolio volatility and calculating the appropriate adjustment to be obtained from stock index futures or index options contracts. If a portfolio has a high beta (i.e., if it responds more dramatically than the average portfolio to changes in the market averages), hedging that portfolio against market risk on a dollar-for-dollar equivalent basis will not be adequate. The value of the portfolio should be multiplied by the beta. The resulting figure is the appropriate hedge target that the index-equivalent hedge position should offset. If an investor is attempting to use index options as a substitute for a long common stock portfolio and the investor is in the habit of investing in stocks with below-average beta, the lower portfolio beta should be taken into account in constructing the option position. The combination of beta and the hedge ratio should help fine tune the risk control. Beta is discussed in Chapter 13.

OPTION EVALUATION

The hedge ratio is of value in understanding the concept of option evaluation. Option valuation discrepancies are the major reason, if not the only reason, for using options rather than futures contracts. Evaluation of stock index and index futures options is beyond the scope of this chapter, but any investor using options should be certain that he or she has a thorough understanding of the principles of option evaluation. There is no reason why every option investor should understand the mechanics of an option evaluation model or be prepared to develop detailed volatility estimates for the underlying optionable instrument. Every option investor should, however, understand that the principal decision variable in the process of option evaluation is the price volatility of the underlying instrument, be it a common stock, a debt instrument, or an index.

The major gains from astute evaluation of common stock options are possible in part because common stocks tend to have greater price volatility than do debt instruments and indexes. The fact that the underlying instrument in debt and index options is inherently less volatile means that the scope for significant over- and underevaluation is less pronounced. Also, stock market and interest rate volatilities tend to be more widely analyzed than does the volatility of an individual stock. If a typical stock option is mispriced by 15 to 25 percent, careful analysis of that degree of over- or underpricing should enable an astute portfolio manager to add several percent per year to the total return of a portfolio compared to the return on a stock-equivalent portfolio created using underlying common stocks alone. Because the index is less volatile than the stocks that it comprises, a similar degree of mispricing on the index options would provide a far smaller potential for improved return. If closer analysis of market volatility leads to more efficient markets for index options, the potential is further reduced. In addition, the transaction costs associated with the use of index options would be increased by the fact that an index option position will probably have to be adjusted more frequently than a stock option position that is part of a diversified portfolio of stock and option positions. On balance, most users of index options will probably find that the most they can expect from their activities in these options is to achieve the desired degree of risk adjustment and cover their transaction costs through astute use of option evaluation. Because transaction costs (the bid-asked spread as well as commissions) will be material, option evaluation is worthwhile. The investor who is on the wrong side of the option contract (e.g., short calls rather than long puts to offset the risk of a long stock portfolio) will be creating a risk adjustment position inefficiently. Transaction costs *and* the valuation premium or discount will be working against this investor. Thus, while option evaluation is unlikely to do as much for an investor in stock index or stock index futures options as it will for an investor in stock options, the transaction cost offset opportunity alone makes the evaluation exercise worthwhile.

Futures contracts can also be mispriced, but the mispricing is different from option mispricing and can either add to or offset it. If a futures contract is the underlying instrument, it is theoretically possible that a mispriced futures contract alone (without any option position) might be a more efficient way of undertaking a given degree of risk adjustment. When the calculation lag and related effects leading to futures contract mispricing are taken into account, what at first appears to suggest the purchase of an undervalued put may actually require the sale of an overvalued call.

There are relatively minor differences in valuation between options on index futures and cash settlement options priced on the indexes themselves. The circumstances that are likely to give rise to early exercise are similar but not identical. Given the pattern of ex-dividend dates, there is perhaps a somewhat greater possibility of early exercise of stock index options than of stock index *futures* options. When remaining dividends are high relative to the level of interest rates, there may be an incentive to exercise in-the-money cash settlement index calls to capture remaining dividends. When interest rates are high relative to dividends, the opposite effect may encourage exercise of in-the-money puts to capture cash that is likely to return more interest than the remaining likelihood of a decline in the index is worth.

Calculation lag also adds to the possibility of early exercise of stock index options should these options be significantly in-the-money. If index options are priced as if the settlement price were a futures price corrected for calculation lag and so forth, the actual closing price may encourage early exercise of some in-the-money options. This will probably not happen with stock index futures options because the futures contract price can adjust more quickly than the cash index value.

Index options and index futures options are affected by interest rates in slightly different ways. The terms of a specific contract should be carefully checked. In general, however, the price of a call option on an index (SEC-regulated) will reflect the fact that a buyer of that call will enjoy participation in gains in the value of the index without having to put up cash to buy the underlying stocks. The price of an index put should reflect the interest that could be earned by a short seller who has access to the proceeds of the short sale of the stocks underlying the index. These interest components of option value are complicated by the dividend pattern of the stocks in the index. The owner of an index call has the right to participate in changes in stock prices reflected in the index, but not directly in cash dividends. Likewise the index put owner's position would not be affected by dividends paid out on implicit short sales of underlying stocks. On the other hand, when a stock trades *ex dividend,* its price reflected in the index generally falls by roughly the amount of the dividend. The dividend adjustment must be computed stock by stock and must reflect the actual timing of ex-dividend dates. Taking a single annualized dividend rate for the index and subtracting it from the interest rate can give seriously misleading results. An interest rate adjustment can be based on the bond-equivalent yield of a Treasury bill expiring concurrently with the option.

Early exercise of an American-type index option is largely a function of interest rates and the relationship of interest rates and dividends. Because the volatility of an index is lower than that of most individual stocks, early exercise of index calls will be common when remaining dividends and interest rates are high and the option is in the money. Under these circumstances the discounted value of the index at expiration will be close to the current spot index, making opportunities for appreciation less valuable. The present value of the cash tied up in an in-the-money option can be greater than the value of the option's appreciation potential. Exercising the option gives call buyers cash on which they can earn interest immediately.

American-type index puts are most likely to be exercised when they are in the money, interest rates are high, and remaining dividends are small. In this case the high rates make early receipt of the cash settlement more valuable, and the low dividends make appreciation in the index somewhat more likely and appreciation in the put less likely.

European-type index options like the S&P 500 options listed on the CBOE and the AMEX Institutional Index options cannot be exercised early and, consequently, do not need an early-exercise adjustment. These contracts were designed for the portfolio insurance market where early exercise is not valued highly. Because these options cannot be exercised early, their premiums should be lower than the premiums on American-type index options, and they may sell below parity when they are in the money. Exchange specialists and market makers have tended to overprice the European-type index options relative to their American-type counterparts. This overpricing is probably due to a slightly greater interest by buyers than by sellers in these options and the tendency of market makers and specialists to offset S&P 500 index (SPX) options positions with S&P 100 index (OEX) options positions and to offset AMEX Institutional Index (XII) options positions with Major Market Index (XMI) options positions.

Index futures options have their own peculiarities. Both index options and index futures options settle for cash on their expiration dates. The cash payment in each case is equal to the difference between the option strike price and the closing index price on that date times the index multiplier, usually $100 or $500. If exercise occurs before the expiration date, the American-type index option settles in the same way, with the settlement based on the closing value of the index on the date of exercise. Early exercise of an index *futures* call option, however, gives the holder of the call a long position in the underlying futures contract, and early exercise of an index *futures* put gives the holder a short position in the index futures contract. Because a futures position is marked-to-the-market daily, exercise of an index futures option gives the holder cash from variation margin equal to the difference between the striking price and the closing futures price on the exercise date times the multiplier. Early exercise of an index futures option is almost totally a function of the interest that can be earned on variation margin over the remaining life of the futures contract and the likely index volatility. While the early exerciser of an index futures option can close out the futures position at about the same time the futures option is exercised, futures options and SEC-regulated index options are not identical. The settlement price of an early-exercised futures option where the futures contract is also closed out is based on the futures price. The settlement price of an early-exercised SEC-regulated index option is the closing value of the "spot" index on the date of exercise. These prices will rarely be the same. The futures price will usually be higher unless (1) short-term interest rates are below the annualized rate of dividends due to be paid before expiration and/or (2) futures are underpriced relative to the "spot" index as a result of risk adjustment by market participants that has temporarily disturbed the futures-spot parity relationship.

As if these difficulties were not enough, there is another possible problem in the evaluation of stock index and stock index futures options. Many stock option evaluation models assume that the distribution of common stock returns is lognormal.[2] Empirical studies show that when the time period involved is less than a year, this assumption may be invalid.[3] Regardless of the shape of the underlying stock return distribution, problems may occur when a variety of stocks with different volatilities (standard deviations) and similarly shaped distributions are combined in a weighted index. The resulting index will have a different variance or standard deviation (invariably lower than that of the average of the component common stocks), and the distribution may have a different shape. Fortunately, many potential problems with the lognormal assumption seem to wash out in the evaluation of index and index futures options. The lognormal approximation is a reasonable description of the actual distribution. Furthermore, because the volatility of an index is less than the average volatility of its components, the importance of the volatility variable and the shape of the distribution are diminished. While the widely

---

[2] Common stock prices are said to have a lognormal distribution if the logarithm of the price has a normal distribution. Thus, if a stock is priced at $100 and prices have a normal distribution, then the distribution of prices is the familiar bell-shaped curve centered at $100. But if the prices have a lognormal distribution, then it is the logarithm of the price which has a bell-shaped distribution about $\log 100 = 4.6051702$. Assuming the logarithm of the standard deviation is .6931472, the logarithm of the prices is equally likely to be 5.2983174 or 3.912023, i.e., $4.6051702 \pm .6931472$ corresponding to prices of $200 and $50, respectively. If the probability density curve is plotted as a function of price, rather than as a function of the logarithm of price, the curve will appear skewed and with tails more nearly depicting the actual observed behavior of stock prices.

[3] R. R. Officer, "The Distribution of Stock Returns," *Journal of the American Statistical Association,* December 1972, pp. 807–12.

used Black-Scholes model is not useful in valuing stock index and index futures options, the problems are with dividend corrections rather than with lognormality.[4]

An investor who is called on to accept a model to evaluate stock index or stock index futures options should ask the following questions.

1. What is the Nature of the Model Used?   If the answer is that it is a Black-Scholes or similar model adapted from stock option evaluation, the investor should use the results with an appropriate degree of skepticism.[5] A binomial model such as the Cox-Ross-Rubinstein model is probably the best choice given the importance of dividend adjustments.[6]

2. How Is the Dividend Adjustment Handled?   The answer to this question should reflect some of the material contained in this book, and explicit adjustments should be made for dividends for each day of the life of the option.

3. How Are Interest Rate Levels Handled?   The answer to this question should be complex. The way an interest rate adjustment is handled for a futures option is different from the way an interest rate adjustment is handled for a stock index option with cash settlement. The significance of the difference is related to the value of the underlying instrument and the probability of early exercise.

4. What Volatility Estimate Is Being Used, and How Was It Developed?   The answer to this question should include more than a discussion of historic and implied volatilities. No specific approach to volatility estimation is inherent to any model, and mechanically derived volatility estimates should be viewed with

---

[4]Fischer Black and Myron Scholes, "The Pricing of Options and Corporate Liabilities," *Journal of Political Economy*, May–June 1973, pp. 637–54.

[5]For a discussion of option evaluation models, see Gary L. Gastineau, *The Options Manual* (New York: McGraw-Hill, 1988), pp. 163–223.

[6]See John C. Cox, Stephen A. Ross, and Mark Rubinstein, "Option Pricing: A Simplified Approach," *Journal of Financial Economics* 7 (1979), pp. 229–63.

suspicion. For example, any weighting of historic and implied volatility is arbitrary at best. Analysis of the underlying factors affecting volatility should be incorporated.

The investor should ask anyone who provides a stock index or stock index futures option model the same questions that would be asked of anyone providing a common stock option model. While investors have a right to expect that these questions have been answered by the services that provide a commercial option evaluation model, these services are rarely up to the state of the art. Many services are guilty of misleading their subscribers, and skepticism is appropriate.

SECTION THREE

APPLICATIONS

CHAPTER 12

PORTFOLIO INSURANCE

Hayne Leland, Ph.D.
Professor of Finance
University of California, Berkeley
and
Director
Leland, O'Brien and Rubinstein Associates

"Portfolio insurance" has grown from miniscule to gargantuan in five years, with over $60 billion in assets now being protected by this technique. This size, coupled with its potential impact on equity markets, has attracted considerable attention. Nonetheless, the advantages and disadvantages of portfolio insurance are imperfectly understood by the much of the investment community. In this chapter, we hope to address a number of questions related to portfolio insurance and how it can be used as an effective investment tool.

Many skeptics are asking whether this is yet another "hot" investment fad that will quickly fade from the scene, leaving a few people richer and many poorer. History would seem to be on the side of the skeptics.

Most discredited products have promised high returns based on the offerors' ability to predict the best-performing assets. Investment history is littered with such discredited claims. Portfolio insurance has a fundamental difference: *it is a form of efficient risk management* that does not depend on or claim the ability to predict the market's future.

We will focus here on several aspects of portfolio insurance:

1. How does it work?
2. How can it be used?
3. What are the most important problems associated with implementation?
4. What future developments and extensions are likely?

Our analysis will be nontechnical, using examples rather than developing theory. References are provided for the reader wishing to explore the theory in greater depth.

Before plunging into details, however, we give a brief description of how both the theory and implementation of portfolio insurance evolved.

THE ROOTS OF PORTFOLIO INSURANCE IN FINANCIAL THEORY[1]

In 1973 Fischer Black and Myron Scholes published "The Pricing of Options and Corporate Liabilities."[2] They showed that, over a short period of time, an option position could be hedged by a changing (i.e., dynamic) stock and cash position. The hedged portfolio, being riskless, must return the risk-free rate.

Given the key assumptions that the stock's return had constant variance and that the risk-free rate did not change over time, Black and Scholes derived a formula for the correct price of options.

Options may not seem closely related to portfolio insurance, but there is a close connection between the two.

Say you purchase a stock at $100. Simultaneously, you buy a three-month put option on the stock with striking price 95, for a cost of $2. For a cost of 2 percent of the initial stock value, you have assured a maximum loss of 5 percent on your $100 stock

---

[1]For a further description of the development of portfolio insurance, see H. Leland and M. Rubinstein, "An Early History of Portfolio Insurance," in Donald Luskin, *Portfolio Insurance* (New York: John Wiley & Sons, 1988).

[2]Fischer Black and Myron Scholes, "The Pricing of Options and Corporate Liabilities," *Journal of Political Economy*, May–June 1973.

investment (or a maximum loss of 7 percent on your total investment of $102). Why? If the value of your stock falls below $95, you exercise your put option, and realize a profit on that option which compensates dollar for dollar on stock losses beyond the initial $5 decline.

Thus the parallel between purchasing a protective put option and purchasing portfolio insurance is precise. The investor must find a put option on the security (or portfolio) he holds, with maturity and striking price equal to his desired period of protection and protection level.

Until 1983, no options were available on broadly based portfolios. Even today, when options exist on such broad indexes as the S&P 500, the maturities desired by most institutional investors are not available.[3] This lack of markets would seem to preclude portfolio insurance.

However, in 1976 the author realized that the Black-Scholes argument could be used to actually replicate options on a stock— or on a portfolio. By dynamically altering the proportion of funds invested in the underlying portfolio and a risk-free instrument such as Treasury bills, any option-like return could be created!

The exact nature of the option replicating strategy is explained elsewhere.[4] It requires the investor to start with an initial hedge (proportion of funds in a risk-free asset) which depends on the protection horizon, the level of protection, the available risk-free rate of a zero-coupon bond with maturity equal to the horizon, and the risk of the portfolio to be protected.

As the value of the insured portfolio rises, the hedge can be reduced since the minimum return is less likely. Conversely, if the value of the portfolio falls, the minimum is more likely and the hedge must increase. The *dynamic* nature of the hedge position distinguishes portfolio insurance from traditional static forms of risk-reduction.

---

[3]There is a recent proposal to extend available maturities to two years on S&P 500 Index options. Even so, the horizons of many institutional investors are considerably longer than this.

[4]Mark Rubinstein and Hayne Leland, "Replicating Options with Positions in Stock and Cash," *Financial Analysts Journal,* July–August 1981, pp. 3–12.

The dynamics enable the upside cost of the hedge to be limited (to the equivalent of the put premium), since the hedge position is wound down to zero in up markets. The dynamics also permit the positive control of downside losses, since if the portfolio continued to lose value, all funds would ultimately be invested in the risk-free hedge.

Of course, if markets vibrate, there is also a cost to the dynamics: with hindsight, the program appears to "buy high, sell low." The cost of such hedging, however, will be limited to the put premium. Just as the holder of a put option sees the time value of his option fall if the market vibrates through time but remains where it began, the dynamic hedger will incur a similar limited cost from his hedging decisions.

In short, whether the market rises, falls, or simply vibrates, the dynamic hedge will give the same result as having bought a put option on the portfolio.[5]

IMPLEMENTATION

Cash Market Implementation

Between 1976 and 1981, the author worked with a colleague at the Berkeley Business School, Mark Rubinstein, to develop a practical program for implementing portfolio insurance.

The theory was successfully tested over a six-month period in 1979 when Rubinstein moved funds between Vanguard's Index Fund and Money Market Fund to achieve a protected return. This experiment was the first practical implementation of portfolio insurance. In 1981, LOR (Leland, O'Brien Rubinstein Associates) was formed to make the product available to institutional investors.

Early portfolio insurance programs required buying and selling stocks as the hedge ratio needed to be changed. This was feasible with reasonably liquid stocks since a typical program's

---

[5]This will be the case if the portfolio's volatility is constant at the level initially anticipated. When volatility is different than anticipated, dynamic hedges will not give exactly the same result as options.

annual turnover varied between 25 percent and 60 percent, depending on the program's horizon and the insured portfolio's volatility.

Implementation in the cash market, however, gave rise to several practical problems. First, large potential clients worried about the liquidity of markets in at least some of the stocks they held. Second, if clients had multiple managers, they had to decide which managers would implement the required buy-and-sell decisions. While all could buy or sell on a pro-rata basis, the complication of coordinating many managers discouraged many potential users. Finally, managers sometimes claimed that the hedging process interfered with their style of management.

These problems associated with implementation in cash markets were largely removed with the introduction of stock index futures.

Index Futures Implementation

The majority of protection programs currently use stock index futures for hedging. Hedging with futures overcomes many of the obstacles encountered when using cash markets.

The use of futures is based on a simple fact: A long futures position is equivalent to (1) buying stock, and (2) borrowing at the interest rate relevant to the expiration date of the futures contract (typically three to six months). This relationship follows from simple arbitrage conditions between futures and cash markets. "Program traders" or arbitrageurs will find it profitable to act when futures prices deviate significantly from this theoretical value. Indeed, hedgers using stock index futures rely on arbitrageurs to keep futures prices "fair".

To illustrate the use of futures, consider the example of a well-diversified equities fund. Assume that initially it is invested entirely in equities, perhaps with several managers. If the initial hedge should be (say) 15 percent of asset value, a short position equivalent to 15 percent of the portfolio value should be taken in index futures.[6]

---

[6]If the equities were best tracked by the S&P 500 index, this should be used as the hedging future. Most equity funds, however, can better be tracked by a basket of futures including the NYSE and Value Line contracts as well as the S&P.

Assume the portfolio's value falls. A profit will be made in the index futures account which will compensate for a fraction of losses. The optimal short futures position must now be increased, necessitating the sale of additional contracts. If the market falls further, the larger short position will generate an even greater cushion of profits to help offset portfolio losses.

Ultimately, the short futures position could become as great as the value of the portfolio, thereby eliminating virtually all further losses. Because futures prices are somewhat higher than the spot index prior to expiration, the short futures position will be generating the equivalent of interest at short-term rates.

When the portfolio's value rises, the short futures position is bought back. Ultimately, the short position could be entirely eliminated if the required hedge is negligible. This limits the potential losses on the short futures position to a fixed amount, equivalent to the insurance premium (or cost of the protective put position).

While generating essentially the same results as cash market implementation, futures markets implementation has some distinct advantages. The S&P 500 Index Futures is one of the most liquid contracts in the world. Hedge positions of more than $100 million can be implemented in a matter of minutes, with small market impact. Trading costs tend to be low. And the use of futures is "nonintrusive" on individual managers: they need not buy or sell stocks for the protection program. Indeed, they might not even know the hedging is taking place!

There are some costs to using futures markets, however. Futures do not always sell at exactly "fair value."[7] Another problem is cross-hedge risk. To the extent that a fund deviates from holding stocks in the same ratios as an index (or basket of indexes), the hedge will not be perfect. The fund's value will not move in lock-step with the value of the futures.

In this case, downside protection cannot be exact. If the fund's stocks moved down while the index moved up, the fund

---

[7]See Donald Luskin, *Index Options and Futures* (New York: Wiley, 1987), pp. 63–78. Measuring fair value is also complicated in fast-moving markets, where the index tends to lag behind its true value due to the nonsynchronous trading of stocks.

would lose money on the hedge as well as on its stocks. Nonetheless *market* risks—which typically account for 90–95 percent of most funds' variability—can be protected with index futures. The "alpha" or fund-specific risk must still be borne by the client. But presumably he is taking these risks because he feels the return is warranted. If he did not, he should own an index fund, and protection would be exact.

Index Options Implementation

Portfolio insurance programs can also use listed options in providing portfolio insurance. An insurance program is equivalent to buying a put option on a portfolio, so why not simply purchase put options?

There are two important advantages to using options. First, a well-designed option position can minimize the amount of trading that must be done in cash or futures markets. This is because an option position "automatically" adjusts the exposure to the underlying index, reducing the adjustment required in futures. Worries related to trading in fast-moving markets are minimized.

Second, options are less sensitive to realized market volatility. Programs which are implemented dynamically have costs that depend on the realized volatility in markets. At times this volatility may be higher than anticipated, with consequent higher costs.[8] An option, however, has a final payoff which is invariant to the volatility actually realized over its life: the option's initial cost reflects *expected* volatility.

Nonetheless, short-term options are not a complete cure to the problem of unanticipated volatility. The implicit volatility (and therefore cost) of options changes dramatically through time. If the market becomes more volatile, it will not affect the final return of the option currently held. But when it comes time to roll over the options, the next round may be more costly. Thus realized volatility over the program's life will affect program costs, whether options or futures are used. But the problem may be less acute when options are used.

---

[8] Of course if volatility is lower, costs will also be lower.

There are some significant problems associated with using options, however:

1. Options may not exist on the appropriate portfolio.
2. Options typically don't have expiration dates as distant as the insurance program's horizon.
3. Many options are American-style rather than European-style.
4. Option position limits may be restrictive.

Options generally exist on the same set of indexes as futures. If the fund to be protected is closely related to a single index (e.g., an equity fund similar to the S&P 500), options can be used as a means of protection. If the fund is a mixture of indexes (e.g., 50 percent stock, 50 percent long-term bonds) then options cannot be used to achieve a result similar to futures.

This problem stems from a fundamental principle: an option on a portfolio is not the same as a portfolio of options. Futures could be used to construct a put option on the portfolio of stocks and bonds. But when options are used, they amount to having separate protection on the stocks and on the bonds and this approach tends to be less desirable.[9]

The relatively short expiration dates of options pose two problems. First, short maturity means frequent rolling forward of options positions and this can be expensive. Second, short-term options must be used to achieve a desired long-term result. Considerable skill is required in selecting short-term options to mimic long-term options. If a sufficient number of striking prices is not available, futures will be needed in conjunction with options.

New, longer-term options are being proposed. In addition, the trend seems to be toward European-style options that can be exercised only at maturity. Since insurance programs typically provide a minimum value only at maturity, European options are better suited for use. American options cost more because

---

[9]Insuring each asset separately provides more insurance than is needed. For example, if one asset rises in value and another falls by the same amount, no insurance would be needed. But there would be a payoff if each asset were insured separately. This payoff is reflected in a higher-than-necessary premium when assets are protected separately, with a consequent lower expected return.

they can be exercised at any time until maturity. The extra cost does not provide a useful benefit for most portfolio insurance programs.

A final encouraging note is the proposed relaxation of option position limits. Position limits may limit the effectiveness of portfolio insurers who seek the benefit of using options. They also may force a proliferation of smaller (and perhaps less efficient) firms, simply to spread the limits more broadly. Manipulation should not be a problem if options are used for legitimate hedging purposes.

In sum, options offer considerable potential for supplementing current techniques of providing portfolio protection. They will become more useful as longer-term, European options are introduced and position limits are relaxed.

SOME REAL WORLD PROBLEMS OF IMPLEMENTATION

Uncertain Volatility

Until recently, all portfolio insurance programs were based on replicating options. The assumptions underlying this approach are quite restrictive. In particular, it is not accurate to assume that stock volatility will remain constant. Historically, the volatility of the S&P 500 has varied from a low of about 10 percent per year in the 1950s to a high of over 30 percent per year in the 1930s. Even the best predictors of futures volatility are subject to considerable error.

Yet the optimal hedge depends on the predicted volatility of the assets being protected. If the volatility turns out not to have been as expected, the initial hedge will have been incorrect. Higher than expected volatility will lead to greater hedging costs, because "whipsaws" tend to be more frequent.

How much will extra volatility cost a program? The cost depends on the actual path of stock prices. If extra volatility occurs when option replication requires little trading, there will be minimal extra cost to volatility using traditional option replicating techniques. If the replication requires large trades, as will be the case when the option is at-the-money, the costs of additional volatility are considerable.

In some circumstances, option replication will be considerably more expensive than expected. (Of course, if volatility is less, the replication will be less expensive).

Recognizing this problem, LOR has developed nontraditional hedging programs to minimize the uncertainty of costs associated with unexpected volatility. So-called perpetual or time-invariant strategies have two advantages over the traditional option-replicating techniques:

1. The costs of extra volatility can be quantified.
2. Time does not explicitly enter the hedging process.

The costs of additional volatility are predictable. Higher volatility will be more costly, but by a quantifiable amount per unit of extra volatility.

The second property addresses an undesirable feature of option-replicating programs: they become fully hedged if the ending portfolio value is as little as $1 under the minimum specified return, but fully unhedged if the ending value is just over the minimum return. Clients renewing their protection policies understandably wonder why it was optimal to be 100 percent hedged on December 31, but (for example) only 25 percent hedged on January 1.

"Perpetual" policies, being time invariant, require hedges that move continuously with ending asset value. They can be left in place as long as the client desires, incurring costs on a "pay as you go" basis. If the insured period is extended, there is no required shift in the current hedge ratio.

Sensitivity to unexpected volatility may be reduced through the use of index options. The joint use of nontraditional hedging techniques and options implementation will substantially reduce the problem of unexpected volatility in the future.

Trading Costs

Real-world portfolio insurance must also deal with trading costs. The Black-Scholes model assumed continuous revision of the optimal hedge position. While giving great accuracy, continuous trading would be ruinously costly. The more frequent the revision, the greater the turnover required for option replication.

Therefore any real-world application of portfolio insurance must specify the rules under which hedge ratios are revised. Early strategies focused on waiting until the market had moved by a certain amount before revision occurred. LOR has used trading bounds ranging from 3 to 5 percent. The greater the cost of transacting, the wider the bounds were chosen.

More recently, theory has suggested that optimal trading should not move to the ideal hedge, but should lag behind.[10] Such lagged trading strategies offer transactions savings of up to 30 percent while providing equivalent accuracy of replication. The optimal lag depends on the magnitude of transactions costs and the protection program being implemented.

How great is the turnover related to portfolio insurance? This depends on many factors: the risk of the portfolio being protected, the protection horizon, and the degree of accuracy required. But typical annual turnover rates for policies have ranged from 15 percent to 60 percent—less than the turnover associated with the average actively-managed pension account. When futures are used for implementation, the expected costs associated with trading can be expected to lie between 3 and 12 basis points per year.[11]

WHO SHOULD BUY PORTFOLIO INSURANCE

We have focused on how portfolio insurance works and some of the problems associated with real-world implementation. These are technical questions. For most investment funds, the important questions are

1. Does portfolio insurance make sense for us?
2. If it does, which policy should we choose?

---

[10]See, for example, Michael Magill and George Constantinides, "Portfolio Selection with Transactions Costs," *Journal of Economic Theory* 13, October 1976.

[11]In addition, the futures position must be rolled over two to four times per year, depending on the maturity of the contracts purchased. The fraction of funds which will be hedged at rollover times will of course vary.

Portfolio insurance is similar to other forms of insurance, but it is different in at least one fundamental respect. Most other insurance involves *risk pooling*. If you buy fire insurance on your house, your premium goes into a pool that covers the expected costs of houses burning down (and a profit for the insurance company!). Traditional insurance buyers pool their funds via the insurance company, and bear *average* costs, thereby smoothing out the magnitude of individual losses.

In contrast, portfolio insurance is *not* risk pooling. The risks avoided by a portfolio insurer are passed on to the rest of the market, which extracts a price for this transfer through the cost of the put option (or cost of the dynamic strategy).

This means that for any buyer of portfolio insurance, there must be a seller. The market as a whole cannot in aggregate buy or sell: for every investor following a strategy which purchases portfolio insurance, other investors who trade with the insurer must (consciously or not) be selling portfolio insurance, by taking the other side of the insurer's trades.

Currently, those taking the other side include rebalancers (who keep constant asset *proportions* and therefore sell stocks when they have done relatively well) and timers (who typically buy after market declines and sell after rises).

The fact that not everyone can simultaneously buy portfolio insurance raises a key question: who should buy, and who should sell? Theory suggests that there are distinct classes of investors who should buy portfolio insurance.[12]

The most important class of investors are those with particular sensitivity to downside risks. These might be investors who have relatively small wealth, or pension funds with fiduciary obligations to pay future retirement benefits. Investors who feel less sensitive to downside risks might well choose to sell portfolio insurance by following opposite strategies.

In comparison with static risk-management techniques, portfolio insurance offers important benefits to investors concerned

---

[12]For a full but technical discussion, see Hayne Leland, "Who Should Buy Portfolio Insurance," *Journal of Finance,* May 1980.

with downside risk. Consider the following example of two investment funds sensitive to downside risk.

Fund A is reasonably aggressive, and can tolerate a maximum annual loss of 12 percent. Fund B is reasonably conservative, and wishes to avoid losing money in any year.

Given estimates of equity risk and return at the time of this writing—expected return of 14 percent and standard deviation of 16 percent—and current interest rates of 6 percent, a static mix of equities and Treasury bills would have the following properties:

Percent Allocation to:		Expected Return (percent)	Maximum Loss (percent)
Stocks	Bonds		
75	25	12	12
25	75	8	0

where maximum loss is the loss which would occur if the stock fell two standard deviations beneath its expected return. (Of course, even greater losses *could* occur.)

Hence, when looking at static policies, Fund A would choose the first strategy and Fund B the second strategy. This is because the strategies offer reasonable assurance of not exceeding the maximum permissible loss.

Consider replacing these static policies with dynamic policies based on portfolio insurance. Given the same parameters for interest rates, market risk, and market return, a dynamic strategy could be set up to assure losses not exceeding 12 percent and 0 percent respectively:

Maximum Loss (percent)	Initial Mix (percent)	Expected Return (percent)
12	52	13.3
0	87	11.0

In moving to a portfolio insurance strategy, Fund A can raise expected returns by 130 basis points per year, and still have the same downside risk protection as a 75/25 static strategy. Fund B can raise expected return by 300 basis points per year!

Is this a free lunch—substantially greater average returns, but equivalent (or better) downside risk protection? No, because *on average* the insured strategies have a higher stock exposure than the static strategies, and thus have greater average volatility. But the dynamic strategies reduce equity exposure exactly when needed for protection, and thus provide positive control of downside risks.

Our example shows that portfolio insurance can be used to *increase* long-run returns. Why is there the popular misconception that the strategy *reduces* return? Because most analysis has focused on protecting an all-equity portfolio, and comparing returns with and without insurance. This is mixing apples and oranges—such strategies don't have equivalent risks. When the proper downside risk comparison is made, portfolio insurance can be shown to increase returns in virtually every case.

What is the optimal horizon of a fund? This depends on the nature of important liabilities. An insurance company's internal fund may have an annual horizon, since the ability to write insurance in the subsequent year will depend on the year-end value of its assets. A pension fund might have a longer horizon, related to the duration of its promised benefits. As a general principle the horizon of a protection program should match the duration of the fund's liabilities.

What is the optimal protection level for a fund? Again, liabilities could be examined to determine the minimum acceptable future value. Or one could "back out" the minimum acceptable return from current (static) investment policies. Say a fund currently has a 50/50 mix and a horizon of five years. The probability is small (two standard deviations) that the annual return will be less than 2.8 percent compounded over the five year horizon. Thus, a five-year program could be instituted which would assure a minimum return over the five-year period of 2.8 percent. Such a policy would have substantially higher expected returns than the 50/50 static policy.

FUTURE DIRECTIONS

The methodology of portfolio insurance lends itself to many applications. Our examples have focused on protection of equity portfolios. But virtually any portfolio of tradable assets can be protected with this technique. Bond and balanced (bond and stock) funds have been successfully protected, as well as internationally diversified portfolios.

With new accounting rules, increasing attention has been focused on pension fund surplus—the difference between the market value of the fund's assets and liabilities. Hedging programs can be implemented to protect surplus to a predetermined level. The theory underlying such protection is different from Black-Scholes, because of the possibility of surplus (unlike stock prices) becoming negative.

Portfolio insurance is but one of many products that can be offered using dynamic strategies. Not all investors will find portfolio insurance appropriate for their investment objectives, but this does not mean that dynamic strategies have no role for such investors. For example, a fund could "sell off" half its returns above a certain level (e.g., 20 percent) in exchange for higher returns at lower levels.

With dynamic strategies, return distributions can be "tailored" to meet virtually any risk profile. Investors now have a powerful new tool at their disposal. As the investment community learns of its potentials, dynamics will become an integral part of every fund's investment strategy.

CHAPTER 13

HEDGING WITH STOCK INDEX FUTURES

Frank J. Fabozzi, Ph.D., C.F.A.
Visiting Professor of Finance
Sloan School of Management
Massachusetts Institute of Technology

Edgar E. Peters
Portfolio Manager
Structured Investment Products Division
The Boston Company, Inc.

The major economic function of futures markets is to transfer price risk from hedgers to speculators. Hedging is the employment of futures as a substitute for a transaction to be made in the cash market. The hedge position locks in the current value of the cash position. If cash and futures prices move together, any loss realized by the hedger on one position (whether cash or futures) will be offset by a profit on the other position. When the profit and loss are equal, the hedge is called a *perfect hedge*. In the stock index futures market, a perfect hedge returns the risk-free rate.

In practice, hedging is not that simple. When hedging with stock index futures, a perfect hedge can only be obtained if the return of the portfolio being hedged is identical to the futures contract. Since it is likely that both the stock portfolio and the futures contract have nonmarket components of return, a perfect hedge will rarely, if ever, happen.

The effectiveness of a hedge on an equity portfolio is determined by:

1. The relationship between the portfolio and the index underlying the futures contract.
2. The relationship between the cash price and futures price when a hedge is placed and when it is lifted.

The difference between the cash price and the futures price is called the *basis*. Consequently, hedging involves the substitution of basis risk for price risk.

A stock index future uses a stock index as its underlying commodity. Since the portfolio to be hedged will have different characteristics than the underlying stock index (unless it is a stock index fund), there will be a difference in the return pattern of the hedged portfolio and the futures contract. This practice, hedging with a futures contract which is different than the commodity being hedged, is called a *cross-hedge*. In the physical and commodities markets, this occurs, for example, when an okra farmer hedges a crop using corn futures. Corn is the commodity with a traded futures contract that may have the strongest price relationship to okra. In the equity markets, the hedger must choose the stock index, or combination of stock indexes with futures contracts, that best tracks the equity portfolio.

Consequently, cross-hedging adds another dimension to basis risk. The non-index related component of return in an equity portfolio will not be hedged by a stock index futures position.

Cross-hedging is the name of the game in portfolio management. There are no futures contracts on specific common stock shares. The only futures traded that are related to the equity markets have specific stock indexes as the underlying commodity. How well the price of a portfolio of common stocks tracks an index and the behavior of the basis will determine the success of a hedge.

The foregoing points will be made clearer in the illustrations presented later in this chapter.

SHORT HEDGE AND LONG HEDGE

In portfolio management, the short hedge is more commonly practiced. Long hedges are generally used in asset allocation strategies. However, it is the short hedge that is referred to as hedging in the marketplace.

A *short hedge* is used by a hedger to protect against a decline in the future cash price of a commodity or a financial instrument. To execute a short hedge, the hedger sells a futures contract (agrees to make delivery of the underlying commodity or financial instrument). Consequently, a short hedge is also known as a *sell hedge*. By establishing a short hedge, the hedger has fixed the future cash price and transferred the price risk of ownership to the buyer of the contract. Three examples of who may want to use a short hedge follow.

1. A corn farmer will sell his product in three months. The price of corn, like the price of any commodity, will fluctuate in the open market. The corn farmer wants to lock in a price at which he can deliver his corn in three months.

2. A corporate treasurer plans to sell bonds in two months to raise $85 million in capital. The cost of the bond issue to the corporation will depend on interest rates at the time the bond issue is sold. The corporate manager is uncertain of the interest rates that will prevail two months from now and wants to lock in a rate today.

3. A pension fund manager knows that the beneficiaries of the fund must be paid a total of $3 million four months from now. This will necessitate liquidating a portion of the fund's common stock portfolio. Should the value of the shares that he intends to liquidate in order to satisfy the benefits to be paid be lower in value four months from now, a larger portion of the portfolio would have to be liquidated. The pension fund manager would like to lock in the price of the shares that will be liquidated.

A *long hedge* is undertaken to protect against the purchase of a commodity or financial instrument in the cash market at some future time. In a long hedge, the hedger buys a futures contract (agrees to accept delivery of the underlying commodity or financial instrument). A long hedge is also known as a *buy hedge*. The following three examples are instances where a party may use a long hedge.

1. A food processing company projects that in three months it must purchase 30,000 bushels of corn. The management of the company does not want to take a chance that the price of corn may increase by the time the company must make its acquisition. It wants to lock in a price for corn today.

2. A bond portfolio manager knows that in two months $10 million of his portfolio will mature and must be reinvested. Prevailing interest rates are high but may decline substantially by the time the funds are to be reinvested. The portfolio manager wants to lock in a reinvestment rate today.

3. A pension fund manager expects a substantial contribution from participants four months from now. The contributions will be invested in the common stock of various companies. The pension fund manager expects the market price of the stocks in which she will invest the contributions to be higher in four months. She therefore wants to lock in the price of those stocks.

Hedging Illustrations

To explain hedging, we will present several numerical illustrations from the commodities area.

Assume that a corn farmer expects to sell 30,000 bushels of corn three months from now. Assume further that the management of a food processing company plans to purchase 30,000 bushels of corn three months from now. Both the corn farmer and the management of the food processing company want to lock in today's price. That is, they want to eliminate the price risk associated with corn three months from now. The cash or spot price for corn is currently $2.75 per bushel. The futures price for corn is currently $3.20 per bushel. Each futures contract is for 5,000 bushels of corn.

Since the corn farmer seeks protection against a decline in the price of corn three months from now, he will place a short, or sell, hedge. That is, he will promise to make delivery of corn at the current futures price. He will sell six futures contracts since each contract calls for the delivery of 5,000 bushels of corn.

The management of the food processing company seeks protection against an increase in the price of corn three months from now. Consequently, it will place a buy, or long, hedge. That is, it will agree to accept delivery of corn at the futures price. Since it is seeking protection against a price increase for 30,000 bushels of corn, it will buy six contracts.

Let's look at what happens under various scenarios for the cash price and the futures price of corn three months from now, when the hedge is lifted.

1. Cash Price of Corn Decreases and No Change in Basis. Suppose that at the time the hedge is lifted the cash price has declined to $2 and the futures price has declined to $2.45. Notice what has happened to the basis under this scenario. Recall that the basis is the difference between the cash price and the futures price. At the time the hedge is placed, the basis is − $0.45 ($2.75 − $3.20). When the hedge is lifted, the basis is still − $0.45 ($2.00 − $2.45).

The corn farmer at the time the hedge was placed wanted to lock in a price of $2.75 per bushel of corn, or $82,500 for 30,000 bushels. He sold six futures contracts at a price of $3.20 per bushel, or $96,000 for 30,000 bushels. When the hedge is lifted, the value of his corn is $60,000 ($2.00 × 30,000). He realizes a decline in the cash market in the value of his corn of $22,500. However, the futures price has declined to $2.45, so that the cost to the corn farmer to liquidate his futures position is only $73,500 ($2.45 × 30,000). He realizes a gain in the futures market of $22,500. The net result is that the gain in the futures market matches the loss in the cash market. Consequently, the corn farmer does not realize an overall gain or loss. When this occurs, the hedge is said to be a *perfect* or *textbook* hedge. The results of this hedge are summarized in Figure 13–1.

The outcome for the food processing company of the buy or long hedge is also summarized in Figure 13–1. Because there was a decline in the cash price, the food processing company would gain in the cash market by $22,500 but would realize a loss of the same amount in the futures market. Therefore, this hedge is also a *perfect* or *textbook* hedge.

This scenario illustrates two important points. First, for both participants there was no overall gain or loss. The reason for this result was that we assumed that the basis did not change when the hedge was lifted. Consequently, if the basis does not change,

FIGURE 13–1

Perfect Hedge: Cash Price Decreases

Assumptions

Cash price at time hedge is placed	$2.75 per bu.
Futures price at time hedge is placed	$3.20 per bu.
Cash price at time hedge is lifted	$2.00 per bu.
Futures price at time hedge is lifted	$2.45 per bu.
Number of bushels to be hedged	30,000
Number of bushels per futures contract	5,000
Number of futures contracts used in hedge	6

Short (Sell) Hedge by Corn Farmer

Cash Market	Futures Market	Basis

At time hedge is placed

Cash Market	Futures Market	Basis
Value of 30,000 bu.: 30,000 × $2.75 = $82,500	Sell 6 contracts: 6 × 5,000 × $3.20 = $96,000	−$0.45

At time hedge is lifted

Cash Market	Futures Market	Basis
Value of 30,000 bu.: 30,000 × $2.00 = $60,000	Buy 6 contracts: 6 × 5,000 × $2.45 = $73,500	−$0.45
Loss in cash market = $22,500	Gain in futures market = $22,500	
Overall gain or loss = $0		

Long (Buy) Hedge by Food Processing Company

Cash Market	Futures Market	Basis

At time hedge is placed

Cash Market	Futures Market	Basis
Value of 30,000 bu.: 30,000 × $2.75 = $82,500	Buy 6 contracts: 6 × 5,000 × $3.20 = $96,000	−$0.45

At time hedge is lifted

Cash Market	Futures Market	Basis
Value of 30,000 bu.: 30,000 × $2.00 = $60,000	Sell 6 contracts: 6 × 5,000 × $2.45 = $73,500	−$0.45
Gain in cash market = $22,500	Loss in futures market = $22,500	
Overall gain or loss = $0		

a perfect hedge will be achieved. Second, notice that the management of the food processing company would have been better off if it had not hedged. The cost of corn would have been $22,500 less in the cash market three months later. This, however, should not be interpreted as a sign of poor planning by management. Management is not in the business of speculating on the price of corn in the future. Hedging is a standard practice to protect against an increase in the cost of doing business in the future.

2. Cash Price of Corn Increases and No Change in Basis. Suppose that when the hedge is lifted the cash price of corn has increased to $3.55 and that the futures price has increased to $4. Notice that the basis is unchanged at −$0.45. Since the basis is unchanged, the cash and futures price we have assumed in this scenario will produce a perfect hedge.

The corn farmer will gain in the cash market since the value of 30,000 bushels of corn is $106,500 ($3.55 × 30,000). This represents a $24,000 gain compared to the cash value at the time the hedge was placed. However, the corn farmer must liquidate his position in the futures market by buying six futures contracts at a total cost of $120,000, which is $24,000 more than the cost when the contracts were sold. The loss in the futures market offsets the gain in the cash market, and we have a perfect hedge. The results of this hedge are summarized in Figure 13–2.

The food processing company would realize a gain in the futures market of $24,000 but would have to pay $24,000 more in the cash market to acquire 30,000 bushels of corn. The results of this hedge are summarized in Figure 13–2.

Notice that under this scenario the management of the food processing company saved $24,000 in the cost of corn by employing a hedge. The corn farmer, on the other hand, would have been better off if he had not used a hedging strategy and simply sold this product on the market three months later. However, it must be emphasized that the corn farmer, just like the management of the food processing company, employed a hedge to protect against unforeseen adverse price changes in the cash market.

3. Cash Price Decreases and Basis Widens. In the two previous scenarios we have assumed that the basis does not change

FIGURE 13–2

Perfect Hedge: Cash Price Increases
Assumptions

Cash price at time hedge is placed	$2.75 per bu.
Futures price at time hedge is placed	$3.20 per bu.
Cash price at time hedge is lifted	$3.55 per bu.
Futures price at time hedge is lifted	$4.00 per bu.
Number of bushels to be hedged	30,000
Number of bushels per futures contract	5,000
Number of futures contracts used in hedge	6

Short (Sell) Hedge by Corn Farmer

Cash Market	Futures Market	Basis

At time hedge is placed

Value of 30,000 bu.:	Sell 6 contracts:	
30,000 × $2.75 = $82,500	6 × 5,000 × $3.20 = $96,000	− $0.45

At time hedge is lifted

Value of 30,000 bu.:	Buy 6 contracts:	
30,000 × $3.55 = $106,500	6 × 5,000 × $4.00 = $120,000	− $0.45
Gain in cash market = $24,000	Loss in futures market = $24,000	
Overall gain or loss = $0		

Long (Buy) Hedge by Food Processing Company

Cash Market	Futures Market	Basis

At time hedge is placed

Value of 30,000 bu.:	Buy 6 contracts:	
30,000 × $2.75 = $82,500	6 × 5,000 × $3.20 = $96,000	− $0.45

At time hedge is lifted

Value of 30,000 bu.:	Sell 6 contracts:	
30,000 × $3.55 = $106,500	6 × 5,000 × $4.00 = $120,000	− $0.45
Loss in cash market = $24,000	Gain in futures market = $24,000	
Overall gain or loss = $0		

when the hedge is lifted. There is no reason why this must occur. In the real world the basis does in fact change between the time a hedge is placed and the time it is lifted. In the following four scenarios we will assume that the basis does change and look at the impact on the hedger.

Assume that the cash price of corn decreases to $2, just as in the first scenario; however, assume further that the futures price decreases to $2.70 rather than $2.45. The basis has now widened from −$0.45 to −$0.70 ($2.00 − $2.70).

The results are summarized in Figure 13–3. For the short (sell) hedge, the $22,500 loss in the cash market is only partially offset by the $15,000 gain realized in the futures market. Consequently, the hedge resulted in an overall loss of $7,500. There are several points to note here. First, if the corn farmer did not employ the hedge, the loss would have been $22,500, since the value of his 30,000 bushels of corn is $60,000 compared to $82,500 three months earlier. Although the hedge is not a perfect hedge because the basis widened, the loss of $7,500 is less than the loss of $22,500 that would have occurred if no hedge had been placed. This is what we meant earlier in the chapter when we said that hedging substitutes basis risk for price risk. Second, the management of the food processing company faces the same problem from an opposite perspective. An unexpected gain for either participant results in an unexpected loss of equal dollar value for the other. That is, the participants face a zero-sum game. Consequently, the food processing company would realize an overall gain of $7,500 from its long (buy) hedge. This gain represents a gain in the cash market of $22,500 and a realized loss in the futures market of $15,000.

The results of this scenario demonstrate that when *(a)* the futures price is greater than the cash price at the time the hedge is placed, *(b)* the cash price declines, and *(c)* the basis widens, then:

The short (sell) hedger will realize an overall loss from the hedge.

The long (buy) hedger will realize an overall gain from the hedge.

FIGURE 13–3

Hedge: Cash Price Decreases and Basis Widens
Assumptions

Cash price at time hedge is placed	$2.75 per bu.
Futures price at time hedge is placed	$3.20 per bu.
Cash price at time hedge is lifted	$2.00 per bu.
Futures price at time hedge is lifted	$2.70 per bu.
Number of bushels to be hedged	30,000
Number of bushels per futures contract	5,000
Number of futures contracts used in hedge	6

Short (Sell) Hedge by Corn Farmer

Cash Market	Futures Market	Basis

At time hedge is placed

Cash Market	Futures Market	Basis

Value of 30,000 bu.:
    30,000 × $2.75 = $82,500
	Sell 6 contracts:
	    6 × 5,000 × $3.20 = $96,000
		−$0.45

At time hedge is lifted

Cash Market	Futures Market	Basis

Value of 30,000 bu.:
    30,000 × $2.00 = $60,000
	Buy 6 contracts:
	    6 × 5,000 × $2.70 = $81,000
		−$0.70

Loss in cash market = $22,500	Gain in futures market = $15,000	
Overall loss = $7,500		

Long (Buy) Hedge by Food Processing Company

Cash Market	Futures Market	Basis

At time hedge is placed

Cash Market	Futures Market	Basis

Value of 30,000 bu.:
    30,000 × $2.75 = $82,500
	Buy 6 contracts:
	    6 × 5,000 × $3.20 = $96,000
		−$0.45

At time hedge is lifted

Cash Market	Futures Market	Basis

Value of 30,000 bu.:
    30,000 × $2.00 = $60,000
	Sell 6 contracts:
	    6 × 5,000 × $2.70 = $81,000
		−$0.70

Gain in cash market = $22,500	Loss in futures market = $15,000	
Overall gain = $7,500		

4. Cash Price Increases and Basis Widens. Suppose that the cash price increases to $3.55 per bushel, just as in the second scenario, but that the basis widens to −$0.70. That is, at the time the hedge is lifted the futures price has increased to $4.25. The results of this hedge are summarized in Figure 13–4.

As a result of the long hedge, the food processing company will realize a gain of $31,500 in the futures market but only a $24,000 loss in the cash market. Therefore, there is an overall gain of $7,500. For the corn farmer, there is an overall loss of $7,500.

The results of this scenario demonstrate that when *(a)* the futures price is greater than the cash price at the time the hedge is placed, *(b)* the cash price increases, and *(c)* the basis widens, then:

The short (sell) hedger will realize an overall loss from the hedge.

The long (buy) hedger will realize an overall gain from the hedge.

These two results are identical to the results we found in the previous scenario, where we assumed that the cash price declined. The magnitude of the overall gain or loss, $7,500, is the same in both scenarios because in each scenario it was assumed that the basis widened to −$0.70.

5. Cash Price Decreases and Basis Narrows. In the two previous scenarios it was assumed that the basis widened. In this scenario and the one that follows, we will assume that the basis narrows to −$0.25.

Suppose that the cash price declines to $2. Since we are assuming that the basis narrows to −$0.25, the futures price at the time the hedge is lifted is assumed to be $2.25. Figure 13–5 summarizes the outcome for the hedge. The corn farmer realizes an overall gain of $6,000. The food processing company, on the other hand, realizes an overall loss of $6,000.

The results of this scenario demonstrate that when *(a)* the future price is greater than the cash price at the time the hedge

FIGURE 13–4

Hedge: Cash Price Increases and Basis Widens
Assumptions

Cash price at time hedge is placed	$2.75 per bu.
Futures price at time hedge is placed	$3.20 per bu.
Cash price at time hedge is lifted	$3.55 per bu.
Futures price at time hedge is lifted	$4.25 per bu.
Number of bushels to be hedged	30,000
Number of bushels per futures contract	5,000
Number of futures contracts used in hedge	6

Short (Sell) Hedge by Corn Farmer

Cash Market	Futures Market	Basis

At time hedge is placed

Value of 30,000 bu.: 30,000 × $2.75 = $82,500	Sell 6 contracts: 6 × 5,000 × $3.20 = $96,000	−$0.45

At time hedge is lifted

Value of 30,000 bu.: 30,000 × $3.55 = $106,500	Buy 6 contracts: 6 × 5,000 × $4.25 = $127,500	−$0.70
Gain in cash market = $24,000	Loss in futures market = $31,500	

Overall loss = $7,500

Long (Buy) Hedge by Food Processing Company

Cash Market	Futures Market	Basis

At time hedge is placed

Value of 30,000 bu.: 30,000 × $2.75 = $82,500	Buy 6 contracts: 6 × 5,000 × $3.20 = $96,000	−$0.45

At time hedge is lifted

Value of 30,000 bu.: 30,000 × $3.55 = $106,500	Sell 6 contracts: 6 × 5,000 × $4.25 = $127,500	−$0.70
Loss in cash market = $24,000	Gain in futures market = $31,500	

Overall gain = $7,500

FIGURE 13–5

Hedge: Cash Price Decreases and Basis Narrows

Assumptions

Cash price at time hedge is placed	$2.75 per bu.
Futures price at time hedge is placed	$3.20 per bu.
Cash price at time hedge is lifted	$2.00 per bu.
Futures price at time hedge is lifted	$2.25 per bu.
Number of bushels to be hedged	30,000
Number of bushels per futures contract	5,000
Number of futures contracts used in hedge	6

Short (Sell) by Corn Farmer

Cash Market	Futures Market	Basis

At time hedge is placed

Value of 30,000 bu.: 30,000 × $2.75 = $82,500	Sell 6 contracts: 6 × 5,000 × $3.20 = $96,000	−$0.45

At time hedge is lifted

Value of 30,000 bu.: 30,000 × $2.00 = $60,000	Buy 6 contracts: 6 × 5,000 × $2.25 = $67,500	−$0.25
Loss in cash market = $22,500	Gain in futures market = $28,500	
Overall gain = $6,000		

Long (Buy) Hedge by Food Processing Company

Cash Market	Futures Market	Basis

At time hedge is placed

Value of 30,000 bu.: 30,000 × $2.75 = $82,500	Buy 6 contracts: 6 × 5,000 × $3.20 = $96,000	−$0.45

At time hedge is lifted

Value of 30,000 bu.: 30,000 × $2.00 = $60,000	Sell 6 contracts: 6 × 5,000 × $2.25 = $67,500	−$0.25
Gain in cash market = $22,500	Loss in futures market = $28,500	
Overall loss = $6,000		

is placed, *(b)* the cash price decreases, and *(c)* the basis narrows, then:

> The short (sell) hedger will realize an overall gain from the hedge.
> The long (buy) hedger will realize an overall loss from the hedge.

6. Cash Price Increases and Basis Narrows. Figure 13–6 summarizes the outcome of the hedge if the cash price increases to $3.55, as in scenario 4, and the basis narrows to −$0.25 (that is, the futures price when the hedge is removed is $3.80). The food processing company realizes an overall loss of $6,000. The corn farmer realizes an overall gain of $6,000.

The results of this scenario demonstrate that when *(a)* the futures price is greater than the cash price at the time the hedge is placed, *(b)* the cash price increases, and *(c)* the basis narrows, then:

> The short (sell) hedger will realize an overall gain from the hedge.
> The long (buy) hedger will realize an overall loss from the hedge.

This outcome is the same as that of the previous scenario, in which the cash price decreased.

Table 13–1 summarizes the outcome of the overall gain or loss for a short hedge and a long hedge for all possible changes in the cash and futures price.

Cross-Hedging

Not all commodities have a futures market. Consequently, if a hedger wants to protect against the price risk of a commodity in which a futures contract is not traded, he may use a commodity that he believes has a close price relationship to the one he seeks to hedge. This adds another dimension of risk when hedging. The cash market price relationship between the commodity to be hedged and the commodity used to hedge may change.

FIGURE 13–6

Hedge: Cash Price Increases and Basis Narrows
Assumptions

Cash price at time hedge is placed	$2.75 per bu.
Futures price at time hedge is placed	$3.20 per bu.
Cash price at time hedge is lifted	$3.55 per bu.
Futures price at time hedge is lifted	$3.80 per bu.
Number of bushels to be hedged	30,000
Number of bushels per futures contract	5,000
Number of futures contracts used in hedge	6

Short (Sell) Hedge by Corn Farmer

Cash Market	Futures Market	Basis

At time hedge is placed

Value of 30,000 bu.: 30,000 × $2.75 = $82,500	Sell 6 contracts: 6 × 5,000 × $3.20 = $96,000	−$0.45

At time hedge is lifted

Value of 30,000 bu.: 30,000 × $3.55 = $106,500	Buy 6 contracts: 6 × 5,000 × $3.80 = $114,000	−$0.25
Gain in cash market = $24,000	Loss in futures market = $18,000	

Overall gain = $6,000

Long (Buy) Hedge by Food Processing Company

Cash Market	Futures Market	Basis

At time hedge is placed

Value of 30,000 bu.: 30,000 × $2.75 = $82,500	Buy 6 contracts: 6 × 5,000 × $3.20 = $96,000	−$0.45

At time hedge is lifted

Value of 30,000 bu.: 30,000 × $3.55 = $106,500	Sell 6 contracts: 6 × 5,000 × $3.80 = $114,000	−$0.25
Loss in cash market = $24,000	Gain in futures market = $18,000	

Overall loss = $6,000

TABLE 13–1
Summary of Basis Relationships for a Hedge

Price		Absolute Change in Basis	Overall Gain (+) or Loss (−) When at Time Hedge Is Placed, Cash Price Is Less than Futures Price	
Cash	Futures		Short Hedge	Long Hedge
Decreases	Decreases by same amount	No change	0	0
Decreases	Decreases by a smaller amount	Widens	−	+
Decreases	Decreases by a greater amount	Narrows	+	−
Increases	Increases by same amount	No change	0	0
Increases	Increases by a smaller amount	Narrows	+	−
Increases	Increases by a greater amount	Widens	−	+
Decreases	Increases	Widens	−	+
Increases	Decreases	Narrows	+	−

Since cross-hedging is involved when stock index futures are used to hedge an individual common stock or a portfolio of common stocks, we will first illustrate the key elements associated with a cross-hedge for a commodity.

Suppose that an okra farmer plans to sell 37,500 bushels of okra three months from now and that a food processing company plans to purchase the same amount of okra three months from now. Both parties want to hedge against price risk. However, okra futures contracts are not traded. Both parties believe that there is a close relationship between the price of okra and the price of corn. Specifically, both parties believe that the cash price of okra will be 80 percent of the cash price of corn. The cash price of okra is currently $2.20 per bushel, and the cash price of corn is currently $2.75 per bushel. The futures price of corn is currently $3.20 per bushel.

Let's examine various scenarios to see how effective the cross-hedge will be. In each scenario, the difference between the cash price of corn and the futures price of corn at the time the cross-hedge is placed and at the time it is lifted will be assumed to be unchanged at $-\$0.45$. This is done so that we may focus on the importance of the relationship between the two cash prices at the two points in time.

Before proceeding, we must first determine how many corn futures contracts must be used in the cross-hedge. The cash value of 37,500 bushels of okra at the cash price of $2.20 per bushel is $82,500. To protect a value of $82,500 using corn futures with a current cash price of $2.75, the price of 30,000 bushels of corn ($82,500/$2.75) must be hedged. Since each corn futures contract involves 5,000 bushels, six corn futures contracts will be used.

1. Cash Price of Both Commodities Changes in the Same Direction and by the Same Percentage. Suppose that the cash prices of okra and corn decrease to $1.60 and $2 per bushel, respectively, and that the futures price of corn decreases to $2.45 per bushel. The relationship between the cash price for okra and the cash price for corn that was assumed when the cross-hedge was placed holds when the cross-hedge is lifted. That is, the cash price of okra is 80 percent of the cash price of corn. The basis for the cash price of corn and the futures price of corn is still $-\$0.45$ at the time the cross-hedge is lifted. The outcome for the short and long cross-hedge is summarized in Figure 13–7.

The short cross-hedge produces a gain of $22,500 in the futures market and an exact offset loss in the cash market. The opposite occurs for the long cross-hedge. There is neither an overall gain nor a loss from the cross-hedge in this case. That is, we have a perfect cross-hedge. The same would occur if we assume that the cash price of both commodities increases by the same percentage and the basis does not change.

2. Cash Price of Both Commodities Changes in the Same Direction but by a Different Percentage. Suppose that the cash price of both commodities decreases but the cash price of okra falls by a greater percentage than the cash price of corn. For example, suppose that the cash price of okra falls to $1.30 per bushel, while the cash price of corn falls to $2.00 per bushel. The futures price of corn falls to $2.45 so that the basis is not changed. The cash price of okra at the time the cross-hedge is lifted is 65 percent of

FIGURE 13-7

Perfect Cross-Hedge: Cash Price Decreases for Both Commodities by Same Percentage

Assumptions

Price of okra	
Cash price at time hedge is placed	$2.20 per bu.
Cash price at time hedge is lifted	$1.60 per bu.
Price of corn	
Cash price at time hedge is placed	$2.75 per bu.
Futures price at time hedge is placed	$3.20 per bu.
Cash price at time hedge is lifted	$2.00 per bu.
Futures price at time hedge is lifted	$2.45 per bu.
Number of bushels of okra to be hedged	37,500
Number of bushels of corn to be hedged assuming ratio of cash price of okra to corn is 0.8	30,000
Number of bushels per futures contract for corn	5,000
Number of corn futures contracts used in hedge	6

Short (Sell) Cross-Hedge by Okra Farmer

Cash Market	Futures Market	Basis*

At time hedge is placed

Cash Market	Futures Market	Basis*
Value of 37,500 bu.:	Sell 6 contracts:	
37,500 × $2.20 = $82,500	6 × 5,000 × $3.20 = $96,000	−$0.45

At time hedge is lifted

Cash Market	Futures Market	Basis*
Value of 37,500 bu.:	Buy 6 contracts:	
37,500 × $1.60 = $60,000	6 × 5,000 × $2.45 = $73,500	−$0.45
Loss in cash market = $22,500	Gain in futures market = $22,500	

Overall gain or loss = $0

Long (Buy) Cross-Hedge by Food Processing Company

Cash Market	Futures Market	Basis*

At time hedge is placed

Cash Market	Futures Market	Basis*
Value of 37,500 bu.:	Buy 6 contracts:	
37,500 × $2.20 = $82,500	6 × 5,000 × $3.20 = $96,000	−$0.45

At time hedge is lifted

Cash Market	Futures Market	Basis*
Value of 37,500 bu.:	Sell 6 contracts:	
37,500 × $1.60 = $60,000	6 × 5,000 × $2.45 = $73,500	−$0.45
Gain in cash market = $22,500	Loss in futures market = $22,500	

Overall gain or loss = $0

*Basis = Cash price of corn − Futures price of corn.

the cash price of corn rather than the 80 percent that was assumed when the cross-hedge was constructed. The outcome for the long and short cross-hedge is shown in Figure 13–8.

For the short cross-hedge, the loss in the cash market exceeds the realized loss in the futures market by $11,200. For the long cross-hedge, the opposite is true. There is an overall gain of $11,200 from the cross-hedge.

Had the cash price of okra fallen by less than the decline in the cash price of corn, the short cross-hedge would have produced an overall gain, while the long cross-hedge would have generated an overall loss.

3. Cash Price of Both Commodities Moves in the Opposite Direction. Suppose that the cash price of okra falls to $1.60 per bushel, while the cash price and the futures price of corn rise to $3.55 and $4, respectively. The results of the cross-hedge are shown in Figure 13–9.

The short cross-hedge results in a loss in both the cash market and the futures market. The overall loss is $46,500. Had the okra farmer not used the cross-hedge, his loss would have been limited to the decline in the cash price, $22,500 in this instance. The long hedger, on the other hand, realizes a gain in both the cash and futures market, and therefore an overall gain.

Figure 13–10 shows the outcome for the short and long cross-hedge if the cash price of okra increases to $3 per bushel, while the cash price and the futures price of corn decline to $2 and $2.45, respectively. In this case the long cross-hedge results in a loss in both the cash and futures markets. The total loss is $52,500. The loss would have been only $30,000, the loss in the cash market, had the management of the food processing company not employed a cross-hedge with corn.

HEDGING WITH STOCK INDEX FUTURES

We have demonstrated in this chapter that a successful hedge strategy will depend on what happens to the basis between the time the hedge is placed and the time the hedge is lifted. When hedging with stock index futures, however a *perfect* or *textbook*

FIGURE 13–8

Cross-Hedge: Cash Price of Commodity to Be Hedged Falls by a Greater Percentage than the Commodity Used for the Hedge

Assumptions

Price of okra	
Cash price at time hedge is placed	$2.20 per bu.
Cash price at time hedge is lifted	$1.30 per bu.
Price of corn	
Cash price at time hedge is placed	$2.75 per bu.
Futures price at time hedge is placed	$3.20 per bu.
Cash price at time hedge is lifted	$2.00 per bu.
Futures price at time hedge is lifted	$2.45 per bu.
Number of bushels of okra to be hedged	37,500
Number of bushels of corn to be hedged	
assuming ratio of cash price of okra to corn is 0.8	30,000
Number of bushels per futures contract for corn	5,000
Number of corn futures contracts used in hedge	6

Short (Sell) Cross-Hedge by Okra Farmer

Cash Market	Futures Market	Basis*

At time hedge is placed

Cash Market	Futures Market	Basis*
Value of 37,500 bu.:	Sell 6 contracts:	
37,500 × $2.20 = $82,500	6 × 5,000 × $3.20 = $96,000	−$0.45

At time hedge is lifted

Cash Market	Futures Market	Basis*
Value of 37,500 bu.:	Buy 6 contracts:	
37,500 × $1.30 = $48,750	6 × 5,000 × $2.45 = $73,500	−$0.45
Loss in cash market = $33,750	Gain in futures market = $22,500	
Overall loss = $11,250		

Long (Buy) Cross-Hedge by Food Processing Company

Cash Market	Futures Market	Basis*

At time hedge is placed

Cash Market	Futures Market	Basis*
Value of 37,500 bu.:	Buy 6 contracts:	
37,500 × $2.20 = $82,500	6 × 5,000 × $3.20 = $96,000	−$0.45

At time hedge is lifted

Cash Market	Futures Market	Basis*
Value of 37,500 bu.:	Sell 6 contracts:	
37,500 × $1.30 = $48,750	6 × 5,000 × $2.45 = $73,500	−$0.45
Gain in cash market = $33,750	Loss in futures market = $22,500	
Overall gain = $11,250		

*Basis = Cash price of corn − Futures price of corn.

FIGURE 13–9

Cross-Hedge: Cash Price of Commodity to Be Hedged Falls while the Cash Price of Commodity Used for the Hedge Rises

Assumptions

Price of okra	
Cash price at time hedge is placed	$2.20 per bu.
Cash price at time hedge is lifted	$1.60 per bu.
Price of corn	
Cash price at time hedge is placed	$2.75 per bu.
Futures price at time hedge is placed	$3.20 per bu.
Cash price at time hedge is lifted	$3.55 per bu.
Futures price at time hedge is lifted	$4.00 per bu.
Number of bushels of okra to be hedged	37,500
Number of bushels of corn to be hedged assuming ratio of cash price of okra to corn is 0.8	30,000
Number of bushels per futures contract for corn	5,000
Number of corn futures contracts used in hedge	6

Short (Sell) Cross-Hedge by Okra Farmer

Cash Market	Futures Market	Basis*

At time hedge is placed

Cash Market	Futures Market	Basis*
Value of 37,500 bu.:	Sell 6 contracts:	
37,500 × $2.20 = $82,500	6 × 5,000 × $3.20 = $96,000	−$0.45

At time hedge is lifted

Cash Market	Futures Market	Basis*
Value of 37,500 bu.:	Buy 6 contracts:	
37,500 × $1.60 = $60,000	6 × 5,000 × $4.00 = $120,000	−$0.45
Loss in cash market = $22,500	Loss in futures market = $24,000	
Overall loss = $46,500		

Long (Buy) Cross-Hedge by Food Processing Company

Cash Market	Futures Market	Basis*

At time hedge is placed

Cash Market	Futures Market	Basis*
Value of 37,500 bu.:	Buy 6 contracts:	
37,500 × $2.20 = $82,500	6 × 5,000 × $3.20 = $96,000	−$0.45

At time hedge is lifted

Cash Market	Futures Market	Basis*
Value of 37,500 bu.:	Sell 6 contracts:	
37,500 × $1.60 = $60,000	6 × 5,000 × $4.00 = $120,000	−$0.45
Gain in cash market = $22,500	Gain in futures market = $24,000	
Overall gain = $46,500		

*Basis = Cash price of corn − Futures price of corn.

FIGURE 13–10

Cross-Hedge: Cash Price of Commodity to Be Hedged Rises while the Cash Price of Commodity Used for the Hedge Falls

Assumptions

Price of okra	
Cash price at time hedge is placed	$2.20 per bu.
Cash price at time hedge is lifted	$3.00 per bu.
Price of corn	
Cash price at time hedge is placed	$2.75 per bu.
Futures price at time hedge is placed	$3.20 per bu.
Cash price at time hedge is lifted	$2.00 per bu.
Futures price at time hedge is lifted	$2.45 per bu.
Number of bushels of okra to be hedged	37,500
Number of bushels of corn to be hedged	
assuming ratio of cash price of okra to corn is 0.8	30,000
Number of bushels per futures contract for corn	5,000
Number of corn futures contracts used in hedge	6

Short (Sell) Cross-Hedge by Okra Farmer

Cash Market	Futures Market	Basis*

At time hedge is placed

Cash Market	Futures Market	Basis*
Value of 37,500 bu.:	Sell 6 contracts:	
37,500 × $2.20 = $82,500	6 × 5,000 × $3.20 = $96,000	− $0.45

At time hedge is lifted

Cash Market	Futures Market	Basis*
Value of 37,500 bu.:	Buy 6 contracts:	
37,500 × $3.00 = $112,500	6 × 5,000 × $2.45 = $73,500	− $0.45
Gain in cash market = $30,000	Gain in futures market = $22,500	
Overall gain = $52,500		

Long (Buy) Cross-Hedge by Food Processing Company

Cash Market	Futures Market	Basis*

At time hedge is placed

Cash Market	Futures Market	Basis*
Value of 37,500 bu.:	Buy 6 contracts:	
37,500 × $2.20 = $82,500	6 × 5,000 × $3.20 = $96,000	− $0.45

At time hedge is lifted

Cash Market	Futures Market	Basis*
Value of 37,500 bu.:	Sell 6 contracts:	
37,500 × $3.00 = $112,500	6 × 5,000 × $2.45 = $73,500	− $0.45
Loss in cash market = $30,000	Loss in futures market = $22,500	
Overall loss = $52,500		

*Basis = Cash price of corn − Futures price of corn.

short hedge will return the risk-free rate of interest, not zero. Therefore, an S&P 500 index fund (with no tracking error) fully hedged with S&P 500 futures selling at fair-value will return the risk-free rate.[1] It will be the equivalent of selling the stock and placing the proceeds in a cash equivalent investment. This point has already been illustrated in Chapter 8, but is crucial to any equity hedging strategy. The cost of carry, which has already been discussed in Chapter 8, is the theoretical basis of a stock index futures contract. If the basis were always equal to the cost of carry, there would be little basis risk since the cost of carry can be estimated with a fair degree of accuracy.

Mispricing, then, is the major portion of basis risk. It can be defined as the difference between the actual futures price and its theoretical price according to the cost-of-carry model, or

$$v = \frac{[F - I(1 + R_f - Y)]}{F}$$

where

v = Mispricing in percent,
F = Actual futures price,
I = Actual index price,
R_f = Risk-free return to expiration of the futures contract,
Y = Dividend yield of the index to expiration of the futures contract, and
$R_f - Y$ = The cost of carry.

We will see later that mispricing is random, and therefore is the major source of basis risk.

We have also seen in this chapter that when cross-hedging the price risk of a portfolio of common stocks will depend on the pricing of the futures relative to the underlying cash or spot index. Since a stock index futures contract will often be used to hedge a portfolio that is not identical in composition to the underlying stock index, any hedge employing stock index futures is a cross-hedge. Therefore, a relationship between the value of the stock index and the stock portfolio must be estimated.

---

[1]The application of stock index futures to index fund management is the subject of Chapter 16.

Finally, the relationship between the stock index future and its underlying index will also be important. The return of the two instruments can vary significantly due to the speculative mispricing. So in implementing a cross-hedge, it should be recognized that the relationship between the common stock portfolio and the underlying stock index must be adjusted for the imperfect relationship between the index and the stock index future. This is a particularly important point when determining the appropriate hedge ratio for implementing a cross-hedge using stock index futures.

Before illustrating how stock index futures can be used for hedging, we will explain the relationship between a portfolio of common stocks and a market index. How the relationship is statistically estimated is explained in most investment textbooks.

The Relationship between the Price Movement of an Individual Stock or a Portfolio of Common Stocks and a Market Index

The statistical technique of regression analysis is used to estimate the relationship between the price of an individual stock or a portfolio of common stocks and a market index. The relationship estimated is as follows:

Percentage change in price of a stock (or value of a portfolio) in period t

$$= \text{Alpha} + \text{Beta} \left(\begin{array}{c} \text{percentage change in} \\ \text{the value of the market} \\ \text{index in period } t \end{array} \right) + \begin{array}{c} \text{Error term in} \\ \text{period } t \end{array}$$

This relationship is known as the *market model*. Strictly speaking, the market model shows the relationship between rates of return (price changes plus cash dividends) rather than price changes. However, one study has demonstrated that the estimate of beta will be for all practical purposes the same whether the relationship involves rates of return or simply price changes.[2]

---

[2]William F. Sharpe and Guy M. Cooper, "Risk-Return Classes of New York Stock Exchange Common Stocks," *Financial Analysts Journal*, March–April 1972, pp. 46–54, 81.

The data to estimate the parameters of the model, alpha and beta, are the observed price changes for the stock (or market value change for the portfolio) and the change in the market index value over some time period.

In practice, the market model has been estimated by using monthly and weekly data. The value of the parameters estimated will differ depending on whether monthly or weekly data are employed. The value of the parameters will also differ depending on the number of observations (e.g., two years of monthly or weekly data versus one year of monthly or weekly data) used to estimate the market model.

The parameter of interest to us is beta, the slope of the market model. This parameter tells us how volatile the individual stock or the portfolio of common stocks is relative to the market index. A value of beta greater than one indicates that the stock or the portfolio is more volatile than the market index. If beta is less than one, the stock or portfolio is less volatile than the market index. If beta is one, the stock or portfolio mirrors the market index. It is rare to find a beta that is negative.

However, the value of beta is not the only important piece of information that we must have in order to assess the likelihood of success of a hedge. We must know how good the relationship is. Look back at the last term in the expression for the market model. The size of the error term indicates how well the stock or portfolio tracks the movement of the market index. If there is a strong relationship between the movement of the stock or portfolio and the market index, the error term will be small.

A statistical measure of the strength of the relationship is the coefficient of determination, or "R-squared" (R^2). This measure indicates the percentage of the variation in the movement of the stock or portfolio explained by the market index. The coefficient of determination can range from zero to one. The closer the coefficient of determination is to one, the stronger is the statistical relationship. The coefficient of determination is directly related to a concept that most individuals are familiar with—the correlation coefficient. The correlation coefficient is equal to the square root of the coefficient of determination. Whether the correlation coefficient is positive or negative is determined by the sign of beta. For example, if the coefficient of determination is .7 and the beta is 1.2, the correlation coefficient is + .84.

A major problem with the market model for individual common stocks is that the coefficient of determination is small, typically between .01 and .65. Statistical techniques are available to determine whether the relationship is statistically significant, that is, whether beta is significantly different from zero. For example, depending on the number of observations used to estimate the market model, a coefficient of determination of .2 may be statistically significant. That is, even though the market model indicates that only 20 percent of the variation in the movement of the price of the stock is explained by the market index, from a purely statistical perspective such a relationship is significant. However, a portfolio manager may have serious reservations about using the relationship to hedge a stock.

As the number of stocks in a portfolio increases, the error term tends to decrease. In the jargon of the portfolio manager, price movements not associated with the movement in the market, the error term, are diversified away as the number of issues in the portfolio increases. One study has shown that only 12 to 18 issues are needed to diversify the risk not associated with the movement of the market.[3] Consequently, a diversified common stock portfolio does a better job of tracking the market index than does an individual stock issue. In statistical terminology, the coefficient of determination approaches one as the number of issues in the portfolio increases. However, keep in mind that even if the coefficient of determination is one for a portfolio relative to a market index, this does not mean that the beta for the portfolio will equal one. The beta tells us how volatile the portfolio is relative to a market index. The coefficient of determination and the correlation coefficient indicate how good the relationship is.

Table 13–2 presents the beta, the coefficient of determination, and the correlation coefficient for 19 randomly selected NYSE stocks. The market model was estimated using weekly price changes for the 33-week period October 5, 1981, to May 17,

---

[3]John L. Evans and Stephen H. Archer, "Diversification and the Reduction of Dispersion: An Empirical Analysis," *Journal of Finance,* December 1968, pp. 761–67.

TABLE 13-2
Estimates of Beta, Coefficient of Determination, and Correlation Coefficient for 19 Randomly Selected Stocks*

Company	Based on S&P 500 Composite Index			Based on NYSE Composite Index		
	Beta	Coefficient of Determination (R^2)	Correlation Coefficient	Beta	Coefficient of Determination (R^2)	Correlation Coefficient
Amerada Hess	1.883	.460	.678	1.960	.472	.687
American Brands	0.412	.158	.397	0.418	.154	.393
American Broadcasting	0.911	.152	.390	0.983	.168	.409
CP National	0.595	.164	.405	0.649	.185	.430
CSX	1.150	.333	.577	1.221	.356	.597
Crown Zellerbach	1.614	.458	.677	1.722	.494	.703
Crum & Foster	0.982	.171	.414	0.942	.149	.387
Ford	0.635	.063	.250	0.645	.061	.248
Procter & Gamble	0.595	.390	.625	0.615	.396	.629
Rohr Industries	1.054	.206	.453	1.104	.214	.462
Rollins	1.690	.400	.632	1.710	.388	.623
Schering Plough	0.994	.315	.561	1.036	.325	.570
Schlumberger Ltd.	1.812	.647	.804	1.790	.599	.774
Scott Paper	1.075	.339	.582	1.113	.344	.587
G. D. Searle	0.711	.243	.493	0.754	.260	.509
Sears Roebuck	0.618	.155	.394	0.666	.170	.413
Stokely-Van Camp	0.482	.043	.207	0.568	.056	.237
Eastman Kodak	0.891	.479	.692	0.934	.499	.706
Eaton	0.623	.147	.383	0.625	.140	.374
Portfolio†	0.940	.860	.927	0.976	.878	.937

*Weekly data used to estimate the market model—October 5, 1981, to May 17, 1982.
†Portfolio consisting of one share of common stock of each company.

1982, and estimated for both the S&P 500 Composite Index and the NYSE Composite Index. Also shown on Table 13–2 are the corresponding values for a portfolio consisting of an equal number of shares of each of the 19 issues. Notice that the correlation for the portfolio is considerably higher than the correlation for any of the stocks comprised by the portfolio and that the correlation is close to one.

The Minimum Risk Hedge Ratio

It is tempting to use the portfolio beta as a hedge ratio because it is an indicator of the sensitivity of the portfolio returns to the stock index return. It appears, then, to be an ideal sensitivity adjustment. However, applying beta relative to a stock index as a sensitivity adjustment to a stock index futures contract assumes that the index and the futures contract have the same volatility. If futures always sold at their fair price, this would be a reasonable assumption. However, mispricing is an extra element of volatility in an index futures contract. A recent study has shown that mispricing adds 20 percent to the volatility of the futures contract.[4] Since the futures contract is more volatile than the underlying index, using a portfolio beta as a sensitivity adjustment would result in a portfolio being over-hedged.[5]

The most accurate sensitivity adjustment would be the beta of the portfolio relative to the futures contract. However, there are a number of operational problems in doing so. First, futures contracts have an element of "seasonality" to them that make beta estimates for individual stocks highly unstable. Second, the calculation of these beta estimates adds an additional computational burden on the hedger.

---

[4]Ed Peters, "Hedged Equity Portfolios: Components of Risk and Return," *Advances in Futures and Options Research*, Vol. 1B, 1986, pp. 75–92.

[5]When a hedge is held until expiration, or if the hedger has the luxury of waiting until the future is fairly priced, the return to mispricing is no longer an unknown factor. Using beta as a hedge ratio locks in the mispricing as an element of return. Strategies known as synthetic cash or cash-and-carry arbitrage use this relationship to achieve incremental returns above the risk-free rate. However, if the duration of the hedge is unknown, then the return due to mispricing is also unknown, making it an extra element of risk. Then beta is not an appropriate hedge ratio.

A recent study has shown that the beta of the portfolio relative to the futures contract is equivalent to the product of the beta of the portfolio relative to the underlying index and the beta of the index relative to the futures contract.[6] For widely used indexes, such as the S&P 500 and the NYSE Composite Index, the former is plentiful. The latter number can be easily computed.

Therefore, the minimum risk hedge ratio (h) can be expressed as:

$$h = B_{PI} B_{IF}$$

where

h = The minimum risk hedge ratio
B_{PI} = The beta of the portfolio relative to the index, and
B_{IF} = The beta of the index relative to the futures contract

While the beta of the index relative to the futures contract may still be unstable, it will be significantly more stable than the beta of individual stocks relative to futures contracts.

This minimum risk hedge ratio plays the same role in hedging a stock portfolio that the relations between the cash price of okra and the cash price of corn did in our cross-hedging example earlier in the chapter. The coefficient of determination will indicate how good the relationship is and will allow the hedger to assess the likelihood of success of the hedge.

Examples of Hedging Using Stock Index Futures

To demonstrate how stock index futures can be used to hedge the market risk of a portfolio of common stocks, actual cases will be used.

Suppose the investor had $1 million in an S&P 500 index fund on July 1, 1986 and wished to hedge against a possible market decline. The account was to be hedged for July 1, 1986 through August 31, 1986. To hedge against an adverse market move during the period, the investor decides to enter into a short hedge by selling S&P 500 futures contracts.

---

[6]Peters, "Hedged Equity Portfolios."

The first thing the investor has to do is to determine how many contracts to sell. This depends on the portfolio's beta (B_{PI}), the beta of the index relative to the futures contract (B_{IF}), and on the dollar value of a S&P 500 futures contract. The steps for determining the number of contracts are as follows:

Step 1.   Determine the "equivalent market index units" of the market by dividing the market value of the portfolio by the current index price of the futures contract.

$$\text{Equivalent market index units} = \frac{\text{Market value of the portfolio}}{\text{Current index value of the futures}}$$

Step 2.   Multiply the equivalent market index units by the two-beta hedge ratio to obtain the "beta-adjusted equivalent market index units."

$$\text{Beta-adjusted equivalent market index units} = B_{PI} \times B_{IF} \times \text{Equivalent market index units}$$

Step 3.   Divide the beta-adjusted equivalent market index units by the multiple specified by the futures contract. For S&P 500 contracts the multiple is $500.

$$\text{Number of contracts} = \frac{\text{Beta-adjusted equivalent market index units}}{\$500}$$

In our illustration, the September 1986 S&P 500 contract was selling at 250.01 on July 1, 1986, the day the hedge was to be initiated. The beta (B_{PI}) of the S&P 500 is, of course, 1.00. The beta relative to the futures contract has been estimated by a regression analysis to be 0.745. Therefore, the number of contracts needed to hedge a $1 million S&P 500 index is computed as follows.

Step 1.

$$\text{Equivalent market index units} = \frac{\$1,000,000}{253.95}$$
$$= \$3,937.78$$

Step 2.

$$\begin{aligned}\text{Beta-adjusted equivalent market index units} &= 1.00 \times .745 \times \$3{,}937.78 \\ &= \$2{,}933.648\end{aligned}$$

Step 3.

$$\begin{aligned}\text{Number of contracts} &= \frac{\$2.933.648}{\$500} \\ &= \quad 5.87\end{aligned}$$

This number will be rounded up to six contracts. This means that the futures position was equal to $761,850 (6 × 500 × 253.95). On August 31, 1986, the hedge was removed. The S&P 500 index fund returned −6.80 percent or a loss of $67,965.40. The futures contract was selling at 233.15 for a gain of 8.19 percent or $62,400. This results in a trivial loss of $5,565.40. This short hedge is summarized in Figure 13–11.

Let us analyze this hedge to determine why it was successful. As explained earlier, in hedging we exchange basis risk for price risk. Consider the basis risk. At the time the hedge was placed, the index was at 252.04. The September 1986 S&P futures contract was selling at 253.95. The basis was equal to 253.95 − 252.04 = 1.91. The cost of carry was equal to 1.26 index units, thus, mispricing equaled 0.65 index units.

When the hedge was removed at the close on August 31, 1986, the index stood at 234.91. The futures contract was selling at 233.15, or a discount of 1.76 units. The basis had changed by 3.67 index units alone or $1,835 per contract. This means that the basis alone returned $11,010 ($1,835 × 6 contracts). The index dropped 17.13 index units for a gain of $8,565 per contract or $51,390.

Thus, the futures position returned $11,010 due to basis change, and $51,390 due to the change in the index. Combined, this comes out to the $62,400 gain in the futures position. Since the index fund suffered a loss of $67,965.40 that period, the net position lost $5,565.40 or −0.56 percent.

In this example, the two-beta hedge ratio minimized the effect of the basis which swung 3.67 index units. If B_{PI} had been used rather than the two-beta hedge ratio, the number of con-

FIGURE 13–11

Hedging a $1 Million S&P Fund Using S&P 500 Futures

Situation

Own $1 million in a S&P 500 Index Fund on 7/1/86.
Need to hedge against an adverse market move.
Time the hedge is held is unknown at the start.
Hedge is lifted 8/31/86.

Facts

	7/1/86	8/31/86
Cash price of S&P 500	252.04	234.91
Price of 9/86 S&P 500 futures	253.95	233.15

Beta of the portfolio relative to the index = 1.000
Beta of the index relative to the futures = .745
Minimum risk hedge ratio = 1.000 × .745 = .745

Outcome

Cash Market	Futures	Cost of Carry	Mispricing
7/1/86—*Time hedge is placed*			
Own $1,000,000, portfolio	Sell 6 9/86 S&P 500 futures contracts at 253.95	+1.26	+ .65
8/31/86—*Time hedge is lifted*			
Own $942,034.60	Buy 6 9/86 S&P 500 futures contracts at 233.15	+ .43	−2.19
Loss in cash market = $67,965.40	Gain in futures market = $62,400		
Overall loss = $5,565.40			

---

tracts for hedging would have been calculated to be eight rather than six. This would have resulted in a 1.5 percent gain in the position. While it is usually preferable to have a gain rather than a 0.56 percent loss, the purpose of hedging is to neutralize the equity exposure. The two-beta hedge ratio gave a return much closer to zero.

In this example, we examined basis risk. Since we were hedging a S&P 500 Index Fund with S&P 500 futures, there was no price risk. However, most portfolios are not S&P 500 funds. When hedging those portfolios with S&P 500 futures, we are cross-hedging. As we have discussed, cross-hedging entails price risk when the portfolio being hedged does not behave as predicted by its beta.

Suppose you owned the Dow Jones Industrials and hedged that portfolio from July 1, 1986 to August 31, 1986. The Dow Jones in a regression analysis is shown to have a beta relative to the S&P 500 of 1.05 percent and an R^2 (coefficient of determination) equal to 93.3 percent. We follow the same procedure to calculate the number of contracts needed for a $1 million portfolio:

Step 1.

$$\text{Equivalent market index units} = \frac{\$1,000,000}{253.95}$$
$$= \$3,937.78$$

Step 2.

$$\text{Beta-adjusted equivalent market index units} = 1.05 \times .745 \times 3937.78$$
$$= \$3,080.328$$

Step 3.

$$\text{Number of contracts} = \frac{\$3,080.328}{\$500}$$
$$= 6.16$$

Again, this would be rounded to six contracts. This means that the futures position would return $62,400, as in the previous example.

According to the market model, the Dow Jones should have returned −7.14 percent as predicted by its beta [1.05 × (−6.80)]. However, the Dow actually returned −7.35 percent for a loss of $73,500. This means that the hedge position returned −1.11 percent, or a loss of $11,100. If this had been a perfect hedge, the portfolio would have lost $71,400. The hedge would have lost $9,000, or 0.99 percent. Overall, the hedge worked well, losing 0.2 percent due to price risk. Figure 13–12 summarizes this hedge.

In both cases, the transaction costs would have been a trivial $150, or $25 per contract round trip.

FIGURE 13–12

Hedge a $1 Million Dow Jones Industrial Index
Fund Using S&P 500 Futures

Situation

Own $1 million worth of Dow Jones Industrial stocks on 7/1/86.
Need to hedge against an adverse market move.
Time the hedge is held is unknown at the start.
Hedge is lifted 8/31/86.

Facts

	7/1/86	8/31/86
Value of portfolio	$1,000,000	$927,500
Cash price of S&P 500	252.04	234.91
Price of 9/86 S&P 500 futures	253.95	233.15

Beta of the portfolio relative to the S&P 500 = 1.05
Beta of the index relative to the futures = .745
Minimum risk hedge ratio = 1.05 × .745 = .782
Coefficient of determination (R^2) = 93.3 percent.

Outcome

Cash Market	Futures Market	Cost of Carry	Mispricing
7/1/86—Time hedge is placed			
Own $1,000,000 portfolio	Sell 6 9/86 S&P 500 futures contracts at 253.95	+1.26	+ .65
8/31/86—Time hedge is lifted			
Own $927,500 portfolio	Buy 6 9/86 S&P 500 futures contracts at 233.15	+ .43	−2.19
Loss in cash market = $73,500	Gain in futures market = $62,400		
Overall loss = $11,100			

MARGIN

As explained in Chapter 5, an investor who wants to employ stock index futures contracts for hedging must be prepared to meet the initial margin requirement and must make provisions to furnish variation margin. Chapter 22 explains how variation margin risk can be controlled.

SUMMARY

Stock index futures can be employed to hedge against adverse stock price movements of a portfolio of common stocks. However, because hedging with stock index futures involves cross-hedging, a strong relationship must exist between the market index that underlies the futures contract and the portfolio being hedged. The effectiveness of the hedge depends on making a good estimate of this hedge. The minimum risk hedge ratio was found to be the product of two numbers. The first is the well-known beta of the portfolio relative to the index underlying the futures contract. The second is the beta of the index to the futures contract itself. These betas are calculated using a statistical technique known as regression analysis.

CHAPTER 14

USING STOCK INDEX FUTURES FOR "UNCERTAIN ARBITRAGE"

Crisostomo B. Garcia, Ph.D.
Professor of Management Science
Graduate School of Business
University of Chicago

Floyd J. Gould, Ph.D.
Hobart W. Williams Professor of Applied
Mathematics and Management Science
Graduate School of Business
University of Chicago

In this chapter we will consider profit potential for spreads (i.e., "uncertain arbitrage strategies") between S&P 500 index futures and the stocks comprising (or tracking) the underlying index. There are two types of such trades. One, initiated by cheap futures, is a yield enhancement on the index (i.e., creation of a high-powered synthetic index fund). The other, initiated by rich futures, is a yield enhancement on a T bill (i.e., creation of a high-powered synthetic bill). These uncertain arbitrage strategies differ from straightforward arbitrage (or what we think of as normal arbitrage) in two respects: (1) The first leg of the spread is identical to the first leg of a normal yield enhancement or normal synthetic T bill arbitrage, but the uncertain arbitrage spreads will be put on, in general, before the normal arbitrage opportunities exist; and (2) The normal arbitrage opportunities are able to promise guaranteed results by holding the position until the futures price and the index value are identical, which is assured when the futures contract expires, if not sooner. The results of the uncertain arbitrage spread are probabilistic (hence our term uncertain arbitrage) with positive results provided only by a sufficiently high degree of intraday volatility in the spread between futures and cash (i.e., intraday volatility in the number "futures value – cash value"). Without such volatility, uncertain arbitrage strategies can lose. Moreover, the successful uncertain arbitrage trades are typically only one-day trades or trades that last at most for several days, in contrast to trades that are held to expiration.

Prospects for profit opportunities with uncertain arbitrage strategies will be assessed by analyzing actual intraday data for the month of April 1987. The data consist of 1,722 "approximately simultaneous" observations of near futures price and index value.[1]

THE STRATEGIES

From a textbook point of view, so-called program traders occupy themselves with two distinctly different types of arbitrage transactions: yield enhancement on the index and yield enhancement on a T bill.

A Yield-Enhancement on the Index

When futures are sufficiently cheap relative to the underlying stock index, an index fund manager may enter into a sell program, meaning he will buy the relatively cheap futures (and T bills) and sell a basket of stocks which closely replicates the index. The motive is to enhance the yield relative to index fund performance and this is achieved when the position is taken off. This may occur in several ways.

---

[1]Since the index is not traded, and due to the nature of its composition, its value at any given time may not be precisely realizable as a "price" of an underlying basket. To this extent our analysis is necessarily an approximation to results that actually would have been obtained.

Lifting at Expiration.   Depending on where (i.e., at what relative price levels of futures and stocks) the position was entered, and on the path of the market thereafter, it may be desirable to hold the long futures position until contract expiration. At that time the contract is cash settled, T bills expire, and stocks are repurchased with a market-on-close (or, if appropriate, market-on-open) order. To achieve a *certain* (i.e., *guaranteed*) yield enhancement via this strategy, the original futures contract would, because of transaction costs (meaning market impact plus commissions) need to be purchased at a considerable discount to the familiar fair futures price, F^*, defined as

$$F^* = (1 + r_T - d_T)S_0.$$

In this formula, r_T and d_T are, respectively, the interest and dividend rates over the time interval to expiration, and S_0 is the price of the underlying index at the time the futures is purchased. We assume that the annual riskless rate and dividend rate are, respectively, 5.5 percent and 4.4 percent. Typically the original futures contract would have to trade below F^* by at least, roughly, 15 to 17 percent of S_0.[2] In other words, when the index value S_0 is at 300, then the future would need to be 1.5 to 2.10 (depending on the magnitude of the transaction costs the trader is subject to) points below S_0. In the first case, the futures price F_0 would need to be less than 298.5; in the second case the futures price would need to be less than 297.9. When an investor purchases futures that are maximally this cheap (i.e., less than these values) then the yield enhancement is *guaranteed*. In the sense that such a strategy will produce a known outcome, it may be thought of as *certain*.[3] In order to produce this certainty, futures had to trade below a specified threshold relative to the index. A less stringent requirement (for entry) will produce a possibility, but not a certainty, for a yield-enhancement trade, as described next.

---

[2]See F. J. Gould, "Stock Index Futures: The Arbitrage Cycle and Portfolio Insurance," *Financial Analysts Journal,* forthcoming, 1988.

[3]The strategy is certain in the following sense: Whatever the index fund yield over the time horizon to expiration of the future (including the possibility of a negative yield), the sell program will, in the described scenario, enhance that yield by (at the minimum) a known amount.

Lifting on a Reversal, Prior to Expiration. Suppose a sell program had been initiated when the futures was trading at F_0 and the index at S_0, with F_0 at *a discount* to S_0 (i.e., $F_0 < S_0$). Prior to expiration of the futures contract, a reversal occurs, meaning that the futures price goes to a premium relative to the underlying index. Let F_1 and S_1, with $F_1 > S_1$, denote the reversed futures and cash prices, respectively. Then, if the reversal is sufficient (i.e., if F_1 is sufficiently larger than S_1), a yield enhancement will be realized if the position is lifted at prices F_1 and S_1.[4]

This chapter provides an empirical inquiry concerning the possibilities of yield-enhancement trades using a reversal strategy, such as just described.

A Yield Enhancement on a T Bill

The second type of arbitrage transaction, using index futures and the underlying basket, is the so-called buy program, wherein relatively cheap stocks are purchased and (relatively) expensive futures are sold. The resulting position, long stocks and short futures, is a synthetic T bill (meaning that a known rate of return is created with certainty). A synthetic T bill can, in some opportune circumstances, produce a yield higher than the yield on the T bills available in the market. Such an enhanced T bill position is created when futures are relatively expensive (compared to the index). As in the previously discussed yield enhancement on the index strategy, there are two ways to exit.

Lifting at Expiration. Parallel to the same exit strategy for the yield enhancement on the index, it may be desirable to hold the synthetic T bill until futures and stocks have the same price. This is guaranteed to occur when the short futures position expires, at which time the futures contract is cash settled and stocks are sold with the appropriate order. To achieve a certain yield

---

[4]The extent of the reversal required to achieve a given level of enhancement will depend not only on F_0 and S_0, but also on S_1, as discussed in the appendix to this chapter.

enhancement of the T bill rate (i.e., a guaranteed rate of return in excess of the return on actual T bills) via this strategy the original futures would need to be sold at a considerable premium to F^*.[5] Roughly, F_0 would have to trade above F^* by at least as much as .5 to .7 percent of S_0. However, a less stringent requirement on the entry point produces the *possibility* for a high-powered T bill.

Lifting on a Reversal, Prior to Expiration.   Suppose the buy program had been initiated with $F_0 > S_0$. Suppose that, at some time prior to expiration of the futures contract, a reversal occurs, meaning we find prices F_1 and S_1, such that $F_1 < S_1$. If the reversal is sufficient a synthetic T bill with enhanced yield will have been created and the position can be lifted.

We will study the possibilities for profit opportunities created by reversals and lifting prior to expiration (i.e., reversal-seeking strategies).

THE ANALYSIS

A simulation program was written to study intraday data for the month of April 1987. Behavior of the near futures contract (the June contract) is shown in Figure 14–1.

Roughly, every five minutes, observations of the pair (near futures price, index value) were recorded. This produced a record of 1,722 chronologically ordered observations. Our study is based on a partition of the futures prices into various intervals relative to the fair value F^*. The motive for this partition derives from the following facts. If we define

S = value of the underlying index when the price of the near futures contract is F

T = total trading costs from transactions in both futures and stock, expressed as a fraction of S (where T incorporates both brokerage costs and market impact)

$LO = F^* - TS$

$HI = F^* + TS$

---

[5]For a detailed analysis, see Gould, "Stock Index Futures."

FIGURE 14–1
The June 1987 S&P 500 Futures Prices, April 1987

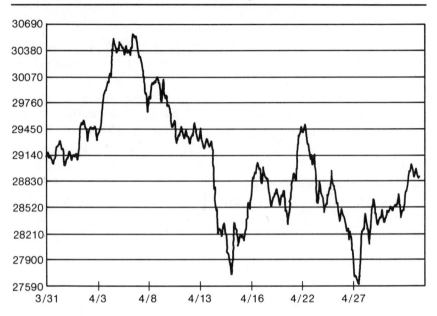

then it can be shown that:[6]

1. Normal yield enhancement on the index (via sell programs) begins to be triggered when prices are such that $F < LO$.
2. Normal yield enhancement on T bills (via buy programs) begins to be triggered when prices are such that $F > HI$.

The difference $HI - LO$ is called the *no arbitrage window,* or *no opportunity window.*[7] If we let W denote the size of this window, then

$$W = HI - LO = 2TS$$

---

[6]For a detailed analysis, see Gould, "Stock Index Futures."

[7]This window was referred to as *the twilight zone* by Gregory M. Kipnis and Steve Tsang, in "Arbitrage," Chapter 10, in *Stock Index Futures,* eds. Frank J. Fabozzi and Gregory M. Kipnis (Homewood, Ill.: Dow Jones-Irwin, 1984), p. 125.

Thus, for any agent the size of the window will depend on the size of his transaction costs T. The lowest-cost transactor will have the smallest window W (and therefore will have earlier opportunities than other transactors).

Now we partition the possible futures prices into various intervals as follows.

Interval 1: $F \le LO \equiv F^* - TS$
Interval 2: $LO < F \le LO + .125W \equiv F^* - .75TS$
Interval 3: $LO + .125W < F \le LO + .25W \equiv F^* - .5TS$
Interval 4: $LO + .25W < F \le LO + .75W \equiv F^* + .5TS$
Interval 5: $LO + .75W < F \le LO + .875W \equiv F^* + .75TS$
Interval 6: $LO + .875W < F \le LO + W = HI \equiv F^* + TS$
Interval 7: $HI < F$

Note that the normal arbitrage strategies require entries from Intervals 1 and 7.

Our study was performed with two different assumptions on T: In Case 1 with low transaction costs, we assume $T = .005S_0$. In Case 2 with higher transaction costs, we assume $T = .007S_0$. Each specific value of T gives a specific set of seven intervals which partition futures prices.

The analysis also identifies different yield enhancement (YE) levels, such as a yield enhancement (in absolute amount) of between 0 and .25 percent, between .25 percent and .5 percent, etc. In other words, a yield enhancement of 1.7 percent would mean that either the index yield (over the period of the trade) was increased by 170 basis points or the T bill rate (over the period of the trade) was increased by 170 basis points.

Now we can describe the simulation. The model identifies the first observation for which the futures price is in some interval other than 4. This interval is recorded and we assume the appropriate *uncertain arbitrage strategy* is triggered.

That is, if the futures price is in levels 1, 2, or 3, the futures is cheap. Hence futures is purchased and stock is sold, creating a synthetic index fund. If the futures is in levels 5, 6, or 7, the futures is expensive. Hence the futures is sold and stock is purchased, thereby creating a synthetic T bill.

Next, we identify the first time that this transaction succeeds in producing a level 1 yield enhancement (if there is such an occurrence). This occurrence and the time it requires (i.e., the amount of time the position is held) is recorded. Then we continue with the same position, examining more observations until, possibly, a level 2 yield enhancement is produced, again recording the occurrence and the time to occurrence. In this way we continue through the entire set of observations. It is possible that no yield enhancement at level 1 (or any higher level) occurs, relative to this particular position. If that is the case, a loss is recorded.

The model then identifies the second observation for which the futures price is in some interval other than 4. The appropriate strategy is triggered and relative to these new positions the model again makes a forward pass through all observations gathering relevant statistics.

No positions were initiated within the last three days of the data set so as to allow a reasonable amount of time (at least three days) for a profitable reversal to arise. Also the prices in the first five minutes and last five minutes of each trade were ignored because of possible distortions on the open and close. The results of this simulation are now given.

EMPIRICAL RESULTS

Tables 14–1 through 14–3 apply to the low transaction cost scenario (Case 1 as defined above). Tables 14–4 through 14–6 are for the higher transaction cost case. Table 14–1 shows the number of times the futures price was observed in various intervals, which is then converted to a probability statement. These observations in Table 14–1 represent the totality of possible entry points for trading. Note that after omitting the last three days and the first and last five minutes of each day, there are 1,440 possible entry points.

For example, if one is creating a synthetic index fund, it would be better to begin in the lowest possible intervals, meaning that an entry from interval 1 is preferred to an entry from 2, and 2 is preferred to 3. The fact that only 9 of the 1,440 futures prices fell into interval 1 means the probability of entering an uncertain

TABLE 14-1
Probabilities of Various Entries (low transaction cost)

Interval	1	2	3	4	5	6	7
Number of occurrences	9	5	18	691	300	221	196
Probability of occurrence	.006	.003	.01	.48	.21	.15	.14

TABLE 14-2
Yield Enhancement Possibilities from Low-End Entries (low transaction cost)

YE Level (percentage)	0–.25	.25–.5	.5–.75	.75–1	1–1.25	1.25–1.5	1.5–1.75
Number of occurrences	31	16	10	5	4	4	1
Probability, given 1, 2, or 3 entry	31/32	16/32	10/32	5/32	4/32	4/32	1/32
Average time (days)	1.1	.76	1.45	.95	1.02	2.95	1

TABLE 14-3
Yield Enhancement Possibilities from High-End Entries (low transaction cost)

YE Level (percentage)	0–.25	.25–.5	.5–.75	.75–1	1–1.25	1.25–1.5	1.5–1.75
Number of occurrences	709	707	707	707	444	37	2
Probability, given 5, 6, or 7 entry	709/717	707/717	707/717	707/717	444/717	37/717	2/717
Average time (days)	3.06	3.94	4.39	4.39	4.60	6.01	6.5

TABLE 14–4
Probabilities of Various Entries (high transaction cost)

Interval	1	2	3	4	5	6	7
Number of occurrences	6	2	9	936	314	149	24
Probability of occurrence	.004	.001	.006	.65	.22	.10	.02

TABLE 14–5
Yield Enhancement Possibilities from Low-End Entries (high transaction cost)

YE Level (percentage)	0–.25	.25–.5	.5–.75	.75–1	1–1.25
Number of occurrences	12	5	4	4	1
Probability, given 1, 2, or 3 entry	12/17	5/17	4/17	4/17	1/17
Average time (days)	2.84	.28	.99	1.21	1

TABLE 14–6
Yield Enhancement Possibilities from High-End Entries (high transaction cost)

YE Level (percentage)	0–.25	.25–.5	.5–.75	.75–1	1–1.25	1.25–1.5
Number of occurrences	480	480	480	235	5	2
Probability, given 5, 6, or 7 entry	480/487	480/487	480/487	235/487	5/487	2/487
Average time (days)	4.09	4.23	4.23	5.20	5.24	6.5

index fund enhancement from interval 1 is .006. This also implies very limited opportunity for normal *low-end arbitrage* (strategies for certain yield enhancement on the index fund). Table 14–1 suggests that at least for this set of data the opportunities for *high-end entries* (intervals 5, 6, and 7) are much greater than at the low end of the window. For example, there are only 32 possible entries from intervals 1, 2, or 3, while there are 717 possible entries from levels 5, 6, or 7. This would suggest more opportunity for yield enhancement on T bills than on the index fund.

Table 14–2 shows the number of trades that could have terminated at various *YE* (yield enhancement) levels, given that an entry occurred in intervals 1, 2, or 3 (of which, from Table 14–2, there were 32 possibilities). Also shown is the average time to realize the trade's potential.

Table 14–3 shows analogous data for entries from intervals 5, 6, or 7. Tables 14–4 through 14–6 show data for the high transaction cost runs.

INTERPRETATIONS, CONCLUSIONS, AND CAVEATS

It must be emphasized that this analysis applies to a very limited data set. The conclusions are strictly applicable only to this set of data and only reflective of what one might encounter over longer horizons. In this limited sense the study has produced some interesting results. In another sense, the study can be interpreted as presenting a framework for a more extensive analysis which the practicing arbitrageur may wish to conduct in the development of his particular systematic trading strategies. Our observations follow.

1. Since no positions were initiated within the last three days of the data set, the last positions initiated could be held for a maximum of three (trading) days. Positions initiated at the outset could be held for a maximum of 20 trading days. Thus the average maximum holding period is about 12 days. In practice, the trader would have two or three times this amount of time, if needed, to realize a desired target level of yield enhancement. In that sense our results sharply exaggerate the possible risk.

2. The low transaction costs implicitly incorporate two assumptions about the physical basket of stocks being purchased: (1) the basket tracks the actual index very closely; and (2) the basket can be traded, simultaneously with the futures trade, at the value of the quoted index (at the time of the futures trade). The first assumption says the basket tracks the index and hence the two are essentially equivalent. The second assumption says the index (i.e., the basket) is actually tradable at a price equal to quoted index levels. To the extent that either of these assumptions is violated more risk is introduced. For our purposes, the high transaction cost can be interpreted as incorporating some downside due to violations of either of these implicit assumptions.

3. From Tables 14–2 through 14–4 one sees that, with the low transaction cost runs, there is much more opportunity for yield enhancement on T bills than on index funds. On the other hand, it takes longer for the opportunity on T bills to be realized than on index funds. This enhanced opportunity on the high end may be due to the fact that T bill holders typically are very risk averse and the high powered T bill strategies do involve some risk. In this sense, T bill holders may not be inclined to enter into uncertain arbitrage at the high end. At the other end, the index fund holders are risk-takers who have probably exhausted reversal-seeking enhancement strategies at the low end, for such strategies would not seem to significantly add to the index fund risk. Stated differently, those willing to take risk may have concentrated on the low end of arbitrage, overlooking potential at the other end, for the April data suggests there may have been significant profit potential for risk bearing traders *at the high end of the window*. In particular, enhancements of at least 75 basis points over the T bill yield occurred with probability close to 1, given that the trade was entered from the intervals 5, 6, or 7. Moreover, almost half of the observed entry opportunities (717 of 1,440) were in the intervals 5, 6, or 7. For such trades the average holding time (as shown in Table 14–3) was about four days. Consequently there may have been four or five non-overlapping opportunities to make at least 3/4 of a percent over T bills on each trade, yielding an aggregate enhancement of 3 or 4 percent for the month.

4. An index fund holder who wishes to engage in reversal-seeking high end arbitrage has even more profit potential for he or she is already long the stocks and hence can create a long stock, short futures position (a synthetic T bill) with less transaction cost than incurred by a trader not already in stocks. Hence, for the index fund holder, the month of April offered the opportunity to make perhaps 5 or 6 percent above the T bill yield for the month. Of course, in this case any upside yield on the index would be foregone. Since the index growth could be 10 percent in a month, a switch from low end to high end could impose significant opportunity cost.

5. We find a substantial difference between the case of a low transaction cost run, and the case of a higher transaction cost run. In the latter, high profit opportunities (75 basis points or higher) are no longer probable. Thus, there is a premium for high efficiency in implementation.

APPENDIX: FORMULAS FOR YIELD ENHANCEMENT

Let T_S denote transactions costs (commissions and market impact) from purchase or sale of stocks, expressed as a fraction of stock price. Let T_{FM} denote market impact from purchase or sale of futures, expressed as a fraction of futures price, and let T_{FB} denote futures brokerage (round trip, paid when the position is lifted), approximated as a fraction of futures price.

1. Synthetic Index Fund. Assume the trader is holding one S&P unit of physical stock and buys one cheap futures contract at F_0 when index value is S_0, and sells the physical stocks. Later, when the futures price is expensive, the trader sells the futures at F_1 when the index value is S_1 and buys back physical stock. On the entry, we obtain $(1 - T_S)S_0$ dollars from stock sale, and buy one futures contract at the price $(1 + T_{FM})F_0$.

When the position is lifted we sell the futures contract at $(1 - T_{FM})F_1$ and pay commissions T_{FB}. Thus we have, in dollar terms,

$$(1 - T_S)S_0 + (1 - T_{FM})F_1 - (1 + T_{FM})F_0 - T_{FB}F_0 = D \text{ dollars.}$$

This buys $\dfrac{D}{(I + T_S)S_1}$ shares of stock selling at (i.e., with last trade at) S_1, and hence we end with

$$\frac{(1 - T_S)S_0 + (1 - T_{FM})F_1 - (1 + T_{FM} + T_{FB})F_0}{1 + T_S}$$

dollars worth of stock. The yield enhancement, expressed as a fraction, is

$$YE = \frac{\left[\dfrac{(1 - T_S)S_0 + (1 - T_{FM})F_1 - (1 + T_{FM} + T_{FB})F_0}{1 + T_S} - S_0)\right]}{S_0}$$

$$- \frac{(S_1 - S_0)}{S_0}$$

$$= \frac{(1 - T_S)S_0 + (1 - T_{FM})F_1 - (1 + T_{FM} + T_{FB})F_0}{(1 + T_S)S_0} - \frac{S_1}{S_0}$$

2. Transaction Costs. In a low-transaction-cost case we take $T_S = .0035$, given by a market impact of ⅛ per share (i.e., 12½ cents per share) and 5 cents/share commission (one-way) and average stock price of $50/share. That is

$$T_S = \frac{.125 + .05}{50} = .0035 = \text{One way transaction cost.}$$

For low-transaction cost market impact in futures, we take 10 points and assume futures trading at 300. Hence

$$T_{FM} = \frac{10(5)}{300(500)} = .00033$$

For futures commissions we use $15 per round trip. Hence, expressed as a fraction of F_0,

$$T_{FB} = \frac{15}{(300)(50)} = .0001$$

In a high-transaction-cost case we let $T_S = .005$, $T_{FM} = .00067$ and again $T_{FB} = .0001$.

3. Synthetic T Bill. Sell one expensive futures contract at F_0 and buy stock at S_0. Thus we are short one contract at $F_0(1 - T_{FM})$ and are holding $\dfrac{1}{1 + T_S}$ shares of stock.

When the position is lifted, buy the futures back at $F_1(1 + T_{FM})$. Sell stock at $(1 - T_S)S_1$. We end with D dollars, where

$$D = F_0(1 - T_{FM}) - F_1(1 + T_{FM} + T_{FB}) + \frac{(1 - T_S)S_1}{1 + T_S}$$

Hence

$$YE = \frac{D}{S_0} - (1 + r)$$

where r is the interest from a T bill over the period the synthetic bill was held.

CHAPTER 15

MECHANICS OF TRADING FOR INDEX ARBITRAGE

Donald L. Luskin
Senior Vice President
Wells Fargo Investment Advisors

Chapter 14 dealt with index arbitrage, in which portfolios of stocks are bought (or sold) to offset positions in overpriced (or underpriced) index options or futures. The concept behind this strategy is simple and straightforward—index arbitrage is a synthetic Treasury bill. But actually implementing an index arbitrage can be extraordinarily complex.

Consider the difficulties you might encounter in implementing an arbitrage in futures contracts on the S&P 500 Index. For openers, you'd have to buy all 500 stocks, in the exact proportions in which they are represented in the index—most are traded on the New York Stock Exchange, but a handful are traded over-the-counter and would have to be purchased from NASDAQ dealers. If the task of buying 500 stocks simultaneously doesn't intimidate you, don't forget that you'd also have to short-sell the futures contracts traded on the Chicago Mercantile Exchange—*also simultaneously*—hoping that a favorable price differential could be preserved amidst all your activity.

To help deal with these difficulties, a number of aggressive brokerage firms have devised a set of methodologies known loosely as *program trading*. These methodologies enable an investor to negotiate a net price for an entire index arbitrage position—stocks and derivatives together as a single package.

Arbitrage trading has frequently been the subject of sensationalistic coverage in the popular business press, especially as it relates to the supposed increase in volatility of stock prices. The result has been to promote an irrational fear of arbitrage trading, without explaining its mysteries and methodologies or its surprising popularity. Whatever its impact, arbitrage trading evidently fills an important need in the marketplace—it was virtually unheard of a few years ago, and now is said to account for upwards of 25 percent of daily New York Stock Exchange share volume. This chapter explains exactly how arbitrage trading is accomplished.

To see how arbitrage trading works, let's follow a $25 million S&P 500 Index futures arbitrage transaction all the way from its inception to its unwinding at expiration. In this transaction we will initially buy the stocks that compose the underlying index and simultaneously short sell the futures. When the futures expire, they will be settled in cash while we simultaneously sell our stocks.

ORGANIZE THE LIST OF STOCKS TO BUY

Using a list of the relative weightings of the 500 stocks in the index, we can determine how many shares of each stock must be bought. We will multiply $25 million by each stock's index weighting, and then divide the result by the stock's price. For example, if a stock's weighting is 5 percent, and its price is $100, we will buy 12,500 shares, as shown below.

$$(\$25,000,000 \times 5 \text{ percent}) \div \$100 = 12,500 \text{ shares}$$

SET UP THE LIST OF STOCKS IN EXECUTION FACILITY

The key to executing a list of stocks with approximate simultaneity is thorough preparation well in advance of the trade. If the executions are to be carried out on the New York Stock Exchange, the tickets used to document floor transactions should be preprinted with each stock's symbol, the appropriate number of shares, and a codeword that serves to identify the list—let's say it will be "Swordfish." These tickets should be distributed among a network of floorbrokers strategically positioned so that each one is relatively nearby the specialist posts that handle the stocks on his tickets. For the over-the-counter stocks in the index, similar tickets are distributed to a NASDAQ dealer. When it is time to execute the list, the brokers are told to buy list "Swordfish"— they locate the tickets bearing this codeword and execute them immediately at the best prices then prevailing.

Alternatively, lists can be executed through the New York Stock Exchange's automated D.O.T. system (Designated Order Turnaround). Instead of preparing tickets, the list of stocks is stored as a file on a computer in communication with D.O.T. When it is time to execute the list, a single keystroke sends it to the NYSE for immediate execution.

DETERMINE HOW MANY FUTURES CONTRACTS TO SELL

This is calculated simply by multiplying the current price of the underlying index by the futures contract multiplier ($500 for S&P futures), and dividing $25 million by the result. For example, if the index is trading at $250, we will sell 200 contracts, as shown below.

$$\$25,000,000 \div (\$250 \times \$500) = 200 \text{ contracts}$$

In large arbitrage positions it may be desirable to adjust the number of futures contracts to offset the effects of variation margin cash flows that will accrue to the position. To do this, the arbitrageur begins with the number of futures contracts as calculated above, and multiplies it by the inverse of one plus the annualized interest rate at which he can borrow and lend times the percentage of a year remaining until the futures expire. For example, if the interest rate is 10 percent and the futures contracts will expire in three months, the arbitrageur will sell only 195 contracts.

$$200 \times \frac{1}{1 + (0.10 \times 0.25)} = 195$$

KEEP THE LIST UPDATED

As time goes by, the list must be constantly updated to account for changes that can occur within the S&P 500 Index. When a component stock undergoes a split, the number of shares to be bought has to be adjusted. For example, if the stock in the example above had a two-for-one split, the number of shares to be bought would have to be adjusted from 12,500 to 25,000. Adjustments in the number of shares for all 500 stocks are required when a stock is dropped from the index and replaced by a new one. Neither of these changes requires an adjustment in the number of futures contracts to be sold.

Price movements in the index do not require adjustments either in the number of shares to be bought or futures contracts to be sold. As the index price fluctuates, the total value of the list of stocks will deviate from the initial value of $25 million, but the relative proportions of each individual stock, and of all the stocks together in relation to the futures contracts, never vary.

SET A TARGET RATE-OF-RETURN
FOR THE ARBITRAGE

The annualized yield of an index arbitrage position can be calculated by subtracting the index price from the futures price, adding the expected value of dividends, dividing the result by the index price, and annualizing. For example, for a position to be held for 91 days, if the index is priced at $250, the futures are priced at $253, and the expected dividends are $1.50, the arbitrage will yield 7.22 percent annualized, as shown below.

$$[(\$253 - \$250 + \$1.50) + \$250] \times (365 \div 91) = 7.22\%.$$

This calculation can be adjusted by estimated market impact and brokerage commission costs required to establish and unwind the position.

Because an index arbitrage position compares to a synthetic Treasury bill, its yield competes with the yield of actual Treasury bills. Each arbitrageur must decide by how much the yield of the arbitrage must exceed that of Treasury bills to justify its administrative complexity, and thus trigger him to initiate a position. It is possible to restate the yield calculation formula in such a way as to produce the differential between the index price and the futures price that will serve as a trigger-point. For example, an arbitrageur might be willing to initiate an arbitrage position whenever its yield exceeds Treasury bills by 1.00 percent. If Treasury bills were yielding 5.00 percent, the yield of 6.22 percent realized when the futures were trading $3.00 above the underlying index, would be more than sufficient to trigger a trade. The precise trigger-point would be realized whenever the futures traded only $2.86 above the underlying index, as shown below.

$$[(6.00\% + 1.00\%) \times 250) \div (365 \div 91)] - \$1.50$$
$$= \$2.86$$

INITIATE A TRADE

An arbitrageur needs to do little more than inform his broker of his trigger-point, and keep him informed periodically as it is revised with the passage of time or fluctuations in Treasury bill yields. From then on, it is the broker's responsibility to monitor the futures markets for the opportunity to actually initiate a position.

CONFIRM THAT THE TRADE WAS IMPLEMENTED SUCCESSFULLY BY THE BROKER

The broker is responsible for managing the risky complexities of the multiple executions required to initiate an index arbitrage position. But after a trade, the arbitrageur should personally check to make sure that the broker has done his job properly. To do this the arbitrageur creates a divisor, by dividing the total value of the stocks by the index price (both as of the previous day's close). For example, if the total value of the stocks is $25 million and the index price is $250, the divisor will be 100,000 ($25,000,000 ÷ $250).

As soon as trade reports are available from the broker, the arbitrageur calculates the actual total cost of buying stocks—for example, a cost of $25,343,232. Dividing this cost by the divisor calculated above provides a result of $253.43 ($25,343,232 ÷ 100,000).

If the arbitrageur had given his broker a trigger-point of $2.86, the broker would have had to sell the futures contracts for at least $256.29—$2.86 above 253.43.

If the futures prices reported by the broker to the arbitrageur are below $256.29, the broker has failed to meet the arbitrageur's trigger-point. In such circumstances the broker may either cancel the trade entirely (thus taking it into his own inventory account) or make a cash adjustment in the arbitrageur's account in the amount of the shortfall.

AGAIN, ORGANIZE A LIST OF STOCKS AND KEEP IT UPDATED

Now that the trade has been initiated, it is important that the execution of its unwinding be carried out perfectly. Therefore, the list of stocks to sell must be constantly updated to account for stock splits and index membership changes. Again, mere price movements in the index do not require adjustments either in the stocks or the futures.

UNWIND THE POSITION AT EXPIRATION

On the day the futures contracts expire, it is a simple matter to sell the stocks at the exact moment the futures contracts are cash-settled. As of this writing, that moment is the opening of trading on the third Friday of March, June, September, and December, so all the broker need do is place market-on-open orders with the New York Stock Exchange specialists.

CHAPTER 16

APPLICATIONS OF STOCK INDEX FUTURES TO INDEX FUND MANAGEMENT

Frank J. Fabozzi, Ph.D., C.F.A.
Visiting Professor of Finance
Sloan School of Management
Massachusetts Institute of Technology

T. Dessa Fabozzi, Ph.D.
Senior Security Analyst
Financial Strategies Group
Merrill Lynch Capital Markets

Edgar E. Peters
Portfolio Manager
Structured Investment Products Division
The Boston Company, Inc.

Index funds represent a passive equity approach to portfolio management. The manager of the portfolio does not attempt to identify under- or overvalued stock issues based on fundamental security analysis. Nor does he attempt to forecast general movements in the stock market and to structure the portfolio so as to take advantage of those movements. Instead, index funds are designed to track the total return performance of a visible market index of stocks.

The indexing approach to portfolio management found its beginning in studies of the efficiency of the equity market in the late 1960s and early 1970s. The first category of studies of market efficiency concerned whether investors could use historical price patterns to develop trading rules for earning consistent abnormal risk-adjusted rates of return. This is the so-called "weak form" of the efficient market hypothesis. With few exceptions, empirical studies found support for the hypothesis that the market is efficient in the weak form. The implication of these findings is that technical analysis, that is, analysis based on the belief that stock prices move in trends that persist, will not be useful in enhancing investment performance.

A second class of empirical studies investigated whether stock prices fully reflected not only information about historical prices but also all other publicly available information, such as earnings and dividends. This is called the "semistrong" form of efficiency. The evidence of these studies on balance supports the view that the stock market is efficient in the semistrong form. The implication is that if the prices of securities embody all publicly available information, then fundamental security analysis will not enhance a portfolio's return.

The "strong form" of market efficiency contends that stock prices reflect all information, both public and private. A third class of empirical studies examined this form of market efficiency by looking at the performance of corporate insiders, stock exchange specialists, and professional money managers. The results were mixed. Corporate insiders and stock exchange specialists did outperform the market on a risk-adjusted basis. However, the performance of professional money managers supported the strong form of market efficiency. Since compared to the information available to corporate insiders and stock exchange specialists, the information available to professional money managers is more indicative of the information available to the average market participant, these studies furnished strong evidence for some observers that the market is efficient in the strong form.

If the findings of market efficiency are accepted, then the costs associated with active equity portfolio management may not enhance the return on a portfolio. These costs consist of the research costs associated with uncovering mispriced stocks, the transaction costs in buying and selling stocks to take advantage of mispricing, and the transaction costs associated with trying to time the market. Consequently, a passive approach to equity portfolio management may be more appropriate for the typical sponsor of a fund. About 30 percent of the total defined benefit assets of the 200 largest pension funds were indexed as of September 1986, with half having some funds under index management. Almost one third used stock index futures in managing an index fund.[1]

In this chapter we will demonstrate how under certain pricing conditions for the futures relative to the actual index, a portfolio manager can use stock index futures contracts and Treasury bills to create an index fund. An index fund so created will have lower transaction costs and can therefore be expected to outperform an actual index portfolio. Furthermore, if the futures are sufficiently underpriced, the index fund created by the futures and Treasury bills will outperform the target market index, including dividends.

CONSTRUCTING AN INDEX FUND

The index fund approach is only one form of passive portfolio management. The view that a portfolio designed to replicate the performance of the "market" is the best approach to passive portfolio management is supported by the work of Harry Markowitz in 1952 on the construction of optimal and efficient portfolios[2] and by capital market theory as developed by William F. Sharpe[3] and John Lintner.[4] The Sharpe-Lintner analysis demonstrated that a market portfolio offers the highest level of return per unit of risk in an efficient market. The theoretical market portfolio consists of all risky assets. Each risky asset is given a weight in the market portfolio equal to its percentage of the aggregate market value of all risky assets. That is, the market portfolio is a capitalization-weighted portfolio of all risky assets.

---

[1] *Pension and Investment Age*, January 26, 1987, p. 16.

[2] Harry M. Markowitz, "Portfolio Selection," *Journal of Finance,* March 1952, pp. 77–91.

[3] William F. Sharpe, "Capital Asset Prices: A Theory of Market Equilibrium under Conditions of Risk," *Journal of Finance,* September 1964, pp. 425–42.

[4] John Lintner, "Security Prices, Risk, and Maximal Gains from Diversification," *Journal of Finance,* December 1965, pp. 587–616.

When applying the concept of an index fund to manage an equity portfolio, the manager of the fund cannot be totally passive. The first decision that he must make is to select the target market index. Most index funds are indexed to the S&P 500. Of course, this is not the "theoretical" market portfolio used in the development of capital market theory, because it does not consist of all risky assets (common stock, bonds, real estate, etc.) or of all equity shares.

Once a target market index has been selected, the manager of the index fund must decide whether to replicate the target market index by buying every stock in the index in proportion to their market weights (full-capitalization weighting approach) or by buying only a sample of issues in the index (stratified sampling approach). Either approach will entail transaction costs associated with (1) the purchase of the shares held to construct the index, (2) the reinvestment of cash dividends, and (3) the adjustment of the portfolio if the composition of the issues in the target market index changes.[5] Although the full-capitalization approach will track the target index better, the transaction costs will be higher. Thus the fund manager must evaluate the costs and benefits of this approach. If the stratified sampling approach is adopted, the cost of the initial construction of the index fund is reduced. However, transaction costs will be incurred to rebalance the index fund over time so that the characteristics of the replicating portfolio will continue to mirror the performance of the target market index. These costs would not be incurred with the full-capitalization weighting approach.

Transaction costs plus management fees result in a divergence between the return on the target market index and that of the index fund. In the case of full-capitalization weighting, the return will be less than that of the index. Whether the return on the index will be greater than or less than that of the index fund

---

[5]For example, if the S&P 500 has been used as the target index in 1976, the fund manager would have had to restructure because of the dramatic change in the components of the index. Specifically, the industrial component of the S&P 500 was reduced from 425 issues to 400 issues, the utility component was reduced from 60 to 40 issues, and a finance component was introduced.

constructed using the stratified sampling approach depends on whether the issues excluded underperform or outperform the issues included in the sample.

USING STOCK INDEX FUTURES AND TREASURY BILLS TO CONSTRUCT AN INDEX FUND

If stock index futures contracts are priced according to their theoretical value, a portfolio consisting of a long position in stock index futures and Treasury bills will produce the same portfolio return as that of a portfolio of common stocks constructed to replicate the underlying index. To see this, suppose that a fund manager who wishes to index his portfolio has $9 million in new money to invest and seeks to replicate the performance of the S&P 500. Also assume the following:

1. The S&P 500 is currently 300.
2. The S&P futures index with six months to settlement is currently selling for 303.
3. The expected dividend yield for the S&P 500 for the next six months is 2 percent.
4. Six-month Treasury bills are currently yielding 3 percent for six months.

Recall from Chapter 8 that the theoretical price for the futures contract is the current index value times the net carry adjustment. The net carry adjustment is essentially the difference between the Treasury bill yield and the expected dividend yield multiplied by the current value of the index. In our illustration the net carry adjustment is 1 percent (3 percent minus 2 percent) times 300, or 3. The theoretical price is then 303, which in our example is the current price for the S&P 500 futures contract.

The construction of the futures/T-bill portfolio first requires the determination of the number of contracts to purchase. In terms of the underlying index, to purchase $9 million of equivalent equity if the current index is 300, 60 contracts must be purchased, since each contract is $500 times the value of the current index. Consequently, the two strategies that the index fund manager may select are:

Strategy 1: Direct purchase of $9 million of equity in such a way as to replicate the performance of the S&P 500.

Strategy 2: Buy 60 S&P 500 futures contracts with a settlement six months from now at 303 and buy $9 million of six-month Treasury bills.[6]

We can now examine the portfolio value for each strategy under various scenarios for the price of the index when the contracts settle six months from now. Three scenarios will be investigated: the S&P 500 increases to 330, remains unchanged at 300, and declines to 270. At settlement the futures price converges to the value of the index. Figures 16–1 through 16–3 show the value of the portfolio for both strategies for each of the three scenarios. As can be seen, for a given scenario Strategy 1 (long position in the stock portfolio) and Strategy 2 will produce the same value for the portfolio.

There are several points that should be noted. First, in Strategy 1 the ability of the portfolio to replicate the S&P 500 depends on how well the portfolio is constructed to track the index. On the other hand, assuming that expected dividends are realized, the futures/T-bill portfolio (Strategy 2) will mirror the performance of the S&P 500 exactly. Second, the cost of transacting is less for Strategy 2. For example, if the cost of one S&P contract is $12.50, then the transaction costs for Strategy 2 would be $750 (60 contracts times $12.50 per contract). This would be considerably less than the transaction costs associated with the acquisition of a broadly diversified equity portfolio constructed to replicate the S&P 500. Finally, in the analysis of the performance of each strategy, the dollar value of the portfolio at the end of the six-month period is the amount in the absence of taxes. For Strategy 1, no taxes will be paid if the securities are not sold, though taxes will be paid on dividends. For Strategy 2, taxes must be paid on the interest from the Treasury bills and on any gain, from

---

[6]In this illustration, margin requirements are ignored. The T bills can be used for initial margin as explained in Chapter 5.

FIGURE 16–1
Comparison of Portfolio Value from Purchasing Stocks to Replicate an Index and a Futures/T-Bill Strategy When There Is No Mispricing and Market Increases

Assumptions
1. Amount to be invested = $9 million
2. Current value of S&P 500 = 300
3. Value of the S&P 500 at settlement (six months later) = 330
4. Current value of S&P futures contract = 303
5. Expected dividend yield = 2 percent
6. Yield on Treasury bills = 3 percent

Strategy 1: Direct Purchase of Stocks

Increase in value of index	= 330/300 − 1 = .10
Market value of portfolio that mirrors the index	
1.10 × $9,000,000	= $ 9,900,000
Dividends	
.02 × $9,000,000	= $ 180,000
Value of portfolio	= $10,080,000
Dollar return	= $ 1,080,000

Strategy 2: Future/T-Bill Portfolio

Number of S&P 500 contracts to be purchased = 60

Gain from sale of one contract		
Purchased for	303	
Sold for	330	
Gain per contract	27	
Gain for 60 contracts		
60 × $500 × 27		= $ 810,000
Value of Treasury bills		
$9,000,000 × 1.03		= $ 9,270,000
Value of portfolio		= $10,080,000
Dollar return		= $ 1,080,000

the disposal of the futures contract or due to the inability to post-pone any gain at the end of a tax year because of the unique tax treatment of futures contracts.[7] Because of this complication, the use of the futures/T-bill strategy would be more appropriate for funds not subject to taxation.

---

[7]Cornell and French argue that it is this tax option that causes futures to trade at a discount to their theoretical value. (See Bradford Cornell and Kenneth French, "Taxes and the Pricing of Stock Index Futures," *Journal of Finance*, June 1983, pp. 675–94.)

FIGURE 16–2
**Comparison of Portfolio Value from Purchasing Stocks to
Replicate an Index and a Futures/T-Bill Strategy When
There Is No Mispricing and Market Does Not Change**

Assumptions
1. Amount to be invested = $9 million
2. Current value of S&P 500 = 300
3. Value of the S&P 500 at settlement (six months later) = 300
4. Current value of S&P futures contract = 303
5. Expected dividend yield = 2 percent
6. Yield on Treasury bills = 3 percent

Strategy 1: Direct Purchase of Stocks

Change in value of index	= 300/300 − 1 = 0
Market value of portfolio that mirrors the index	
1.00 × $9,000,000	= $9,000,000
Dividends	
0.02 × $9,000,000	= $ 180,000
Value of portfolio	= $9,180,000
Dollar return	= $ 180,000

Strategy 2: Future/T-Bill Portfolio

Number of S&P 500 contracts to be purchased = 60

Loss from sale of one contract	
Purchased for	303
Sold for	300
Loss per contract	3
Loss for 60 contracts	
60 × $500 × 3	= ($90,000)
Value of Treasury bills	
$9,000,000 × 1.03	= $9,270,000
Value of portfolio	= $9,180,000
Dollar return	= $ 180,000

ENHANCING RETURNS WHEN THE FUTURES CONTRACT IS UNDERVALUED

The use of stock index futures and Treasury bills to construct an index fund that would reproduce the performance of the underlying index if the futures were priced according to their theoretical value was demonstrated in Figures 16–1, 16–2 and 16–3. However, when the futures price is less than the theoretical price,

FIGURE 16–3

Comparison of Portfolio Value from Purchasing Stocks to Replicate an Index and a Futures/T-Bill Strategy When There Is No Mispricing and Market Declines

Assumptions
1. Amount to be invested = $9 million
2. Current value of S&P 500 = 300
3. Value of the S&P 500 at settlement (six months later) = 270
4. Current value of S&P futures contract = 303
5. Expected dividend yield = 2 percent
6. Yield on Treasury bills = 3 percent

Strategy 1: Direct Purchase of Stocks

Decrease in value of index	$= 270/300 - 1 = -.10$
Market value of portfolio that mirrors the index	
0.84 × $9,000,000	= $8,100,000
Dividends	
0.02 × $9,000,000	= $ 180,000
Value of portfolio	= $8,280,000
Dollar return	= ($720,000)

Strategy 2: Future/T-Bill Portfolio

Number of S&P 500 contracts to be purchased = 60

Loss from sale of one contract		
Purchased for	303	
Sold for	270	
Loss per contract	33	
Loss for 60 contracts		
60 × $500 × 33		= ($990,000)
Value of Treasury bills		
$9,000,000 × 1.03		= $9,270,000
Value of portfolio		= $8,280,000
Dollar return		= ($720,000)

the index fund manager can enhance the portfolio return by buying the index and Treasury bills. That is, the return on the futures/T-bill portfolio will be greater than that on the underlying index when the position is held to the expiration of the futures contract.

To see this, suppose that in our initial example the current futures price was 301 instead of 303; that is, the futures contract is undervalued. Figure 16–4 shows the value of the portfolio from

FIGURE 16-4
Enhancement of Portfolio Return for a Futures/T-Bill
Portfolio When Futures Contract Is Underpriced

Assumptions
1. Amount to be invested = $9 million
2. Current value of S&P 500 = 300
3. Current value of S&P 500 futures contract = 301
4. Expected dividend yield = 2 percent
5. Yield on Treasury bills = 3 percent
6. Theoretical price of futures contract = 303

If value of index at settlement is 330

Value of portfolio for Strategy 1 (direct purchase of stocks)
(from Figure 16–1) = $10,080,000

Value of portfolio for Strategy 2 (futures/T-bill portfolio)
Gain per contract = 330 − 301 = 29

Gain for 60 contracts = 60 × $500 × 29 =	$ 870,000
Value of Treasury bills	$ 9,270,000
Value of portfolio	$10,140,000

If value of index at settlement is 300

Value of portfolio for Strategy 1 (direct purchase of stocks)
(from Figure 16–2) = $9,180,000

Value of portfolio for Strategy 2 (futures/T-bill portfolio)
Loss per contract = 300 − 301 = 1

Loss for 60 contracts = 60 × $500 × 1 =	($30,000)
Value of Treasury bills	$9,270,000
Value of portfolio	$9,240,000

If value of index at settlement is 270

Value of portfolio for Strategy 1 (direct purchase of stocks)
(from Figure 16–3) = $8,280,000

Value of portfolio for Strategy 2 (futures/T-bill portfolio)
Loss per contract = 270 − 301 = 31

Loss for 60 contracts = 60 × $500 × 31 =	($930,000)
Value of Treasury bills	$9,270,000
Value of portfolio	$8,340,000

each strategy for each scenario. As can be seen, the value of the portfolio is $60,000 greater by buying the futures contracts and Treasury bills.[8]

STOCK INDEX FUTURES AND INDEX FUND MANAGEMENT

Thus far we have seen how index futures and T bills can be used to create an index fund. Despite the appeal of this strategy (due to its simplicity and low transaction costs) traditional index fund management is still needed for those periods when index futures are overpriced, as well as for institutions, such as pension funds, which may have restrictions on the amount of futures which can be held in their accounts. Still, index futures have applications in traditional index fund management. They include: (1) short-term investment of cash income and contributions, (2) index swaps, and (3) high beta or "levered" funds.

Short-Term Investment

Index funds receive income in the form of dividends. This income is usually held in cash until it reaches a large enough size (say .5 percent of the holdings) to be used in rebalancing the fund by purchasing stock. The cash held is a primary source of tracking error because index returns always assume immediate reinvestment. While .5 percent in cash may not seem like a large enough holding to matter, for an index fund it can be a significant problem. Index funds are measured not by how much they beat the market, but by how closely they track the market. For an S&P 500 index fund, this goal is usually to track the index within .1 percent per year. Therefore, if the S&P 500 is up 25.25 percent, the index fund should be up between 25.35 percent and 25.15 percent. Any higher or lower return would be considered poor per-

---

[8]The gain on each contract will be $1,000 greater (2 times $500) for each scenario. Since there are 60 contracts, the gain will be $60,000 greater. When there is a loss as a result of the decline in the index value at settlement, the loss is $1,000 less per contract, or $60,000 for 60 contracts.

formance. It is possible that a continuous holding of .5 percent cash could account for more than .1 percent tracking error in a year. The index fund manager must decide how to keep cash at a minimum while controlling transaction costs.

The answer is to buy stock index futures in an amount equal to the amount of cash held. When the cash position is large enough, the futures are sold and stocks are bought for the fund. This is a classic long hedge as described in Chapter 13.

An index mutual fund must keep a cash balance to handle daily contributions and withdrawals. Using stock index futures can minimize the tracking error which must be experienced from holding large sums of cash.

Finally, when a substantial contribution is received into the fund, futures can again be used as a long hedge. That is, futures can be bought in an amount equal to the face value of the contribution for instant market exposure. Stocks are then bought over time and the futures position is unwound. This type of long hedge eliminates the price risk associated with a long buy program.

Index Swaps

Index futures can also be used to enhance the returns of an index fund. If a futures contract is underpriced, the fund manager may be able to enhance returns by liquidating the existing portfolio and buying futures and Treasury bills. That is, the fund manager could "swap" an index fund for a long position in the underlying futures contract and Treasury bills. Once the futures contract becomes overpriced by a sufficient amount, the fund manager could swap out of the futures/T-bill portfolio and back into a stock portfolio designed to replicate the index. Program trading would be used to buy and sell the stocks.

Whether an index swap strategy will enhance the portfolio return depends on the degree of mispricing and the transaction costs associated with (1) liquidating an existing portfolio, (2) buying it back if the contract becomes overpriced, and (3) acquiring a long position in the stock index futures. These transaction costs coupled with the costs associated with monitoring and executing an index swap must be assessed before the swap is undertaken. As noted earlier in this chapter, the construction of a portfolio of equities to create an index fund also has transaction and monitoring costs. Therefore, it is imperative to examine portfolio returns under either strategy for indexing after all associated costs are considered.

High Beta Index Funds

One assumption built into the Sharpe-Lintner Capital Asset Pricing Model is the ability to borrow and lend at the risk-free rate of interest. The model has been criticized as unrealistic since one can lend at the risk-free rate by purchasing T bills, but borrowing at the risk-free rate is impossible. As a result, the only way to increase the return of a portfolio was to buy high-beta stocks and incur additional nonmarket risk as well as market risk.

However, by combining an index fund and index futures, it is now possible to create a high-beta fund by "borrowing" at the risk-free rate. This effect occurs because buying futures requires no capital outlay.

The return of a portfolio of stocks and stock index futures has been shown as being:

$$R_H = \alpha + E + (\beta + L)\, R_I + R_B$$

where

R_H = Return of the stock portfolio
α = Expected nonmarket return of the stock portfolio
E = Unexpected nonmarket return of the stock portfolio
R_I = Return of the underlying index
R_B = Return due to the basis of the futures
β = Portfolio beta relative to the underlying index
L = Percent of the portfolio to be levered

For an index fund, $\alpha = 0$, and $E = 0$. Therefore, the beta of the portfolio can be changed by the leverage factor L. An index fund with a beta of 1.00 can be changed to 1.20 by buying an additional 20 percent of stock index futures.

The return due to the basis of the futures contract must be considered. If the future is selling at fair value, the return due to the basis will be a small negative number since the cost of carry will decline over time.

If the basis is wider or narrower than the cost of carry, the futures contract is mispriced and the return due to mispricing becomes a source of nonmarket return. It is crucial to examine the basis to assure that the contract is not overpriced enough to make the strategy inefficient.

As an example, consider an investor with $10 million invested in an S&P 500 fund who wishes to increase his beta to 1.30. According to the formula, this would require buying $3 million worth of S&P 500 futures. If the index were at 300, this would mean buying 12 contracts. The monetary requirements for this is $60,000 in Treasury bills ($5,000 per contract) and $150 in commissions ($12.50 per contract). A cash account is also needed to handle the daily marking-to-market (see Chapter 5).

From this we can see that index futures and index funds can be combined to create high-beta portfolios which are "efficient" in the capital market sense.

SUMMARY

Index funds have gained in popularity in recent years. Although the construction of an index fund is simple in principle, a good deal of judgment on the part of the fund manager is required to design a portfolio that will track the target index. Stock index futures provide a fund manager with a less costly alternative strategy for constructing a portfolio to mirror the performance of the index when the price of the futures contract is equal to its theoretical price. When the futures contract is underpriced, a futures/T-bill portfolio will outperform the underlying index. Under certain circumstances, index swaps may be employed to enhance portfolio returns. In addition, it is possible to combine index futures and index funds to create a high-beta fund which is efficient in the capital market sense. That is, it is possible to borrow at the risk-free rate of interest using index futures.

CHAPTER 17

PENSION FUNDS, PROGRAM TRADING, AND STOCK INDEX FUTURES

W. Gordon Binns, Jr.
Chairman of the Committee on Investment
of Employee Benefit Assets (CIEBA)
Financial Executives Institute*

Program trading and the uses of equity index funds, index futures, and portfolio insurance are a complex and not widely understood area of investment management. Program trading is a very useful trading strategy or investment technique that permits pension funds both to control market risk and substantially reduce transaction costs in investing or disinvesting in the equity markets. Financial futures also facilitate such activities. Furthermore, such activities as portfolio insurance, which use index futures, can be useful risk-management or hedging strategies.

---

*The Committee on Investment of Employee Benefit Assets (CIEBA) of the Financial Executives Institute has approximately 40 members and more than 100 advisory members who are responsible for the investment of their firms' employee benefit funds, all of which are governed by ERISA. CIEBA members are responsible for more than $300 billion, and the employees and retirees covered by these plans number in the millions. Chapter 17 is a slightly abbreviated testimony presented by Mr. Binns before the House Energy and Commerce's Subcommittee on Telecommunications and Finance on July 23, 1987. Mr. Binns is also Vice President and Chief Investment Funds Officer, General Motors Corporation.

Prudently investing a multi-million or multi-billion dollar portfolio is a difficult and time-consuming task. CIEBA members seek to be prudently diversified. We carefully invest our assets in different proportions in this nation's equity markets, in this nation's debt instruments, and in smaller proportions in venture capital markets, in real estate, and in international equity and bond markets. The act of allocating large sums can in itself move markets against you and can result in substantial transaction and market impact costs. It is a classic example of supply and demand—how much of anything can one buy or sell without moving its price? In addressing these concerns, advances have been made in computer and telecommunication technologies that substantially reduce the risks and costs of these transactions and have made possible the trading method commonly called "program trading."

PROGRAM TRADING

Program trading is the purchase or sale of a "basket" of different securities rather than the discrete purchase or sale of each of the individual securities. Program trading first came to the attention of major pension funds after they had placed large portions of their funds in passively managed index funds. Assets held in index funds are managed to replicate the investment performance of a particular index, either by holding all of the underlying securities of the index or a portion of such securities which replicates the index. For example, S&P 500 Index fund managers hold either all 500 stocks of the S&P 500 Index or a portion statistically designed to track this index.

As the program trading or package trading activities grew, these terms were used to describe trading groups of stocks which constituted a "slice" of an index fund or an entire portfolio. In addition, after equity index futures contracts became available in 1982, program trading was extended to arbitrage activities to exploit, and as a by-product mitigate, mispricings between the futures markets and underlying securities markets. Program trading is employed in several different investment strategies and distinguishing these strategies is helpful in evaluating market impacts stemming from its use.

Pension funds want to be exposed to the U.S. equity markets. Program trading is a method of cost-effectively accomplishing that. It involves buying or selling a large number of stocks, indeed perhaps all the stocks comprising the S&P 500 Index or the NYSE Index. Program trading does not imply computers simply churning out orders. Computers only provide data analyzed by people making investment decisions and help implement decisions, again made by people, in order to enhance the value of the assets.

Using program trading can significantly reduce transactions costs, which are made up principally of commission cost and execution, or market impact, cost. Prior to the development of program trading, large pension funds experienced average commission costs of about 7 cents to 10 cents per share. For transactions executed through program trading, these costs have declined dramatically to about 2 cents to 3 cents per share. In addition, with respect to execution costs, it is believed that the aggregate market impact costs from trading an entire portfolio in one transaction are significantly less than the aggregate costs of a series of separate trades of individual stocks, although the exact extent of this savings is not known precisely.

INDEX FUTURES

An *equity index future* is a contract to deliver at a future date an amount in cash which is some dollar multiple (500 in the case of the S&P 500 Index future) times the difference between the value of the index at the close of the last trading day and its value when purchased or sold. (The daily mark-to-market feature of financial futures, that adds financial integrity to the futures market, results in a daily cash flow that on a cumulative basis is roughly equivalent to the price difference from inception to termination of contract ownership.) At contract expiration, settlement is made in cash, not in the underlying stocks of the index.

Program trading and the use of stock index futures have each contributed to the development of the other activity. As futures evolved, investment brokers were able to improve the pricing on program trades to their clients since they could immediately hedge their market risk through the futures markets. As the futures market grew in liquidity and depth, larger pension funds increased their participation in this market; this in turn further increased the liquidity and depth of the market. Consequently, large pension funds which, of course, represent the funds set aside for retirement benefits for millions of employees and retirees, as well as smaller investors, now can quickly and inexpensively enter or exit the market and have an ability to effectively hedge market risks. As a result of this progress, pension funds are in a better position to hold larger equity exposures.

Importantly, the stock index futures markets are directly linked to the underlying stock markets. As indicated earlier, this has resulted in greater liquidity in both markets. Broad, deep, liquid markets are healthy markets. They are the types of markets pension funds need to invest in. Our willingness to hold equity portfolios enhances capital formation in liquid markets. Because of this linkage and corresponding liquidity, pension funds use both index funds and futures as investment vehicles to implement specific investment strategies, sometimes interchangeably or concurrently.

While the use of program trading has dramatically reduced some commission and market-impact costs, it is estimated that such costs are even lower when using futures. On the other hand, because futures may be mispriced relative to the underlying securities, program trading may be less expensive at times. Because of this mispricing, pension funds prefer the choice of using the more cost-effective approach in implementing an investment decision.

PENSION FUND USES OF PROGRAM TRADING AND FUTURES

Pension funds benefit from using program trading and futures in a number of ways.

Most pension funds receive contributions from their sponsors in relatively large lump sums and then face a difficult task of quickly and cost-effectively deploying these assets in the stock and bond markets. The ability to invest these funds quickly and cost effectively via program trades or via equity futures is of substantial value to pension funds. Even when the fund eventually plans to deploy new receipts in actively managed equity market sectors, perhaps managed by a number of different external managers, the fund can almost instantly gain equity market exposure through futures, thus largely eliminating the opportunity cost of the entire market advancing quickly while the fund is still carrying out its equity deployment.

If a fund wishes to withdraw assets from a particular investment manager and then redeploy the assets, the pension fund can immediately hedge the assets using S&P 500 Index futures, thus buying time for determining how and when the assets being withdrawn should be placed with another manager. Alternatively, pension funds can withdraw securities from a manager, quickly sell slices of a portfolio, or the entire portfolio, and give the proceeds to another manager to invest. Similarly, an investment manager receiving the funds can quickly acquire market exposure via either futures or program trades.

Another case where the new techniques can be useful to a pension fund is where the fund wishes to restructure its mix of stocks, bonds, or cash to reflect changes in economic and financial expectations. Equity index or bond futures, as well as program trading techniques, allow a pension fund to quickly and cost effectively implement such an asset mix shift. For example, a large pension fund holding a mix of 70 percent S&P 500 Index funds and 30 percent bonds and cash equivalents can quickly and cost effectively change this mix through either the purchase (sale) of index funds (via program trading of the underlying securities) or futures, whichever is felt to be the least costly choice. Being able to execute quickly at a relatively known price reduces the pension funds' exposure to adverse market moves while implementing such an activity. Since the action can be relatively inexpensive with a fairly certain cost, fund managers can make asset allocation decisions that better reflect the total estimated costs associated with their actions.

S&P 500 Index futures provide significant benefits in carrying out other investment activities. For example, if a *temporary* reduction in equity exposure were considered prudent, it could be achieved by selling equity futures rather than having the equity manager liquidate the portfolio. In this instance, significant transaction and manager rebalancing costs (if a partial liquidation is being carried out) can be eliminated. Furthermore, in situations where active equity managers (distinguished from passively managed funds like index funds) are expected to provide value above the S&P 500 Index, reducing equity exposure by using S&P 500 Index futures permits the added return from the active managers to flow through to the pension fund while reducing the risk specific to the equity market as a whole.

Portfolio insurance is an investment activity which has become widely employed by many pension funds over the past several years as a means of hedging assets which have appreciated substantially. So-called *portfolio insurance* is known by various other names as well, including *dynamic asset allocation, dynamic return management, dynamic hedging,* and *portfolio downside protection*. In most of these arrangements, portfolio insurance generally does not have an up-front fee as does an insurance policy on a car or home. In addition, while the loss of the latter property would result in full recovery (less the deductible) from the insurance carrier, the recovery provided by portfolio insurance is uncertain. This is because such programs are not precisely predictable in advance, and the outcome in a particular case could deviate widely from the average results to be expected over time.

More specifically, portfolio insurance typically calls for systematically reducing equity exposure, and increasing cash equivalent exposure, in a predetermined fashion based on specific equity market declines. This strategy is designed to protect pension assets from losses stemming from further market declines by systematically shifting the mix toward a greater cash exposure while also continuing to make available all or most of the upside participation opportunity should the equity market continue to advance (the strategy can be operated in reverse fashion in market rises).

Many of the practices or procedures of pension funds noted above—such as asset mix shifts and the investment of large lump sum corporate contributions—are not daily occurrences; in fact, these are relatively infrequent, major events in the life of a pension fund and the decisions made in connection with these occurrences are made with care and deliberation. As a consequence, it is *not* generally the case that the pension funds are employing these techniques on a day-in day-out basis.

CONCERNS

Our concerns center on the unknown, concern for appropriate safeguards, and concern for the continued financial integrity and viability of the financial markets—the concerns we would have about any investment innovation. ERISA and other fiduciary standards of prudence obviously require our focus on these concerns.

Market Decline Concerns

One concern stems from the possibility that portfolio insurance could, theoretically, drive markets further downward in a period of declining prices. The terms *cascading* or *spiraling* markets or, in the words of one prominent observer, *market meltdown,* have been used in this connection. As indicated earlier, portfolio insurance coupled with program trading is designed to allow fund managers to transfer assets from the equity markets to cash equivalents when prices of the equity markets decline to a level which the investor has chosen in advance. For example, a decline of x percent in the equity market might translate into a strategy of removing y percent of assets from equity markets to Treasury bills. A further decline of a certain percentage might again dictate a further transfer from the equity portfolio. Thus, the concern is that selling pressures set off by portfolio insurance programs could generate more selling pressures resulting in a downward cascading of prices.

In thinking about the possibility of this type of market decline, some market participants have pointed out that futures activities are being carried out to a significant extent by thinly capitalized entities—both independents and subsidiaries of the large investment banking houses. Should one or more of these thinly capitalized firms experience financial difficulty in this type of decline—as a result of a client being unable to meet a daily margin call—the presumed financial strength of the futures market might not be available. In such a situation, while the exchange would call on its members to provide funds, these funds would be limited to the guarantees provided by the thinly capitalized firms and, in the case of the subsidiaries, the financial strength of the parent investment houses would not be present. Conceivably, in any such failure, the overall futures market could experience a downward spiral which could spill over or cause a cascading effect in other markets. It appears that some changes to practices might be useful in this area.

Another concern discussed by pension funds is that portfolio insurance has not truly been tested in a substantial market decline or bear market. While some of these strategies have been back-tested using historical data, this type of test may be deficient since it does not reflect the fact that, in the past, portfolio insurance was not a widespread activity. The evolution and growth of portfolio insurance has occurred during one of the longest bull markets in history.

Because of the advances in technology permitting quicker execution of large transactions, the time period for a market decline could be much shorter. Should the markets fall precipitously, or should futures—the common vehicle to implement portfolio insurance—become significantly undervalued, portfolio insurance techniques might not be workable or might prove to be significantly more expensive for pension funds than originally anticipated.

While recognizing these concerns, it should be understood that portfolio insurance strategies involve only one category of market participant. Other participants are in the market and they act. When prices decline below fundamental values, numerous participants are likely to commence buying securities, reversing the trend. Bargain hunters exist—they are speculators, individuals, and institutions. Evaluating fundamentals is still very much with us. At some point, the pension funds themselves could be expected to detect undervalued conditions and change or reverse their portfolio insurance disciplines. Furthermore, pension funds use a number of investment strategies, based on relative valuation models, which would provide an offset to this downward market pressure. The firms that offer such investment strategies alter the mix of stocks, bonds, and cash depending on relative market movements. As the stock market declines, these approaches would tend to call for increasing equity and reducing cash and bond exposure, thus providing a counterweight to the activities of those portfolios employing portfolio insurance approaches.

As the use of portfolio insurance has matured, many users have modified the parameters of their programs so as to avoid "whipsaw" losses resulting from frequent, small changes in market direction. These modifications have tended to reduce the sensitivity of the insurance programs to small market movements which might cascade into larger movements.

Imbalance Concerns

Another concern is that program trading might move markets so that supply and demand imbalances could occur, thus causing mispricings between the futures markets and the actual underlying securities. However, this phenomenon brings arbitrageurs into the market. For example, if futures prices decline substantially more than the underlying basket of securities (decline below fair value), arbitrageurs (principally index funds holding the securities or brokers who either hold the securities or are willing to sell securities short) would step in and buy futures and simultaneously sell the basket of securities as a program trade. Such actions by the arbitrageurs would draw the two markets back together. This process would also normally lead to increased activity and liquidity in both the underlying stocks and in the equity futures. In short, arbitrage works to bring prices in the different markets into proper alignment.

In this connection, a specific concern stems from the fact that futures and underlying securities are subject to different rules and regulations—particularly the SEC up-tick rule—that could prevent arbitrage from working in its normal price-aligning role just described. Specifically, the up-tick rule precludes the short sale of securities unless the securities experience an up or zero tick on the sale of the security. In a declining market in which futures prices decline substantially below the fair value of the underlying securities, an arbitrage participant, such as a broker, would be precluded from selling securities short and thus arbitraging the mispricing between the equity futures and the index.

This decoupling of the index funds and the futures price apparently occurred on September 11 and 12, 1986 as index funds available for this activity were pretty much exhausted. It should be noted that, at that time, a limited number of plan sponsors with index funds permitted their index fund managers (such as Wells Fargo, Bankers Trust, or Mellon Capital) to engage in this activity. As a measure of the self-correcting nature of the markets, it is our understanding that since then the number of pension funds permitting this activity within their index funds, and the amounts involved, have increased two- to three-fold to meet potential future demands. Nevertheless, it appears that the uptick rule may be preventing useful arbitrage which otherwise would take place. We are not, however, suggesting that the uptick rule be dropped, but believe that the issue merits further study.

Market Depth Concerns

Another possible concern is whether the rise in stock index futures trading, and the practice of arbitraging between the cash market and the futures market, have affected stock market bid and asked spreads and depth. Some traders feel that the growth of program trading may have caused spreads to widen and the depth of the markets for individual stocks to have lessened.

It is important to note that spreads on individual stocks can be impacted by other factors. For example, continuing pressure for lower commission rates on both institutional and individual trades, on balance, may cause spreads to widen. Changes in patterns of ownership of individual stocks could have a similar effect.

In our opinion, it is not easy to draw a causal relationship between the growth in index futures trading, stock market volatility, and bid-ask spreads or trading depth of individual stocks.

In any event, on balance, we believe that program trading and a viable futures market enhance market efficiency and reduce aggregate transactions costs for most pension funds.

Limitation Concerns

Another area of concern, particularly for sponsors of large pension funds, is the limitation on the maximum open position which a plan sponsor may have. While a sponsor can apply for a higher maximum level, it appears that such approval does not come readily and the application process itself is somewhat time-consuming. The process for obtaining approval to hold larger futures positions needs to be reviewed and expedited.

Volatility Concerns

Two types of volatility that particularly concern pension funds are that volatility which arises from supply and demand imbalances and volatility which results from changes in economic and financial expectations. Expiration day volatility, such as when options, futures, and options on futures expire at the same time (the "triple witching hour"), is one form of volatility resulting from supply and demand imbalances. These imbalances can lead to abrupt price reversals. This volatility can then be viewed as the cost of providing liquidity to the market to bridge the supply/demand imbalance. While program trading may be a source of some of this volatility from time to time, as more market participants (including pension funds) structure their assets to be more quickly mobilized, one would expect this type of volatility to diminish. The decline of volatility on options and futures expiration days over recent months indicates the self-correcting or self-adjusting nature of the financial markets—this appeared to be evolving even before the most recent changes involving market procedures on expiration days. Continued attention to the procedures regarding expirations could well be helpful in diminishing unnecessary volatility.

Another source of volatility can be caused by reversals in financial and economic expectations. The time period for the investment process for all market participants has been compressed by advances in computer and telecommunication technologies. These advances have sped up the timely flow of economic and financial information, increased the ability of managers to analyze such information quickly and to revise investment strategies accordingly, and have provided the means to implement changes to strategies quickly and cost-effectively. Having current prices reflect all readily available and public information is viewed by pension funds as a benefit since these prices would tend to be fair market prices. Pension funds, as well as other market participants, would be concerned if prices did not reflect all current information. For example, anyone purchasing a stock at a time when negative information was available but not reflected in the stock's price, would be disturbed if, after purchasing it, the price fell drastically. From this standpoint, an increase in volatility stemming from the advances in technology and investment management could be viewed as a sign of more rapid dissemination of information.

As a final point, there are several statistical studies that indicate that volatility of inter-day price movements in the broad market indexes, such as the S&P 500, is no greater now, and in fact may be less, than it has been in the past. On the other hand, evidence from studies of *intra*-day price volatility suggests that it may have increased, so that further analysis and study would be warranted. It is interesting to note, however, that the extreme case of intra-day volatility—last January 23 [1987], when the Dow moved over 100 points within a single hour—has not been repeated, perhaps due to the markets self-adjusting to accommodate better the increased trading volumes associated with the new techniques.

Small Investor Concerns

One criticism often raised is that the small investor may be disadvantaged relative to the larger institutions that constantly monitor market movements and engage in sophisticated investment strategies. To the extent this may be true, it is hoped that it will prove to be a temporary situation.

Indeed, by investing in mutual funds, the small investor now has access to several of these sophisticated strategies. A small investor can quickly and easily shift assets from one equity mutual fund to a bond or cash equivalent mutual fund or vice versa without the concerns about market impact and transaction costs that pension funds must consider. In addition, a small investor can readily liquidate his entire position; in contrast, pension funds with many millions invested in the market cannot readily liquidate their entire portfolios and as a consequence must devise alternative strategies such as program trading or use strategies which use futures to reduce large exposures to the market.

Another example of the small investor having access to sophisticated strategies is the money market instrument recently introduced by a major New York bank. Over a set period of time, this instrument, which is issued in $1,000 denominations, pays interest based on the S&P 500 Index price appreciation while returning to the investor the amount originally invested should the market decline. This could be viewed as a repackaged form of portfolio insurance (which is hedged by the bank using futures and options contracts). In our free market environment, money management firms will continue to seek out the small investor by developing new approaches to meet investors' needs.

Finally, it should be remembered that pension funds act on behalf of many small investors, inasmuch as pension funds are the stewards of assets set aside to meet the existing and future pension benefits for plan participants and beneficiaries of differing income levels. Our funds are comprised of billions of dollars that provide benefit security to millions of individual Americans, many of whom are small investors.

Market Manipulation Concerns

Pension funds have no desire to engage in activities in markets that could be manipulated. Pension funds engage in program trading or futures activities either through in-house personnel or external managers; thus, such activities are closely monitored and reviewed by the investment managers, the pension funds themselves and, in many cases, outside consultants. While charges of manipulation are difficult to substantiate, the potential for manipulation is a concern and the possibility of abuse needs to be considered and addressed.

POTENTIAL APPLICATION OF PROGRAM TRADING AND FUTURES IN INTERNATIONAL MARKETS

With the coming of age of major overseas markets, the primary reasons for international investment by pension funds are the opportunities to realize higher portfolio returns and to reduce portfolio risk. Reduced risk is possible, in part, because of the timing differences in business and market cycles among major countries, as well as differences in long-term real economic growth rates, inflation, and currency values. In addition, some overseas markets tend to be less efficient than the U.S. market, meaning that careful and astute investors may more easily identify misvalued securities in overseas markets and use this knowledge to add incremental return. At the same time, lower risk is possible because international investment provides opportunities to diversify into a much wider selection of financial assets and asset diversification tends to reduce risk.

To the extent pension funds prudently invest some assets in international markets, clearly we would welcome effective financial futures and options as *hedging* instruments for those market exposures. Furthermore, we believe that most U.S. pension funds would prefer using international futures contracts traded on U.S. markets falling under U.S. jurisdiction because this would provide the comfort of readily available legal remedies, as well as the surveillance, regulation, and oversight provided by the Commodity Futures Trading Commission (CFTC), Securities and Exchange Commission (SEC), and National Futures Association (NFA). Nevertheless, as pension funds continue to participate in global markets, they will use hedging instruments offered in those countries to the extent it is considered prudent to do so.

SUMMARY

In recent years a great number of financial innovations—including index funds, index futures, program trading, and portfolio insurance—have been developed; these on balance have been useful, enabling pension funds to discharge better their fiduciary responsibilities. We expect there will be continued innovations in the future. To achieve this, continued cooperation is necessary between regulators, legislators, policymakers, and market participants to ensure that financial stability and viability, as well as market efficiency and liquidity, remain hallmarks of the U.S. capital markets. In this period of major financial innovation and growth, we have concerns which have been discussed in this testimony. At the same time, we have been reassured by the obvious strength and demonstrated self-correcting capability of the U.S. capital markets which have developed over the years.

CHAPTER 18

THE USE OF STOCK INDEX OPTIONS IN CORPORATE CASH MANAGEMENT

Keith C. Brown, Ph.D.
Assistant Professor of Finance
Graduate School of Business
University of Texas at Austin

Roger G. Clarke, Ph.D.
Managing Partner and Chief Investment Officer
TSA Capital Management

Meir Statman, Ph.D.
Associate Professor of Finance and Chairman
Department of Finance
Leavey School of Business and Administration
Santa Clara University

Companies keep a portion of their assets in liquid balances for transactions for precautionary and speculative motives. Some of these assets are in cash; the rest are in marketable securities.

Which criteria do cash managers use as they choose among marketable securities? A recent study reported that preservation of capital is the most important criterion.[1] Second in

---

[1] R. R. Kamath, S. Khaksari, H. H. Meier, and J. Winklepleck, "Management of Excess Cash: Practices and Developments," *Financial Management* 14 (Autumn 1985), pp. 70–77.

importance is the rate of return, followed by liquidity, company policy, convenience, and restrictions such as those imposed by creditors.

Which securities do cash managers select? The same study reported that repurchase agreements were the most popular security, used by 76.5 percent of the companies in the sample. Following repurchase agreements, in order of popularity, were negotiable certificates of deposit, commercial paper, foreign short-term securities, Treasury securities, banker's acceptances, and tax-exempt securities. Variable (adjustable rate) preferred stocks are mentioned as one in the group of "other securities." Regular preferred stocks and common stocks are entirely absent from the list.

The list of securities for cash management portfolios seems consistent with the selection criteria used by cash managers; preservation of capital is more important than high rates of returns. Common stocks offer expected rates of return that are higher than those of repurchase agreements and 70 percent of dividends on stocks are free from federal corporate income tax (when less than 20 percent of the distributing corporation's stock is held). But returns on common stocks come with high risk. Common stocks, represented by the Standard & Poor's 500 Index, had a mean annual return of 12.01 percent over the 60-year period 1926–1985, a return that is 8.55 percent higher than the 3.46 percent mean return on U.S. Treasury bills. However, the standard deviation of the returns on stocks was 21.37 percent, more than six times higher than the 3.38 percent standard deviation of the returns on U.S. Treasury bills.[2]

Preferred stocks are less risky than common stocks, and they offer the tax advantages associated with dividends. However, while preferred stocks are stable relative to common stocks, they are quite volatile relative to U.S. Treasury bills and similar securities.[3]

---

[2]Data are from Roger G. Ibbotson and Rex A. Sinquefield, *Stocks, Bonds, Bills, and Inflation* (SSBI); updated in *SSBI 1986 Yearbook* (Ibbotson Associates: Chicago 1986).

[3]See M. D. Joehnk, O. D. Bowlin, and J. W. Petty, "Preferred Dividend Rolls: A Viable Strategy for Corporate Money Managers?" *Financial Management* 9 (Summer 1980), pp. 78–87.

Some of the risk of preferred stock is due to the fact that dividends remain constant when returns on alternatives, such as Treasury securities, increase. Adjustable-rate preferred stocks eliminate some of that risk with dividends that rise and fall with the yields on Treasury securities. Yet dividends on adjustable-rate preferred stocks are not as secure as interest coupons. Moreover, many adjustable-rate preferred stocks have caps on dividends and, like other stocks, preferred or common, they are not immune to significant declines in value.[4] It is no wonder that one researcher noted that "most corporate investors regard adjustable-rate preferred stock as the most risky investment in their portfolio and limit their exposure."[5]

This chapter suggests that index options, both puts and calls, can be a useful part of cash management portfolios. The principal role of options is to expand the patterns of portfolio returns available to investors. Cash managers can use options to create return distributions that might fit their objectives better than the return distributions available from Treasury and similar low-risk securities. We focus on two strategies. The first, fully covered calls, consists of writing (selling) call options while holding an identical number of shares of the underlying stock portfolio. The second, which we call insured stocks, combines holding put options and an identical number of shares of the underlying stocks.

COVERED CALLS, INSURED STOCKS, AND RISK

Preservation of capital is the most important criterion in the selection of securities for cash management portfolios with rates of return a secondary consideration. Cash managers are often restricted to a few low-risk securities, and higher risk securities may be excluded even when they have exceedingly high expected returns. Cash managers are also likely to be penalized more severely for losses than they are rewarded for gains. The criteria

---

[4]L. R. Walbert, "Aftertax Is What Counts," *Forbes,* June 17, 1985, p. 214.

[5]J. C. Van Horne, *Financial Management and Policy,* 7th Edition, Englewood Cliffs, N. J.: Prentice-Hall, 1986, p. 431.

used by cash managers seem to follow the safety first rule in the form suggested by Telser; they attempt to maximize the expected return on their invested funds, subject to the condition that the probability that the return will fall below a predetermined minimum return is less than some acceptable level.[6]

Both covered calls and insured stocks offer lower risk and lower expected returns than holding only the underlying stock. The option provides a hedge against fluctuations in the price of the underlying stock. But the characteristics of the hedge implicit in covered calls are different from the characteristics of the hedge implicit in insured stocks. In particular, insured stocks provide a predetermined floor for losses—a floor that can be designed to limit losses to a small amount or even assure a gain. However, losses on covered calls can be substantial. In the extreme case where the stock price declines to zero, a holder of a covered call is left only with the option premium, and the loss is limited only to the difference between the purchase price of the stock and the premium received for the call option.

We restrict our attention to the S&P 500 Stock Index. Options on the index are traded on the Chicago Board of Trade. The value of the index at the close of trading on Friday, March 13, 1987 was 289.89. Options with expiration dates in March, April, and June were available with exercise prices ranging from 225 to 305. We will focus here, for simplicity, on options expiring in April with exercise prices of 280, 290, and 300.

Consider a covered call consisting of buying the S&P 500 Stock Index at $289.89 and selling (writing), for $6.75, an April call option on the index with an exercise price of $290. The $6.75 option premium was the price at the close of trading on March 13. What would be the profit on the covered call position if the value of the index increased to 300 by the option's expiration date? The gross profit would be $7.77, composed of the gains on the index, the option premium, and the dividend. The $.11 gain on the index is the difference between the $289.89 purchase price of the index, and the $290 exercise price. The call premium is

---

[6]L. G. Telser, "Safety First and Hedging," *Review of Economic Studies* 23 (1955–56), pp. 1–16.

$6.75 and the dividend on the index is approximately $.91. The dividend is an estimate, based on a 3 percent annual dividend yield over the one and one-quarter months between March 13 and the expiration date of the April option. The gross profit is subject to a 34 percent federal corporate income tax. However, 70 percent of the dividend is exempt from the tax. The after-tax profit is $5.35.

After-tax profits of covered calls with exercise prices of $280, $290, and $300 over a range of index values at the option's expiration date are presented in Figure 18–1. The figure also presents the after-tax profits that are associated with buying and holding the index, without writing call options.

Observation of Figure 18–1 confirms that covered calls have lower risk than the underlying security. They reduce the loss, by the amount of the option premium, when the index falls substantially. The price for the lower loss is an upper limit of profits. The

FIGURE 18–1
Profits (after-tax dollars) on Covered Calls on the S&P 500 Stock Index

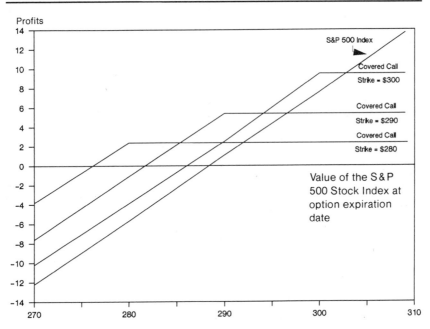

index offers higher profits than do covered calls when the index increases substantially.

Now consider an insured index consisting of buying the S&P 500 Stock Index at 289.89 and buying, for $5.375, an April put option on the index with an exercise price of $290. As in the case of calls, these are the closing prices on March 13, 1987. What would be the profit on the insured stock position if the value of the index increased to $290 by the option's expiration date? The position will register a gross loss of $4.36, composed of an $.11 gain on the index, a $.91 dividend, and a $5.375 loss of the option premium. The after-tax loss is $2.88.

After-tax profits of an insured index with exercise prices of $280, $290, and $300 over a range of index values at the option's expiration date are presented in Figure 18–2. The figure also presents the after-tax profits that are associated with buying and holding the index, without buying put options.

FIGURE 18–2
Profits (after-tax dollars) on Insured S&P 500 Stock Index

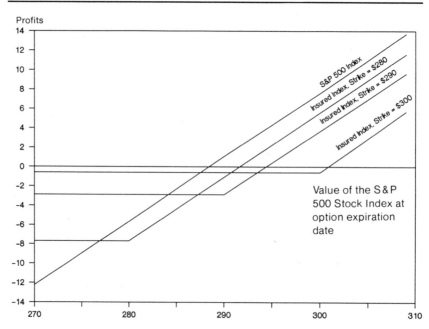

Observation of Figure 18–2 confirms that an insured index has lower risk than the index itself. Losses on an insured index are lower relative to losses on the index when the index decreases substantially. The lower risk comes with lower expected return. In particular, profits on an insured index are lower than profits on the index when the index increases substantially. Most important is the fact that, unlike covered calls, the reduction in risk in an insured index *limits losses to a small amount or even to a gain.* For instance, the after-tax loss on an insured index with an exercise price of $290 cannot exceed −$2.88.

COVERED CALLS, INSURED STOCKS, AND TAXES

Covered calls are not very good at satisfying the preservation of capital criterion. As is evident from Figure 18–1, they offer little protection against significant declines in the value of the index. Indeed, the attraction of covered calls is rooted primarily in their ability to satisfy the second criterion, the rate of return.

Specifically, some covered calls allow cash managers to capture the benefits of the exemption of 80 percent of dividends from federal corporate income tax, while undertaking levels of risk that are lower than the levels of risk associated with holding only the index.

The tax reform laws of 1984, 1986 and 1987 affected the attractiveness of covered calls as a dividend capture system.[7] Indeed, one purpose of the 1984 law was to increase the risk borne by cash managers as they benefit from dividend capture programs.

Dividend capture is allowed only when cash managers are at risk. Forcing cash managers to be at risk helps ensure that they will not receive preferential tax treatment without bearing risk. The 1984 law specifies that covered calls qualify for the exemption of dividends from tax only when a call option has an exercise price that is no higher than the least in-the-money option avail-

---

[7]See Chapter 19 for a further discussion of dividend capture strategies. See also K. C. Brown and S. L. Lummer, "The Cash Management Implications of a Hedged Dividend Capture Strategy," *Financial Management* 13 (Winter 1984), pp. 7–17; and T. Zivney and M. Alderson, "Hedged Dividend Capture with Stock Index Options," *Financial Management* 15 (Summer 1986), pp. 5–12.

able. Prior to 1984, even deep in-the-money call options qualified. Covered calls with deep in-the-money options are more effective at reducing risk than covered calls that employ options with higher exercise prices. Since deep in-the-money options are almost certain to be exercised, they are similar to contracts to sell the stock at guaranteed prices. The existence of contracts to sell at guaranteed prices is considered to be evidence that cash managers are not at risk.

The restriction on the options that qualify for dividend exemption forces cash managers who wish to capture dividends to select from a set of call options with relatively high exercise prices. These options have premiums that are low, and they provide little protection against declines in the price of the stocks that are part of the covered call positions. The 1984 law also increased the risk exposure of cash managers by lengthening from 16 to 46 days the period a stock has to be held before the dividend qualifies for exemption.

The 1986 change in the tax law also diminished the attractiveness of covered calls by reducing the exempted portion from 85 to 80 percent while the 1987 tax law reduced the exemption percentage to 70 percent.

After-tax returns on covered calls, presented in Figure 18–1, are based on the 1987 tax law. Covered call positions where calls have exercise prices of $290 and $300 are eligible for the exemption of 70 percent of dividends from taxes, but the covered call where the call has an exercise price of 280 does not qualify because that exercise price is below 285, the exercise price of the least in-the-money call option available.

Insured stocks are not considered as at risk positions since the put option is a contract to sell the stock at a guaranteed price. Therefore, no insured stock position is eligible for the exemption of any portion of the dividends from taxes.

COVERED CALLS, INSURED STOCKS, AND RATES OF RETURN

Covered calls and insured stock are both likely to be useful for cash managers, and each comes in many varieties, defined by the ratio of the exercise price of the option to the current price of the stock. What are the available varieties and what combinations of risk and return do they offer? We answer these questions using a simulation program developed by Bookstaber and Clarke[8] and data for the 60-year period 1926–1985 from Ibbotson Associates.

The mean annual risk premium on stocks over the period 1926–1985 was 8.55. This is the mean of the difference between the rate of return on stocks, represented by the S&P 500 Stock Index (including dividends), and the risk-free rate of return, represented by U.S. Treasury bills. The standard deviation of the rate of return of the S&P 500 Stock Index over the period was 21.37 percent.

We assumed that the dividend yield on the S&P 500 Stock Index is 3 percent and that the risk-free rate of return is 5 percent. The expected rate of return on the S&P 500 Stock Index is 13.55 percent, the sum of the 5 percent risk-free rate and the 8.55 percent risk premium.

Consider a covered call with an exercise price that is equal to the purchase price, or value, of the S&P 500 Stock Index. The results of the simulation show that it has an expected return of 8.42 percent with a standard deviation of 8.87 percent. The expected return on this covered call is lower than 13.55 percent, the expected return on the S&P 500 Stock Index. The standard deviation of returns is also lower than the 21.37 percent standard deviation of the returns of the S&P 500 Stock Index. However, the lower standard deviation of this covered call should not be interpreted in its entirety as a reduction in risk. As is evident in Figure 18–3, most of the reduction in standard deviation is the result of the upper limit on the rate of return, a limit that marks all covered calls. The upper limit on the return of this covered call is 12.69 percent. The probability that a sizable portion of the invested capital will be lost is substantial.

Before-tax, as well as after-tax, returns for a range of covered calls that vary by the ratio of the exercise price of the option to purchase price of the index are presented in Table 18–1. Covered calls that are way out-of-the-money offer expected returns and standard deviations of returns that are similar to those of the in-

---

[8]R. Bookstaber and R. Clarke, "Option Portfolio Strategies: Measurement and Evaluation," *Journal of Business* 57 (October 1984), pp. 469–92.

FIGURE 18–3

Distribution of Annual Returns of a Covered Index, Established with an Exercise Price Equal to the Index

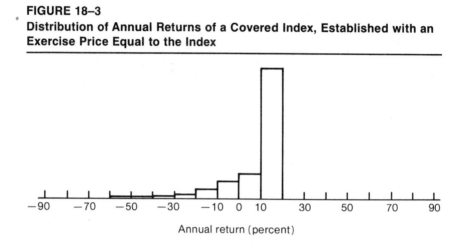

Annual return (percent)

dex itself. For example, a covered call where the ratio of the exercise price of the option to the purchase price of the index is 1.3 has an expected return of 13.03 percent, a return not much lower from the 13.55 percent expected return on the index itself. The standard deviation of the returns on that covered call is also not much lower than the standard deviation of the returns of the index. At the other extreme, covered calls with deep in-the-money options offer expected returns and standard deviations of returns that are similar to those of the risk-free asset. For example, a covered call where the ratio of the exercise price of the option to the purchase price of the index is 0.7 has an expected return of 5.13 percent, a return not much higher from the 5 percent assumed return for U.S. Treasury bills. However, the standard deviation of that covered call is not much higher than the zero standard deviation of the returns on a risk-free asset. Note also that this deep-in-the-money covered call is not likely to qualify for any exemption of dividends from taxes. The figures in Table 18–1 were calculated under the assumption that exercise prices that are 10 percent or more in-the-money are lower than the least in-the-money option available and do not qualify for any exemption of dividends from taxes.

Now consider an insured index with an exercise price that is equal to the purchase price, or value, of the S&P 500 Stock Index.

TABLE 18–1

Expected Annual Returns and Their Standard Deviations for Covered Call Options on the S&P 500 Stock Index

Ratio of the Exercise Price of the Option to the Purchase Price of the Stock	Mean Return (percent)		Excess of Mean Return over the Risk-Free Rate (percent)		Standard Deviation of Before-Tax Returns	Minimum Return (percent)	
	Before Tax	After Tax	Before Tax	After Tax		Before Tax	After Tax
1.3	13.03	9.31	8.03	6.01	18.12	34.59	23.54
1.2	12.00	8.63	7.00	5.33	15.54	26.06	17.91
1.1	10.37	7.56	5.37	4.26	12.29	18.62	13.00
1.0	8.42	6.27	3.42	2.97	8.87	12.69	9.08
0.9	6.69	4.41	1.69	1.11	5.81	8.60	5.68
0.8	5.58	3.68	0.48	0.38	3.45	6.31	4.16
0.7	5.13	3.39	0.13	0.09	1.87	5.37	3.54

Source: These results are based on a simulation using an algorithm by Bookstaber and Clarke in "Option Portfolio Strategies: Measurement and Evaluation," *Journal of Business* 57 (October 1984), pp. 469–92. The standard deviation of the returns of the S&P 500 Stock Index was assumed to be 21.37 percent per year, and the risk premium was assumed to be equal to 8.55 percent per year. These are equal to the mean standard deviation and risk premium over the period 1926–1985. The risk-free rate was assumed to be 5 percent, and the dividend yield was assumed to be 3 percent. The tax rate used is 34 percent, the marginal corporate income tax rate. Covered calls with a ratio of exercise price of the option to the purchase price of the stock of 0.9 or lower were assumed to be ineligible for the exemption of 70 percent of dividends from corporate income tax.

The results of the simulation show that it has an expected return of 10.25 percent with a standard deviation of 15.86 percent. The expected return on this insured index is lower than 13.55, the expected return on the S&P 500 Stock Index. The standard deviation of returns is also lower than the 21.37 percent standard deviation of the returns on the S&P 500 Stock Index. However, while the standard deviation of returns on covered calls understates their true downside risk, the standard deviation of returns on insured stocks overstates their loss potential. As is evident in Figure 18–4, much of the reduction in the standard deviation of returns is the result of a lower limit on the rate of return, a limit that marks all insured stocks. The maximum possible loss for this insured index is 4.57 percent.

Both before- and after-tax returns for a range of insured stocks that vary by the ratio of the exercise price of the option to the purchase price of the index are presented in Table 18–2. Insured indexes that are way-out-of-the-money offer expected returns and standard deviations of returns that are similar to those of the unhedged index itself. For example, an insured index where the ratio of the exercise price of the option to the purchase price of the index is 0.7 has an expected return of 13.51 percent—a return that is only marginally lower than the 13.55 expected return on the index itself. The standard deviation of the returns on

FIGURE 18–4
Distribution of Annual Returns of an Insured Index, Established with an Exercise Price Equal to the Index

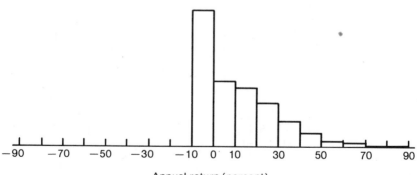

Annual return (percent)

that insured index is 20.83 percent, which is only marginally lower than the 21.37 percent standard deviation of returns on the index. However, note that the maximum possible loss on this insured index is 27.28 percent. At the other extreme, insured indexes with options that are way-in-the-money, offer expected returns that are similar to those of the risk-free securities, and standard deviations that are considerably higher. However, insured index positions offer minimum returns that result in a small loss or even a gain. For example, an insured index where the ratio of the exercise price of the index to the purchase price of the stock is 1.2 has an expected return of 6.70 percent, a return that is somewhat higher than the 5 percent return on the risk-free security, along with a standard deviation of 9.24 percent, a figure much higher than the zero standard deviation of the risk-free security. However, note that this insured index assures complete preservation of capital. The minimum possible return is 2.09 percent.

THE USE OF INDEX OPTIONS IN CASH MANAGEMENT

Common stocks offer expected returns and standard deviations that are considerably higher than those of low-risk or risk-free securities, such as U.S. Treasury bills. Stocks satisfy well the expected rate of return criterion, but not the preservation of capital criterion of the cash manager. On the other hand, risk-free securities satisfy well the preservation of capital criterion, but not the rate of return criterion. Options allow cash managers to construct portfolios with return distributions that might jointly satisfy the two criteria better than unhedged stocks or risk-free securities alone. We have focused our discussion on index options used in covered call positions and insured index positions. The purpose of this section is to discuss issues that are likely to arise as cash managers use index options in their portfolios.

Both covered calls and the insured index require holding the index portfolio. That index can be the S&P 500 Stock Index, the S&P 100 Stock Index, or other indexes where options are available.

TABLE 18–2
Expected Annual Returns and Their Standard Deviations for Insured Index on the S&P 500 Stock Index

Ratio of the Exercise Price of the Option to the Purchase Price of the Stock	Mean Return (percent)		Excess of Mean Return over the Risk-Free Rate (percent)		Standard Deviation of Before-Tax Returns	Minimum Return (percent)	
	Before Tax	After Tax	Before Tax	After Tax		Before Tax	After Tax
1.3	5.68	3.75	0.68	0.45	6.12	3.57	2.36
1.2	6.70	4.42	1.70	1.12	9.24	2.09	1.38
1.1	8.32	5.49	3.32	2.19	12.66	-.48	-.32
1.0	10.25	6.77	5.25	3.47	15.86	-4.57	-3.02
0.9	11.97	7.90	6.97	4.60	18.36	-10.49	-6.92
0.8	13.07	8.63	8.07	5.33	19.97	-18.21	-12.02
0.7	13.51	8.92	8.51	5.62	20.83	-27.28	-18.00

Source: These results are based on a simulation using an algorithm by Bookstaber and Clarke, "Option Portfolio Strategies," pp. 469–92. The standard deviation of the returns of the S&P 500 Stock Index was assumed to be 21.37 percent per year, and the risk premium was assumed to be equal to 8.55 percent per year. These are equal to the mean standard deviation and risk premium over the period 1926–1985. The risk-free rate was assumed to be 5 percent, and the dividend yield was assumed to be 3 percent. The tax rate used is 34 percent, the marginal corporate income tax rate.

Constructing portfolios that duplicate an index, such as the S&P 500 Stock Index, is likely to involve a high ratio of transaction costs to the value of the portfolio in all but very substantial portfolios. The Vanguard Index Trust offers an alternative for managers of smaller portfolios. Index Trust is a no-load mutual fund that duplicates the S&P 500 Stock Index. It offers investors returns that are approximately 0.5 percent lower than those of the S&P 500 Stock Index itself.

Another way to reduce transaction costs is to use covered calls and insured stocks with single stocks rather than an index. Indeed, such a strategy can increase the return on covered calls. Specifically, cash managers can time the purchases and sales of individual stocks to capture as many dividends as possible while satisfying the requirement that each stock be held for at least 46 days. However, this strategy has risks. An index represents a diversified portfolio where most of the unsystematic risk is eliminated. In contrast, the holder of a portfolio including just a few stocks bears its entire risk, both systematic and unsystematic. Corporate cash managers can also purchase shares in mutual funds that are designed for dividend capture.

Unlike covered calls, insured stocks can be quite effective even when constructed with a single stock. Since insured stocks limit risk as they insure a minimum return, there is no need for diversification as a risk-reducing device; a single insured stock is sufficient. Insured stocks with a single stock may also be useful when cash managers want a combination that insures complete preservation of capital (i.e., no loss) and where the available range of put options on the S&P 500 Stock Index does not provide options that accomplish that goal. Options on individual stocks come in a great variety of exercise prices and expiration dates, and cash managers should be able to choose among many stocks to create insured stocks where preservation of capital is assured. However, note that an insured stock position with a well-diversified portfolio of stocks brings returns that are similar to the average returns of all stocks. In contrast, returns on an insured stock position with a single stock are likely to deviate substantially from the average returns of all stocks.

Insured stocks require the use of options, and options are likely to connote high risk and speculation to those not familiar with them. Of course, high risk is precisely what cash managers attempt to avoid. Proper framing of the insured index program is important for its acceptance. We have chosen to use the term insured index rather than protective puts or covered puts to deemphasize the role of options and emphasize the role of insurance. If this seems a trivial concern, consider the experiment by two researchers.[9] They used two frames, a gamble frame and an insurance frame of a choice problem that is identical from an expected utility perspective. They found that more people were willing to pay when the payment is labeled as an insurance premium than when it is labeled as a loss.

The potential failure of decision makers to distinguish frame from substance is also important in the assessment of the implications of put-call parity. Put-call parity suggests that the return distribution of an insured index can be duplicated by investing a portion of the funds in risk-free securities, such as Treasury bills, and purchasing call options with the remainder.[10]

It is not difficult to see how such a position guarantees a minimum return. For example, no more than 2 percent of all funds can be lost if 98 percent of the funds are invested in Treasury bills and 2 percent are invested in call options, even if the options expire worthless.

Given that a position with calls is identical in substance to a position with puts, how should a cash manager choose? If the focus is only on substance, a cash manager should choose the position that entails the lowest transaction costs. However, there is considerable evidence that frames may be just as important as substance. Conservative money managers may be receptive to the idea of buying puts, since puts are easily framed as insurance. They may be less receptive to the idea of buying calls, which are likely to be framed as speculation. Still, not every money manager is subject to the effect of frames. If the effect of frames is eliminated, then the choice between positions involving puts and calls will turn on their relative transaction costs.

---

[9]P. Schoemaker and H. Kunreuther, "An Experimental Study of Insurance Decisions," *Journal of Risk and Insurance* 46 (December 1979), pp. 603–18.

[10]See H. R. Stoll, "The Relationship Between Put and Call Option Prices," *Journal of Finance* 24 (December 1969), pp. 801–24.

Cash managers who are limited to short-term risk-free securities should also avoid the temptation to try to beat the market. The use of covered calls and insured stocks might expose cash managers to this temptation. Care must be exercised in the implementation of such programs so that what has been designed as insurance would not turn into a bet by cash managers who are overconfident in their ability to beat the market. That can be achieved if cash managers are constrained to hold stocks and options only as paired covered calls or insured stocks.

SUMMARY

Cash managers have traditionally limited their holdings of marketable securities to Treasury bills, commercial paper, and the like, and shunned common or even preferred stock. They are willing to sacrifice the high returns of common stock for the low risk that comes with investment in Treasury bills and commercial paper. Are cash managers sacrificing *too much* return for the reduction in risk of loss that they desire? Possibly.

Covered calls and insured index offer alternatives to short-term risk-free debt instruments used in cash management. We focused here on stock indexes, the S&P 500 Stock Index in particular, rather than on individual stocks. A covered index consists of holding the index while selling a call option on that index. An insured index consists of holding both a put option and the underlying index.

Covered calls offer lower risk than common stocks along with expected returns that are higher than those of risk-free securities and the advantages of the exemption, under certain conditions, of 70 percent of dividends from federal corporate income tax. For example, a covered call with an exercise price equal to the index offers an expected annual return that is higher than the risk-free rate by 3.42 percent per year before tax, or 2.97 percent per year after tax.

Insured stocks offer higher expected returns than the risk-free rate, along with a reduction of risk in the form of an insured minimum return. For example, an insured index with an exercise price equal to the index offers an expected return that is higher than the risk-free rate by 5.25 percent per year before tax, or 3.47 percent per year after tax, and where the minimum return is restricted to a loss of 4.57 percent before tax, or 3.02 percent after tax.

Of course, insured stocks are not superior to stocks or Treasury bills for all cash management portfolios. Stocks offer higher expected returns than either covered calls or insured stocks. Treasury bills, at the other end, offer minimum returns that are higher than those offered by insured stocks. Our point is that covered calls and insured stocks can be useful cash management vehicles alongside stocks, Treasury bills, and other securities.

CHAPTER 19

THE USE OF FUTURES AND OPTIONS IN DIVIDEND CAPTURE STRATEGIES

David T. Posen
First Vice President
Equity Arbitrage Group
Shearson Lehman Hutton Inc.

Bruce M. Collins, Ph.D.
Vice President
Equity Arbitrage Group
Index Products Research
Shearson Lehman Hutton Inc.

Dividend capture is a term that broadly encompasses all corporate cash management strategies that attempt to generate high dividend income. These types of strategies have existed for quite some time, but have flourished in recent years as new instruments have been introduced that enable investors to better control risk. Corporations enjoy a significant after-tax benefit from qualified dividend income because it is taxed at only 30 percent of the regular rate. Therefore, a corporation which is normally taxable at 34 percent on ordinary income will pay only 10.2 percent on qualified dividend income. This means that a corporation must generate over $1.36 of ordinary income to retain the same amount after taxes as they would from $1.00 of dividend income.

In order for a dividend to qualify for advantageous tax treatment, a corporation must hold the common or preferred stock of another company for a minimum of 46 days. During this time, the equity investment must be subject to a reasonable degree of economic risk. If the stock is leveraged, the amount of the dividend received deduction is reduced proportionately. The 46-day holding period is suspended during any period in which the taxpayer has reduced the risk of loss by virtue of holding positions of substantially similar property. This means that attempts to hedge the risk to the equity portfolio, in fact, introduce a tax risk through the loss of the dividend deduction holding period. Should this happen, the strategy is no longer possible because the dividends do not qualify for the tax exemption.

The extension of the corporate dividend holding period to 46 days and restrictions regarding leverage and risk reduction strategies were introduced in the 1984 Deficit Reduction Act. Many dividend capture strategies have had to be modified to conform to the guidelines developed in that landmark legislation. Therefore, if historical returns are used to project the expected performance of a dividend capture strategy, then the period subsequent to the 1984 tax act is certainly the most relevant period to assess. Additionally, the tax revisions made in the tax acts in 1986 and 1987 affected the strategy by reducing the dividend received deduction from 85 percent to 80 percent in 1987 and to 70 percent in 1988. Further revisions are currently pending in Congress.

RISKS

Traditionally, corporations have invested their cash in highly liquid and secure short-term credit instruments such as Treasury bills and certificates of deposit. But the prospect of higher after-tax yields has been shifting interest to dividend capture strategies. However, if a corporation is going to become involved in dividend capture it must first understand that these strategies have significantly different risk characteristics than more traditional investments. All dividend capture programs share the following six differences relative to short-term riskless instruments: lower liquidity, longer time horizon, greater volatility, a tax advantage, active management skill, and audit risk. Any corporation considering dividend capture must determine if the first three characteristics are compatible with their risk tolerance before they can conclude that dividend capture is consistent with their investment objectives. Furthermore, the tax advantage is contingent on the firm earning an operating profit.

The first four differences between dividend capture and traditional short-term cash investments explain much of the reason for the higher expected return associated with dividend capture strategies. In an efficient market, an investor willing to accept lower liquidity, a longer time horizon, and greater volatility should be compensated by a correspondingly higher rate of return. However, the tax advantage to a corporation from dividend income adds significantly to the return without a corresponding increase in investment risk. Thus, the first three characteristics of dividend capture simply place the corporation at a different spot than Treasury bills along the Security Market Line. The tax benefit, however, introduces a regulatory friction or inefficiency into the market which places the return above the Security Market Line.

A final unifying feature of dividend capture programs is that all performance is determined to a large degree by active management skill. Dividend capture is not a simple tax arbitrage. Real economic risk must be taken and the success of any dividend capture program is heavily influenced by the skill with which the strategy is implemented. Since so much of the performance results from individual management decisions, and because the many types of programs are so varied, comparison between different forms of dividend capture is often extremely difficult. Nevertheless, despite the rather significant differences among dividend capture programs, the common objective of all investment managers involved in this strategy is to achieve significantly higher after-tax rates of return on corporate cash than can be achieved using traditional money market instruments. Audit risk refers to the possibility that the IRS may audit the strategy and deem it does not incur a significant amount of risk.

UNHEDGED PROGRAMS

The oldest and most basic dividend capture programs can be classified as unhedged programs. These programs generally entail constructing portfolios of high yield common and/or preferred stock, and timing the purchases and sales of equities around the different securities ex-dividend dates which makes the company holder of record on the record date. Therefore, purchases would generally involve stocks that are going ex-dividend within 46 days and sales would transpire on or after ex-dividend date.

The type of stock used in unhedged dividend capture programs is generally utility or preferred stock. These stocks usually have a high yield and are perceived to be inherently stable in price. Nonetheless, even though utilities and preferred stock tend to be less volatile than the S&P 500, they are extremely volatile relative to cash. In addition, because the universe of stocks to choose from is limited to a few interest rate sensitive sectors, the portfolios are subject to greater residual risk than a more broadly diversified equity portfolio. Consequently, an unhedged dividend capture portfolio can generate a high level of dividend income, but it will also have considerably greater risk than traditional money market instruments.

USE OF FUTURES AND OPTIONS

The revolution in dividend capture strategies occurred with the introduction of risk hedging instruments, namely options and futures. Options and futures allow a corporation to construct a high-yield portfolio to capitalize on the tax benefits of dividend income while simultaneously offsetting much of the risk of adverse price movements associated with an equity portfolio. By skillful use of derivative instruments, a dividend-capture manager can attempt to generate an after-tax rate of return which is significantly higher than that of money market instruments while keeping both short-term and long-term volatility at a minimum. In dividend capture strategies, it is generally insufficient to focus only on long-term results. Corporate cash investments are unlike pension investments with respect to the relevant time frame. Pension fund investments are designed to match projected liabilities and, depending on the actuarial assumptions, have time frames considerably longer than one year. Corporate cash investments, on the other hand, must be available as the need arises. Because there may be periods of inferior performance due to adverse market moves against a cross-hedged position, a corporation should commit to a dividend capture program with a minimum one year time horizon, while keeping the quarterly and monthly principal fluctuations to a minimum.

Hedged dividend capture programs can be classified by what is being hedged and by the instruments used to implement the hedge. The most basic decision in hedged dividend capture strategies is whether to hedge the entire equity portfolio, the individual issues within the portfolio, or a combination of the two. When hedging the entire portfolio, a manager will generally try to address two components of risk: equity market risk and interest rate risk. The derivative instruments available to hedge the market risk of an equity portfolio are stock index futures, index options, and options on index futures. Interest rate sensitivity is based on the observation that high yield equity portfolios have durations comparable to long Treasury bonds. Managers have tried to hedge these types of portfolios by using Treasury bond and note futures, options, and options on futures. A third hedging alternative, which handles both equity and interest rate risk at the same time, is to set up a cash market hedge by taking an offsetting short portfolio position. Although this third approach does not employ derivative instruments, it is an alternative analogous to a short futures position and has been used successfully in a few dividend capture programs.

Before discussing specific types of dividend capture programs and the hedging techniques employed in those programs, it makes sense to analyze the relationship between options and futures and the underlying cash instrument. Futures can be viewed as an alternative to a fully leveraged position in the underlying cash instrument where the theoretical price of the futures should reflect the cost of carry in the cash market. For example, S&P 500 stock index futures exhibit the same return distribution as a position in the S&P 500 cash index. The difference in absolute price levels reflects the cost of carrying the equivalent position in the cash market, as shown below.

$$\text{Theoretical value} = \text{Cash index} \times (1 + \text{Cost of carry})$$

where

$$\text{Cost of carry} = \text{Cost of money} - \text{Annualized dividend yield}$$

For example, assume:

$$
\begin{aligned}
\text{Cash index} &= 270 \\
\text{Cost of money} &= 6\% \\
\text{Annualized dividend yield} &= 3.5\% \\
\text{Days to expiration} &= 75
\end{aligned}
$$

then

$$
\begin{aligned}
\text{Theoretical value} &= 270 + 270 \times (6\% - 3.5\%) \times (75/365) \\
&= 270 + 1.39 \\
&= 271.39
\end{aligned}
$$

Bond and note futures are similar to stock index futures in that they have virtually identical return distributions to equivalent positions in the underlying cash market and their theoretical value reflects the cost of carrying the underlying cash positions. If the yield curve is positively sloped the futures should trade at a discount to the cash markets because the relevant carrying cost should reflect the differential between short-term and long-term interest rates. In addition, because there is no single underlying instrument for note and bond futures contracts, but instead a conversion into a theoretical bond or note, and because of certain peculiar elective options concerning the delivery procedure, bond and note futures cannot be valued using strictly a cost of carry model. However, despite these nuances, debt futures can still be viewed as a fully leveraged alternative to a position in the cash market with a theoretical price adjusted for time.

Having established that futures represent an alternative to an underlying position in the cash market, then the only application for futures within the context of a dividend capture program is to offset the risk of a long equity portfolio with a short futures position. Futures have the potential to fully offset a decline in the underlying market, and an investor using futures doesn't have to pay a premium to gain full coverage. However, an investor using futures will also have an unbounded liability in a rising market, and losses on the futures may equal or exceed any gains on the underlying equity portfolio.

The major risks in using futures for dividend capture are tracking error, pricing risk, and tax risk. Tracking error is the risk that the futures price will perform differently than the underlying portfolio. Consequently, losses on the portfolio may exceed gains on the futures, or losses on the future may exceed gains on the portfolio. The opposite scenario may also occur and an investor will add incremental profit because the portfolio outperforms the hedge. In either case, the presence of tracking error prevents the elimination of volatility in dividend capture strategies and should be considered as a real economic risk.

Pricing risk is simply the risk that futures may be adversely mispriced at the time you want to use them. Although futures prices are linked to their theoretical value by arbitrage pressure, market factors can cause mispricing that will persist until arbitrage corrects it. In addition, arbitrage has transaction costs associated with it so that futures contracts will remain mispriced if the mispricing is less than the transaction costs of the arbitrage. Mispricing in the futures market will affect dividend capture returns if it is evident at the time the hedge is established, when it is lifted, or when the position needs to be rolled. Like tracking error, pricing risk can also have a favorable as well as a detrimental impact.

Recall that the 46-day holding period must be satisfied to qualify for the dividend received deduction, and is jeopardized when the corporation holds positions in substantially similar property. Selling futures against an equity portfolio may constitute a tax risk if the Internal Revenue Service deems that the futures contract used mimics the portfolio being hedged. This, of course, presents an interesting "Catch-22": *A dividend capture manager must try to minimize the risk of holding an equity portfolio, but must also be aware that if his hedge is regarded as substantially similar to the stock position, the dividend received deduction may be forfeited.*[1]

Rather than hedging the risk of an equity portfolio with futures, a dividend capture manager may elect to use options or options on futures instead. There are two kinds of stock index options: cash settled options and options on futures. Upon exercising, the holder of a cash settled option receives the intrinsic

---

[1]The dividend received deduction is also subject to substitution-payment risk should the portfolio be kept in street name. This is, however, a minor consideration for dividend-capture strategies.

(in-the-money amount) value of the option based on the closing price of the index on the evening it is exercised. In the case of an option on an index future, an actual futures contract is delivered on assignment.

Assignments in options on bonds and notes result in the delivery of the underlying debt instrument, while the exercise of options on debt futures are satisfied with delivery of the underlying futures position. All index options are priced similarly and have similar return distributions regardless of the delivery mechanism on assignment. The same is true of options on debt instruments. For example, there are options on S&P 500 futures and cash settled S&P 500 index options. Two options of the same class and series will be priced identically and will have the same sensitivity to price changes in the underlying index even when one is cash settled and the other is on a futures contract. The decision on what type of option to use is, therefore, a function of liquidity and the correlation between the portfolio and the underlying index rather than one of settlement feature or underlying instrument.

In using options to hedge portfolio risk, the two available alternatives are buying puts and selling calls. The decision whether to buy puts or sell calls is similar to deciding whether to sell insurance or buy insurance. When an investor buys puts he pays a single premium to gain full protection against a market decline, and will also continue to participate in market appreciation by an amount diminished only by the insurance premium paid. When selling calls, the investor takes in the premium income, but forgoes a great deal of participation in subsequent market appreciation. Moreover, protection against a market decline is limited to the amount of premium taken in by the sale of calls. A call selling strategy will generally outperform a put buying strategy in a flat market, but will underperform a put hedging strategy during a large decline or large rise in the market.

HEDGED PROGRAMS

Strategies that hedge portfolio risk with futures tend to use either equity or debt futures, but not both. One such program involves hedging a perpetual preferred portfolio with short Treasury bond futures. The premise of such a strategy is that perpetual preferreds are extremely sensitive to changes in interest rates and have a comparable duration to government long bonds. The objective of this strategy is to neutralize price risk while capturing the dividend stream from the preferred stock portfolio. If successful, this type of strategy could be expected to return 4–6 percent after tax in the 1988 market environment.

This strategy, however, has numerous liabilities. The duration of perpetual preferreds and Treasury bonds is a reasonably good match for hedging purposes for small changes in yields. Duration changes are significant, however, when yield changes are large. This is due to convexity—a measure of change in duration for changes in yield that is not the same for preferreds and Treasury bonds. Preferred stocks and bonds can move in opposite directions, and negative returns are possible (and even probable) over periods of time—an intolerable situation for many corporations. The relatively low liquidity of many of the issues in the preferred market can result in high transaction costs and the inability to liquidate a program quickly without extreme expense if the cash is needed for other corporate purposes. Finally, the preferred stock market displays certain industry group concentration which may introduce an additional element of residual risk due to sector concentration.

Another strategy which hedges equity portfolio risk, this time by selling stock index futures, can be seen as a tax enhanced variation of stock index futures arbitrage. A portfolio is constructed using optimization techniques to create a subset of the stocks in the S&P 500 index. This portfolio is designed to minimize tracking error with the S&P 500 index but may contain as few as 50 individual issues. These stocks are selected both because they constitute a portfolio which is highly statistically correlated to the S&P 500, and because they have the highest possible dividend yield consistent with the goal of correlation. S&P 500 stock index futures are then sold against the 50-stock optimized portfolio and the return consists of the dividend income from the portfolio plus the premium on the future.

In addition to selecting stocks that have a high yield, dividend income can be maximized by rotating stocks around their position in the dividend cycle. This is similar to the unhedged utility stock roll where stocks are purchased prior to their ex-dividend dates and sold afterwards. However, when rotating stocks around the dividend stream it is extremely important to be aware of how tracking is affected and the size of the transaction costs.

This type of program can return 4–6 percent after tax in the current (mid 1988) market environment and probably provides the most dependable protection against a severe market decline. Nonetheless, this strategy also has some significant liabilities. As was mentioned previously, hedged strategies will have basis risk, pricing risk, and tax risk. Tracking error is statistically quantifiable, and can probably be limited to approximately 2 percent. This means that there is a one standard deviation (65 percent) probability that the portfolio's annual change in value will be within 2 percent of the S&P 500 index, and a two standard deviation (95 percent) probability that the portfolio will track the index within a 4 percent range.

Recently, pricing risk has been extremely evident as stock index futures have traded on many occasions at steep discounts to their theoretical value. In addition, the spread between the front month on the future and the back month has also been trading at a discount to fair value. In both of these cases, adverse futures mispricing will reduce the returns to this type of dividend capture strategy.

Finally, the tax risk of this type of a program is, of course, subjective. The concern is that if the S&P 500 future mimics the equity portfolio, then the dividend received deduction may be disallowed. The tax code does not define what mimic means, but instead it relies on nebulous terms such as *substantially similar properties* and *substantial diminution of risk*. Proponents of this strategy claim that a 50-stock portfolio is not a substantially similar property to a 500-stock index. Opponents claim that because the portfolio is designed specifically to correlate as highly as possible with the S&P 500 index, the future does mimic the portfolio and risk is substantially diminished.

A final point about this program and the strategy of hedging perpetual preferred stock with short bond futures is that their expected return is lower than most other dividend capture strategies. The objective of these strategies is to generate high dividend income and to minimize the risk of price movement. Most other dividend capture strategies try to generate both dividend income and capital gains either by option premium income or price appreciation. An example of a strategy which retains the potential for capital appreciation but also hedges the risk of a portfolio price decline is hedging a portfolio of perpetual or sinking fund preferred stock by purchasing put options on Treasury bond futures.

This hedging technique will underperform the strategy of selling futures in a flat or declining market, but will significantly outperform in a rising market. The price appreciation that would be expected on a preferred stock portfolio in a declining interest rate environment will be diminished only by the premium paid for the puts. Tracking error and pricing risk are also evident in this strategy, but tax risk is not a concern, because the hedging vehicle is a fixed income security.

Just as perpetual preferreds are often hedged with options on bond futures, some dividend capture programs will hedge a utility common and preferred stock portfolio with options on bond futures or combinations of options on bond futures and note futures, and options on stock index futures. These programs will generally purchase a utility portfolio and combinations of equity and debt puts. These portfolio hedges attempt to neutralize interest rate risk and equity market risk. The risk/reward profile of this strategy is similar to that of the perpetual preferred portfolio hedged with puts on bond futures.

Although returns from perpetual preferred strategies can be high, they are accompanied by significant volatility. This is due to the portfolio's large residual risk and a departure from its fixed income characteristics. For example, when the Chernobyl nuclear disaster occurred, the utility market declined while government bonds rallied, resulting in a loss on both the portfolio and the hedge. The residual risk in this kind of portfolio resulting from sector concentration and stock selection simply cannot be hedged away with Treasury bond options and index options. Essentially, the use of derivative instruments to hedge the stock portfolio exchanges market risk for residual risk. Although a hedged position is less volatile than an unhedged position, it may exhibit greater short-term volatility than is acceptable to many corporations.

A third alternative for hedging a utility and preferred stock portfolio is to take an offsetting short position in a portfolio of similar equities. The major advantage of this approach is that it can have a significantly lower tracking error than a hedge using equity and debt derivative instruments. The total risk to an equity portfolio consists of market risk, sector risk, and stock specific risk. A cash market hedge addresses both the market risk and the sector risk of owning an equity portfolio while diversification reduces stock specific risk. Thus, a cash market hedge can address the risk of owning an equity portfolio in a way that a simple interest rate hedge can not.

The major remaining risk is issue specific. The success of this strategy is essentially predicated on skillful stock selection. Very simply, if long positions outperform short positions, profits will result. In addition, dividends will be received on the long positions and interest will be earned on the short position. If dividends are paid out on the short position, it will directly offset dividend income from the long portfolio. Therefore, purchases and sales on both the long portfolio and the hedge must be oriented around the ex-dividend dates of the component stocks. The management objective is to maximize dividend income, avoid dividend outflow, and profit from the relative performance of the long portfolio versus the hedge.

Two problems with cash market hedges are diversification and cost. A cash market hedge is essentially a relative value play. After taking dividend considerations into account, a manager implementing a cash market hedge is trying to profit from the change in value of his long positions relative to his short positions. In this strategy, a manager must construct both well diversified long and short portfolios. If the short portfolio is not well diversified, an unpalatable level of stock specific risk may exist. A short position in half a dozen stocks may be more of a speculation than a hedge, especially if there are a large number of issues in the long portfolio.

The second consideration is that transaction costs can be significantly higher in the cash markets than they are in the derivative markets. Transaction costs are composed of both commission costs and market impact.[2] At commission rates of $.05 per share

---

[2]Market impact refers to the difference between the price of an asset when the decision to transact was made and the execution price. Market impact on a portfolio of stocks is measured on a weighted average basis.

on stock, and $25 round turn on stock index and bond futures, commission costs are roughly 10 times higher in the cash markets than in the futures market. Market impact costs are much more difficult to estimate, but these are also generally believed to be significantly higher in the cash market than in the futures market. Therefore, the potential benefit of lower basis risk must be weighed against the detrimental impact of higher trading costs.

The final dividend capture strategy to be profiled is the buy-write strategy. The buy-write strategy is the only dividend capture strategy which directly hedges both market risk and stock specific risk. In the buy-write, stocks are purchased and, simultaneously, qualified covered calls are sold to hedge the individual equity positions. Table 19–1 contains the specifics of what qualifies as a covered call. The total return to the investor is the sum of the call time premium and the dividend income on the stock less commission costs, while the downside protection is the full price of the short call option plus the dividend.

Consider the following example: General Motors is purchased at 69¼, and the GM March 60 calls are simultaneously sold for 9⅝. As long as General Motors is above $60 per share at expiration, the calls will be exercised and the stock will be sold at $60. Because a price of 9⅝ was received at the time the calls were sold, the effective sales price for the stock is 69⅝ (60 + 9⅝). The dividend on General Motors is $1.25 per share, and the commission on a buy-write is generally about $0.125. Therefore, the total return on this trade is $1.50 (effective sale price minus purchase price minus commission plus dividend income) of which $1.25 is dividend income and $0.25 is a trading profit. The cost basis on this investment is 59¾ (stock price minus call price plus commission), and assuming a marginal tax rate of 34 percent, the after-tax rate of return is 2.15 percent. Buy-write rates of return are generally quoted on an annualized basis; if there were 60 days left between trade date and contract expiration, the annualized after-tax rate of return is 13.11 percent.

An important consideration in evaluating a buy-write return is whether an early exercise prior to receiving the dividend will materially lower the annualized return on the investment.[3] If we

---

[3]For a discussion of early exercise conditions, see John Cox and Mark Rubinstein, *Options Markets* (Englewood Cliffs, N. J.: Prentice-Hall, 1985), Chapter 4, 139–144.

TABLE 19–1
Qualified Covered Call Options

Applicable Stock Price*	Minimum Strike Price of Qualified Calls†		Applicable Stock Price*	Minimum Strike Price of Qualified Calls†	
	31–90 Days until Expiration	Over 90 Days until Expiration		30–90 Days until Expiration	Over 90 Days until Expiration
5⅛ – 5⅞	5 or more	5 or more	100⅛ – 105	100 or more	95 or more
6 – 8¾	7.50 "	7.50 "	105⅛ – 110	105 "	100 "
8⅞ – 11¾	10 "	10 "	110⅛ – 115	110 "	105 "
11⅞ – 14⅝	12.50 "	12.50 "	115⅛ – 120	115 "	110 "
14¾ – 17½	15 "	15 "	120⅛ – 125	120 "	115 "
17⅝ – 20	17.50 "	17.50 "	125⅛ – 130	125 "	120 "
20⅛ – 22½	20 "	20 "	130⅛ – 135	130 "	125 "
22⅝ – 25	22.50 "	22.50 "	135⅛ – 140	135 "	130 "
25⅛ – 30	25 "	25 "	140⅛ – 145	140 "	135 "
30⅛ – 35	30 "	30 "	145⅛ – 150	145 "	140 "
35⅛ – 40	35 "	35 "	150⅛ – 155	150 "	145 "
40⅛ – 45	40 "	40 "	155⅛ – 160	155 "	150 "

Stock Price Range		Strike			Stock Price Range		Strike	Strike		
45⅛ — 50	=	45	=	=	160⅛ — 165	=	160	155	=	=
50⅛ — 55	=	50	=	=	165⅛ — 170	=	165	160	=	=
55⅛ — 60	=	55	=	=	170⅛ — 175	=	170	165	=	=
60⅛ — 65	=	60	=	=	175⅛ — 180	=	175	170	=	=
65⅛ — 70	=	65	=	=	180⅛ — 185	=	180	175	=	=
70⅛ — 75	=	70	=	=	185⅛ — 190	=	185	180	=	=
75⅛ — 80	=	75	=	=	190⅛ — 195	=	190	185	=	=
80⅛ — 85	=	80	=	=	195⅛ — 200	=	195	190	=	=
85⅛ — 90	=	85	=	=	200⅛ — 210	=	200	195	=	=
90⅛ — 95	=	90	=	=	210⅛ — 220	=	210	200	=	=
95⅛ — 100	=	95	=	=	220⅛ — 230	=	220	210	=	=

*The applicable stock price is the last closing price of the stock prior to the day on which the option is granted. If the opening price of the stock is more than 110 percent of its prior close, then the opening price becomes the applicable stock price.

†An assumption is made that strike prices are at $2.50 intervals up to $25.00, $5.00 intervals from $25.00 to $200.00, and $10.00 intervals above $200.00. Note that if a stock splits, strikes will vary temporarily.

Source: Chicago Board Options Exchange (compiled by Louis Napoli when he served as Manager of Institutional Services).

assume that the ex-dividend date on General Motors is 10 days after the trade date, then the worst time for early exercise is nine days later. If you are assigned on or after the ex-dividend date, the full return is earned over a shortened holding period. It is only if the assignment occurs before ex-dividend date that the return may be impaired. If the exercise occurs the day before ex-date, then only $.25 (effective sale price minus purchase price minus commission) is earned over a nine-day holding period, and the annualized return is 11.20 percent.

The downside protection in a buy-write is as important a consideration as the return. In the General Motors example, the stock can decline 13.82 percent to 60 before the rate of return is adversely affected. Furthermore, the stock can decline an additional 2.5 percent to 58½ before the investor is at a break even. This is the major benefit of the buy-write strategy. An investor can suffer through fairly significant declines before losing money, and can prosper in a positive, flat, or even slightly negative market environment.

In addition to hedging the individual issues within the portfolio, risk can be further reduced by purchasing stock index puts. Thus, both the stock specific risk and the market risk are hedged. Because short calls provide an initial degree of downside protection, it isn't necessary to insure the first part of a market decline. Generally speaking, put protection is intended to begin where the call premium leaves off. If the average short call position is providing 8–10 percent of downside protection, then index puts will be purchased 8–10 percent out-of-the-money. The additional put premium will reduce the return of the buy-write portfolio in a flat or rising market, but it provides substantial protection against a large market decline. In this respect, it can be viewed as disaster insurance that has been purchased at a cost of approximately 1½ to 2 percent per year.

The buy-write dividend capture strategy has some distinct advantages which have helped to make it the most popular of the dividend capture programs. It is the only type of dividend capture program which hedges both the stock specific risk as well as the market risk of owning equities. In addition, because there is a universe of approximately 500 optionable stocks, buy-write portfolio managers have a large number of stocks they can choose from, giving them the ability to construct well-diversified portfolios. This helps to avoid the sector bias that is manifest in other types of dividend capture programs. These factors contribute in making buy-write programs among the least volatile of the dividend capture programs, rivaled only by the optimized equity portfolios hedged with stock index futures. The annualized standard deviation of monthly returns for buy-write programs range from 2–4 percent. In addition, the annual rates of return realized by buy-write programs have normally ranged from 6–16 percent after tax over the last three and a half years, making this style of dividend capture very attractive on a risk-adjusted basis.

In addition, a dividend capture strategy can be implemented using an index buy-write.[4] Essentially, the previous strategy involved a portfolio of buy-writes, such that calls were written on individual stocks. Index buy-writes, on the other hand, involve holding a portfolio of stocks that comprise the index and writing index calls. This strategy is applied selectively during peak dividend periods when after-tax return targets can be met. There are several advantages to index buy-writes. Index options often are more overvalued than individual equity options and thus provide a higher degree of protection. In addition, the ability to write calls on a broad market index reduces the concern for stock selection or the need to maintain a high level of return across the entire range of individual equity calls written. Additional protection is available through the purchase of index puts. Because of the cash settlement feature of index options no stock changes hands on assignment. Moreover, index buy-writers normally need not be concerned with early assignments that often precede an ex-dividend date of individual equities. There are, nevertheless, early assignment risks peculiar to index options. Essentially, if the options are exercised early,[5] the investor is left with an unhedged equity position and its accompanying risks. The choices

---

[4]As of this writing, the Treasury Department has not defined a qualified covered call for index options. The question of diminution of risk due to the short call remains a gray area. Some investors use qualified calls on individual stocks as a guideline.

[5]Because there is no fixed ex-dividend date to focus on with indexes, but a distribution of dates, the buy-write position must be monitored closely before and during peak dividend periods.

are to sell new calls, or to sell the stocks. Either action may have a detrimental impact on return due to adverse pricing or price movement.

The index buy-write strategy is illustrated using an XMI buy-write. Since the XMI is a price-weighted index, this strategy is implemented by purchasing equal shares of the 20 stocks comprising the index. The number of calls to sell is determined by multiplying the divisor by the number of hundred round share lots of each issue held. The returns to the index buy-write are calculated in the same way as buy-writes on individual equities.

$$\text{Return} = \frac{\text{Time premium} + \text{Dividends} - \text{Commissions}}{\text{Cost basis}}$$

$$\text{Cost basis} = \text{Index value} + \text{Commissions} - \text{Option premium}$$

The information required to determine the returns to the buy-write strategy is given below.

Major Market Index Buy-Write

Spot Index	373.57
Feb 370 call	13.06
Dividends	2.42
Commissions	.432*
	.09†
Days to expiration	65

*Commission based on $.08/share.
†Option cost 4.50 per option one way.

The static annualized after-tax return is computed by adjusting the return formula. Using the above data and assuming the tax rate is 34 percent, the annualized after-tax return is 12.59 percent.

$$\frac{(\text{Time premium} - \text{Commissions} + (1 - .7) \times \text{Dividends}) \times (1 - \text{Tax rate}) + .7 \times \text{Dividends}}{\text{Cost basis}} =$$

$$\frac{(9.49 - .522 + .726) \times .66 + 1.694}{361.032} \times \frac{365}{65} = 12.59 \text{ percent}$$

The preceding example cites an annualized return as a means of comparison with alternative investments. The XMI buy-write usually has a trade duration of one to three months. Since this strategy can be implemented several times over the course of a year, the annualized return for any one period does not necessarily represent the realized return for one year.

The XMI buy-writer receives premium income but relinquishes some, if not all, of the potential for portfolio appreciation. The return to the strategy depends on the time premium of the option and dividends paid on the portfolio. The premium provides an element of protection in a declining market. In our example, once the index declines below 370, the level of return is reduced. The break-even point of the strategy (before transaction costs) is 360.51. While a buy-write is considered one of the most conservative option strategies, the loss of a significant portion of the investor's principal is not precluded. After-tax returns are enhanced by the tax treatment of dividends. The risk of early assignment jeopardizes the return because the investor is left with an unhedged long stock position. Under most circumstances, the debit incurred as a result of assignment will be offset by the gains realized on the long portfolio. The early exercise risk lies with the possibility that the gains realized on liquidation of the portfolio do not fully offset the debit created by the assignment.

SUMMARY

In summary, dividend capture is a generic term that describes a wide array of techniques designed to generate high levels of dividend income. Innovative hedging programs involving options, futures, and the cash market allow corporate investors to generate high after-tax returns through equity investments while concurrently offsetting much of the price risk associated with holding stock. Although not all dividend capture programs involve options and futures, it is safe to say that derivative instruments have contributed markedly to investor interest in dividend capture strategies.

CHAPTER 20

ASSET ALLOCATION USING FUTURES CONTRACTS

Mark A. Zurack, C.F.A.
Vice President
Goldman Sachs & Company

*Ravi E. Dattatreya, Ph.D.**
Director
Financial Strategies Group
Prudential Bache Capital Funding

Allocating a portfolio's total assets to equities, long-term bonds, and money market securities has been the focus of considerable research in the investment community. Less effort has been focused on better ways of implementing an asset allocation revision. Typically, an investment manager will restructure his portfolio by buying and selling individual equities, bonds, and money market securities or by trading in portfolios of securities in a formal program. Another method of restructuring a portfolio is to use interest rate and stock index futures contracts to change the portfolio's exposure to the equity and fixed-income markets. By altering the portfolio's risk using stock index and interest rate futures contracts, an investment manager is changing asset allocation; nonetheless, capital does not move from one market to the

---

*Dr. Dattatreya was employed at Goldman Sachs at the time this chapter was written.

other. Therefore, we can assume that a change in an asset's exposure to the risk of the market is, in effect, a change in asset allocation. In this chapter, we explore how interest rate and stock index futures contracts can be used in asset allocation and show: (1) why using futures in portfolio restructuring programs may be more efficient, (2) how asset allocation can be changed in the futures market, and (3) how futures pricing should influence the decision.

Many of the exhibits in this chapter draw off 1984 data. Although market conditions have changed, the concepts introduced in this chapter still hold true.

WHY USE INTEREST RATE AND STOCK INDEX FUTURES CONTRACTS IN ASSET ALLOCATION DECISIONS

Futures contracts on fixed income securities and stock market indexes are efficient portfolio restructuring tools for four major reasons: (1) The specific futures contracts are based on cash instruments that broadly represent their markets, (2) futures allow the manager of a large pension fund to separate the asset allocation decision from the security selection process, (3) equity and interest rate futures markets are very liquid, and (4) the total costs of trading futures are, on average, less than those of trading individual stocks and bonds.

Broad Market Representation

Investors who use interest rate and stock index futures contracts in their portfolios are able to change their exposure to equities and bonds with one or two transactions. In the interest rate futures market, two contracts are traded actively, the Chicago Board of Trade (CBT) 15-year long bond contract and the CBT 10-year note contract. Because the price movements of both contracts correlate closely with changes in corporate and government bond prices, an investment manager can use bond and note futures contracts to adjust the exposure of the portfolio to match his desired level of interest rate risk.

In the equity market, two futures contracts are traded aggressively by institutional investors, the S&P 500 Index contract and the NYSE Composite Index contract. Most pension fund managers use the S&P 500 Index to measure the relative performance of an equity portfolio to the stock market. In addition, the industry and sector characteristics of most pension funds are similar to the S&P 500. An analysis of all equity portfolios by Wilshire Associates quantifies this.[1] In 1984, 86 percent of the variability of equity returns for the median pension fund could be explained by the behavior of the S&P 500 Index. The NYSE Composite Index contains more issues than the S&P 500 (1,700 versus 500), making it slightly more representative of the broad stock market. Both indexes are market capitalization weighted and contain most of the Fortune 500 companies. The performance of both indexes is influenced by the price movement of large companies. Some 80 percent of the capitalization of the NYSE is included in the S&P 500, and the correlation between the two indexes is very high.[2] Therefore, most equity portfolios can be successfully hedged with either the S&P 500 or NYSE futures contracts; the exceptions are small stock funds and equity portfolios with concentrated positions in stocks not well represented in the broad market indexes.

Separation of Security Selection and Asset Allocation Decisions

Many large corporations apportion their pension assets to different investment managers who purchase and sell securities for the pension fund on a discretionary basis. In this way the pension fund can establish positions in different capital markets. Portions of the base of the pension fund are allocated to different managers who are instructed to maintain positions in stocks, bonds, cash, and whatever other asset classes are desired.

Prior to the introduction of interest rate and stock index futures, the pension fund manager had to implement an asset allocation change by instructing his portfolio managers to revise their

---

[1] Median R^2 of all equity portfolios in the fourth quarter of 1984. Source: Wilshire Associates Trust Universe Comparison Service.

[2] Standard & Poor's Research Services estimate, December 1984.

exposures in equities and fixed income securities or by changing managers. With the advent of futures contracts on stock market indexes and government bonds, a pension fund can manage its asset mix without disrupting its investment manager's day-to-day activities.

Liquidity

Investors will only use interest rate and stock index futures contracts in their portfolios if they believe the markets are large enough for them to change the portfolio's exposure to stocks and bonds quickly and inexpensively. Fortunately, the equity and interest rate futures markets are extremely liquid as measured by all standard indicators of market activity.

In the fixed-income market, it is more difficult to compare dollar trading activity between Treasury notes, Treasury bonds, and Treasury bond and note futures contracts because most cash bond trading is done in dealer markets rather than on exchanges. We estimate that dollar volume in longer-term interest rate futures contracts is three to four times that of the cash bond market. We also expect that differences in trading volume between equity and fixed income securities and interest rate and stock index futures contracts will become more dramatic as institutional investors become more comfortable using futures in their portfolios. This does not mean that trading volume in the securities themselves will be adversely affected. For many, liquid futures markets lead to strategies that result in more securities trading.

Trading Costs

Liquid futures markets provide a low-cost means of accepting and transferring market risk. One justification for using futures in a portfolio restructuring program can be a savings in trading costs relative to buying and selling individual stocks and bonds. We break down trading costs into two components:

$$
\begin{array}{ccc}
\text{Total} & \text{Commissions} & \text{Spread between} \\
\text{trading} \; = & \text{(generally for} \; + & \text{last sale and} \\
\text{costs} & \text{equities only)} & \text{the transacted price} \\
& & \text{(market impact)}
\end{array}
$$

We mentioned above that dollar trading volume in futures contracts consistently exceeds that in the cash market. In addition, at any point in time most trading activity in futures occurs in four contracts: CBT nearby Treasury bond futures, CBT nearby Treasury note futures, S&P 500 nearby futures, and NYSE nearby futures. In the securities markets, trading is spread among many individual equities and bonds.

An implication of concentrated trading in futures is that there is fierce competition between members to make markets, which induces tighter spreads than in the cash markets. Tighter spreads imply that a trade in interest rate or stock index futures contracts has a lesser impact on the futures market than a comparable transaction in equities or bonds. By reducing market impact, a portfolio manager will incur lower trading costs using futures contracts to change asset allocation.

USING FUTURES TO CHANGE THE MIX OF A PORTFOLIO IN CASH, STOCKS, AND BONDS

We will use two examples to show how futures can be used to implement asset allocation strategies. In the first case, we start with a pension fund of $1 billion, 60 percent invested in equities, 25 percent in bonds, and 15 percent in cash. The fund's investment policy committee decided to change its asset mix to 50 percent equities, 30 percent bonds, and 20 percent cash.

To restructure the portfolio, the pension fund manager must reduce the fund's exposure to equities by $100 million and raise its position in bonds and money market securities by $50 million. Normally, the manager would sell stocks and purchase fixed income and money market securities to change the portfolio.

Alternatively, the portfolio manager can use interest rate and stock index futures contracts to implement the allocation change. The portfolio's exposure to the stock market is changed by selling enough stock index futures to offset the risk of a $100-million position in the portfolio. If the equity portion of the fund is run by more than one portfolio manager, the aggregate risk of the total equity position should be analyzed. We use two statistical risk factors to quantify the effect of adding stock index futures to an equity portfolio. The market risk measures the sensitivity of total return to the movements in an index that proxies the stock market. The statistical measurement for market risk is the portfolio beta. The higher the beta, the greater the market risk for a given investment in the portfolio, and the more futures contracts required to hedge that risk. The number of contracts required to hedge an equity investment is calculated as follows:

$$\text{Number of index futures contracts} = \frac{\text{Desired change in portfolio value}}{500 \times \text{index}} \times \text{Portfolio beta}$$

Our example assumes that the S&P 500 Index is at 165 and the portfolio beta at 1; the number of S&P 500 futures contracts to sell short equals:

$$\text{Number of S\&P 500 futures contracts} = \frac{\$100 \text{ million}}{500 \times 165} \times 1 = \text{1212 March S\&P 500 futures contracts}$$

The nonmarket risk, also known as statistical tracking error, will influence the performance of selling futures against a portfolio relative to selling stocks and raising cash. Statistical tracking error equals the difference in total return between the portfolio and the index used to hedge that portfolio. It also reflects the portion of total return that is unrelated to movements in a stock market index and thus cannot be offset in the futures market. Statistical tracking error is minimized by selecting the index (or combination of indexes) most closely correlated to the entire equity position.[3] The greater the tracking risk, the less ideal will selling futures be as a substitute for selling stocks.

To use bond futures to alter the portfolio's exposure to changes in interest rates, we must also establish a convention to measure the fund's current and desired levels of risk. We analyze the portfolio's dollar duration to determine current interest rate risk. The duration of a bond measures the sensitivity of its price to interest rate movements. Numerically, it equals the percent change in the price of a bond for a one-point change in its yield. Duration is a function of a bond's remaining life, coupon, and

---

[3]See Chapter 13 for an expanded discussion of the risk of hedging equity portfolios.

yield to maturity. A long bond would have a higher duration than a money market security, while the duration of a zero coupon bond would be greater than that of a high-coupon bond with the same maturity. Specifically, duration measures vary from less than one for money market instruments, to over eight for long Treasury bonds, to over 35 for long zero coupon bonds. A natural indicator of a portfolio's interest rate exposure is its dollar duration. The dollar duration for a fixed-income portfolio equals the dollar change in portfolio value per 100-basis-point change in interest rates; it is determined by multiplying the portfolio's duration by its market value divided by 100.

In one simple asset allocation process, we change the portfolio's dollar duration to restructure the fixed income portion of the portfolio. In our example, the average duration of all bonds and notes in the portfolio equals four. Thus, a $250-million investment in the market translates into a portfolio dollar duration of $10 million. Assume that in this example the manager, by increasing his dollar commitment to fixed income securities in the fund to $300 million, desires to increase the dollar duration to $12 million. Interest rate futures contracts can be used to adjust the portfolio's dollar duration because they respond to rate changes in a predictable way.[4] The dollar duration of a Treasury bond or note futures contract is determined by dividing the duration of the assumed deliverable bond by the factor associated with that bond and multiplying the result by 1,000 ($100,000 par value per futures contract divided by 100). (See the appendix to this chapter for more detail.)

For example, on November 27, 1984, the March bond future 7⅞ of 11/15/07 priced at 72¹²/₃₂. The dollar duration of the bond was 6.24. The delivery factor associated with the cheapest to deliver bond was 0.9883; thus, one futures contract had a dollar duration of 6,314.

---

[4]Duration hedging using interest rate futures contracts works well for a parallel shift in the yield curve. If the portfolio's change in yield is very different from the yield change in the deliverable bond, the hedge will not work as well as expected.

We recommend following the sequence of steps below to determine the number of Treasury futures needed to increase dollar duration to $12 million.

Step 1. Current dollar duration = $250 million × 4/100 = $10 million

Step 2. Desired dollar duration = $300 million × 4/100 = $12 million

Step 3. Change in dollar duration = $12 million − $10 million = $2 million

Step 4. Number of Treasury bond futures contracts = $\dfrac{\$2\ \text{million}}{\$6,314}$ = 317 March Treasury bond futures contracts

In this example, the portfolio manager would be long 317 Treasury bond futures contracts. Once the futures transactions are executed, one of three things will generally happen: (1) The futures contract positions will be reversed gradually as portfolio revisions are made in the equity, bond, and money markets; (2) the manager's view of the market will change and his futures contracts will be closed, allowed to expire, or go to delivery; or (3) the manager will keep all current futures contract positions.

In the second example, we examine a $1 billion pension fund with a policy of maintaining an asset mix of 60 percent equities, 30 percent bonds, and 10 percent cash. The relative performance of the three markets will cause the mix to vary. The portfolio manager of this fund rebalances his positions quarterly to keep his asset mix constant. At the close of the current quarter, the equities are valued at $550 million, long bonds at $340 million, and cash at $110 million. Normally, the manager would buy $50 million stocks, sell $40 million in long bonds, and reduce the cash reserve by $10 million. Instead, the manager might also realign the portfolio with stock index and interest rate futures contracts.

With the S&P 500 Index at 165 and the beta of the equity port-folio equaling one, he would buy long

$$\frac{\$50 \text{ million}}{500 \times 165} \times 1 = \frac{606 \text{ S\&P 500}}{\text{March futures contracts}}$$

to increase the portfolio's equity exposure to $600 million.

In this example, the manager desires to maintain a fixed-income portfolio dollar duration of $15 million. Market condi-tions indicate a dollar duration of $17.85 million. Assuming the same duration measure on the bond futures contract as in the previous example, the manager would sell short

$$\frac{\$17.85 \text{ million} - \$15.00 \text{ million}}{\$6,314} = \frac{451 \text{ March Treasury bond}}{\text{futures contracts}}$$

to rebalance the portfolio's exposure to interest rates.

UNIQUE CHARACTERISTICS OF THE FUTURES MARKETS

We stated above that the use of interest rate and stock index fu-tures contracts to implement asset allocation decisions can in-crease the portfolio's total return by lowering its trading costs. The validity of this statement depends on the creation of a long or short futures position providing the same rate of return before transaction costs as the purchase or sale of stocks and bonds. Three factors influence how the returns from using futures con-tracts compare with returns for a similar strategy traded in the cash markets: (1) the prices at which the futures contracts are executed and closed out relative to the value of the underlying security or portfolio of securities, (2) the price at which near-term futures contracts can be rolled over into longer-term positions, and (3) variation margin.

Valuation

The initiation of a long or short position in a futures contract does not cause cash to change hands between the buyer and the seller. The owner of a futures contract participates in the price movement of the underlying commodity or security without an initial capital outlay, thus making the transaction similar to buying a security and financing 100 percent of it. The difference is that the owner of a fully leveraged security collects income (interest, dividends) on that security, while the owner of a futures contract does not. There are also differences in collateralization and day-to-day margin settlement. Therefore, the buyer or seller of a futures contract would expect to trade that contract at a price relative to the spot security based on the difference between the financing cost of the underlying security or portfolio of securities and the benefits that would accrue to the owner of those securities. The spread between the spot security and the futures contract, also called the *basis,* should be positive when financing costs exceed future income and vice versa. When the basis trades at its expected value, the futures contract is said to be fairly priced. If the contract is not trading at fair value, and the basis is lower (higher) than expected, the buyer (seller) of futures contracts achieves a higher return (excluding trading costs) using futures in asset allocation than he would transacting in the securities markets.

In one of our previous examples, a manager sold short S&P 500 futures contracts to reduce his portfolio's exposure to the stock market instead of selling stocks to raise cash. If the total return of the long stock/short futures position (before trading costs and ignoring tracking error) is greater than the short-term interest rate, the portfolio manager has taken advantage of a mispricing in the futures market. Generally, interest rate and stock index futures contracts are driven toward fair value by an active arbitrage market, but they occasionally reflect other factors. As shown in Figures 20–1 and 20–2, the return achieved on the entire portfolio by an investor who sells stock index and interest rate futures contracts rather than stocks or bonds to raise cash can be very different from a money market yield.

In the previous section, we described two strategies involving the creation of long and short positions simultaneously in interest rate and stock index futures contracts. Many asset allocation revisions using futures will operate in this manner. Therefore, investors who use interest rate and stock index futures contracts must know whether there is a predictable relationship

FIGURE 20–1

Short–Term Interest Rate versus the Return Achieved by Selling the Nearby S&P 500 Future against the S&P 500 Index (4/28/82–11/30/84)

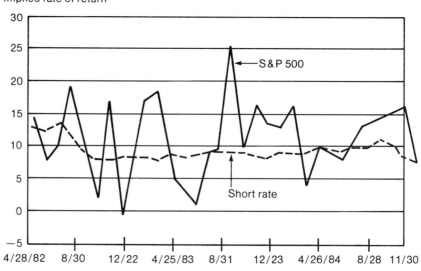

between occurrences of mispricing in the equity and interest rate futures markets. In other words, the manager is interested in determing whether, if he creates a short position in rich S&P 500 futures contracts, he will consistently be long over- or undervalued in Treasury bond futures contracts. To analyze the premium relationship of the Treasury bond and S&P 500 futures markets, we compare the implied money market returns for a long bond/short nearby Treasury bond futures position with the purchase of the S&P 500 Index combined with a short position in the nearby S&P 500 futures contract. A regression using monthly data between April 1982 and November 1984 was run on the return information; as shown in the following table and in Figure 20–3, there is no quantifiable relationship between premium variations in the equity and interest rate futures markets. Therefore, the investor who purchases rich S&P 500 futures should not expect to consistently sell rich or cheap Treasury bond futures.

Regression Results*		
T Statistic	Slope (Beta)	Correlation Coefficient
1.49	0.103	0.26

*Long deliverable bond/short bond future is the dependent variable.

The pricing of equity and interest rate futures must be considered in deciding whether to include futures contracts in the portfolio. This does not imply that unattractively priced futures contracts should never be used to implement a change in asset allocation, since the benefits of added flexibility and lower transaction costs may more than offset unappealing futures contract prices. Moreover, unless the contracts are held until expiration or delivery, it is impossible to measure the impact of prevailing futures premiums on total return. We believe the analysis of premi-

FIGURE 20–2
Short-Term Interest Rate versus the Return Achieved by Selling the Nearby Bond Future against the Deliverable Treasury Bond
(4/28/82–11/30/84)

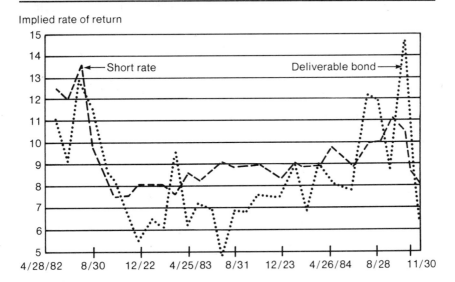

Implied rate of return

FIGURE 20–3
**Short–Term Interest Rate versus the Return Achieved by Combining the
S&P 500 and the Deliverable Bond with Their Respective Nearby Futures
Contracts** (4/28/82–11/30/84)

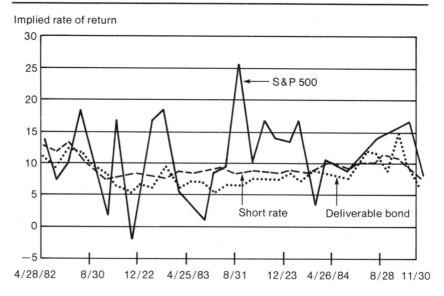

ums is very helpful in timing entry into and exit from the interest
rate and stock index futures markets; this should be done before
a transaction is made.

Rolling Over Near Month Futures into
Later Expiration Months

We mentioned in the previous section that when interest rate and
stock index futures contracts are used in asset allocation, the positions must be (1) reversed along with transactions in the securities markets; (2) closed, allowed to expire, or delivered; or
(3) left in place. If the third approach is followed, the manager
must address the issue of how to maintain the same positions in
the futures market for a long time period.

Earlier, we stated that most interest rate and stock index futures trades are in contracts with a life of three months or less.
The investor with a horizon greater than three months must close

his current positions and set up new ones in later contract months to maintain a constant market exposure. This process subjects the portfolio manager holding futures to additional pricing risks.

To illustrate the pricing risk of rolling short-term futures, we refer to the example in which the portfolio manager sold 1,212 March S&P 500 futures contracts and bought 317 Treasury bond futures to restructure the portfolio. As the March expiration draws near, the March S&P 500 and Treasury bond futures contracts will have to be rolled into June to avoid the risks that the equity position will become unhedged after the March futures expire and that delivery of fixed income securities will be necessary.

In the S&P 500 futures market, the spread between the March contract's repurchase price and the sale price for the June futures contract will affect the return of the hedged portfolio between March and June. In our first example, if the trades are done at fair value, the return on the long stocks/short futures positions should equal the risk-free rate between March and June. If not, the return on the hedged portfolio will differ from the return on cash by the extent of mispricing. To measure the impact of rollover risk on portfolio return in the equity futures market, we compare the spread between the nearby and second nearby S&P 500 futures contract with its fair value each day during the month before the near-term futures expiration. To quantify pricing risk, we have adopted a trading rule: As soon as the spread reaches fair value or better, we roll the position. If it never equals fair value, the transaction is made on the last date of the analysis.

Table 20–1 and Figures 20–4, 20–5, 20–6, and 20–7 show the results of four separate spreads rolled between November 1983 and September 1984. During this period, a buyer of S&P 500 futures would have lost nearly 1 percent in total return due to unfavorable futures rollover.

In Treasury bond futures, the spread market is more efficient for two reasons: (1) It is easier and cheaper to arbitrage pricing discrepancies between bonds and futures, and (2) the second nearby bond futures contract is more liquid than its corresponding S&P 500 contract. Figure 20–8 shows that the difference between the short-term interest rate and the implied yield from the nearby/second nearby futures spread stays fairly constant over

TABLE 20–1
Impact of the S&P 500 Futures Rollover on Total Portfolio Return

	Buyer of Futures		Seller of Futures	
	Execution under (over) Fair Value	Impact on Return	Execution over (under) Fair Value	Impact on Return
Dec. 1983–Mar. 1984	0.24	0.15	0.01	0.01
Mar. 1984–Jun. 1984	(0.71)	(0.45)	0.09	0.06
Jun. 1984–Sep. 1984	0.10	0.06	0.12	0.08
Sep. 1984–Dec. 1984	(1.13)	(0.67)	0.41	0.24
	(1.50)	(0.91)	0.63	0.39

time. The yield implied by the futures spread is consistently lower than the short-term interest rate because of the variability of delivery dates and deliverable bonds for bond futures contracts.[5]

The pricing risk of rolling short-term futures contracts will exist as long as actual prices deviate from their cost-of-carry values. This risk can be minimized by placing a limit spread order at fair value as soon as the position is established, given the liquidity limitation in later contract months.

Variation Margin

An investor who buys or sells futures to change asset allocation should consider the effect of variation margin on total return. The futures exchanges require that all futures positions be marked-to-the-market daily and settled in cash. The cash flow arising from a change in value in the futures position is called variation margin and is added to or taken from the investor's cash account each day. To show how variation margin works, we refer to the previous section in which we recommended that a fund manager sell 606 S&P 500 futures contracts to reduce his equity exposure by $50 million. We assume that with the S&P 500 Index at 165, the manager sold 606 three-month futures contracts at 167.50. One

---

[5]See the appendix to this chapter for an expanded discussion of the delivery option for bond futures.

FIGURE 20–4
Three-Month Interest Rate versus the Yield Implied by the Dec. 83–March 84 S&P 500 Futures Spread (daily information, 11/15–12/13/83)

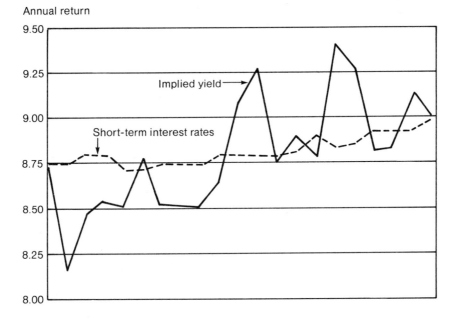

day later, the futures contract price increases $1 to 168.50. The next morning, the manager who sold 606 futures contracts had to transfer $303,000 (500 x $1 x 606) in cash to his broker as variation margin for the day.

The implications of variation margin flow for the fund manager are twofold. The fund must maintain a cash reserve to cover negative variation margin flows. The size of the reserve required is a function of the dollar value of the futures position, the expected length of the hedge, and a forecast of how far the market can move against the position during the life of the hedge. In the case of a $50-million stock index futures position with a three-month hedging horizon, we would expect a cash reserve of $5 million to cover variation margin calls most of the time.[6]

---

[6]Assuming market volatility of 20 percent per annum, a $5 million cash reserve could cover variation margin flows 83 percent of the time.

FIGURE 20–5
Three-Month Interest Rate versus the Yield Implied by the March–June 84 S&P 500 Futures Spread (daily information, 2/15–3/13/84)

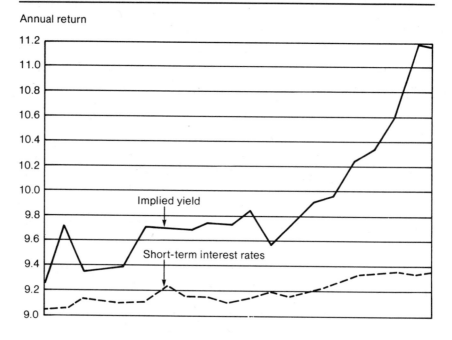

In addition, the pension fund will receive or pay out interest income on the cash resulting from variation margin inflows or outflows. For longer-term positions, the interest on variation margin cash flow can be important. In our example, the portfolio manager had to transfer $303,000 in cash out of his account. If the interest rate on a three-month Treasury bill is 10 percent per year, the manager would lose $7,575 ($303,000 x 3/12 x 0.1) in interest due to variation margin flows. Had the market gone the other way, total return on the hedge would have increased by $7,575. We do not believe that variation margin biases total return in a positive or negative direction. However, we do think that over any one period, the interest received or lost due to margin flows will cause actual return to deviate from expected return.

It is possible to mitigate the short-term effects of variation margin by adjusting the original futures position. We showed that

FIGURE 20–6
Three-Month Interest Rate versus the Yield Implied by the June–Sept. 84 S&P 500 Futures Spread (daily information, 5/15–6/14/84)

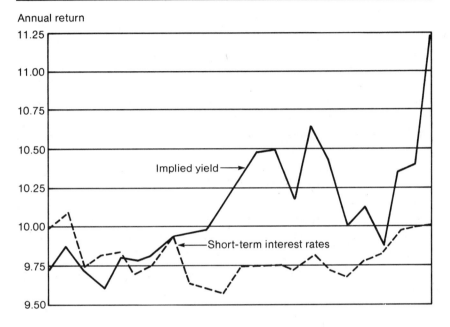

the manager who sold 606 three-month S&P 500 Index futures contracts would lose $303,000 in variation margin and $7,575 in interest on that margin. The manager can offset the added interest on margin flow by reducing the number of futures contracts traded by the cost of money between the date the position is evaluated and the contract's expiration date.

$$\text{Adjusted futures position} =$$

$$\frac{\text{Original futures position}}{1 + (\text{Daily risk-free rate}) \times (\text{No. of days until futures expiration})}$$

In the example, the adjusted futures contract position results in 591 three-month S&P 500 futures being sold instead of 606. A $1 increase in the futures market would result in a variation margin call of $295,500 and lost interest income of $7,388, for a total loss of $302,888 for the revised position. The decline in asset

FIGURE 20–7

Three-Month Interest Rate versus the Yield Implied by the Sept.–Dec. 84 S&P 500 Futures Spread (daily information, 8/15–9/14/84)

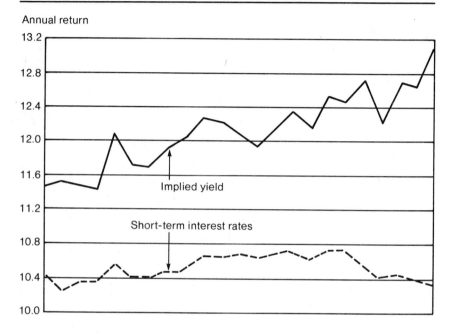

value of $302,888 is very close to what would have occurred had 606 contracts been sold and the position not marked-to-the-market. As the expiration date for the futures contract approaches, the futures contract position should be changed to reflect the declining cost of financing daily variation margin flows.[7] In the example, approximately once a week, the 15-contract adjustment in the futures position should be revised, resulting in the sale of one additional futures contract.

SUMMARY

Institutional investors can use interest rate and stock index futures to change a portfolio's sensitivity to bond and stock returns. The two most liquid bond and stock index futures contracts, the

---

[7]Adjustments may occur more often if interest rates change significantly during the period.

FIGURE 20–8
Implied Yield from the Bond Futures Spread versus Short-Term Interest Rates (by quarters, 10/83–3/85)

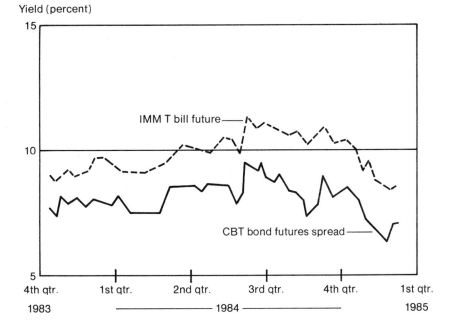

CBT 15-year bond contract and the S&P 500 Index contract, are useful hedging vehicles because they correlate closely with most bond and equity portfolios. Pension fund managers gain added flexibility by using futures in their portfolios because they are able to revise asset allocation without disturbing the day-to-day activities of their investment managers. Dollar trading volume for interest rate and stock index futures contracts exceeds that of the stock and bond markets. Liquid futures markets create tighter bid/ask spreads in futures than in individual stocks or bonds, thereby lowering trading costs and increasing returns for the portfolio manager who judiciously uses interest rate and index futures contracts in a portfolio restructuring program.

In this chapter, we have illustrated two ways investment managers can revise asset allocation with futures contracts. In the first case, the manager uses futures contracts to restructure the portfolio so it matches his desired change in investment strategy. In the second example, futures contracts are used to rebalance the portfolio to maintain constant percentages in stocks, bonds, and cash. Although there are other potential uses for interest rate and stock index futures in asset allocation, we believe these two examples are the most popular. Investors who use futures contracts to restructure a portfolio should understand the unique characteristics of interest rate and stock index futures before they use them. Interest rate and stock index futures contracts do not always trade at their fair value. Often, premiums are determined partly by factors such as market sentiment. The most liquid interest rate and stock index futures contracts have lives of three months or less. An investor looking to maintain a futures position longer than three months runs the risk that his position will be rolled into a later contract month at an unfavorable price. Variation margin impacts total return because the portfolio manager will receive or pay out interest on cash inflows or outflows resulting from daily marked-to-the-market futures contract positions.

APPENDIX: THE BASIS IN CBT BOND FUTURES

The trading unit for the Chicago Board of Trade bond future is $100,000 of long-term bonds issued by the United States Treasury. An 8 percent coupon (annual interest rate, as a percent of face value) is nominally assumed for pricing the futures. However, Treasury bonds with other coupons may also be delivered; the main requirement is that the bond have at least 15 years remaining before the first redemption (maturity or call). Most deliverable bonds are callable at par five years prior to maturity. Delivery may take place on any business day during the delivery month.

A price adjustment is made at delivery to compensate for the coupon rate of the deliverable bond. This adjustment uses a *delivery factor,* which, when multiplied by the final settlement price, gives the delivered bond's invoice price (to which must be added the accrued interest as of the delivery date). Thus, the factor works like a quality premium or discount: It adjusts upward the price of a bond with a coupon greater than 8 percent and it adjusts downward the price of a bond with a coupon less than 8 percent. Roughly speaking, the factor is the price at which the delivered bond gives an 8 percent yield to call. In more precise terms, the factor is the price of the deliverable bond that gives a yield to call of 8 percent, with the following variations: The term to call is computed by starting on the first possible delivery date, ending on the first call date, and rounding down to the nearest whole quarter-year; and the price is expressed in decimal, divided by 100, and rounded to four decimal places. Note that every bond has a unique factor for a given delivery month, but the factors for different months' deliveries of the same bond are usually different.

The Major Influences on Bond Futures Pricing: Arbitrage

The cost of carry is by far the biggest influence on the basis in bond futures. The end result of taking a long position in bond futures and taking delivery is ownership as of the future delivery date. The same result could be achieved by buying Treasury bonds in the cash market, borrowing the money to pay for them, and paying off the loan on the futures delivery date. Either way, the investor fixes a price today for bonds he pays for in the future. Bond futures prices tend to equate the cost of the two methods of forward ownership. The interest on the loan used to finance holding the cash bond is called *cost of carry*. It is offset to some extent by the coupon income from the cash bond. Because repurchase agreements, or *repos,* are the cheapest generally available method of financing a position in Treasury bonds, term repo rates play a major role in pricing bond futures. Knowledge of Treasury bond prices and term repo rates allows for a rough estimate of the price of the nearby bond future by dividing the delivery factor into the sum of the bond price and the net cost of carry.

Similarly, knowledge of the price of a deliverable bond and a bond future allows the inference of a term repo rate; the implied repo rate is the breakeven financing rate between cash and futures. For the unleveraged investor who is long cash and short futures, the implied repo rate is the rate of return he will earn from the coupon on the bond adjusted for any difference between the purchase price of the bond and the sale price implied by that particular delivery month's futures price. By comparing the implied repo rates available, an investor can see how closely cash prices are in line with futures prices.

Arbitrageurs watch the implied repo rates because any time a bond can be financed from cash settlement to futures delivery date at less than the implied repo rate, it is a virtually risk-free way to profit from price aberrations. The cumulative effect of many arbitrageurs' buying cash and selling futures when an implied repo rate gets too high is to drive down futures prices relative to cash, and prevent any implied repo rate from getting significantly above actual term repo rates. This activity is known as buying the implied repo.

Similarly, it is possible to sell the implied repo, although this poses greater risks. Whereas the investor who buys the implied repo and carries through to delivery knows what bond he owns, an investor who sells the implied repo must "borrow a bond versus cash" (on which the rebate may be as low as 3 percent or 4 percent annual interest), sell it, and then take delivery on his long futures position to return the borrowed bond. The delivered bond may not be the same bond he borrowed, and he may lose on the exchange. Still, selling the implied repo is attractive when the implied repo rates on all deliverable bonds are low for a given delivery month. The cumulative effect of many arbitrageurs' selling cash and buying futures is to push up futures prices relative to cash, and prevent all the implied repo rates from being very low at once. (The rebate on borrowing a bond may be thought of as a very low repo rate.) The overall effect, then, of arbitrage on implied repo rates is to keep them all at or below actual term repo rates, and also to keep the implied repo for at least one deliverable bond above 3 percent or 4 percent. A good definition of "normal" basis is as follows: The implied repo rate for at least one deliverable bond is close to actual repo rates, but no implied repo is above.

Other Influences on the Basis: Expectations and Timing of Delivery

Expectations play a role in determining the level of implied repo rates within the bounds set by arbitrage. A shift in expectations from falling to rising interest rates can cause a large volume of short hedging. This depresses futures prices relative to cash prices, with the result that implied repo rates will all fall below actual repo rates. When interest rates are perceived as falling, many short hedged positions are lifted. Buying all those bond futures causes the implied repos to rise to—and perhaps exceed for a short time—repo rates available on the market. Hedging or speculative activities of unusually large volume can also cause aberrations in the basis, although this happens infrequently.

One key assumption that must be made in figuring the implied repo is the number of days to delivery. Since delivery is allowed on any business day of the delivery month (at the option of the short), there can be as much as a 30-day difference in how long a delivery-bound arbitrageur must finance his position. A good rule of thumb for deciding between early and late delivery is: Deliver late when the "current yield" (coupon divided by cash price) exceeds the financing rate (or implied repo, for an unleveraged investor), and deliver early if the financing rate exceeds the current yield. This stems from a comparison of the extra income from holding the bond, the additional accrued interest as a percentage of the price paid for the bond, with the expense of holding the bond for the longer period of time. Another factor in the decision is variation margin: If the short had to borrow more to meet margin calls, he may be more inclined to deliver early.

CHAPTER 21

ACTIVE PORTFOLIO MANAGEMENT

Stanley J. Kon, Ph.D.
Professor of Finance
Graduate School of Business Administration
University of Michigan

The recent availability of stock index futures contracts has provided portfolio managers and individual investors with a unique set of investment opportunities that were nonexistent prior to the new contract. These opportunities will allow investment managers to obtain the maximum benefits from their special skills and enhance the risk-adjusted return to their clients.

It is well recognized that the return on a common stock investment can be attributed to both firm-specific and market-wide events. The inherent advantage of using stock index futures contracts in portfolio management lies in the fact that such contracts make it possible to unbundle and manage these two sources of return on investment separately. Without stock index futures contracts a manager might pass over an incremental investment in a new security because its contribution to the stock selection performance of the fund may be contrary to its contribution to the market timing performance of the fund. For example, an investment in a high-market risk stock that the manager believes to be undervalued due to a new technological discovery or the introduction of superior management skills might be passed over because of a bear market forecast and the unfavorable high-beta characteristic of the stock.[1] With a position in stock index futures contracts the manager can have his cake and eat it too. That is, he can purchase the undervalued stock to achieve positive stock selectivity performance and simultaneously sell the index futures contract to hedge away the effect of general market movements. If he is very confident that the general market will move downward, he can sell more contracts than are required to eliminate market risk and thus make a profit if the market declines. All of this can be done at a trivial commission cost. Consequently, managers can no longer blame general market movements for their lack of success in selecting undervalued securities, since bearing market risk is no longer a prerequisite to bearing and profiting from the management of firm-specific risk.

In order to analyze the contribution that positions in stock index futures contracts can make to the performance of a managed portfolio, we begin in the next section by introducing the principles of both stock selectivity and market timing performance. The balance of the chapter discusses the risk-return properties of using index futures relative to a specific common stock portfolio and presents the solution to the optimal futures position for a managed pension portfolio of undervalued stocks.

PERFORMANCE MEASUREMENT

The investment management process can be dichotomized into the activities of stock selection and market timing. Stock selection is based on forecasts of company-specific events, and hence the prices of individual securities. Market timing, however, refers to forecasts of future realizations of the market (index) portfolio. If an investment manager believes he can make better than average forecasts of market portfolio returns, he will adjust his portfolio risk level in anticipation of market movements. If the manager can also make better than average predictions of firm-specific events for a group of stocks, then this portfolio will be levered up in anticipation of a bull market and down in anticipa-

---

[1]Beta measures the sensitivity of a security's return relative to the market.

tion of a bear market. If successful, he will earn abnormal returns relative to an appropriate benchmark for each activity.

Consider an investment manager of a $100 million stock portfolio that he believes is undervalued by $5 million and that he believes the marketplace will revalue within one year. Assuming that prices are determined by the Sharpe-Lintner capital asset pricing model,[2] then:

$$E(R) = r + \beta[E(R_M) - r] \qquad (21\text{--}1)$$

That is, the expected rate of return on any security or portfolio, $E(R)$, is equal to the riskless rate, r, plus a risk premium that depends on its level of systematic risk, β, and the excess return on the market portfolio, $[E(R_M) - r]$.

Equation (21–1) is known as the ex ante security market line (SML) and is illustrated in Figure 21–1 as the ray rA. Risk-averse investors will set prices today such that the greater the systematic (nondiversifiable) risk of an asset, the greater the expected return must be to compensate them. For example, if the current rate on one-year treasury issues is 0.1 (10 percent) and the expected return on the market portfolio is 0.2, then the expected return on a portfolio with a β of 0.8 is 0.18 [= 0.1 + 0.8 (0.2 − 0.1)]. This is point P in Figure 21–1.

A model that describes the actual or ex post returns on securities or portfolios, R, over the next year is:

$$R = r + \beta(R_M - r) + \epsilon \qquad (21\text{--}2)$$

One difference between Equations (21–1) and (21–2) is the replacement of the expected return on the market portfolio, $E(R_M)$, with what actually occurred, R_M. This determines the effect on a security's return from market-wide events, and the magnitude depends on the security's sensitivity to these events. The measure of this sensitivity is its level of systematic risk, or beta (β). Therefore, $R = r + \beta(R_M - r)$ represents the ex post security market

---

[2]William F. Sharpe, "Capital Asset Prices: A Theory of Market Equilibrium under Conditions at Risk," *Journal of Finance*, September 1964, pp. 425–42; and John Lintner, "The Valuation of Risk Assets and the Selection of Risky Investments in Stock Portfolios and Capital Budgets," *Review of Economics and Statistics*, February 1965, pp. 13–37.

FIGURE 21–1

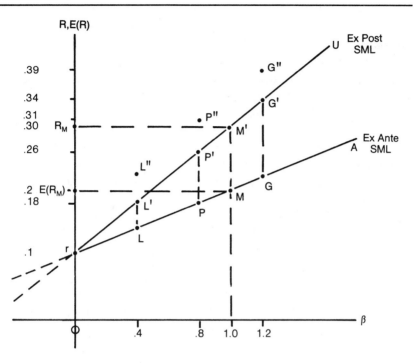

line. Ray rU in Figure 21–1 is an example of a bull market outcome of 0.3, in which all stocks will do better than expected just due to the general market movement.

It is this ex post return on the market portfolio that market timers are forecasting and betting on. A shift to a higher level of sensitivity to market outcomes will magnify the portfolio's return in a bull market. For example, it would be preferable to have selected portfolio G with a $\beta = 1.2$ rather than P in a bull market, since the ex post return at G' of 0.34 $[= 0.1 + 1.2(0.3 - 0.1)]$ is considerably greater than the $0.26 = [0.1 + 0.8(0.3 - 0.1)]$ at P'. The difference of 0.08 $(= 0.34 - 0.26)$ has two components: compensation for the incremental risk increase from 0.8 to 1.2 and the timing performance gain for correctly predicting the bull market. The change in expected return for an additional 0.4 of systematic risk can be calculated with the risk premium term in Equation (21–1), $\beta(E(R_M) - r)$. Therefore, one expects 0.04 $[=$

0.4 (0.2 − 0.1)] as compensation for bearing the additional 0.4 of systematic risk. The gain for a correct market forecast will depend on the size of the market turn and the magnitude of the change in the risk level. The market timing performance resulting from the decision to depart from the assumed target risk level of 0.8 must be measured relative to the gain or loss that would have occurred had the manager decided to remain at the target level (passive or no timing decision). Hence the net gain is that from point *G* to *G'* (for having selected a portfolio risk level of 1.2 during a bull market of 0.3) less the gain from point *P* to *P'* that would have occurred anyway had the manager maintained the target risk level of the fund. Therefore, the market timing performance is measured by the distance *G'G* = 0.12 (= 0.34 − 0.22) less the distance *P'P* = 0.08 (= 0.26 − 0.18). The difference of 0.04 (= 0.12 − 0.08) represents the gain for this correct market timing decision. The *market timing performance* component can be generalized to the following equation.[3]

$$\tau = [(\beta_A - \beta_T)(R_M - E)(R_M)] \qquad (21\text{--}3)$$

Note that the timing performance measure does depend on the magnitude of the risk-level change from the target level, β_T, to the actual risk level selected, β_A. The target risk-level value depends on the stated objectives of the managed portfolio. The actual risk level selected will deviate from the target level based on the magnitude of the bull or bear market prediction, the degree of confidence in the prediction (forecast error), and the risk-return trade-off that the fund is willing to assume based on its stated objectives.[4] The size of the market turn is also included

---

[3]See Eugene F. Fama, "Components of Investment Performance," *Journal of Finance,* May 1972, pp. 551–67; Stanley J. Kon and Frank C. Jen, "The Investment Performance of Mutual Funds: An Empirical Investigation of Timing, Selectivity, and Market Efficiency," *Journal of Business,* April 1979, pp. 263–89; Stephen Figlewski and Stanley J. Kon, "Portfolio Management with Stock Index Futures," *Financial Analysts Journal,* January–February 1982, pp. 52–60; and Stanley J. Kon, "The Market Timing Performance of Mutual Fund Managers," *Journal of Business,* July 1983, pp. 323–47.

[4]See Michael C. Jensen, "Optimal Utilization of Market Forecasts and the Evaluation of Investment Performance," in *Mathematical Methods in Investment and Finance,* ed. G. P. Szego and K. Shell (Amsterdam: North-Holland, 1972); and Kon and Jen, "Investment Performance of Mutual Funds."

in this timing measure by the deviation of the actual return on the market portfolio, R_M, from its expected level, $E(R_M)$. In the numerical example τ is again equal to 0.04 [$= (1.2 - 0.8)(0.3 - 0.2)$].

Furthermore, note that Equation (21-3), the timing performance equation, is symmetric. That is, if the manager was predicting a bear market and moved the risk level of the fund to 0.4 during a bull market return of 0.3, then $\beta_A - \beta_T = 0.4 - 0.8 = -0.4$ and the performance would be -0.04. This is the distance of $L'L$ minus the distance $P'P$ in Figure 21-1. Therefore, penalties for inferior market timing performance will also be assessed. This measure captures the manager's ability to predict bear markets as well. In Figure 21-2 ray rA is the same ex ante security market line as in Figure 21-1 and ray rD in the ex post security market line for a bear market of $R_M = -0.2$. The performance measure for having predicted a bull market and selected a high risk level of 1.2 in a bear market is -0.16 [$= (1.2 - 0.8)(-0.2 - 0.2)$]. This is the negative distance $G'G$ minus the smaller negative distance $P'P$ in Figure 21-2. If the manager had correctly predicted a bear market and lowered the portfolio risk level to a beta of 0.4, the performance would be a positive 0.16 [$= (0.4 - 0.8)(-0.2 - 0.2)$]. This is the negative distance $L'L$ less the larger negative distance $P'P$ in Figure 21-2.

The last term in Equation (21-2), ϵ, represents the effect on a security's return due to firm-specific events that will occur over the next year. This is the variable that is being forecast in the stock selectivity activity. Today the consensus of investors is that the value of ϵ will be zero for all stocks. Our hypothetical investment manager, however, *expects* his portfolio of undervalued stocks with a β of 0.8 to have an ϵ of 0.05 ($5 million/$100 million). If he has no special information concerning general market movements and the target risk level of the fund is also 0.8, then if he is exactly right about the firm-specific events and there is a bull market ($R_M = 0.3$), the total return on the portfolio will be 0.31. This is represented by point P'' in figure 21-1. The 0.31 return is made up of a 0.26 return associated with the bull market outcome and the systematic risk level of the portfolio and a 0.05 return from the previous selection of undervalued securities. It is this 0.05 return that is known as the "Jensen measure" of supe-

FIGURE 21–2

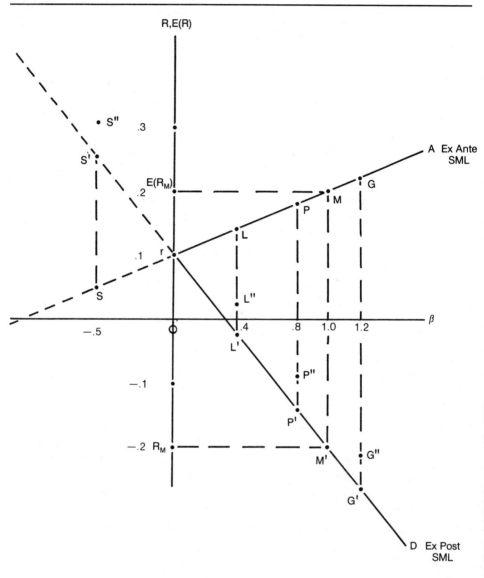

rior selectivity performance.[5] Since the final decision was to select a portfolio risk level equal to the target level, the market timing performance was zero, as indicated by Equation (21–3) and the definition of a passive timing policy.

Now we can examine some of the conflicts of interest that can arise when investment managers participate in timing and selectivity activities simultaneously. In our continuing example, if the manager still believes that the portfolio of stocks with a beta of 0.8 is undervalued by a 0.05 return and that there will be a bull market, then financial *theory* tells us to lever up that stock portfolio by borrowing at the riskless rate and investing the proceeds and initial wealth in the undervalued portfolio until the risk level reaches a beta of 1.2. In general, however, regulated funds are restricted from borrowing for speculation, so that in practice a manager must sell low-risk securities and buy high-risk securities to achieve the high-beta position. First, this more realistic alternative requires large transaction costs and presents possible liquidity problems for large positions in some stocks. Second, no manager wants to sell undervalued stocks and purchase correctly priced stocks. A manager will engage in this trade-off only if the perceived benefits of the timing activity exceed those of the selectivity activity.

But why give up either, since it will be shown that the purchase of stock index futures can be used as a perfect substitute for levering up the undervalued stock portfolio with a beta of 0.8 to a beta of 1.2 at trivial commission charges. Therefore, correct stock selectivity and bull market forecasts will yield a total return of 0.39. The result is represented by point G'' in Figure 21–1. This point is obtained by levering portfolio P to point G with index futures contracts and obtaining a market timing performance of 0.04 from the bull market outcome at G' (return of 0.34) and a 0.05 selectivity performance from the revaluation of securities in the portfolio to reach G''. Then a total (timing plus selectivity) investment performance of an incremental 9 percent can be achieved without sacrificing one activity for another.

---

[5]Michael C. Jensen, "The Performance of Mutual Funds in the Period 1945–1964," *Journal of Finance*, May 1968, pp. 389–416.

Similar conflicts of interest can be resolved with the index futures contract even when fund managers are being passive with respect to market timing. For example, stock index futures can be used if the research analysts are currently finding that most of the undervalued securities are low-beta stocks such that an optimal portfolio of these stocks would have a beta of 0.4, whereas the stated objectives of the fund are more consistent with a portfolio having a beta of 0.8. In the absence of special information about general market movements, it is the obligation of the investment manager to select a portfolio with a constraint that the beta be equal to the target level. This is crucial to fund clients who have other wealth invested elsewhere and are making an optimal personal account portfolio decision based on the manager's adherence to stated objectives concerning risk. Rather than forgo selectivity profits by selling some low-beta undervalued stocks and buying high-beta correctly priced stocks to achieve a portfolio beta of 0.8, the manager can buy stock index futures contracts to lever up the underlying stocks and maintain the gains to selectivity performance. In Figure 21–1 this is illustrated by levering portfolio L to obtain point P. If the manager is correct about the individual security events, in a bull market point P'' will result.

Another interesting portfolio strategy that is not readily attainable without index futures contracts involves taking maximum advantage of bear market forecasts. In principle, a bear market forecast is usually implemented by selling high-beta stocks and purchasing low-beta stocks. As noted before, this may involve giving up positive selectivity performance. But more interestingly, the strategy is limited by the lack of negative beta stocks available and is only considered a loss-minimizing strategy. This is illustrated by the rule of thumb of selling stocks and buying Treasury securities with a zero beta in anticipation of a bear stock market. This is equivalent to selecting point r in Figure 21–2 and giving up any expected positive selectivity performance. However, being able to construct portfolio S with a beta of -0.5 will result in an outcome of S' in a bear market, and if this can be done by selling index futures and holding undervalued portfolio P, then the final outcome of the strategy will be point S'', with the selectivity performance of 0.05 still intact. The additional market timing performance will be 0.52 [$= (-0.5 - 0.8)(-0.2 - 0.2)$] for a bear market of -0.2. This is a total investment performance of 57 percent *above* the performance required to compensate investors for risk bearing.

PORTFOLIO OPPORTUNITIES WITH STOCK INDEX FUTURES

In an article by Figlewski and Kon the pricing and risk-return properties of the index futures contract are analyzed by considering a portfolio of cash holdings of an index fund and enough sales of the index futures contracts to eliminate all risk.[6] A riskless portfolio must earn the rate of return that exists for other risk-free assets, such as Treasury bills. Otherwise, arbitrageurs will step in and engage in a strategy to earn riskless returns above the riskless rate. This will bid the prices in the cash and futures markets to values at which there are no further arbitrage opportunities. At this point the pricing relations will hold.

An investor holding the index portfolio can lock in a future value by *selling* stock index futures and *transferring* the full risk of fluctuations in the market to the buyer, who requires compensation for risk bearing. It is clear from the security market line in Figure 21–1 and Equation (21–1) that for the market index with a $\beta_M = 1.0$, the risk premium required is $E(R_M) - r$. Therefore, given a specific stock portfolio, the change in expected portfolio return for an incremental long position in the index future is:

$$E(R_F) = E(R_M) - r \qquad (21\text{–}4)$$

For example, if an investment manager is currently holding portfolio P in Figure 21–1 on the security market line and is forecasting a bull market, he can attain point G without selling any of his undervalued stocks by buying index futures contracts. If the manager is forecasting a bear market, point S in Figure 21–2 can be attained by selling enough index futures contracts. Since the risk premium on the index futures return is the same as the

---

[6]Stephen Figlewski and Stanley J. Kon, "Portfolio Management with Stock Index Futures."

slope of the security market line, all points on the line are obtainable with positions in the index futures from any cash market position. Furthermore, since all fluctuations in the index are being transferred from the seller to the buyer of the index futures contract, the variance of the index futures' return (σ_F^2) is the same as that of the market (σ_M^2),

$$\sigma_F^2 = \sigma_M^2; \tag{21–5}$$

the beta of the index futures return (β_F) is the same as the cash market index return (β_M),

$$\beta_F = \beta_M = 1.0; \tag{21–6}$$

and the covariance of the return on any stock portfolio J (R_J) with the index futures' return (R_F) is the same as that with the index itself,

$$Cov(R_J, R_M) = Cov(R_J, R_F) \tag{21–7}$$

Since there is no initial investment in an index futures contract, the rate of return on a futures position can only be measured relative to the cash value of a specific stock portfolio.[7] A convenient standardization is to measure the stock portfolio value and the position in the index futures market in index units based on the current value of the index. Therefore, define N_J as the number of index units in the given stock portfolio J. This is the current market value of portfolio J divided by the current value of the index. Define N_F as the number of index units sold short in the index futures market. N_F will be negative for long positions in the index futures market. Then,

$$h = N_F/N_J \tag{21–8}$$

is the hedge ratio, which can be varied to obtain an entire set of portfolio risk-return combinations with the following characteristics.

---

[7]For index futures the margin requirement is essentially a modest collateral requirement that can be satisifed with a portion of the portfolio's existing assets (e.g., with Treasury bills). Since there is no reduction in the return from the collateral asset, the margin requirement for index futures does not represent any additional cash outlay.

The portfolio consisting of stock portfolio J and hedge position h in the index future has an expected return of

$$E(R) = E(R_J) - hE(R_F), \qquad (21\text{--}9)$$

variance of return of

$$\begin{aligned} \sigma^2 &= \sigma_J^2 + h^2\sigma_F^2 - 2hCov(R_J, R_F) \\ &= \sigma_J^2 + h^2\sigma_M^2 - 2hCov(R_J, R_M), \end{aligned} \qquad (21\text{--}10)$$

and portfolio systematic risk of

$$\begin{aligned} \beta &= \beta_J - h\beta_F \\ &= \beta_J - h \end{aligned} \qquad (21\text{--}11)$$

Now we can see how the choice of hedge ratio affects the β of the portfolio of stocks and index futures. If h is selected to equal β_J, then the portfolio $\beta = 0$ and all market risk is hedged away and only nonmarket (diversifiable) risk remains. Recall that ex post returns can be described by Equation (21–2):

$$R = r + \beta(R_M - r) + \epsilon$$

Hence a portfolio with $\beta = 0$ will have returns equal to the riskless rate plus deviations due solely to firm-specific events. Therefore, an investor who believes that a mutual fund contains a positive $E(\epsilon)$, but does not want to incur the fund's level of systematic risk, can hedge the market risk away by selecting a hedge ratio equal to the beta of the fund and keep the expected positive selectivity performance. The variance of the return process in Equation (21–2) is

$$\sigma^2 = \beta^2\sigma_M^2 + \sigma_\epsilon^2 \qquad (21\text{--}12)$$

so that only the last term associated with firm-specific risk is left when all market risk is hedged away ($\beta = 0$). The important result here is that market risk can be controlled *independently* of the firm-specific return and risk. If the manager in our earlier example, with stock portfolio P in Figure 21–1 with a beta of 0.8, wants to lever up to a β of 1.2 in anticipation of a bull market and keep his undervalued stocks, he can do so by purchasing enough futures contracts to make $h = -0.4$. From Equation (21–8), the number of index units in the futures market to be purchased would be $N_F = hN_J = (-0.4)(100 \text{ million}/165) = 242,424.2424,$

where 165 is the current value of the S&P 500 index. This means that if the futures price for delivery of an index unit in one year is 170, then the manager wants to purchase $(242,424.2424)(170) = \$41,212,121.21$ worth. Since futures contracts in the S&P 500 index sell for 500 times the futures price, this requires a purchase of $41,212,121.21/(500 \times 170) = 484.85$, or approximately 485 contracts. Then, from Equation (21–11) the final portfolio will have a $\beta = 0.8 - (-0.4) = 1.2$.

If the investment manager is predicting a bear market and wants to create a final portfolio with a beta of -0.5, as in point S of Figure 21–2, while preserving the firm-specific ϵ, he can sell enough index futures contracts to make the hedge ratio equal to 1.3. Then, from Equation (21–11) the market risk exposure will be $\beta = -0.5 = 0.8 - 1.3$. The number of index units in the futures market to be sold to achieve a portfolio β of -0.5 is $N_F = hN_J = 1.3(100 \text{ million}/165) = 787,878.78$. This is implemented by selling $N_F/500$, which is approximately 1,576 index futures contracts.

OPTIMAL INDEX FUTURES POSITION FOR A PENSION OR TRUST FUND

In the previous sections of this chapter we have discussed performance measurement and optimal index futures positions when the relevant measure of portfolio risk is the systematic, or beta, risk of the managed portfolio. This is appropriate for the many cases in which the investors in the fund only allocate a relatively small proportion of their wealth to the managed fund. If these investors are well diversified on personal account, then the beta concept of relative contribution to the variance of total portfolio returns is a reasonable approximation. This is frequently the case for mutual fund shareholders. However, in many cases an individual's entire wealth is being managed by one investment adviser. Pension funds, trusts for widows and orphans, and personal investors are some possible examples. Then variance or standard deviation of portfolio returns is the relevant measure of risk.

This problem has been explored by Figlewski and Kon and will be elaborated on here.[8] The ray rA in Figure 21–3 is the capital market line (CML), which represents all efficient portfolio opportunities as perceived by the consensus of all investors. The consensus views portfolio P as inefficient, with an expected value of returns to firm-specific events of zero. However, our superior skilled investment manager believes that this portfolio is undervalued and has an expected return on firm-specific events of 10 percent. He has considerable confidence in his prediction, so that his assessment of the firm-specific standard deviation is about one half that of the consensus. Hence the manager's view of the risk-return dimensions of this portfolio is represented by P' in Figure 21–3. In the absence of an index futures market, the manager would select a point on ray rB that is consistent with the investors' risk preferences. For example, portfolio R' is preferred to the passive strategy denoted by R at the same level of target risk, σ_R.

Now we can introduce the opportunities that would be available by making the index futures contract available. The curve GH represents the portfolio opportunities of combining stock portfolio P' and the index futures contract. This curve is defined by Equations (21–9) and (21–10) for various choices of the hedge ratio h where the parameters described by portfolio J are replaced by the manager's assessment of P'. At point $P'h = 0$ with no position in the index futures contract. At the point where $h = \beta_P = \beta_P'$, all market risk is hedged away and the expected return to that strategy, r', is equal to the riskless rate plus the return that the fund manager expects on firm-specific events. That is, the distance r to r' represents $E(\epsilon)$, the Jensen measure of expected selectivity performance, discussed earlier. Then points along ray rC are obtainable by combinations of the riskless asset, portfolio P', and a position in the index futures market to hedge away all the market risk in P'. Clearly, these opportunities dominate those along ray rB without a position in the index futures contract. This

[8]Stephen Figlewski and Stanley J. Kon, "Portfolio Management with Stock Index Futures."

FIGURE 21–3

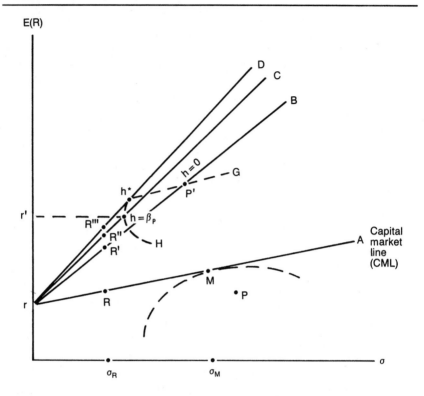

is illustrated by R'' with its dominance of more return than R' at the same level of target risk. However, the most efficient set of opportunities requires the solution to an optimal hedge ratio h^* on the positively sloped segment of the opportunity set offered by P' and positions in the index future. This dominant efficient set as perceived by the fund manager is ray rD. Combinations of the riskless asset, stock portfolio P', and hedge position h^* in the futures contract can be used to construct any portfolio along ray rD, including the preferred risk position in which R''' dominates all others at the target risk level.

If there are restrictions on borrowing at the riskless rate and investing the proceeds in portfolio P', then the perceived efficient frontier becomes the portfolio opportunities along $rh^*P'G$. Portfolios along the segment from r to h^* involve the optimal hedge position in the futures market with portfolio P' and lending at the riskless rate. Portfolios along the curve from h^* to G involve combinations of portfolio P' and a hedge position in the index futures contract with h less than h^*.

The optimal h^* is obtained by selecting the value of h that maximizes the "Sharpe measure" of investment performance.[9] That is,

$$\text{Max } \theta = [E(R) - r]/\sigma$$
$$= \frac{[E(R_{P'}) - hE(R_F) - r]}{[\sigma_{P'}^2 + h^2\sigma_F^2 - 2hCov(R_P, R_F)]^{1/2}} \qquad (21\text{--}13)$$

By taking the derivative of θ with respect to h and setting it equal to zero, we have the optimality condition. Then solving for h yields

$$h^* = \beta_P - [\sigma_\epsilon^2/E(\epsilon)][(E(R_M) - r)/\sigma_M^2] \qquad (21\text{--}14)$$

Note that as the manager's assessment of selectivity performance, $E(\epsilon)$, increases, h^* increases toward the fully hedged against the market position, $h = \beta_P$. This occurs because the curve HG moves up the graph. When the manager is more confident about his forecast, σ_ϵ decreases and the curve moves to the left, so that the optimal solution h^* also moves toward $h = \beta_P$. If the manager is less confident about his forecast or if he perceives less selectivity performance, then h^* will decrease toward G. Note that Equation (21–14) is only appropriate for positive values of expected selectivity performance. The optimal portfolio decision in the absence of special information concerning individual stock prices is along the capital market line (i.e., portfolio R).

---

[9]William F. Sharpe, "Mutual Fund Performance," *Journal of Business,* Supplement, January 1966, pp. 119–38.

CHAPTER 22

CONTROLLING FOR VARIATION MARGIN RISK IN STOCK INDEX FUTURES

Bruce D. Fielitz, Ph.D.
Research Professor of Finance
Georgia State University

Gerald D. Gay, Ph.D.
Associate Professor of Finance
Georgia State University

When participants in the equity futures markets consider initiating investment or hedging programs, attention must be given to the important institutional requirement of daily resettlement or marking-to-market. While initial margin deposits with a futures broker may be in the form of cash, interest-bearing securities, or letters of credit, subsequent gains or losses in the futures position must be settled on a daily basis in cash. The requirement for daily resettlement payments (known as *variation margin*) raises the strong possibility that both long or short positions in the futures market may generate sizable negative cash flows. This can happen even for successful hedge programs, because changes in the value of the underlying equity portfolio are typically on paper only and may not immediately generate the cash flows necessary for meeting margin calls. In such a situation an equity manager runs the risk of having to liquidate a portion of the equity portfolio to satisfy daily resettlement to the detriment of the overall investment strategy.

There is a need for the establishment of a liquidity maintenance program that is consistent with management's risk tolerances and that will allow flexibility in dealing with potential variation margin cash flows. The purpose of this chapter is to provide users of stock index futures contracts with an analytical model for assessing and monitoring their potential funds or liquidity needs during the implementation of index futures trading or hedging programs. First, we briefly review some of the many uses of stock index futures in portfolio management and describe the important relationship that daily resettlement will have in conjunction with these strategies. We then present a model that provides investors with the necessary liquidity requirements to maintain, given the probability they are willing to accept exhausting the liquidity pool, and given their portfolio's size, investment horizon, and risk (beta). The model is adapted to each of the four major stock index futures contracts, namely, the S&P 500, Value Line, NYSE, and Major Market contracts.[1] Next, we present an actual application of the model and illustrate its effectiveness in coping with the serious market decline of September 1986. The final section provides some concluding remarks.

POTENTIAL USES

Several considerations motivate investors to use equity futures contracts. First, an investor with a demonstrated ability in market timing may short futures contracts to reduce the downside risk of an equity portfolio in a declining market environment. He may also take long positions in a rising market to allow for upside gains. A second strategy, related to the first but different enough to warrant separate consideration, is the employment of stock index futures to aid in the asset allocation decision. Managers of large equity portfolios often find that price pressures associated

---

[1]For a review of these contracts and their performance characteristics, see Chapters 3 and 7, respectively.

with moving large blocks of stocks increase the difficulties of quickly implementing decisions to change the cash-stock mix of their portfolios. The use of stock index futures allows for virtually instantaneous implementation of asset allocation decisions regarding the cash-stock mix.

Also, the use of stock index futures can aid in the preservation of positive alphas associated with superior security selection decisions, regardless of the movements of the general market. With the aid of a stock index futures hedging program, an investor can neutralize portfolio return variability (beta risk) associated with day-to-day gyrations of the market, and, at the same time, preserve the positive impact on portfolio return of a security selection process that outperforms the market on a risk-adjusted basis.

The above discussion of potential strategies involving stock index futures is by no means exhaustive, but is sufficient to provide background for the topic of this chapter.

A LIQUIDITY MODEL

A recent article presents a model for determination of the size of the liquidity pool necessary to preserve a futures commitment.[2] The key ingredients of the model are: (1) time, (2), the size of the portfolio, and (3) the probability the investor is willing to accept that the liquidity pool may be exhausted (called the *probability of exhaustion*). More specifically, the probability of exhausting a given liquidity pool associated with meeting variation margin requirements when using stock index futures contracts is given by the expression[3]

---

[2]Bruce D. Fielitz and Gerald D. Gay, "Managing Cash Flow Risks in Stock Index Futures," *The Journal of Portfolio Management,* Winter 1986, pp. 74–78. The theoretical development of this model is presented in Robert G. Kolb, Gerald D. Gay, and William Hunter, "Liquidity Requirements for Financial Futures Investments," *Financial Analysts Journal,* May/June 1985, pp. 60–68.

[3]When applying the following expressions to situations involving the Major Market Index contract, one should use 250 instead of 500 wherever it appears.

TABLE 22–1
Daily Price Change Statistics for Various Stock Index Futures Contracts*

Contract	Exchange	Average Change	Standard Deviation
S&P 500	CME	.087	2.488
NYSE composite	NYFE	.045	1.438
KCVL composite	KCBT	.148	2.339
Major Market	CBOT	.108	3.133

*Data taken from prices of nearby contract during June 1 to August 31, 1986.

Probability of exhaustion $= 2\{1 - N(X/[S \times 500 \times \sqrt{T}])\}$:
where

$X =$ The dollar amount of the liquidity pool required to satisfy the probability of exhaustion criterion for one
contract[4]

$S =$ The standard deviation of the stock index futures daily
price changes

$T =$ The number of trading days in the investment or hedging horizon

$N(\ ) =$ The cumulative distribution function for a standard normal variate

A key input for implementation of the above model is the standard deviation of the stock index futures daily price changes (S). Table 22–1 presents data regarding recent historical values for the nearby contracts of the four stock index futures contracts mentioned above.

Once an estimate of the standard deviation of the stock index futures daily price changes is available, application of the above model is straightforward. To illustrate, assume a pension fund money manager wishes to hedge a $30 million account against potential downside market risk for an arbitrarily selected 20 trading day period when the S&P 500 stock index futures index is at a level of 240. The manager estimates that the standard deviation

---

[4]To determine the probability of exhaustion for a multiple contract position in the futures market, simply divide X in the above expression by the number of contracts.

of daily closing prices for the S&P 500 futures index is currently 2.5 and wishes to maintain a liquidity pool such that there is a 95 percent probability that it will be large enough to satisfy potential variation margin calls over the 20-day period (this means that the probability of exhaustion is 5 percent or .05). The arithmetic proceeds as follows.

Let

$$.05 = 2\{1 - N(X/[S \times 500 \times \sqrt{T}])\}$$

Then

$$.025 = 1 - N(X/[S \times 500 \times \sqrt{T}])$$

So that

$$N(X/[S \times 500 \times \sqrt{T}]) = .975$$

The normal deviate associated with a cumulative normal distribution value of .975 is 1.96; this value is obtained from a cumulative normal distribution table available in any introductory statistics textbook. (For example, if the desired probability of exhaustion is .01, the cumulative normal distribution value would be .99 and the associated normal deviate would be 2.576).

Thus,

$$X/[S \times 500 \times \sqrt{T}] = 1.96$$

and

$$X = 1.96 \times S \times 500 \times \sqrt{T}.$$

Recall that X is the dollar amount of the liquidity pool required to satisfy the probability of exhaustion criterion (in this case .05) for one contract.

Now let $X(m)$ be the dollar amount associated with multiple contracts given by X times M, where $M = A/$(Futures index $\times$ 500) and $A = $ the total dollar value of the available investment funds. Thus, $X(m)/A$ will equal the proportion of the total available funds that should be committed to the liquidity pool.

Continuing with the arithmetic:

$$X(m)/A = (X \text{ times } M)/A$$
$$= (X \text{ times } [A/(\text{Futures index} \times 500)])/A$$

$$= X/(\text{Futures index} \times 500)$$
$$= (1.96 \times S \times 500 \times \sqrt{T})/(\text{Futures index} \times 500)$$
$$= (1.96 \times S \times \sqrt{T})/\text{Futures index}.$$

For the assumptions given above:

$$X(m)/A = (1.96 \times 2.5 \times \sqrt{20})/240 = .091$$

or:

$$X(m) = .091 \times \$30,000,000 = \$2,730,000.$$

The above model is applicable to all four of the most popular stock index futures contracts. Moreover, assumptions regarding the probability of exhaustion, time horizon, futures index level, and standard deviation can be altered as needed depending on current market conditions and user specific parameters.

Figures 22–1, 22–2, and 22–3 present results of the above calculation procedure tailored to S&P 500, NYSE, and Major Mar-

FIGURE 22–1
S&P 500 Futures Index: Horizon 20 Days (exhaustion probability = .05)

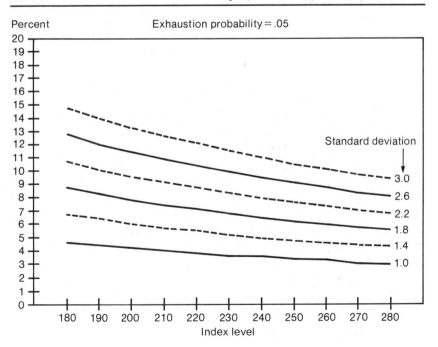

FIGURE 22–2
NYSE Futures Index: Horizon 20 Days (exhaustion probability = .05)

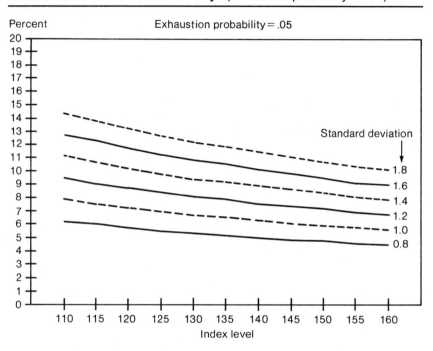

ket contracts. The results in Figure 22–1 are also applicable to the Value Line contract given that its index levels and standard deviation characteristics would fall within the same levels as presented for the S&P 500 contracts. The graphs show the percent of total available funds needed for a liquidity pool when an exhaustion probability of .05 and a 20 trading day horizon are assumed. Differing volatility and index level assumptions for the various contracts are also made. Consider, for example, Figure 22–2 describing the liquidity model as applied to futures contracts on the Major Market Index. If the standard deviation of daily changes in the futures index is 3.2, then Figure 22–3 shows that the liquidity pool should be 9.7 percent of total available funds given that the underlying index level is near 290. Similarly, a liquidity pool of 8.2 percent of available funds is needed if the underlying index is at 340, and so on. Graphs similar to the ones

FIGURE 22–3
Major Market Futures Index: Horizon 20 Days (exhaustion probability = .05)

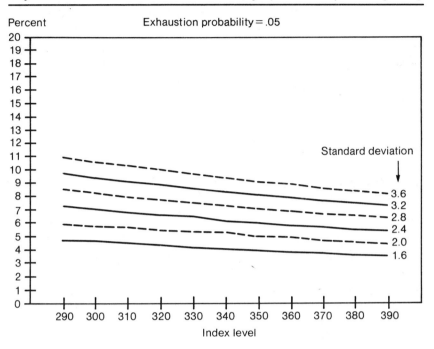

shown here can, of course, easily be constructed for different assumptions.

Interpretation of the results given by the liquidity model can be summarized as follows. First, while Figures 22–1, 22–2, and 22–3 only illustrate the procedure for an exhaustion probability of .05, common sense (confirmed by mathematical calculation) suggests that relaxation of an acceptable probability of exhaustion results in a lower proportion of total funds required for the liquidity pool, all other variables held constant. Second, these graphs confirm that for a given probability of exhaustion and a given level of the futures index, the higher the volatility of the futures index, the higher the proportion of available funds that needs to be committed to the liquidity pool to maintain the given probability of exhaustion. Finally, a lower proportion of available funds is needed for the liquidity pool as the level of the futures index increases, for a given probability of exhaustion and level of volatility. This is because the standard deviation is stated in terms of the index level itself. Thus, a standard deviation of 1.6 for the futures index when the index is at 100 represents twice as much volatility as a standard deviation of 1.6 associated with an index of 200.

We have chosen to present the graphs in terms of a 20-day trading horizon, which is consistent with a monthly hedging operation. Liquidity pools for shorter or longer periods are easily derived via the previously illustrated arithmetic. In our opinion, however, establishing liquidity pools commensurate with a monthly hedging program allows adequate response time for flexible adjustments to liquidity requirements in succeeding periods via equity security sales or purchases, dividend receipts, and futures gains and losses. Too short a period may provide flexibility difficulties, and too long a period may allow estimation errors to become significant.

An implicit but important assumption reflected in Figures 22–1, 22–2, and 22–3 is that the underlying equity portfolio being hedged is of average market risk, or that its beta is near 1.0. The values in these graphs can be adjusted to portfolios of other risk levels simply by multiplying them by the actual portfolio beta. Thus, for example, if the equity portfolio for our earlier example had a beta equal to .8, the appropriate size of the liquidity pool is .8 × .091 × $30,000,000 = $2,184,000.

The key input variables for the above model are the probability of exhaustion, time, and the standard deviation. The proper method for estimation of the standard deviation requires additional research, but calculations based on a moving window of time series data should be sufficient for most purposes. Values for the probability of exhaustion and time are a function of the money manager's style, the desire for trading flexibility regarding the underlying equity portfolio, the client relationship regarding risk/return tradeoff opportunities, and marketability of the underlying equity securities.

Needless to say, the conditions surrounding determination of an optimal probability of exhaustion and time are complex considerations that are difficult to resolve. In fact, they may never be fully resolvable in a quantitative sense for every conceivable set of circumstances. However, the example problem considered next should provide useful insights into the issue involving determination of the proper exhaustion probability.

AN ILLUSTRATION

Consider a variation of the second strategy described earlier for using futures contracts. At the end of August 1986, a money manager is hired by a large pension fund to manage a $50 million portion of the total fund. As is customary when one manager is hired and another fired, the new manager receives managerial custody of the security positions established by the old manager on behalf of the pension fund, not cash. The new manager's investment style is different from that of the old manager, and it is doubtful that many, if any, of the securities inherited from the old manager will be retained by the new manager. Because of the size of the positions in the inherited portfolio, it will take some time for the new manager to liquidate the holdings without putting substantial price pressure on the securities. Likewise, once the sales are accomplished, additional time will be required to obtain the desired holdings in the new manager's favorite stocks. In the meantime, the new manager is very bullish on the stock market, and wants to participate fully in the up market he expects to continue for the immediate future. He knows it is important to perform quickly regarding the new account, so he decides to commit to a $50 million stock market exposure via S&P 500 futures contracts. The new manager must determine what size of liquidity is needed over the next month so that an orderly liquidation and acquisition program can proceed for the new account.

On August 29, 1986, the S&P 500 December Futures Index closed at 254.35. (Because of the potential for pricing irregularities, we recommend avoiding the nearby contract when it enters its expiration month). To obtain a $50 million exposure to the market, 393 S&P 500 stock index futures contracts are required ($50,000,000/(254.35 × 500)). Obviously, over the next month as various stocks are sold and purchased in the portfolio restructuring program, varying amounts of cash may be available for variation margin requirements. But the manager does not wish to use these funds for this purpose because it involves different transfer agents and custodians than the pension fund normally utilizes. Also, as new positions in the desired securities are established, portions of the $50 million equity market exposure can be eliminated. However, this latter circumstance does not alter the basic nature of the problem; the same proportion of the total dollar commitment to futures must be held in a liquidity pool consistent with a desired exhaustion probability. The actual dollar amount of the pool will decrease as the dollar amount to be hedged decreases, but the proportion will not.

To virtually minimize the chance of exhausting the liquidity pool in the period of transition between money managers, the new manager decides on an exhaustion probability of .01. The manager must then decide on an appropriate level of volatility that he expects the market to experience. Figure 22–4 shows the volatility of the S&P 500 nearby stock index futures contract since its inception in April 1982. (The volatility calculations assume the above mentioned convention of using the next contract prices when the nearby contract enters its expiration month.) The standard deviations reflect a rolling 21-day window (21 days is a slightly more accurate approximation to a trading month than the 20-day assumption employed earlier). Figure 22–4 also shows a three-month moving average of the 21-day standard deviation calculations. To be conservative, the money manager decides to use the higher of the most recent 21-day standard deviation or three-month moving average. As of 8/29/86 the rolling 21-day standard deviation is 1.86, while the three-month moving average is 2.54.

The calculations in the liquidity model are as follows:

$$X(m)/A = (2.576 \times 2.54 \times \sqrt{21})/254.35 = .1179$$

Thus $X(m) = .1179 \times \$50,000,000 = \$5,895,000$ is required in the liquidity pool.[5]

---

[5]We wish to emphasize that the liquidity pool only provides for potential variation margin calls. The dollar commitment in the liquidity pool is in addition to the dollar commitment necessary for initial margin requirements.

FIGURE 22–4
Standard Deviation (Daily) of S&P 500 Futures Index
(rolling 21 days: 5/24/82–8/29/86)

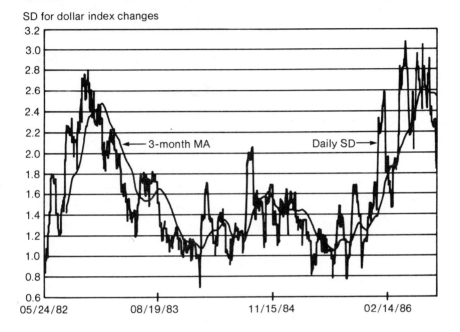

SD for dollar index changes

As noted earlier, 393 contracts are required to establish a $50 million stock equivalent position when the futures index is at 254.35. Ignoring financing and investment aspects with regard to liquidity pool balances, we can easily determine what downside move in the futures market is required to wipe out the liquidity pool cushion by solving for S&P(t) in the following manner:

$$254.35 \times 500 \times 393 - \text{S\&P}(t) \times 500 \times 393 = 5{,}895{,}000$$
$$\text{S\&P}(t) = 224.35.$$

Thus, the S&P 500 futures index would have to fall from 254.35 to 224.35 before the liquidity pool would be exhausted. This represents a price change of 11.79 percent, or precisely the liquidity

TABLE 22–2
Illustration of Application of Futures Liquidity Model

Date	S&P 500 Futures Contract Price	Daily Futures Price Change	Change In Futures Position ($)*	Value of Liquidity Pool†— Exhaustion Probabilities	
				.01	.05
08/29/86	254.35			$5,895,000	$4,500,000
09/02/86	249.40	- 4.95	$(972,675)	4,925,705	3,529,905
09/03/86	252.35	2.95	579,675	5,506,086	4,110,086
09/04/86	255.90	3.55	697,575	6,204,450	4,808,250
09/05/86	251.45	- 4.45	(874,425)	5,330,914	3,934,514
09/08/86	250.45	- 1.00	(196,500)	5,136,707	3,739,706
09/09/86	249.60	- 0.85	(167,025)	4,970,418	3,573,217
09/10/86	248.65	- 0.95	(186,675)	4,784,455	3,387,054
09/11/86	234.90	- 13.75	(2,701,875)	2,083,266	685,665
09/12/86	229.70	- 5.20	(1,021,800)	1,061,765	(336,037)
09/15/86	231.15	1.45	284,925	1,347,146	(51,256)
09/16/86	230.85	- 0.30	(58,950)	1,288,389	(110,214)
09/17/86	230.35	- 0.50	(98,250)	1,190,324	(208,480)
09/18/86	230.95	0.60	117,900	1,308,395	(90,609)
09/19/86	230.50	- 0.45	(88,425)	1,220,157	(179,047)
09/22/86	234.60	4.10	805,650	2,026,332	626,526
09/23/86	236.60	2.00	393,000	2,419,622	1,019,615
09/24/86	235.90	- 0.70	(137,550)	2,282,419	882,211
09/25/86	231.35	- 4.55	(894,075)	1,388,671	(11,737)
09/26/86	231.95	0.60	117,900	1,506,770	106,161
09/29/86	229.55	- 2.40	(471,600)	1,035,386	(365,424)
09/30/86	230.60	1.05	206,325	1,241,860	(159,151)

*The assumed futures position is for 393 contracts.
†Column figures reflect accumulating interest on pool balances.

proportion suggested by the above model with an exhaustion probability set at .01.

Table 22–2 shows the daily performance of the liquidity pool over the month of September 1986. Interest is assumed earned overnight on the previous day's pool balance.[6] The data in Table 22–2 show that in spite of the severe market decline on September 11 and 12, 1986, the liquidity pool was sufficient to avoid variation margin calls during the entire period for a probability of exhaustion of .01.

The last column in Table 22–2 repeats the above exercise using an exhaustion probability of .05 in contrast to the .01 analysis described previously. The analysis shows that the derived liquidity pool of $4,500,000 would not have been sufficient to protect against variation margin calls in the down market of September 1986.

The above examples illustrate the effectiveness of the liquidity model in providing for variation margin cash flow requirements during one of the most dramatic short-term market declines in recent years. Under more normal market conditions there will be a direct relationship between the selected probability of exhaustion and the expected frequency of liquidity pool depletion. For example, for a probability of exhaustion of .01, one would expect to exhaust the liquidity pool in approximately 1 out of 100 applications of this model whereas for a probability of exhaustion of .05 this would expect to happen in 1 out of 20 applications.

SUMMARY

Based on assumptions regarding the probability of exhaustion, the volatility of the futures markets, portfolio risk (beta), and a selected trading period, the model presented in this chapter allows a prospective user of the equity markets to compute the needed liquidity pool for maintaining a futures position. The tech-

---

[6]In the example we have used the prevailing T-bill rate adjusted to a daily basis. A more realistic assumption would be to perhaps use the overnight broker loan rate.

nique allows the money manager to begin consideration of futures hedging or investment programs with some notion of the liquidity requirements associated with such programs. As investment and hedging programs involving stock index futures continue to gain in popularity and use, a model such as the one discussed here should be helpful in determining the proportion of an investment portfolio which should be committed to the liquidity pool.

CHAPTER 23

INVESTMENT OPPORTUNITIES USING VALUE LINE FUTURES

Robert D. Arnott
President and Chief Investment Officer
First Quadrant Corporation

Roger G. Clarke, Ph.D.
Managing Partner and Chief Investment Officer
TSA Capital Management

Since the inception of trading in the Value Line futures contract, there has been a persistent pattern of mispricing. This may be attributed to a fundamental misunderstanding of the nature of the Value Line index. The Value Line index is an equal-weighted geometric index of some 1,700 issues. As such, it has two attributes that have important implications for the performance of the index. First, it has a pronounced small stock bias: While it covers most NYSE & ASE issues, just as much weight is given to Action Industries and Kennametal as is given to IBM and Exxon. The second key attribute is the fact that it is a geometric index, which behaves very differently from any arithmetic indexes.

In terms of composition, 46 percent of the S&P universe has market value greater than $2 billion, versus 17 percent for the Value Line universe. On the small market value side, 56 percent of the Value Line companies are below $500 million and only 15 percent for the S&P. Table 23–1 shows the distribution of market values for both indexes.

TABLE 23–1
Distribution of Market Values

Market Value ($000,000)	Percent of S&P Companies	Percent of Value Line Companies
Less than 500	14.6	56.3
500–900	16.2	15.6
1,000–1,999	23.2	11.3
2,000–4,999	28.0	10.5
5,000–9,999	10.0	3.4
More than 10,000	8.0	2.9
	100.0	100.0

Source: Paine Webber Capital Markets.

THE NATURE OF THE GEOMETRIC INDEX

The best way to understand the implications of a geometric index is to review an example. Suppose there are two stocks in an index, ABC and XYZ. Over the course of a year, ABC rises from 100 to 200, but XYZ drops form 100 to 50. A portfolio with 5,000 shares of each would rise from $1 million to $1.25 million, for a 25 percent rise. The arithmetic index would also rise from 100 to 125, for a 25 percent rise. On the other hand, the geometric index would be unchanged at 100. In this example, the index understates *actual portfolio results* by 25 percent!

In the real world, few stocks double in a year or fall 50 percent in a year. A more typical extra-market standard deviation for stock performance over the course of a year is 25–30 percent. This would correspond to a negative bias in a geometric index of 3.1 percent to 4.5 percent per annum. This means that an equal-weighted portfolio of all Value Line issues *will* outpace the Value Line index *by 3–4 percent each year.*

Perhaps the most telling illustration of the power of this bias can be found by looking at the past 20 years. As an equal-weighted index, Value Line gives as much weight to tiny Action Industries as it gives to IBM and therefore has a pronounced small-stock bias vis-à-vis the S&P 500, or other capitalization-weighted indexes. Thus, the Value Line index should track the behavior of small stocks which have experienced some extraordinary performance in the past 20 years. Yet, from 1965 through 1984, the Value Line index was virtually unchanged relative to the S&P 500. (Indeed, the S&P 500 was slightly stronger.) In the face of several tremendous bull markets in small stocks, this negative bias is most striking.

A FAIR PRICING ARBITRAGE

A futures contract is fairly priced if a portfolio of "risk-free" cash equivalents (Treasury bills) plus stock index futures will match the performance of a direct investment in the stocks in the index. A portfolio of $100 million in Treasury bills plus $100 million worth of S&P 500 futures would forfeit the dividend income earned in stocks, but would earn the higher income available in Treasury bills. With fair pricing, this increased income should be exactly offset by a reduced capital gain on the futures; in other words, the investor should pay a premium price for the futures large enough to offset the higher income available in Treasury bills. In the case of S&P 500 futures, this means that the fair price for a futures contract is defined as:

$$F^{SP} = I^{SP} [1 + (r - d^{SP})] \tag{23-1}$$

where

F^{SP} = Price of the S&P futures contract
I^{SP} = S&P index
r = Treasury bill yield until expiration
d^{SP} = Dividend yield on the S&P 500 until expiration

This pricing mechanism is well understood by arbitrageurs and practitioners in the futures markets. The same mechanism is at work in all stock index futures, *except* for the Value Line futures. For Value Line futures, pricing of the futures contract should reflect the negative bias (B^{VL}) inherent in a geometric index:

$$F^{VL} = I^{VL} [1 + (r - d^{VL}) - B^{VL}] \tag{23-2}$$

Interestingly, the Value Line futures are often priced as if the negative bias inherent in a geometric index did not exist. This provides the investor with some intriguing opportunities as long as this mispricing persists.

Once again, an example is helpful. At the end of September 1985, the S&P 500 futures were priced at 182.80, as compared with an index level of 182.08. This represents a premium to the index level of .40 percent, which is somewhat smaller than the "fair" premium of .88 percent. The Value Line futures were priced at 190.20, a .63 percent premium over the Value Line composite index of 189.01 on that date. This also represents a mispricing vis-à-vis the "fair" premium of .28 percent. Consequently, the S&P future appears to be somewhat overpriced.

Suppose one were to construct a $100 million account consisting of $58,000 invested in each of these 1,700 issues in the Value Line index. Over the subsequent three months, this portfolio would have risen by 15.84 percent including dividends. In contrast, the index rose by 13.68 percent while the future rose by 12.97 percent. If one were to sell $100 million worth of Value Line exposure in the futures market, the return over this period would have been the Treasury bill yield plus the effects of mispricing, or an annualized total return of 11.16 percent compared with the Treasury bill yield of 7.32 percent with no price volatility. Figure 23–1 summarizes these transactions.

To illustrate these results in more detail, consider the following information about returns from September 30, 1985 to December 31, 1985.

	Sept. 30–Dec. 31 Quarterly Return	Estimated Quarterly Dividend Yield	Total Quarterly Return	Total Annualized Return
Portfolio of 1,700 Value Line stocks	15.19	.65	15.84	63.36
Value Line index	13.68		13.68	54.72
December Value Line future	12.97		12.97	51.88
Treasury bill	1.83		1.83	7.32
S&P 500 stocks	16.04	.95	16.99	67.96
December S&P future	15.58		15.58	62.32

FIGURE 23–1
Portfolio Positions to Exploit the Geometric
Index Bias Creating Synthetic Cash

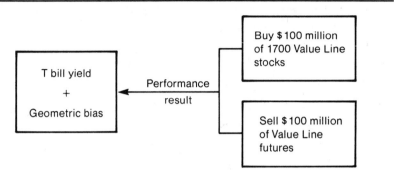

The bias in the geometric effect can be captured by purchasing the portfolio of Value Line stocks and selling an equivalent amount of Value Line futures. The return from this strategy would be:

	Total Quarterly Return	Total Annualized Return
Portfolio of 1,700 Value Line stocks	15.84	63.36
Sell Value Line futures	−12.97	−51.88
Premium adjustments*	−.08	−.32
Total hedge return	2.79	11.16
T bill return	1.83	7.32
Incremental return over T bills	.96	3.84

*The premium adjustment is required to adjust to a common investment base between the initial level of the index and the future. This is noted in more detail in Appendix B.

AN INDEX FUND PLUS ALPHA

Suppose one were to go one step beyond this risk-free arbitrage, and purchase the same exposure in S&P futures, offsetting the short position in Value Line futures. These contracts rose in value by an amount approximately equal to the mispricing in Value Line futures at the start of the quarter plus the mispricing in the S&P 500 future.

To illustrate this effect consider the returns for each of the portfolio components. If the Value Line stocks and a short position in Value Line futures were combined with an equivalent value using contracts in S&P 500 futures, this creates an index fund targeted at the S&P 500 but captures the geometric index bias.

	Total Quarterly Return	Total Annualized Return
Portfolio of 1,700 Value Line stocks	15.84	63.36
Sell December Value Line future	− 12.97	− 51.88
Premium adjustment*	− .08	− .32
Total hedge return	2.79	11.16
Buy December S&P 500 Future	15.58	62.32
Premium adjustment*	.06	0.24
Total portfolio return	18.43	73.72
S&P 500 stocks	16.99	67.96
Incremental return over S&P 500 index	1.44	5.76

*The premium adjustment is required to adjust the futures return to a common investment base between the initial level of the index and the future. See Appendix B.

Notice that the incremental return in the two strategies is a little different. The mispricing of the December S&P 500 future adds a little extra return in the index fund strategy. The net result is an incremental return relative to the S&P 500 slightly more than that achieved relative to the T-bill rate in the arbitrage strategy. Figure 23–2 summarizes these two different positions graphically.

APPLICATIONS

The intriguing thing about this futures mispricing is that is has been consistent since the inception of trading in the Value Line futures. This means that over the past several years it has been

FIGURE 23–2
Portfolio Positions to Exploit the Geometric
Index Bias Creating an Index Fund

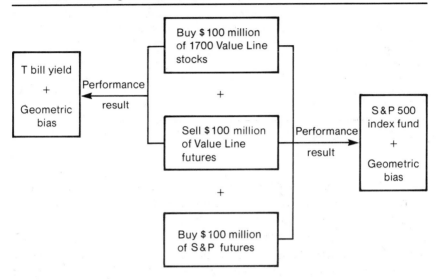

possible to lock in index fund returns with an annual alpha of some 300 basis points simply by using this futures spread between the S&P 500 and the Value Line contracts. Applications of this spread are intriguing:

1. One can construct an index-plus portfolio with a return approximating the S&P 500 stock index plus whatever mispricing exists in the Value Line and S&P futures markets. As long as the Value Line mispricing persists, this can lead to an alpha of some 300–400 basis points.

2. To the extent that a small capitalization bias exists in a portfolio, this bias can be neutralized through a spread between the S&P 500 index and the Value Line index. To the extent that this spread is mispriced and is employed in portfolio management, extra-market performance will be added.

3. A "January effect" in small stock performance has been widely reported in many published articles. Small stocks have historically exhibited a pronounced and consistent tendency to sharply outperform large-capitalization issues virtually every Jan-

TABLE 23–2
January Effect—Short S&P, Long VL

Period	S&P Return (percent)	VL Return (percent)	Spread Profit (in $s)
12/27/82–1/12/83	3.17%	6.07%	$2,586
12/29/83–1/12/84	1.75	3.51	2,220
12/27/84–1/17/85	3.00	5.36	2,936
12/30/85–1/22/86	−3.41	−1.05	1,337
12/19/86–1/14/87	7.92	9.82	2,876

Source: Paine Webber Capital Markets.

uary. If small stocks outperform large stocks by a big enough margin, the natural geometric bias can be overcome and the investor can participate in the January effect using the spread between the futures contracts. For example, by shorting the S&P nearby future and going long an equal dollar amount of nearby Value Line futures near the end of December, a net profit was secured in each of the last five years when the position was closed out in the middle of January. Table 23–2 shows the spread trades assuming a round turn commission of $25 per contract. The Value Line consistently outperformed the S&P in these periods.

4. By neutralizing a small capitalization bias through the use of this spread, a core equity strategy need not have characteristics matching that of the index. A conventional core equity strategy must have holdings in IBM, General Motors, Exxon, and other large issues, whether or not the security selection disciplines suggest that these issues are attractive. If exposure to large issues is provided through the use of a spread, one can focus primary security selection attention on the medium and small capitalization ends of the market, where inefficiencies are likely to be more significant. The resulting small capitalization bias can be neutralized with some additional alpha contributed directly by the spread. In short, to the extent that this mispricing opportunity persists, there is an opportunity which can lead to considerable performance enhancement.

APPENDIX A   GEOMETRIC AND ARITHMETIC INDEXES

The Value Line index is a geometric mean of the performance of some 1,700 issues followed by Value Line. A geometric index is calculated by the formula:

$$\text{Geometric index}_t = C(P_{1t} \cdot P_{2t} \cdot P_{3t} \cdots P_{nt})^{1/n} \qquad \text{(A–1)}$$

where P is stock price and C is a normalizing constant. By implication, the change in the level of the geometric index is:

$$\frac{\text{Geometric index}_{t+1}}{\text{Geometric index}_t} = \left(\frac{P_{1,t+1}}{P_{1,t}} \cdot \frac{P_{2,t+1}}{P_{2,t}} \cdots \frac{P_{n,t+1}}{P_{n,t}} \right)^{1/n} \qquad \text{(A–2)}$$

The most striking attribute of a geometric index is that it will *always* understate the performance of an equal-weighted arithmetic index. This understatement of performance can be rigorously quantified. The change in the level of an equal-weighted arithmetic index can be expressed as:

$$\frac{\text{Arithmetic index}_{t+1}}{\text{Arithmetic index}_t} = \frac{P_{1,t+1} + P_{2,t+1} + \cdots + P_{n,t+1}}{P_{1,t} + P_{2,t} + \cdots + P_{n,t}} \qquad \text{(A–3)}$$

Mathematically, it is impossible for a geometric index to outpace the corresponding arithmetic index:

$$\left(\frac{P_{1,t+1}}{P_{1,t}} \cdot \frac{P_{2,t+1}}{P_{2,t}} \cdots \frac{P_{n,t+1}}{P_{n,t}} \right) = $$
$$k_t \left(\frac{P_{1,t+1} + P_{2,t+1} + \cdots + P_{n,t+1}}{P_{1,t} + P_{2,t} + \cdots + P_{n,t}} \right) \qquad \text{(A–4)}$$

where $k_t \leq 1$ always.

This underperformance can be rigorously quantified. The shortfall is closely approximated by half of the *extra-market* variance of the issues in the index.

$$k_t \approx \frac{1}{2n} \sum_{i=1}^{n} \left(\frac{P_{i,t+1}}{P_{i,t}} - \frac{\text{Arithmetic index}_{t+1}}{\text{Arithmetic index}_t} \right)^2 \qquad \text{(A–5)}$$

To show the accuracy of the formula for the negative bias of the geometric mean, consider the example used in the first section. This example has two stocks with extra-market standard deviation of 75 percent away from the 25 percent mean return. This leads to a 56 percent variance or 28 percent estimated performance understatement as shown below:

$$k \approx \frac{1}{2(2)} [(2.0 - 1.25)^2 + (.50 - 1.25)^2] = .28$$

APPENDIX B   RETURNS USING FUTURES CONTRACTS

Let

VL_t = Value of the 1,700 Value Line stocks in the index at time t
F_t^{VL} = Value of the Value Line future at time t
D_t^{VL} = Dividends on the Value Line stocks at time t

Return on the Value Line Arbitrage Strategy

The return on the strategy of buying the Value Line stocks and selling the Value Line future will be:

$$\begin{aligned}
R &= \frac{VL_1 + D_1^{VL} - VL_0 - (F_1^{VL} - F_0^{VL})}{VL_0} \\
&= \frac{VL_1 + D_1^{VL} - VL_0}{VL_0} - \left(\frac{F_1^{VL} - F_0^{VL}}{F_0^{VL}}\right)\left(\frac{F_0^{VL}}{VL_0}\right) \quad \text{(B–1)} \\
&= R_{Stocks}^{VL} - R_{Futures}^{VL}(1 + P_0^{VL})
\end{aligned}$$

where

$$(1 + P_0^{VL}) = \frac{F_0^{VL}}{VL_0} = (1 + (r - d^{VL}) - B^{VL})$$

and P_0^{VL} is the premium on the Value Line future at the initiation of the position.

Equivalently, by rearranging terms we can write the return as

$$R = \frac{VL_1 + D_1^{VL} - VL_0 - (F_1^{VL} - F_0^{VL})}{VL_0}$$

$$= \frac{D_1{}^{VL} + VL_0\,P_0{}^{VL} + (VL_1 - F_1{}^{VL})}{VL_0} \qquad \text{(B–2)}$$

$$= d^{VL} + P_0{}^{VL} + (R_{Stocks}^{VLC} - R_{Index}^{VL})$$

$$= r - B^{VL} + (R_{Stocks}^{VLC} - R_{Index}^{VL}),$$

where

R_{Stocks}^{VLC} = Return from capital appreciation on the Value Line stocks

R_{Index}^{VL} = Return on the Value Line index

r = Return on the T bill

B^{VL} $= r - d^{VL} - P_0{}^{VL}$

     = Apparent mispricing in the fair value of the Value Line future

Equation (B–2) indicates that the return from the strategy will be equal to the return on the T bill if the apparent mispricing is equal to the actual bias which results from the construction of the geometric index relative to the stock portfolio.

Return on Combined VL and S&P 500 Strategy

The return on the strategy of buying the Value Line stocks, selling the Value Line future and buying an equivalent dollar amount of the S&P future will be:

$$R = \frac{VL_1 + D_1{}^{VL} - VL_0 - (F_1{}^{VL} - F_0{}^{VL}) + \left(\dfrac{VL_0}{SP_0}\right)\left(F_1{}^{SP} - F_0{}^{SP}\right)}{VL_0}$$

$$= \frac{VL_1 + D_1{}^{VL} - VL_0}{VL_0} - \left(\frac{F_1{}^{VL} - F_0{}^{VL}}{F_0{}^{VL}}\right)\left(\frac{F_0{}^{VL}}{VL_0}\right)$$

$$+ \left(\frac{F_1{}^{SP} - F_0{}^{SP}}{F_0{}^{SP}}\right)\left(\frac{F_0{}^{SP}}{SP_0}\right) \qquad \text{(B–3)}$$

$$= R_{Stocks}^{VL} - R_{Future}^{VL}(1 + P_0{}^{VL}) + R_{Future}^{SP}(1 + P_0{}^{SP})$$

Using the relationships from Equations (B–1) and (B–2) we can write (B–3) as

$$R = r - B^{VL} + (R_{Stocks}^{VLC} - R_{Index}^{VL}) + (R_{Stocks}^{SP} - r) \qquad \text{(B–4)}$$

$$= R_{Stocks}^{SP} - B^{VL} + (R_{Stocks}^{VLC} - R_{Index}^{VL})$$

where

$$F^{SP}_t = \text{Value of the S\&P future at time } t$$
$$SP_t = \text{Value of the S\&P stocks and index at time } t$$
$$R^{SP}_{Stocks} = \text{Return on the S\&P stocks}$$
$$R^{SP}_{Future} = \text{Initial premium on the S\&P future}$$

The final result indicates that the return on the Value Line basket of stocks with the spread in futures contracts yields an S&P return plus any incremental return from the bias in the Value Line futures contract.

SECTION FOUR

OTHER CONSIDERATIONS

CHAPTER 24

THE PSYCHOLOGY OF TRADING INDEX FUTURES AND OPTIONS*

B. Thomas Byrne, Jr., J.D.
Vice President
Shearson Lehman Hutton Inc.

Much ado has been made about traders going from rags to riches due to some uncanny "market feel." Market feel is not a type of ESP that some people are endowed with at birth. Some of Wall Street's most respected traders started out by losing sizable sums of money. Market feel comes from study of markets and trading. Just as a batter learns to take advantage of a pitcher's curve balls by stepping up and swinging until he is familiar with the pitcher's tricks, a trader learns to take advantage of the market's curve balls by stepping up and swinging until the market's tricks become familiar rather than intimidating. In either game, if you strike out too often, you try another sport.

Part of understanding the psychology of stock index futures is understanding the mindset of those who populate the trading pits and those who are major institutional or individual traders. Although stock index futures cannot be discussed in a vacuum excluding the stock market itself, my purpose here is not to summarize the vast accumulation of literature on stock market psychology into a few pithy sentences. Rather, it is to focus on key aspects of the psychology of the stock index futures market, and

---

*This chapter is adapted from Chapter 5 of the author's book, *The Stock Index Futures Market: A Trader's Insights and Strategies* (Chicago, Ill.: Probus Publishing, 1987).

to note critical differences between stock market and futures market psychology.

It is important to be aware of certain contrasts between the psychology of the stock market and that of the stock index futures market. Remember that many of the players on the stock side are different people with different investment goals than those in the stock index futures market. On the whole, futures players have a shorter time horizon than do stock players–open interest for stock index futures contracts with less than six months to expiration amounts to over 99 percent of the total. Stock transaction costs are substantially higher, so a stock investor can't afford to change his mind several times in a day or week as a futures trader can. If a stockbroker encouraged the frequency of trading that is common in the futures market, he'd be in trouble for churning.

Further, many stock investors are motivated by the desire to buy "value" in the form of underpriced stocks that are bound to provide a sound return, even if it takes time. In contrast, not all stock index futures traders care about value in the form of underpriced contracts. In fact, many speculators prefer to buy overpriced contracts believing that buying by smart money raises the prices and that there is little downside risk in buying overvalued contracts when it takes only seconds to get out of the market.

Strange, isn't it? One can argue that stock buyers and stock index futures buyers are purchasing essentially the same assets, and yet they often have diametrically opposite outlooks on intrinsic value.

Just as stock traders and futures traders can differ in their outlook, futures traders differ among themselves. In fact, I believe that most floor or "pit" traders have a substantially different approach to the market than position traders, who are attempting to capitalize on market trends of varying duration. Let us discuss each outlook in turn.

PIT TRADING PSYCHOLOGY

Most people are puzzled when I explain that many successful pit traders do not necessarily have any opinion on which direction the market is going. Others seem puzzled by the fact that a trader could be bidding a quarter one minute and offering at a half a minute later. Is it possible to quantify what makes these people operate the way they do?

Understanding the time horizon of someone in a commodity ring is one key to the psychology of pit trading. People who trade on the floor of an exchange tend to have an even shorter-term outlook than futures traders in general. A pit trader generally believes that it is not easy to predict what the market might be doing in two days or two weeks, but predicting what the market is likely to do in the next two minutes is less difficult. To make profits in the trading ring, that is essentially all one must do. For example, two ticks on the S&P futures contract can be loosely equated to a move of approximately 75 cents on the Dow. Thus, a trader who buys 10 contracts and is right about that 75-cent move in the Dow can often pocket two ticks times 10 contracts. That 20-tick profit amounts to $500 in the bank for just a few minutes of work. The faster one can get in and out of a contract, the less time left for anxiety.

Better yet, a pit trader can make profits even without much ability to predict minute-to-minute fluctuations in the market. A pit trader is happiest when doing what is affectionately known as "scalping." Remember that in any market, there is always a bid and an ask price. For instance, if IBM's last trade was at 125, the stock might be 124⅞ bid, offered at 125⅛. Scalpers make money simply by buying contracts at the bid side of the market and selling them as quickly as possible at the offered side of the market (or selling first and quickly covering). For example, by purchasing 10 NYFE contracts at 125.00 and selling them a minute later for 125.05, it is possible to make a profit of $250 for a minimal risk.

In the best of all worlds, both sides of the transaction will occur before the bid-ask fluctuates at all. Even on days when the Dow has climbed more than 30 points, I have made money by selling short and then covering quickly. Since such activity is such a desirable way to make money, it is not always easy to buy at the bid side or sell at the offered side, even in the trading ring.

There are a number of pit traders who usually have no strong conviction about the overall direction of the market. Such a trader knows that the percentages favor him over time if he manages to buy on the bid side of the market and sell at the offered side. Most people who trade in this manner are content to make a one or two tick profit on each contract. This gives some indication as to why a number of people are generally willing to sell even when the market is rising.

I am aware of only one academic study of market-makers in stock index futures.[1] In it, Silber concluded that scalper earnings are positively related to the scalper's ability to buy at his bid and sell at his offer, and negatively related to the length of time a position is held. He found that the two successful scalpers studied tended to lose money on trades held open for longer than three minutes. He also found that these two scalpers held trading positions open for an average time of less than two minutes.

Silber studied a "Mr. X" in great detail. He found that during the 31 trading days studied, Mr. X's daily gross profit averaged $742, which was within the top quartile of scalpers on NYFE. The gross profits ranged from a daily high of $2,250 to a low of $50, and his average net profit (after commissions) was $672. Thus, his net profit was $9.34 per contract in a market where the bid-ask spread was generally $25. Mr. X was able to transact 77 percent of his trades on his side of the market, and he held a trade open for an average of 116 seconds.

Many pit traders do have opinions on the market, at least over a very short time span. Such traders may be very sensitive to retail order flow, to developments in other markets or in key stocks, or to how many buyers step up as the market reaches an important technical support line. These pit traders also often surmise what a major institution or trader is doing just by watching the broker that usually handles those orders. Some pit traders act on their sense of the degree to which other traders in the pit are net long or net short, much as a card counter surmises who holds what at a blackjack table. Thus, many people in the trading crowd not only have opinions on the market, but these opinions are often based on their perception of what others are doing.

---

[1]W. Silber, "Market-Maker Behavior in an Auction Market: An Analysis of Scalpers in Futures Markets," *The Journal of Finance* 39 (September 1984).

POSITION TRADING PSYCHOLOGY

Even the shrewdest position traders know that they are not always right and that the market can confound. People on one of the finest trading desks in the world, at Salomon Brothers, used to drill into my mind that, "You can't outguess the market."

Examples abound in which some economic news changes the fundamental outlook for the market, but the market moves in precisely the opposite direction to what a rational observer would expect. IBM releases lower first-quarter earnings for 1985, and the stock climbs over a point. The consumer price index for March 1985 suggests a possible resurgence in inflation, and the Dow climbs 12 points. On April 11, 1985, it was announced that March retail sales dropped by the largest monthly amount in seven years. Still, the Dow rose eight points in the first 15 minutes of trading and closed up 3.75. Of course, everybody has an explanation in retrospect. But if we dissect these examples, we may be able to discern a few axioms about how traders react.

A first axiom is that traders have a tendency to focus on the short-term impact of economic news, even if the same news might have opposite effects over time.

Consider the announcement that retail sales for March 1985 were off by a surprising 1.9 percent. Most traders couldn't have told you if that 1.9 percent drop was relative to February 1985 or March 1984. But they knew it was a bad number, a possible harbinger of a weakening economy. So do stocks go down? Perversely, they go up. In this instance, the likely explanation is that the prospect of a weaker economy suggested a possible reduction in demand for credit, spurring a bond rally. On that day, lower interest rates were the short-term effect while a weakened economy was a more distant concern.

A second axiom is that traders may perceive varying short-term impacts of seemingly identical news developments at different points in time. Consider a weakening dollar. A weaker dollar is bearish because it portends higher interest rates and a possible trade war. Right? Absolutely, if you traded on April 14, 1987. The yen soared versus the dollar, and the Dow dropped 35 points.

But two years earlier, a weaker dollar was perceived as bullish. On March 19, 1985, gold soared $35 and then the dollar tumbled, suggesting shaken confidence in our financial system. But the Dow soared 21 points. Traders focusing on the short-term apparently concluded that a weaker dollar meant higher profits for blue-chip stocks with a high volume of international sales. Remember, too, that the dollar fell from different levels in 1985 and 1987. In 1985, the greenback was widely viewed as overvalued, so that a decline was welcome. In 1987, the dollar had been trending down for two years, and interest rates soared due to the perception that foreign capital had to be attracted to dollar-denominated assets in order to stabilize the currency. Before you place a sure bet on the fundamentals, have a stop-loss point in mind just in case the market doesn't see it your way.

A third axiom is that traders often think more in relative than absolute terms. This "relative" outlook on the assessment of market developments occurs in two steps: (1) measuring the divergence between a piece of actual news relative to expected news ("news divergence"), and (2) assessing the initial reaction of the market relative to its expected reaction given a particular degree of news divergence (or "news surprise" in the event of a completely unexpected bulletin). This relative way of thinking is perhaps best conveyed by illustration.

Consider April 23, 1985. Inflation had been under control at about 4 percent per year. The March CPI number, due out before the opening, was expected by most forecasters to be up .3 or .4 percent. The actual number was up .5 percent (5.8 percent annualized), a bad number in both absolute and relative terms. So a trader would expect the market to open lower, which in fact it did. But how much lower? Is the market acting more or less resiliently than it has on other occasions when digesting other bad news of similar importance? Traders are very sensitive to the market's initial reaction as compared to what that reaction might have been.

On April 23, the Dow was down only about two points in the early minutes. (See Figure 24–1.) The S&P and NYSE futures traded down to their support lines on a 90-day bar chart but did not penetrate those lines, so the market did not open as low as it might have in the circumstances. This makes any trader, and especially one with a short position, think that if a knockout punch couldn't push the market more than two points lower, nothing would. The market now feels strong. Time for short sellers to cover their positions or place pretty tight stop-loss orders. It is also a good opportunity for traders with no position to "buy low." The Dow gradually climbed throughout the morning. In early afternoon, General Motors announced earnings 34 percent below last year's and also below the estimates of Wall Street analysts. More bad news, both in an absolute and a relative sense. The Dow went down. But more significantly, it only backed up four points and did not reach the morning's lows.

So what does a trader think? If this bearish news doesn't make the market go down, nothing will—at least today. A trader

FIGURE 24–1
Movement of Dow Jones Industrial Average, April 23, 1985

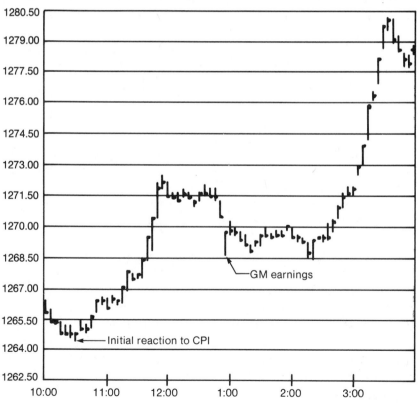

Source: Videcom Service, ADP Comtrend, Stamford, Conn.

who has no position is unlikely to sell into a market that, rationally or not, refuses to go down. The trader realizes that he or she is too small to fight the trend single-handedly. Perhaps more important, traders with short positions begin to worry and to cover their positions at small losses. That kind of thinking was probably responsible for a big part of the final-hour surge. Although I was not especially optimistic about the upside prospects for the market that day, I was one of the buyers just to cover my short position and prevent any significant losses. Once those panics get going, there is no telling whether the Dow might move 10, 20, or 30 points in final-hour trading. On that day, it closed 12 points higher, seven of which were added in the final hour.

Why is the notion of relativity so important? Investors react to information as it develops, using any clue or estimate that might give them an edge. Those reactions move prices. If the actual news varies from the consensus expectation already built into prices, the market reaction can seem puzzling to an observer who just sees news that is bad in absolute terms, rather than news that is not as bad as expected. Perhaps this psychology gave rise to the old market adage, "Buy the rumor, sell the news."

The same psychology is illustrated by the movement of IBM stock when IBM released lower first-quarter earnings for 1985. The stock climbed over a point, but IBM shares had fallen several points earlier in the week because investors had expected the worst. The old adage worked in reverse for bad news: "Sell the rumor, buy the news."

Having established the "why" of relativity, let us turn to the next logical question—the "how" of relativity. How is relativity measured? Relative to what? To answer this question, we must elaborate on the previously mentioned support lines and their counterparts, resistance lines.

A support line is a threshold level formed by a line, which can be horizontal or diagonal, connecting several market bottoms. That line is expected to support the market in its next downtrend. If the market falls below the line, technically oriented traders view it as a sign of weakness. In the ensuing loss of confidence, many traders will sell short, or at least postpone any buying.

Conversely, a resistance line is a threshold level formed by a line connecting several market tops. It is expected to restrain the market the next time it uptrends and approaches that line. If the market goes above the line, traders view this penetration as a sign of strength. Analysis of the market's ability or inability to hold or pierce various support and resistance lines is part of what is generally called "technical analysis."

The general idea behind technical analysis is that the consensus reaction to all fundamental factors is reflected in the movement of share prices and the index as a whole; and, consequently, in the patterns formed by those movements. Thus, a look at the patterns on an index price chart will provide a view of the market's reaction to general economic conditions and fundamental news developments in the context of certain benchmarks.

People seek benchmarks in any field of endeavor. As in physics, everything is relative in the stock market. People need some measuring rod to quantify information and to compare actual results to expectations. People seek patterns in order to find some rhyme or reason and predictive value in quantified information. For instance, if Racehorse A has run four consecutive miles in 1:40 and $\frac{3}{5}$, $\frac{2}{5}$, $\frac{1}{5}$ and 1:40, one might bet on it in a race against a horse that has consistently run 1:40. Or, if a presidential candidate gets 10, 15, and 20 percent of the vote in the first three primaries, he or she will experience a substantial increase in contributions and press coverage as pundits become bullish on his or her prospects. That game of searching for patterns is essentially the same in the stock market.

Technical analysis is rooted in the human desire to find threshold levels to serve as yardsticks of sufficient or insufficient progress in some endeavor. For instance, a salesperson who sells $1 million worth of widgets wins a prize vacation in the Caribbean for the strong performance, while the colleague who sold $999,000 stays home because he did not surpass the threshold. Judging by retailers' pricing strategies, consumers must look very differently at items marked $10.00 and $9.95. So it is in the market. A close on the Dow of 1000 may be judged as strong, while 995 may be considered weak. In absolute terms, there is very little difference between the two levels. But in psychological terms, there may be a world of difference.

Use of support and resistance lines as thresholds is by no means foolproof. But if the market has bounced off a well-defined support line twice before, enough technically oriented traders are likely to decide that it is a good bet to do so again. It is a good bet for two reasons.

The first reason is that if a pronounced bull or bear trend emerges from a particular market pattern often enough, certain traders will anticipate that same trend whenever they see that particular market pattern and buy or sell accordingly. Perhaps there is a Pavlovian aspect to such responses.

Pavlov demonstrated that when it garners a reward for responding in a certain manner to a pattern, even the simplest brain is likely to continue to respond in the same manner whenever the same pattern is presented. Stretching Pavlov's work just a bit, one could hypothesize that if a trader is rewarded frequently enough for responding in a certain manner to a technical pattern that resembles something he has seen before, he is likely to continue responding in the same manner. Thus if a trader has profited 75 percent of the time he bought at a triple bottom, he is likely to buy the next time such a formation presents itself.

I still remember—clear as a bell—the technical patterns that preceded my biggest wins. Those patterns almost get imprinted on one's mind. And I know what I'm going to do the next time I see one of the patterns.

The second reason thresholds are good bets is that support and resistance lines permit a position trader to refine his risk-reward calculus to provide substantial profits if the guess is correct and minimal losses if it is wrong. In other words, if he buys on a support line and the market continues to decline, he takes a small loss by selling as soon as, or shortly after, that support line is cracked. If he is right and captures a new trend, he can let his profits run. A successful trader, knowing that he has an opportunity to make an appreciable profit before a pattern runs its course, will maintain his position until the price reverses by a predetermined amount, causing a sell alarm to go off.

Consider this proposition. Pick a coin of your choice. Now suppose I offer you a game in which you pay me a $25 commission each time you flip the coin. In return, I will pay you $25 every time the coin comes up heads if you will pay me $25 for every time the coin lands on tails. Hopefully, you would decide that this is not a very good game.

But suppose I offer you $100 for every heads if you will pay me $25 (plus a $25 commission) for every tails. Suddenly this is not a bad proposition. Similarly, technical analysis may give you only slightly better than fifty-fifty odds of determining whether the next market move will be up or down. But if you buy on a technical support line and the market disappoints you by going down, you get out as soon as that support line is pierced, thus minimizing your loss. But if you are right, you may have caught a new short-term trend and can make a profit that exceeds the amount of the expected loss should the market move adversely.

I try to outguess the short-term market when a good risk-reward situation presents itself. For instance, if the market is near a technical support line and stocks look cheap relative to bonds, I'll buy. But when I make a bet that I have a fifty-fifty chance of winning, I try to make the expected payoff higher than the expected loss. That's why I use technical analysis. If the market trades in a range from 1240 to 1300 and I buy at 1241, my upside is as much as 60 points and my downside risk is only about five points to the point at which my stop gets hit. Once in a while, the upside is far greater than that 60 points because the market breaks out from its trading range.

Many people use support and resistance levels not only to try to ascertain market direction, but also to establish good odds on each trade. As with anything else in the market, support and resistance levels are not foolproof, and even the most skilled traders are sometimes whipsawed.

Even so, most successful traders are cognizant of the value of technical analysis. But, you may say, technical analysis is nothing more than Wall Street's answer to voodoo. That may well be true, but it is also true that many well-capitalized market participants rely heavily on technical analysis. In fact, since so many traders from the commodity markets, where technical analysis has long been an integral part of trading, have joined the ranks of stock index futures traders, technical analysis has become even more influential in the stock index futures market. Moreover, because so much capital is committed on the basis of technical analysis, the self-fulfilling prophecy aspect of technical analysis, in and of itself, makes it worthwhile to be aware of the technical indicators. Indeed, in today's market, there are computers programmed to buy or sell in response to technical signals.

The more cynical may wish to consider the trader who one day referred to technical analysis as a lot of hocus-pocus. After a time, he revised his view to, "Still a lot of hocus-pocus, but a darn good way to make money." As another highly successful trader put it, "The difference between a fundamentalist and a technician is about three years and three million dollars."

Most traders do not rely on technical analysis in a vacuum. Many employ fundamental analysis on both a macro scale (e.g., fiscal and monetary policy, reaction to government economic statistics, etc.) and on a micro scale (e.g., corporate profits and other indicators of the health of individual companies). Surely, a fundamental news development can move the prices of stock index futures. But on many occasions, prices will move quickly to the nearest salient technical support or resistance line. Then, the focus shifts to the notion of relativity as traders conduct a tug-of-war over whether the news is sufficiently important to move prices through that technical level.

TRENDS AND THE HERD INSTINCT

Few traders will volunteer to be the first to attempt to buck an established market trend. Usually, the goal among speculators is to let someone else be the guinea pig—but to be the first follower once it looks like the pig is getting fat. Out of such motives arises what is fondly known as the herd instinct. Traders recognize the potency of the herd instinct. In fact, in addition to their trading badges, many floor traders wear another badge with the saying, "The trend is your friend."

If all of these traders are just followers, who are the leaders? What precipitates a new trend? Part of the answer is that the leaders are the ones that play with big money. Someone who buys 500 contracts will move the market. If I buy 10, I won't move the market. Since I can't be a leader, my goal is to be a good follower.

But there are a lot of well-capitalized investors. What makes the leaders act rather than react? A news development might do it. The enormous rally in the autumn of 1985 began the day after the Group of Five industrial nations agreed on joint efforts to reduce the value of the dollar. Drops in the dollar have in the past led traders to buy stocks on the theory that U.S.-based multinationals will increase their foreign-source incomes and that U.S. firms will find it easier to export. Developments in another market might do it. Stocks might rise when bond prices rise because stocks offer a relatively more attractive return whenever bond yields fall. Since both the dollar and bonds open for trading in the United States before the stock market does, it pays to know how these markets have opened.

Some market leaders act out of a conviction that a trend has gone too far and that the market is overpriced or underpriced by an amount sufficient to induce them to establish a new long-term position. In fact, such "value-oriented" investors may begin to accumulate a position before the trend is moving their way on the theory that they cannot predict tops or bottoms and that they can "ride out" a short-term movement given the prospects for sizable long-term rewards.

But most market leaders also remain acutely aware of technically important levels in the market. Their trading is often based on the same risk-reward strategy discussed earlier. For instance, in early April 1985, the 180.00 level was recognized as a key technical support line on the S&P 500 June contract. On April 8, the market was poor all day and for the final half-hour, it danced around above and below that number, closing just above it. The market tested that level one more time the next day and stopped four ticks above the previous day's low. That was enough to convince traders that the market was feeling stronger.

The mood changed and the market headed north, with the S&P contract closing at 182.75 for the week. A trader who bought at 180.00 made slightly over $1,300 per contract. Had that trader been wrong, he probably would have been out at about 179.65 (as Figure 24–2 indicates, a tick below the low on April 8) for a loss of $175 per contract. This example is not to suggest that one should rely on technical analysis in a vacuum. This mood change was undoubtedly encouraged by a two-point rally in the bond market during the same period. Nevertheless, the technicals presented a risk-reward scenario that was good in the short-term and

FIGURE 24–2
Five Day Bar Chart, June S&P Futures (April 8–12, 1985)

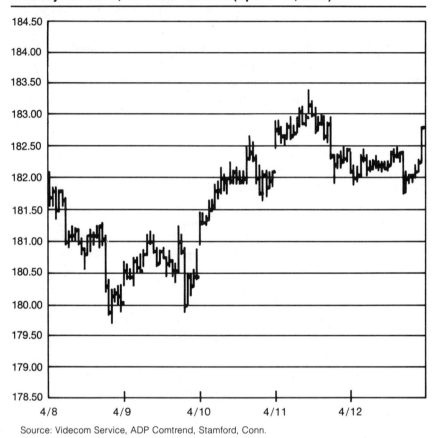

Source: Videcom Service, ADP Comtrend, Stamford, Conn.

even better over the next few weeks as the market climbed sharply in April and May.

Trading psychology is such that if the contract had fallen under the 180 level, briefly pierced it again without being able to maintain it, and traded one to three ticks lower in the final 15 minutes, some traders would have gone home short and been prepared to cover at perhaps 180.20. The difference between 179.90 and 180.10 in terms of movement of the Dow is minuscule, about 1.50 points, but to a trader it could be the difference between the market acting weak or providing some encouragement.

Well-capitalized traders are not always prepared to lead. They too can be followers who just exacerbate herd tendencies. In fact, the role of trend-setter may shift among well-capitalized traders from one major move to the next.

If investors who buy on technical signals or major news developments are often the initial trend-setters, who are the first players to get on the bandwagon? It appears that fear can be a stronger emotion than greed. Often the early stages of a new trend are spurred by liquidation of positions rather than new commitments. A Salomon Brothers study of the start of the bull market in 1982 concluded that:

> The price stampede was probably most influenced by traders who were buying stock to cover short sales. . . . There was also a great deal of short covering in the futures market. . . . The number of contracts available for trading was reduced by 13.9 percent in the first four weeks of the rally. This probably resulted from short traders covering their contracts, thus causing the number of contracts available to shrink, as contracts were canceled. From this, two results ensued: first, the buying drove prices up; and second, fewer contracts were available for subsequent trading.[2]

As Table 24–1 indicates, open interest experienced its sharpest drop of the month during the week between August 13 and 20, when the rally began.

RECORD YOUR MARKET OBSERVATIONS

An appreciation of past market performance under similar conditions can be developed and refined by keeping a trading diary. A trading diary should serve two functions. One is to review actual trades and to write down what you did right and, more importantly, what you did wrong and do not care to repeat. The other is to record your thoughts as to what the market is likely to do in the near term. A month or so later, flip back and read your

---

[2]Laszlo Birinyi, Jr. and Susan L. Field, *Rally on Wall Street—An Anatomy of the Stock Market Performance August 13–October 11, 1982* (New York: Salomon Brothers Inc, November 1982).

TABLE 24–1

Week	Value Line	S&P 500	NYSE	Total	Percent Change from Previous
August 6, 1982	5,740	15,861	6,466	28,067	
August 13, 1982	5,753	15,413	5,886	27,052	−3.6
August 20, 1982	6,388	14,169	4,531	25,088	−7.3
August 27, 1982	5,520	13,749	4,883	24,152	−3.7
September 3, 1982	6,059	14,359	5,333	25,751	+6.6

thoughts and begin to develop a sense of what you anticipated well and what you overlooked. Keeping such a diary is not necessarily an exercise for idlers. Some of those with legendary market feel have kept diaries. The great Jesse Livermore spent an hour each morning recording his thoughts in writing before trading began.[3]

Let me share one entry from my market diary with you. I selected this passage before I had any idea whether my prognostication would prove right or wrong because it relates to an interesting juncture in the market. I was particularly interested in the very long-term charts which are reproduced in Figures 24–3, 24–4, and 24–5.

> January 11, 1985. Good time to sell. Who knows when breakout from this triangle will occur but I say it's down. Economic fundamentals are lousy. Budget woes will resurface after State of Union—traders will say Reagan proposals are not enough. Bank woes, farmers' troubles will also cause selling at major resistance levels. Declining commodity prices make me uneasy. The smart money already fears a crash. A reversal in the dollar would be inflationary, would drain money from our capital markets, and would be terrible psychologically on investor confidence. High premiums on futures contracts tell me there isn't enough pessimism to fuel major advance. There is no follow-through whenever we have a sharp advance in a day. Lower high every time. Individual stocks are getting badly punished if earnings don't meet expecta-

---

[3]Livermore, one of the greatest speculators of all time, provided superb trading insights in a book written using a pseudonym. See Edwin L. LeFevre, *Reminiscences of a Stock Operator* (Fraser Publishing, 1980 reprint).

FIGURE 24–3
Value Line Futures—135-Week Chart (June 1982–January 1985)

Source: Videcom Service, ADP Comtrend, Stamford, Conn.

tions—sign of latent nervousness. Market is paying a high multiple for earnings when net present valued at these rates, just like 1929. Stocks are already strong relative to bonds, so a push from that market is unlikely. Bond futures can't maintain 72.00 anyway. Pretty soon too much money growth will be considered inflationary and too little will be recessionary. If AFC team wins Super Bowl, would make a great short. Traders would freak, just like last year. Otherwise, just sell the resistance level. Cover if S&P finally breaks above 174.50 or Value Line tops 193.50; start appreciating "countervailing influences."

FIGURE 24–4
Value Line Futures—The Aftermath

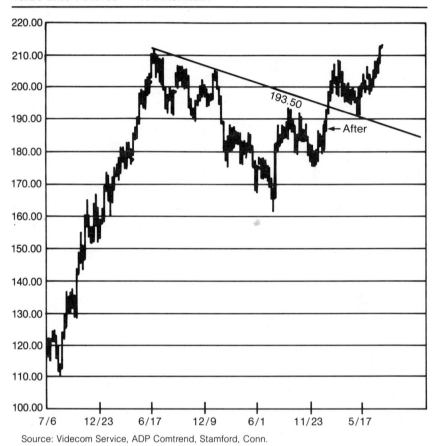

Source: Videcom Service, ADP Comtrend, Stamford, Conn.

Of course, every entry in a trading diary need not be quite this exhaustive, but it is good to organize your thoughts. Part of organizing your thoughts involves consideration of appropriate action in the event that your analysis is wrong, or just plain untimely.

When I walked in Monday morning, one of the brokers remarked to me that it would be a bad day to trade because it was a bank holiday. It turned out to be an expensive holiday for the banks, and could have been an expensive day for me as well had

FIGURE 24–5

135-Week Chart of S&P 500 Futures Showing Major Resistance Level

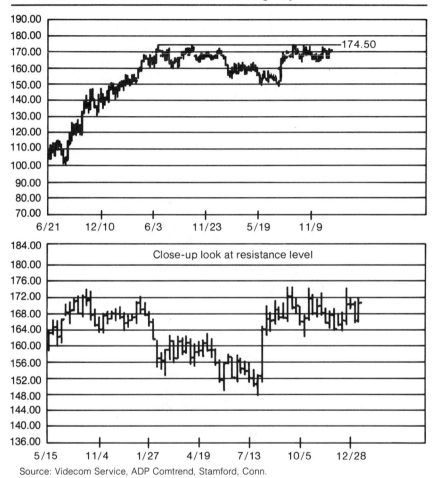

Source: Videcom Service, ADP Comtrend, Stamford, Conn.

I not been mindful of a critical attribute of a trader—flexibility. Even though I was dead wrong on which way the market would go when the Value Line future reached 193.50 and the S&P future reached 174.50, I watched my net worth go up 1 percent a day for the next three days. I started appreciating "countervailing influences" as soon as the S&P traded through 174.50 and the Value Line traded through 193.50. At that point, I decided that my fun-

damental analysis could wait and that it was time to adhere to a
more basic principle: "Don't spit in the wind."

The Dow went up 36 points (or 3 percent) to 1264 that Monday and didn't stop until it flirted with 1300. The newspapers reported that the market rose because investors became more
optimistic on the general economic outlook. Three percent more
optimistic in just one day, I presume. As one superb trader said
to me, "News is a lagging indicator."

Consider this as an alternative hypothesis. Traders, who can
be superstitious, were not about to sell short immediately following an NFC victory in the Super Bowl, because of a spurious
correlation between wins by teams from the original NFL and
bull markets for the ensuing year. In fact, enough traders were
outright buyers to push the market through the triangle-shaped
technical pattern that formed during the previous 135 weeks (see
Figure 24–3). Once that breakout had occurred, the buying just
fed on itself as traders became bullish simply because this crucial
resistance level had been pierced.

A trading diary is a good way to crystallize an opinion, and
to develop an early warning signal to recognize when you are
wrong.

In fact, such an early warning signal led me to my best month
ever in January 1987. I thought the market would be down, but I
got long as soon as the S&P futures traded above an important
technical resistance line (256.40) and held on to half of my position all the way up to 281. Not bad for initially being wrong.

A trading diary is also a good place to record your own observations about market psychology and your personal trading
rules.

A HEAD START—HEED OTHERS' TRADING RULES

Elementary as it may seem, successful traders heed certain market axioms and develop certain trading rules that they have disciplined themselves to follow regardless of ephemeral
countervailing emotions. A trading diary is a good place to record
your own observations and rules as you develop them. For instance, one of my early observations was that, rational or not,

there seems to be a natural human tendency to want to buy and a natural desire to hope that the price goes up. Similarly, the uninitiated often tend to be reluctant to sell something they don't own.

In contrast, an old axiom is that in extreme market conditions, the stock market is capable of dropping more rapidly than it will rise. Many veterans observe that there will always be an offer in a trading crowd, but there will not always be a bid. There seems to be a tendency to be more afraid of being caught long in a market crash than being caught short in a rally—even though the ground is a lot closer than the sky.

A digression on a few other axioms and rules, some of which are more widely accepted than others, will, I hope, enhance your understanding of the psychology of the trading ring and hence of the dynamics of stock index futures trading.

The notion that the "trend is your friend" suggests that momentum tends to push a market in one direction, in both the short and long term, with some backing and filling along the way. As was discussed above, very few successful traders will maintain large positions that go against momentum.

Be Flexible

Particularly if you intend to be a day trader, try not to be habitually bullish or bearish. In other words, don't be a one-way trader. Be flexible. When I was brand new at the stock index game, I was perhaps too habitually bullish. It worked in the practice trading sessions. True enough, we were in the midst of a great bull market, but my second and third weeks of trading happened to be a time when there was a pause in the bull market and in fact a slight retreat from recent highs. I learned rather quickly not to be habitually bullish.

When you have capital to spend on a number of contracts and you wish to establish a position, it often makes sense to buy in at different levels, all the while watching to ensure that the market is confirming your instincts. If the market is not confirming, do not add to a losing position. Add only to good trades. This is just another way of avoiding the mistake of thinking the market eventually has to start moving in your favor. What seems low can always go lower—examples of that axiom would fill another book. It makes sense to withhold any buy orders until downward momentum has stopped.

Cut Your Losses

Some traders maintain that one should never let a profit become a loss. However, I believe that a more sensible approach is to set a firm loss limit when you are initiating a trade and don't start hoping against hope that the market will come back if it reaches your loss limit. Some people lose money simply because they freeze. Others lose because they have some idea in the back of their mind that one particular news factor will move the market in their direction. But other forces they're not yet aware of may in fact be having a more powerful impact. If there are to be such surprises in the market, they're always more welcome when they don't cost you much money.

Some investors are reluctant to take a small loss in the stock market because doing so means paying a big commission. One advantage of trading in futures is that commissions are generally low relative to stock market commissions and will be paid only once anyway, on either the liquidation or expiration of the contract. Thus, commissions should not even be a factor in a decision to take a small loss.

Let Your Profits Run

Cutting losses has always been easy for me, maybe because I'm fairly disciplined, maybe because I get scared easily, or maybe because I've had lots of practice. For me, the tougher maxim has been, "Let your profits run." It has a beguiling ring to it. If you just remember that rule, you get rich. The problem is that it's terribly easy to become giddy, especially when you've had three losing trades in a row and will do anything for a little bit of positive reinforcement.

In my mind, there are two keys to letting your profits run. Rule number one is to avoid deciding to sell based simply on your percentage return. A classic error is made by people who dump a position any time their profits reach some magic number like

$1,000 or double what they put down, even when there is only good news in the market and no major technical resistance level close at hand. Move your stop higher, but don't get giddy and sell for no rational reason.

Rule number two—unwind a profitable position gradually. Even if you master the art of dispassionate trading, you cannot always count on perfectly following the elusive cardinal rule to "buy low, sell high." It is twice as difficult to be absolutely right on both your buy decision and your sell decision on any single contract. Your odds can be greatly improved, however, by selling only part of a position when things seem too good to be true. In fact, that strategy helps to explain who the sellers are on days when the Dow is up 30 points. In other words, if you are long and the market begins to move in your favor, do not maintain your entire position on the assumption that this is the beginning of the Dow's move to 3000. Sell gradually. Unlike the sliding scale commissions on stock trades, your transaction costs are the same when you sell a stock index futures position in several pieces. If you are a small trader who has just scraped together the $10,000 for one S&P contract, try buying two MMI or NYFE contracts.

Conversely, *do not sell all of a profitable position, no matter how strongly you feel that the market has run its course and cannot move any further in your favor.* For instance, at the opening on November 11, 1985, I had a very profitable long position after a period in which the Dow had risen 120 points in the preceding two months. I thought the run was over and was tempted to close out my position at a good profit. As much as I had to clench my teeth to stick to the let-your-profits-run rule, I decided to sell only a quarter of my position on the opening and just leave the rest alone. The Dow closed 27 points higher that day. So much for making money on gut feel.

Do not ever trade more contracts than you can prudently handle. One nice thing about the market is that tomorrow will always bring another opportunity to make money. There is no need to bet the ranch on the strong feeling you have today. Statistically speaking, you have a 50 percent chance of being wrong. Moreover, trading beyond your financial capability is a clear invitation to panic, and panic is the surest way to lose money in the market.

You must not bet the ranch because no matter how strong your feeling is, you cannot think of everything. And if you do, the market won't. I was still in law school when the news of the Iraq-Iran war and attacks on oil supplies broke. At the time, I owned options on Mobil with a week or two to expiration. I decided to hold on because the market would conclude that war means supply interruptions, ergo higher crude prices, ergo inventory profits, ergo higher stock prices. I thought of everything. Nothing happened for three days, so I threw up my hands and sold my options. Then the market thought of everything. The episode reminded me of an adage that I have heard attributed to Joe Kennedy: "I know a lot of guys who have lost their shirt by being right too soon."

Avoid Overtrading

Another maxim is that one should not overtrade. Overtrading has several disadvantages. First, brokerage commissions are likely to eat into whatever profits you make. Second, one who is overly anxious to trade often jumps into the market too quickly, without seeking the best possible execution price. Third, overtrading is sometimes the result of panicking rather than sticking to a well-thought-out strategy where you had perceived good odds. Of course, loss of nerve can be a bad thing, but too much hope can be even worse.

Information and Conclusions

A watershed occurs when a trader is no longer spooked by the market opinions of others, particularly those of successful traders. The world's most experienced traders can be wrong just as often as you, and they may change their mind about the market thirty seconds after talking to you anyway. I am always interested in someone else's opinion because I might have overlooked one factor or another. Accepting *information* from other people is fine because it is free of charge, but accepting *conclusions* from other people may not be free. It is an invitation to trading losses. A trader should be able to weigh and evaluate information from any source, but should be able to draw his own conclusions.

The more subtle rules of the market are not absorbed over-night, nor are they constant. Just as a magician's secret won't earn him much money once it is out, neither will a trader's secret be worth much once it is common knowledge. So when a certain pattern or rule becomes too well known, some players decide that it is time to change the trick. When too many journalists start writing about the Super Bowl theory (i.e., the market finishes the year higher after a victory by a team from the original NFL), it will be time to sell short after an NFC win. So far, the whole notion seems too preposterous for a respectable news story, which is fine by me.

Nevertheless, certain technical and seasonal (e.g., tax sell-ing) patterns are repeated time and time again. Some professional traders do well simply by recognizing the development of recur-ring patterns in a market.

Regardless of how much you study stock index futures, it is inevitable that you will learn from your own mistakes. There is a difference, though, between being wrong and making a mistake. Being wrong is part of the game and a necessary cost. Mistakes are unnecessary costs. They can be minimized.

It pays (or at least saves) to practice before you play, al-ways bearing in mind that any simulation is not quite the real thing. The first time I paper-traded, I "made" $7,000 in a week and became quite worried over how to spend my 50 years of re-tirement. Then I went to a trader's night at the New York Futures Exchange and "made" $700. Retirement was pushed back a bit. On my first day of actual trading, I was lucky to make $50. Suddenly, it seemed clear that retirement by age 30 was not in the works.

But there are valuable lessons in paper trading. Paper trading forces one to focus on market patterns and nuances.

One of the most important observations about the futures markets is that the first 100 trades are the hardest. No matter what you learn by reading this book or any other material, your education will not be complete until you've actually gone and done it—and yes, made a few mistakes. If a book on the stock market costs me $25, I may or may not remember a particular point. If a bad trade costs me $100 that particular type of mistake is less likely to be repeated. The learning curve can be frustrating. It took two years before I had my first $1,000 day. It took another two weeks before I had my second.

The market is influenced by an infinite number of variables. There is no magic formula, no perfect multiple regression that will unfailingly predict the market's direction. The guy with the foolproof black box does not last, or you would have read about him by now.

Although no one has discovered El Dorado, certain people do emerge as consistent winners in the stock market or in stock index futures. They are outnumbered by losers. Fifty years ago, those consistent winners may have been the people who had the most access to inside information. There is virtually no inside information today that will dramatically move the market as a whole. Yet, there are still consistent winners in the stock index futures market.

Can market feel really help if stock prices do indeed take a random walk? Consider a migrating goose. It may appear to be on some sort of random flight, but an ornithologist who has studied the behavior of geese in similar circumstances might feel comfortable making certain predictions about a particular bird. If it's October, that goose is flying south even if it temporarily changes direction for no apparent reason. Maybe it tends to fly at between 1,200 and 1,800 feet. It usually follows a leader. The more you study, the more you know. Even the experts won't know precisely where the thing will land. But to them, its flight does not appear quite so random.

So what is this mysterious market feel? Developing a sense of how the market has reacted to similar circumstances. Assessing what is different about this situation. Talking to people because they might have thought of something you overlooked. Assimilating new information quickly. Adhering to trading rules to keep losses small enough to minimize the amount netted out from the gains. Playing the percentages. Maybe a facility for numbers. Maybe a dash of luck.

CHAPTER 25

ACCOUNTING FOR STOCK INDEX FUTURES AND OPTIONS

Benjamin S. Neuhausen, C.P.A.
Partner
Arthur Andersen & Co.

Accounting for stock index futures contracts is governed by Financial Accounting Standard Board (FASB) Statement No. 80, *Accounting for Futures Contracts,* issued in 1984. Accounting for stock index options is covered in American Institute of Certified Public Accountants (AICPA) Issues Paper 86–2, *Accounting for Options.* While the AICPA issues paper is not authoritative like an FASB Statement, it represents the best guidance currently available on accounting for options. The options accounting described in this chapter generally conforms to the accounting recommended by the AICPA issues paper.

The FASB currently has a major project underway dealing with financial instruments and "off balance sheet financing" issues. Risk management products, including futures and options, are included in the scope of that project. Accordingly, practices in this area may change if the FASB or the Securities and Exchange Commission promulgate new standards. Readers should be aware that this is an evolving area.

BACKGROUND—ACCOUNTING FOR MARKETABLE EQUITY SECURITIES

FASB Statement No. 12, *Accounting for Certain Marketable Securities,* governs the accounting for marketable equity securities. Stock index futures and options do not meet the definition of an equity security, because they do not represent a right to acquire shares—they are settled in cash. However, the accounting requirements of Statement 12 are important for understanding the accounting for index futures or options that hedge positions in equity securities.

Statement 12 comprises two basic sections. The first addresses accounting principles for marketable equity securities for enterprises in industries that do not have specialized accounting practices with respect to marketable securities. The second addresses such principles for enterprises in industries with specialized accounting practices.

Enterprises in Industries That Do Not Have Specialized Accounting Practices

Statement 12 requires that a marketplace equity securities portfolio be carried at the lower of its aggregate cost or market value, determined at each balance sheet date. The amount by which the aggregate cost of the portfolio exceeds its market value is to be accounted for as a valuation allowance. The valuation allowance represents the net unrealized loss (the amount by which the aggregate cost exceeds the market value) in that portfolio.

Statement 12 requires entities with classified balance sheets (those entities that show separate classifications of current assets and liabilities permitting ready determination of working capital) to classify marketable equity security holdings into separate current or noncurrent portfolios to determine the amount, if any, and the disposition of a valuation allowance (i.e., the comparison of aggregate cost and market value for each portfolio). The classification of marketable equity securities into current or noncurrent portfolios is based on existing accounting literature, mainly Accounting Research Bulletin No. 43, Chapter 3. For entities with unclassified balance sheets, all marketable equity securities are considered noncurrent. If the classification of a marketable equity security changes between current and noncurrent, the security is to be transferred between the corresponding portfolios at the lower of its cost or market value at the date of transfer. If a security's market value is less than its cost, its market value becomes the new cost basis. The theretofore unrealized loss should be accounted for as if it were a realized loss and included in net income.

Realized gains and losses on marketable equity security positions are included in income for the period in which they occur. Changes in the valuation allowance for a marketable equity securities portfolio classified as current are included in income for the period in which the changes occur. On the other hand, accumulated changes in the valuation allowance for a marketable equity securities portfolio classified as noncurrent (including portfolios in unclassified balance sheets) are included in a separate component of stockholders' equity.

Enterprises in Industries with Specialized Accounting Practices

Statement 12 recognized that certain industries had specialized accounting principles allowing or requiring marketable equity securities to be carried at market value, rather than at the lower of cost or market. Enterprises in those industries are allowed to continue using market value rather than adopting the general lower-of-cost-or-market method. Examples include the following:

> Brokers and dealers in securities and investment companies carry marketable equity securities at market value and include unrealized gains and losses in income.
>
> Employee benefit plans (for example, pension and profit sharing plans) carry marketable equity securities at market value and include unrealized gains and losses in the change in net assets available for benefits.
>
> Stock life insurance companies and property and casualty insurance companies carry common and nonredeemable preferred stocks at market value and include unrealized gains and losses in

a separate component of stockholders' (policyholders') equity. Upon sale of the securities, the realized gain or loss is included in income. Unrealized losses that are other than temporary are treated like realized losses and included in income.

ACCOUNTING FOR STOCK INDEX FUTURES

Balance Sheet

Consistent with the accounting for other forward and executory contracts, the gross contract amount of an index futures contract is not recorded on the balance sheet. Margin deposits are recorded simply as a deposit, representing a receivable from the broker.

Hedge versus Speculation

The major issue in accounting for stock index futures is whether they are entered into for hedging purposes or whether they are entered into for speculation. For those that are entered into for speculation, gains and losses are recognized in income currently. For those that are entered into for hedging purposes, gains and losses are accounted for symmetrically with the underlying equity positions, that is, the gains and losses on the index futures are deferred initially and are included in income when the equity position is sold or closed out (hedge accounting is discussed further below).

The accounting standards and conventions include criteria for determining when stock index futures are hedges for accounting purposes. Those that do not qualify as hedges for accounting purposes are deemed to be speculative for accounting purposes. In certain cases, index futures may represent economic hedges but fail to meet the criteria to be accounted for as hedges. In this case, the gains or losses on the index futures might be included in income in a period different from the period when the loss or gain on the underlying hedged position is included in income. Assuming the hedge is effective, the cumulative gain or loss on the index futures will equal and offset the cumulative loss or gain on the underlying hedged position, but the offset may be imperfect in particular quarters or years.

Hedge Criteria

Three criteria must be satisfied for an index futures contract to be considered a hedge for accounting purposes:

1. *The underlying position that is being hedged exposes the company to risk.* This means that the company's income will be increased or decreased by the effect of changing stock prices on the position. For example, if the company owns a portfolio of common stocks, income will be affected by changes in stock prices, either when unrealized or realized gains and losses are included in income. Statement 80 requires that the risk exposure be assessed on a total enterprise basis, taking into account other assets, liabilities, firm commitments, and anticipated transactions. Thus, if the parent company is long in stocks and a subsidiary is short in the same stocks, the consolidated enterprise has no stock price risk and, therefore, would not consider any index futures that hedge either the long or the short position to be accounting hedges.

2. *The enterprise designates the futures as a hedge.* This means that the enterprise documents in its records the purpose of the stock index futures and the underlying position(s) that is (are) being hedged.

3. *The futures are effective as a hedge.* This requirement has two parts. First, the enterprise must demonstrate at the inception of the hedge that high correlation is probable between the gains or losses on the index futures and the losses or gains caused by changing stock prices on the underlying hedged position(s). Second, high correlation must actually be achieved while the hedge is in place. If high correlation is not probable at inception, the index futures are accounted for as speculative. If high correlation is probable at inception but is not achieved, the futures would cease to be regarded as a hedge for accounting purposes and would begin to be accounted for as a speculative position. Unless the portfolio to be hedged is an index portfolio designed to closely match the performance of the index underlying the stock index future, this criterion is unlikely to be satisfied.

Types of Transactions That May Be Hedged

Futures may be hedges of existing assets, existing liabilities, firm commitments, or anticipated transactions for accounting purposes. In the case of index futures, the hedge of an existing asset—a portfolio of stocks that correlates well with the index—is the most common. The other types of transactions probably are not relevant.

A firm commitment is an agreement, usually legally enforceable, under which performance is probable because of sufficiently large disincentives for nonperformance. It is difficult to conceive of a transaction that is hedged by stock index futures and would satisfy this definition. For example, a company may agree to purchase or sell a portfolio of stocks that correlates well with an index, but if the transaction will be consummated at market prices, the penalties for nonperformance are likely to be insignificant.

An anticipated transaction is a transaction that an enterprise expects, but is not obligated, to carry out in the normal course of business. In addition to the three criteria described above, an index futures contract would have to satisfy two additional criteria to be considered a hedge of an anticipated transaction for accounting purposes:

a. The significant characteristics and expected terms of the anticipated transaction are identified. These include the expected date of the anticipated transaction and the identity and number of shares to be purchased or sold.

b. It is probable that the anticipated transaction will occur. Considerations in assessing the likelihood that a transaction will occur include (1) the frequency of similar transactions in the past, (2) the financial and operational capability of the enterprise to carry out the transaction, (3) the length of time to the anticipated transaction date, (4) the extent of loss or disruption of operations that could result if the transaction does not occur, and (5) the likelihood that transactions with substantially different characteristics might be used to achieve the same business purpose (for example, an enterprise that expects to have cash to invest may have several investment alternatives ranging from purchasing shares in an index fund to purchasing a portfolio concentrated in just one or two industries). If an enterprise contemplates two or more similar alternative transactions, an index futures contract may qualify as a hedge of the anticipated transaction only if all hedge requirements are met regardless of which alternative is consummated. Because of the number of investment alternatives and the impossibility of all of them correlating well with any particular stock index future, this criterion probably can never be satisfied.

This chapter discusses accounting for hedges of existing assets and liabilities only, because hedges of firm commitments and anticipated transactions do not seem realistic for the reasons stated above.

Accounting Treatment for Hedges

As noted previously, index futures that qualify to be treated as hedges for accounting purposes are accounted for symmetrically with the underlying hedged item. If the underlying hedged items are accounted for at market value, any index futures hedging those items also will be accounted for on a market value basis. (In the insurance industry, where stocks are accounted for at market value with unrealized appreciation and depreciation included in a separate component of stockholders' (policyholders') equity, rather than in income, the gains or losses on index futures contracts that qualify as hedges also would be included in that separate component of equity. The gains or losses on the futures contracts would be allocated in some systematic and rational way to the individual stocks in the portfolio and included in measuring the realized gain or loss on sale of the stocks.)

Outside of those industries with specialized accounting, common and preferred stock portfolios are carried at the lower of cost or market. If an index futures contract qualifies to be treated as a hedge of an existing portfolio or short position carried at lower of cost or market (higher of proceeds or market for a short position), gains and losses on the futures contract are deferred as an adjustment to the carrying amount of the hedged portfolio (short position). Gains on index futures would offset the losses on the hedged portfolio and eliminate or reduce the writedown of the portfolio that might otherwise be required. Losses on index futures would offset the gains on the hedged portfolio and would only require a writedown if the portfolio's aggregate carrying amount, including the deferred loss from the futures contract, exceeds its market value. The deferred gains or losses on index futures are allocated in some systematic and rational way to the individual stocks in the portfolio, and are included in measuring the realized gain or loss when those stocks are sold.

ACCOUNTING FOR STOCK INDEX OPTIONS

The accounting described for stock index futures is generally applicable to stock index option. However, some differences exist. In addition, the accounting for options is complicated by the fact that the option premium may have both time and intrinsic value components.

Balance Sheet

Like index future, the gross contract amount of an index option is not recorded on the balance sheet. Premiums paid for purchased options are recorded as assets; premiums received for written options are recorded as liabilities.

Hedge versus Speculation

As with index futures, the major issue in accounting for index options is whether they qualify as hedges for accounting purposes. Options that are entered into for speculative purposes or that do not qualify to be accounted for as hedges desirably should be accounted for on a market value basis. However, if an enterprise follows lower-of-cost-or-market accounting for its marketable equity investments, it could use the lower-of-cost-or-market basis for speculative stock index options. Speculative stock index options would be valued separately; they would not be included in the equity securities portfolio for purposes of the lower-of-cost-or-market test.

Hedge Criteria—Purchased Options

The same three criteria described for index futures must be satisfied for a purchased index option to qualify as a hedge for accounting purposes. In the first criterion—exposure to risk—assessment of a risk on a total enterprise basis is preferable, but assessing risk on an individual transaction basis also is acceptable. Thus, if the parent company is long in stocks and a subsidiary is short in the same stocks, either one might account for index options as a hedge of its position if all three hedge criteria are satisfied.

Types of Transactions That May Be Hedged

Index options may hedge the same types of transactions described for index futures. For the reasons discussed previously, hedges of firm commitments and anticipated transactions probably are not relevant to stock index options and are not discussed in this chapter.

Accounting Treatment for Hedges—Purchased Options

Similar to index futures, index options that qualify to be treated as hedges for accounting purposes are accounted for symmetrically with the underlying hedged item. If the underlying items are accounted for at market value, any index options hedging those items also will be accounted for on a market value basis. Two different approaches to market value accounting can be followed. The first approach is to mark the option to market based on changes in its quoted market price (the premium that would be received if the option were closed out). The second approach is to split the option premium into time and intrinsic value components. The time value component is amortized systematically to expense over the life of the option, like an insurance premium.

The intrinsic value component is marked-to-market based on changes in the option's intrinsic value. (In the insurance industry, where stocks are accounted for at market value with unrealized appreciation and depreciation included in a separate component of stockholders' (policyholders') equity, rather than in income, the gains or losses on index options that qualify as hedges also would be included in that separate component of equity. If time and intrinsic value were split, however, time value would be amortized to expense, not to the separate component of equity. The gains or losses on the options would be allocated in some systematic and rational way to the individual stocks in the portfolio and included in measuring the realized gain or loss on sale of the stocks.)

Outside of those industries with specialized accounting, common and preferred stock portfolios are carried at the lower of cost or market. If purchased index options qualify to be treated as a hedge of an existing portfolio or short position carried at lower of cost or market (higher of proceeds or market for a short position), the premiums paid should be split into the time and intrinsic value components. The time value component should be amortized to expense systematically over the life of the option. Changes in the intrinsic value of the index options (the gain or loss on the options) are deferred as an adjustment to the carrying amount of the hedged portfolio (short position). Gains on index options would offset the losses on the hedged portfolio and eliminate or reduce the writedown of the portfolio that might otherwise be required. Losses on index options would offset the gains on the hedged portfolio and would only require a writedown if the portfolio's aggregate carrying amount, including the deferred loss from the options, exceeds its market value. The deferred gains or losses on index options are allocated in some systematic and rational way to the individual stocks in the portfolio, and are included in measuring the realized gain or loss when those stocks are sold.

Hedge Criteria and Hedge Accounting—Written Options

Accountants have been somewhat skeptical of applying hedge accounting to written options, because the writer of an option accepts a limited premium for undertaking unlimited risk. The

AICPA issues paper concludes that a written option may be accounted for as a hedge if it meets the same criteria required for a purchased option. However, hedge accounting for a written option would be different. First, the premium received would not be split into time and intrinsic value components. Rather, gain or loss on the option would be computed based on changes in its total value. Second, only gains could be deferred; losses would be charged to expense as incurred.

Some believe another approach should be used for written options. They would add a fourth criterion before hedge accounting could be used—that the option be so deep in the money that it is reasonably assured that the option will remain in the money throughout its term. In this case, the deep in the money option would behave much like a futures contract and should qualify as a hedge if a similar futures contract would qualify as a hedge. Under this approach, both gains and losses would be deferred similar to a purchased option. However, time and intrinsic value would not be split. Because the premiums on deep in the money options are relatively expensive, the market for them often is thin. This makes it unlikely that many companies would use this instrument to hedge.

Multiple Option Positions

A company can create a synthetic index futures contract by buying a put and writing a call at the same strike price with the same expiration date (equivalent to a short futures position) or by buying a call and writing a put at the same strike price with the same expiration date (equivalent to a long futures position). Synthetic futures should be accounted for like futures contracts in accordance with Statement 80 rather than as options.

A company may also enter into an option transaction in which it buys and writes options with the same expiration dates but different strike prices. If the premium paid for the purchased option is greater than the premium received for the written option, the position should be accounted for as a hedge if the purchased option qualifies for hedge accounting. Specifically:

> The excess of the time value paid over the time value received should be accounted for as the time value of a purchased option.

Hedge accounting should be applied to changes in the excess of the intrinsic value of the purchased option over the intrinsic value of the written option.

If the premium received from the written option is greater than the premium paid for the purchased option, the position should be accounted for as a hedge if the written option qualifies for hedge accounting.

DISCLOSURE

A company using index futures and options should disclose:

The nature of the items that are hedged with the index futures or options.

The method of accounting for the index futures and options, including a description of the events that result in recognizing gains and losses on the futures or options in income.

CHAPTER 26

STOCK INDEX FUTURES IN HISTORICAL PERSPECTIVE

Benjamin Wolkowitz, Ph.D.
Principal
Morgan Stanley & Co., Inc.

THE STATISTICAL CASE AGAINST SUCCESS

A significant event in the development of futures contracts occurred in February 1982, when the Kansas City Board of Trade initiated trading in stock index futures contracts. Shortly afterward, the Chicago Mercantile Exchange and the New York Futures Exchange introduced their entries in the new stock index futures market. The reception received by these contracts was immediate and enthusiastic, motivating some observers to predict that stock index futures contracts would become the hot new market of the 1980s. This prediction seemed premature but was not without foundation, given the early experience with these contracts.

Reviewing the usual record of new futures contracts underscores the truly outstanding nature of the reception given stock index contracts. A recent and extensive study by Professor William L. Silber indicated that from 1960 to 1977 only 31.8 percent of new contracts were traded in an annual volume of more than 10,000 after three years, and that only 20.9 percent of contracts representing competitive modifications of existing contracts were traded in that volume.[1] By contrast, all three stock index futures contracts were trading in excess of 10,000 contracts a week shortly after their introduction. In fact, by mid-1982 the average daily trading volume for the three contracts was 35,000.

As Professor Silber's data suggest, the proliferation of contracts infrequently leads to successful trading in competing markets. Moreover, Professor Holbrook Working, long a prominent and incisive analyst of futures markets, observed some time ago that duplicative contracts are unlikely to be successful.[2] Yet all three stock index contracts have been trading successfully, a situation replicated by no other duplicative contracts. A later entrant to the stock index futures market, the Chicago Board of Trade, has also managed a successful contract which makes the experience with stock index futures all the more unprecedented. It could be argued that these stock index contracts are in fact different contracts because the underlying indexes are different (more on this later). Indeed, differences in indexes and contract design affect the behavior of these contracts, but any reasonable measure of relationships, such as coefficients of correlation, shows a close association among the three indexes, indicating that in many respects they are substantially the same.[3] In summary, from the perspectives of both volume and contract proliferation the experience with stock index contracts has been an impressive departure from previously established norms.

ELEMENTS OF SUCCESS

In concept, an equity-based contract should have long seemed a likely candidate for a futures contract. The significant liquidity and depth of the underlying equity markets should have suggested the potential for a derivative contract for the same reasons that

---

[1]William F. Silber, "Innovation, Competition, and New Contract Design in Futures Markets," *Journal of Futures Markets* 1 (Summer 1981).

[2]Holbrook Working, "Whose Markets? Evidence of Some Aspects of Futures Trading," *Journal of Marketing* 19 (July 1951).

[3]Correlation coefficients between various market indexes are presented in Chapter 7.

liquid cash markets in various agricultural products and financial instruments suggested the development of other derivative futures contracts. Besides the liquidity of the underlying cash market, many of the other preconditions associated with successful futures contracts have been characteristic of the equity markets as well. In particular, there is sufficient price volatility so that an equity-based futures contract would hold interest for both hedgers and speculators. Moreover, equity cash prices are competitively determined in markets that disseminate price information widely, quickly, and accurately. In addition, there are a number of widely recognized and easily understood indexes of equity prices that provide an adequate basis on which to price and settle a contract.

Since equities have many of the characteristics needed for a successful derivative instrument and were received with such enthusiasm it seems odd that it took so long for these instruments to be introduced. Indeed, from a business perspective it could be argued that the introduction of this product was long overdue. But from the perspective of contract design and the historical development of futures markets, the introduction of stock index futures contracts occurred at an appropriate time and in many respects at the earliest possible time. To appreciate this seeming contradiction requires reviewing selectively the history of futures trading and contract development in the United States, starting with the very first agriculture-based contracts.

AGRICULTURAL HERITAGE

Futures markets had their start in agriculture, where they provided a method of insulating farmers, distributors, and processors of agricultural produce from the risk of unanticipated price changes. Farmers were seeking a way to secure a price that would yield a spread over their costs early in the harvest cycle, while processors and distributors were interested in guaranteeing an adequate supply of produce at a price that would ensure them a profit. Enabling farmers to contract with distributors and processors to make delivery at a prearranged price, well in advance of the actual delivery date, would satisfy the needs of both farmers and their direct customers. The economic need for such contracts was sufficiently strong that prior to the introduction of exchange-traded agriculture-based futures, off-exchange substitutes, which were in effect forward contracts (also known as "to arrive" contracts), had already developed.

In some ways, these off-exchange contracts served the same purpose as futures contracts. They were an inferior substitute, however, and the inadequacies inherent in forward contracts contributed to the development of futures contracts. One of the key problems with forward contracts was that they carried no assurance of reliability or performance. They were essentially a customized transaction between two parties operating on the basis of trust. If one party to the contract reneged, the other party had no way of being compensated for attendant losses except to take the matter to litigation; obviously, this would have been an unsatisfactory climax to a transaction initiated as a method of minimizing exposure to price risk. In addition, each forward contract had its own method of determining payment and price. Since price information was not generally available, the participants to a contract could never be certain of receiving the best terms. Besides lack of standardization of payment, there was no standardization of the quality of the commodities to be delivered. Consequently, there was no method of easily reselling a contract, even though various potential applications of forward delivery-type contracts do not actually require the delivery of the commodity. For example, speculators interested in profiting from price movements certainly do not need to make or take delivery of the underlying commodity; nor, in fact, do many types of hedgers.

In spite of the shortcomings of forward contracts, until the latter part of the 19th century they were the only available method of arranging for the future delivery of an agricultural commodity. When the Chicago Board of Trade, the first commodity exchange in the United States, was organized in 1848, the objective was largely to locate the forward contracting activity in one central place. Not until 1865 were the first standardized futures contracts in the United States traded at the Chicago Board of Trade. Their introduction revolutionized the process of arranging for forward delivery of a commodity.

The obvious advantages of futures trading compared with off-exchange forward arrangements were apparent, ensuring the success of the concept. Throughout the latter part of the 19th century, a number of exchanges that are still active today were developed.[4] The development of competitive exchanges and the growth of interest in futures contracts encouraged the proliferation of different types of futures contracts. These ultimately spanned a range of "commodities" extending from the original Chicago Board of Trade grain contracts to the recent stock index futures contracts. Unfortunately, the majority of new contracts have always failed to create sustainable trading interest at the outset. Exchanges have been energetic, however, both in designing new contracts based on different cash market instruments and in altering the basic structure of contracts so as to make them better suited to particular trading needs and particular cash instruments. As a result of these efforts, there are now 41 actively traded contracts. These contracts differ not only in the terms of the cash instrument on which they are based but also in key design characteristics. They reflect the evolutionary process that has led up to stock index contracts.

CONTRACT DEVELOPMENT ISSUES— STORABILITY

As previously noted, the first futures contracts were based on grains. Because grains are storable and the contracts are standardized instruments, a trader could take delivery of a futures contract, store the grain, and redeliver the grain on the next contract.

The following hypothetical example illustrates the delivery aspect of these futures contracts.

Step 1: Long 10 December wheat contracts (50,000 bushels) Short 10 March wheat contracts

---

[4]These include the Mid-America Commodity Exchange (1868); the New York Cotton Exchange (1870); the Kansas City Board of Trade (1871); the New York Mercantile Exchange (1872); the Minneapolis Grain Exchange (1881); the Coffee, Sugar, and Cocoa Exchange (1882); and the Chicago Mercantile Exchange (1898). Exchanges continued to be developed in the 20th century, principally the Commodity Exchange (1933) and the New York Futures Exchanges (1980).

Step 2: December 27, take delivery

Step 3: Store until expiration of
March contract

Step 4:   Close out March position by delivering
50,000 bushels

During the period between the two contract maturity dates, the commodity must be stored at a cost that includes the cost of actual physical storage and insurance and the cost of financing. The total of these costs is referred to as the cost of carry. This concept is at the core of a large number of trading strategies for financial as well as nonfinancial futures contracts and is also a major factor in explaining the prices for different months for the same contract. A primary example of a financial futures contract with this cost of carry aspect is the Treasury bond contract. Since insurance and storage costs are minimal for a Treasury bond, most of the cost of carry of Treasury bonds is the short-term financing rate incurred in taking delivery of a bond and re-delivering it on a distant contract. As a consequence, there are a number of trading strategies based on the recognition that the cost of carry for a bond contract is a short-term interest rate.

Of course, many commodities are perishable; that is, they have a limited storage life. Such commodities could not be as easily carried from one futures contract to another as commodities with a long storage life. Introducing futures contracts based on limited or noncarry commodities was a major departure from the original design of futures contracts. The Chicago Mercantile Exchange (CME) opened its operations with a futures contract based on butter. Because of the perishability of butter, this was a noncarry contract. Interestingly, all subsequent CME contracts have been of a limited carry or noncarry variety.

FINANCIAL INSTRUMENTS WITH AND WITHOUT FORWARD MARKETS

The next major contract development leading to the introduction of stock index futures contracts was the opening of the International Monetary Market (IMM), a wholly owned subsidiary of the

CME, in 1972.[5] This exchange was developed to offer an entirely new type of futures contract: futures based on financial instruments. The first listed contracts were based on foreign exchange. Foreign currencies were a logical choice for the first financial futures contracts for much the same reason that futures contracts began with grains. There was already a well-developed, off-exchange forward market. Thus the process of agreeing to make or take delivery at some future time was an established part of the domestic foreign exchange market in the United States prior to the introduction of currency futures. And as with grains, currency futures provided an exchange-traded substitute for what had previously been conducted off-exchange. The usefulness of these contracts is evidenced by the growing trading success of futures contracts in British pounds, Canadian dollars, Japanese yen, Swiss francs, and West German marks.

The Chicago Board of Trade was next with a financial futures contract, introducing the Government National Mortgage Association (GNMA) contract in 1975. This contract was based on a government-guaranteed debt obligation. The GNMA had also been traded in a well-developed forward market and thus was a natural choice for a futures contract.

Logically, the next step in the development of financial futures was to offer a contract based on a financial instrument for which there was no forward market. The IMM took this step in 1976, when it introduced the Treasury bill futures contract. In 1977 the Chicago Board of Trade followed with the introduction of the Treasury bond futures contract. Both contracts have been highly successful, with the Treasury bond contract becoming the most actively traded futures contract in any market. In both cases these contracts trade a larger daily dollar value of commitments than does the underlying cash market. Developing a successful U.S. Treasury note contract proved to be somewhat more difficult with several note contracts failing to develop sufficient trading interest. The Chicago Board of Trade managed to prevail by listing a successful 10-year U.S. Treasury note contract.

---

[5]Although there were a number of significant steps between the opening of the CME in 1898 and that of the International Monetary Market in 1972, from the perspective of this discussion they are of a lesser order of importance.

QUALITY DISTINCTIONS

One characteristic that all government security futures contracts have in common is the uniform and negligible credit risk of the underlying cash instrument. Government securities are differentiated by other characteristics, namely maturity and coupon (for issues of longer original maturity than one year). Indeed, in fulfillment of the obligation under the contract, the Treasury bond futures contract permits delivery of any U.S. Treasury bond with 20 years or more to maturity. To determine the invoice price of a deliverable security requires a simple mathematical transformation from the contract price to the invoice price of an eligible deliverable bond.

When several eligible deliverable securities differ in such characteristics as coupon and maturity, but not in quality, they are likely to be priced in a stable relationship to one another, a situation that is not likely to prevail when quality differences exist. Consequently, if the quality of deliverables were not standardized and controlled, the usefulness of the contracts in hedging, investing, and arbitraging applications would be seriously diminished, and such a contract would be unlikely to succeed.

Concern over controlling credit quality hampered the introduction of financial futures based on private-debt obligations. Whereas it is a straightforward matter to specify all U.S. Treasury bonds as deliverable and then to provide a method of converting each particular U.S. Treasury bond to deliverable units, this is not a straightforward matter for private-debt obligations, for example, certificates of deposits (CDs). For private-debt obligations to provide the basis for successful futures contracts, it is necessary that there be a generally accepted method of identifying obligations of like quality and that at any point in time such like-quality instruments trade at the same price. The solution to quality problems for CDs depended on the existence in the CD secondary market of a convention known as the "no-name" or "on-the-run" list. This is a CD secondary market-determined list of sufficiently similar, top-quality CDs trading with no price distinction based on quality. Cash market traders provide price quotes on no-name CDs applicable to all CDs on this list without differentiation. This informal grading arrangement had worked well in the cash market and therefore could be used as the basis for standardizing quality for a futures contract.

Obtaining good price quotes for uniform-quality private-debt obligations satisfied one necessary condition for having such an obligation serve as the basis for a futures contract. Another characteristic inherent in CDs that facilitated using them as the basis for a futures contract was the feasibility of deliveries. Not only were there no apparent supply problems, but in addition CDs were negotiable instruments, so that transferring ownership posed no particular problems.

In mid–1981 the Commodity Futures Trading Commission (CFTC) authorized three exchanges to trade CD futures contracts.[6] All three contracts relied on the CD secondary market convention to control for quality. Although deliverable grade has since been altered in response to CD secondary market assessment of what constitutes top-quality CDs, there has been no disruption in the orderly trading in these contracts. Their success can be further gauged by the fact that soon after their introduction the daily trading volume in CD futures exceeded the cash market volume. Moreover, deliveries have been conducted in an orderly manner indistinguishable from deliveries of other futures contracts.[7]

CASH SETTLEMENT

Delivery problems were an issue, however, in the consideration of other potential futures contracts. Eurodollar deposit contracts were a reasonable choice to follow CDs because they were also a commercial bank liability. Moreover, reliable price quotes for prime-quality Eurobank names were available through the widely

---

[6]The IMM, CBT, and NYFE all introduced such contracts, although the NYFE and CBT versions no longer trade.

[7]The introduction of Eurodollar futures, discussed later in the chapter, proved to be the undoing of the CD contract. These two contracts behaved too much alike for both to prevail and with the larger constituency for Eurodollars, it has become the dominant contract. The IMM CD contract, although still listed, is for all practical purposes dormant.

quoted London Interbank Offered Rate (LIBOR) and the market was international in scope and vast in size (exceeding $1 trillion). The difficulty with introducing such a contract was that all bank time deposits, including Eurodollar deposits, were not negotiable, thus preventing delivery of a physical instrument in fulfillment of an obligation under a futures contract.

The solution to this delivery problem was to design a cash settlement contract. Unfortunately, cash deliveries of commodity contracts had previously been used only in disreputable off-exchange trading.[8] So-called bucket shops offered wagers based on the performance of a given commodity of futures contract. The person involved in the wager was interested only in the potential of speculative gain and did not have any legitimate commercial need to be involved in the actual contract. These off-exchange activities were conducted outside the jurisdiction of exchanges and their regulatory authorities and were frequently illegal, running afoul of state gaming laws and regularly bilking patrons. As a consequence, exchanges as well as the CFTC shied away from cash settlement contracts and many states had anti-gaming laws explictly prohibiting such contracts.

By 1981 it had become clear to the regulatory authorities that Eurodollars futures, as well as several other potential contracts, would be tabled because of delivery problems unless cash settlement was permitted. The question of whether past abuses associated with cash settlement should prevent the next stage in futures contract development was debated. The CFTC decided in favor of cash settlement, however, and in late 1981 Eurodollar futures contracts were approved.[9] All approved contracts share the same cash settlement procedure. On the delivery day a sample of LIBORs was used as the basis for cash delivery. The delivery procedure is illustrated by the following hypothetical example:

---

[8]A Supreme Court decision in the early 20th century prohibited the trading of commodity contracts settling in cash. The authorizing legislation for the Commodity Futures Trading Commission in effect reopened the issue by granting that agency the authority to determine the definition of a commodity futures contract.

[9]The CBT and the NYFE also applied to the CFTC for authorization to trade a Eurodollar contract relying on cash settlement. Both exchanges were granted authority, but neither has yet listed a Eurodollar contract.

	Day before Delivery	Delivery Day
Contract price	$78.25	$78.50
Dollar value of change in price equals $625 (0.01 = $25)		Shorts transfer $625 per contract to longs ($25 x 25 b.p.)

This system of effecting deliveries has worked well, causing no unique problems or customer abuses. Interestingly, both the London International Financial Futures Exchange (LIFFE) and the Singapore Futures Exchange (SIMEX) had among their first contracts a Eurodollar deposit contract that also settled in cash based on a quote derived by sampling prime Eurobanks.[10]

AN INDEX OF PRICES OF HETEROGENEOUS ITEMS

After the principle of cash delivery had been successfully established for the Eurodollar deposit contract, it could be applied to other contracts in which delivery of the physical instrument was impractical. The only prerequisite was that there exist a reliable widely disseminated and easily understood "price" on which to settle the contract price in order to conduct a delivery.

With the cash delivery issue resolved, the equity market was the logical next focus for a futures contract. Although equity indexes themselves had been published for some time and could have been used as the basis for futures contracts before Eurodollars, the progression from CD to Eurodollar and then to stock index futures was orderly and appeared to suit the regulatory community. Basing a contract on a deliverable bank liability, the CD, and then going to a nondeliverable bank liability, the Eurodeposit, in a sense made the regulatory step to stock index futures with cash delivery less precipitate than it would have

---

[10]The United Kingdom also had to contend with laws that restricted the use of cash settlement contracts. In particular, there was a question as to the legal enforceability of a contract that settled in cash.

been if stock indexes had come immediately after U.S. Treasury obligations contracts. In fact, the Kansas City Board of Trade had proposed its Value Line Stock Index Futures Contract before either the CD or Euro-deposit futures had been proposed, but the Value Line contract was placed in regulatory limbo, receiving serious consideration only after the CD and Euro-deposit contracts establishing the cash settlement arrangements had been approved.

It was logical to approve cash settlement in the Euro-deposit futures contract before considering stock index futures. Although Euro-deposit futures represented a departure from traditional contract design, stock index futures were yet a further departure since these contracts sanctioned the concept of averaging together the prices of related but dissimilar items. The items comprised by the indexes were all securities, but they differed widely as to quality.

The introduction of stock index futures required not only a resolution of the cash settlement issue but also a clarification of the regulatory environment. Commodity trading activity, including trading in financial futures, is regulated by the CFTC, whereas equity trading is regulated by the Securities and Exchange Commission (SEC). Stock index futures contracts posed a jurisdictional issue since the underlying instrument was regulated by one agency and the derivative contract would presumably be regulated by a different agency. To further complicate matters, at about the same time consideration was also being given to trading options both on physical instruments other than individual equity issues (i.e., options on physicals) and on futures contracts (i.e., futures options). The SEC had been regulating equity options since their inception and was therefore a natural candidate to regulate the proposed new option contracts. Because of its responsibility for futures, however, the CFTC was the natural choice as the regulator of commodity options.

This potential regulatory dispute was rather amiably resolved by the chairman of the two regulatory agencies, Philip Johnson (CFTC) and John Shad (SEC). Under what has become known as the Johnson-Shad Agreement, the regulators decided that regulating futures contracts and options on futures, regardless of the underlying instrument, would be the responsibility of the CFTC, while the SEC would have jurisdiction over options on any security, including certificates of deposit, Treasury bills, bonds and notes, and groups or indexes of securities.[11] This agreement, which was publicly announced in December 1981, clarified the regulatory environment, so that the development of stock index futures contracts, commodity options, and options on physicals could proceed in a hospitable environment.

STOCK INDEXES

In designing stock index futures, there was no shortage of widely quoted, reliable and familiar indexes on which to base a contract. The Kansas City Board of Trade specified a contract having a size of $500 times the Value Line Index, a comprehensive geometric average of 1,683 stocks. The Chicago Mercantile Exchange established the value of its contract as equal to $500 times the Standard & Poor's 500 Composite Index, which is a value-weighted index. The New York Futures Exchange specified the value of its contract as $500 times the New York Stock Exchange Composite Index, which is a value-weighted index of over 1,500 NYSE-listed stocks. Basing the contracts on different indexes not only affects the size of the contracts, and consequently the required margin on each contract, but also their price volatility.

The most volatile contract and the largest contract in terms of value is the Value Line Average Composite. In the middle, in terms of both volatility and size, is the S&P contract. The NYSE contract is the smallest, and it tends to be the least volatile. Thus, unlike CD and Euro-deposit contracts, where the differences in indexes have less to do with the composition of the indexes than with the date and time they are constructed, competing stock index contracts have more significant distinctions. One might expect that the more volatile the contract, the more it will appeal to floor traders, whereas the less volatile the contract, the more it will appeal to institutional users. However the early

---

[11]The one area of overlap in jurisdiction is options on foreign currencies.

trading in these contracts offers little evidence in support of this conjecture.

Regardless of the relative volatility of a particular contract, stock index futures permit equity investors to effectively accomplish two objectives; they can buy the market, and they can hedge against market risk. Speculators in equities have had as one objective profiting from general price movement in the markets by buying a bullish market or selling a bearish one. Until the introduction of stock index futures, speculators could satisfy this objective only by dealing in stocks whose price movements were closely related to the general market. This strategy can be unsatisfactory, however, since the prices of individual stocks are continually being influenced by specific information that does not necessarily affect the entire market in the same way. There are mutual funds that comprise groups of stocks selected because their price behavior closely tracks an index of overall market movement. But mutual funds are not particularly well suited to speculation, largely because of their slowness in completing a transaction. Thus stock index futures provided a unique instrument for buying or selling the market.

The introduction of stock index futures contracts also presented hedgers with a unique opportunity. The concern of hedgers is in a sense the opposite of the concern of speculators, since instead of being interested in profiting from general moves in market prices, hedgers are interested in insulating portfolios or individual stocks from such moves. For example, suppose an equity portfolio manager anticipates a bearish period in the market that could erode the value of fundamentally sound portfolio that the manager is unable or unwilling to sell. Stock index futures provide such a manager with the option of shorting the market. If the manager's expectations are correct, the profit on futures will compensate for the loss on the portfolio. Such a strategy is also applicable when a manager has a portfolio that is anticipated to outperform the market but that the manager would like to insulate from possible adverse market moves. In such a case, if the market does deteriorate, the gain in futures will compensate for the loss in portfolio value. These examples of hedger and speculator strategies are indications of the possible applications unique to stock index futures that in part explain their immediate success.

These basic applications suggest the logical direction of continued developments in stock index futures. Hedgers and speculators may have a narrower focus than the entire market; they may be interested in a subset of the market. Evidence that investor attention is frequently focused on segments of the market is suggested by the existence of a variety of sub-indexes constructed by the New York Stock Exchange and Standard & Poor's. Both the New York Futures Exchange and the International Monetary Market have proposed trading in several sub-indexes. In particular, the NYFE has proposed trading futures contracts based on NYSE indexes of industrials, transportation, and utility stocks, and in early November it initiated trading in a futures contract based on the NYSE financial index. Moreover, the NYSE is developing a sub-index of energy stocks that could also be used as the basis for a futures contract. The IMM has proposed trading futures contracts based on the Standard & Poor's finance, utilities, and transportation indexes. Because of the potential for successful futures contracts, Standard & Poor's has agreed to develop three additional indexes based on stocks characterized as high technology, energy, and consumer staples.

The likelihood of success for these sub-index futures contracts would be in part a function of their uniqueness. A sub-index behaving in a distinct manner is more likely to trade successfully than is a contract based on an index closely correlated to other indexes for which contracts exist. In hedging, for example, using a contract based on a given instrument (for example, T-bill futures) to hedge a different cash instrument (for example, banker's acceptances) is a well-established futures trading technique known as cross-hedging. The possibility of successful cross hedges with various sub-index futures contracts diminishes the likelihood that they will all succeed. Speculative interest will similarly be determined by the uniqueness of the sub-indexes. Although not all sub-index contracts will behave distinctively, there is probably a need for more than just a composite stock index contract. Certainly, at least some of the proposed sub-index contracts might eventually establish themselves along with the composite index contracts. Unfortunately experience to date suggests that the enthusiastic support for futures contracts based on broad market indexes has not yet extended to these sub-indexes.

OPTIONS ON FUTURES

Another development in financial futures that is likely to have a direct effect on stock index futures is trading in commodity options, which was introduced in the fall of 1982. The CFTC in 1981 approved a limited pilot program authorizing each designated contract market to trade one option based on a futures contract, subject to CFTC approval. The fact that the IMM, NYFE, and Kansas City Board of Trade all proposed options on their stock index futures testifies to the dramatic early success of these futures.

Options on the cash instrument rather than the futures contract have also been proposed, subject to SEC authorization. Stock index options will also appear in this market: The New York Stock Exchange has proposed options on its composite index, its four sub-indexes, and its newly developed energy index. Both the American Stock Exchange and the Chicago Board Options Exchange also intend to trade stock index options based on their own constructed indexes. As with sub-indexes, initial interest in options on these stock index contracts has not yet been sufficient to develop a successful option contract.

Options on stock index futures and on the indexes themselves may attract to these markets participants who find options better suited to their needs than futures. Moreover, options on stock index futures contracts may serve to further attract participants in equity markets to futures markets. Option trading has become a firmly established adjunct to equity trading since it was introduced in the early 1970s. Equity traders who understand options but have shied away from futures because of a lack of experience with these instruments, may be attracted to this market by the introduction of options on stock indexes. What remains to be seen is which variant—options on cash contracts or options on futures contracts—will dominate. Each has apparent relative advantages and disadvantages, making it difficult to predict which will be successful or whether they can both generate a reasonable market.

One other development that has the potential to significantly affect financial futures trading generally is the increasing overseas involvement with financial futures. In some cases, commodity trading conducted outside the United States has been evolving in much the same way that such trading evolved in the United States. Starting with contracts based on indigenous agricultural products, there has been an evolution to financial instruments. This has been particularly the case in Australia and Canada. Alternatively, new futures exchanges have been developed in the early 1980s which opened offering financial futures only or in combination with traditional commodities such as gold. These exchanges include the London International Financial Futures Exchange (LIFFE), the Singapore Futures Exchange (SIMEX), the Hong Kong Futures Exchange and the Tokyo Futures Exchange.

With the advent of overseas trading in financial futures, trading in a futures contract beyond the closing time of one exchange becomes a very real possibility. The advantage of extended trading hours is that it enables a trader to lay off risk in another market if cash market prices move dramatically after a given exchange has closed. Cash market trading in certain instruments—including Eurodollars, U.S. government securities, precious metals, and foreign exchange—now goes on around the clock. Consequently, traders in one country can either cover their positions by taking offsetting positions in other countries or take advantage of rallies that gravitate from one time zone to another as markets close for the day. This activity has been facilitated by a mutual offset arrangement worked out between the IMM and the SIMEX. A Eurodollar futures order placed on either floor (the contracts are identical) can be either cleared at that exchange or specified as a contract to be cleared at the other exchange; i.e., the exchange not involved in execution. Thus a trader in the United States can after U.S. trading hours initiate a Eurodollar futures contract at the SIMEX which can be identified in such a way as to make it equivalent to a Eurodollar futures contract initiated at the IMM and vice versa. This makes cross-country (and of course cross time-zone) futures trading possible without it being any more difficult than if the trade had been executed domestically. The IMM-SIMEX link has worked so well that it is inevitable that other such links will be attempted.

Whether stock index futures contracts will attract sufficient interest to justify a market outside the United States is problematic. There is, however, active interest in U.S. equities outside the United States, and it is therefore conceivable that an overseas futures market in stock indexes will develop.

THE PROGNOSIS FOR FINANCIAL FUTURES

The probable development of futures markets has aspects of both widening and deepening participation—widening in the sense of additional trading vehicles and deepening in the sense of additional traders. Additional trading vehicles will be motivated by the same concern and objective that has motivated the development of every contract from the very first one offered at the Chicago Board of Trade in 1865: risk transfer. Commercial users, whether farmers, financial institutions, or corporations, have been well served by financial futures that have enabled them to transfer risk to willing speculators. This same objective has been behind the development of sub-index contracts on stock index futures, and it will no doubt lead to a variety of other instruments.

When cash settlement was accepted by the CFTC as an admissible method of delivery on a contract, the possibility of a whole new class of contracts was introduced. There are numerous measurable risks that could certainly be the basis for a contract but for which physical delivery would be either awkward or impossible. The stock index futures contract is a perfect example of a contract that would not have materialized without the cash settlement option. It is likely that exchanges will use cash settlement for contracts based on other private credits, in particular U.S. and foreign corporate debt issues. Efforts have also been made to use cash settlement as the basis for contracts on measurable risks rather than physical commodities. The Coffee, Sugar, Cocoa Exchange has listed a Consumer Price Index contract which has yet to generate widespread interest. Nevertheless it is likely that other such measurable risks will become the basis for contracts.

The deepening of the futures markets comes in part as a function of these products. Institutional investors for the most part watched the early development of financial futures from the sidelines. Institutional investors who had not previously been participants in futures markets were reluctant to become involved.

The trading environment and the instruments themselves were alien to cash market traders. Over time, however, these markets gained acceptance as they grew in size and diversity. Government dealers were quick to incorporate financial futures on government obligations into their trading strategies. In turn, their customers, financial intermediaries, money managers, and financial managers generally have begun to rely increasingly on financial futures.

To a lesser degree nonfinancial corporations have begun to consider the futures markets. Although they control large portfolios and could quickly become a significant factor in the futures markets, their potential still remains less than fully realized. In a similar category are pension and trust managers who for the most part have made little use of futures. This has in part been a consequence of a restrictive regulatory environment. In 1982, however, some liberalization began to be noticed. A Department of Labor opinion letter eased up somewhat on the restrictions on using futures in ERISA portfolios. In addition, the New York State insurance commissioner also indicated a willingness to reexamine a long-standing prohibition against the use of futures by insurance companies.

These regulatory changes have made a noticeable difference in the level of participation on the part of pension funds and insurance companies. This trend is likely to continue since the risk transfer function performed by futures is often not as efficiently or effectively replicated with cash instruments alone even for very large cash market participants. Moreover, a number of institutions needing futures-like risk management but unable or unwilling to enter the market directly have become active participants through intermediaries. Many interest rate insurance and portfolio programs rely on futures for their implementation. Thus over time the number of futures market participants, whether direct or indirect, has continued to grow.

In summary, the outlook seems bright for financial futures in general and for stock indexes in particular. The rapid annual growth rate of financial futures trading volume should continue and perhaps even accelerate as new contracts and new participants join these markets. In the midst of this active environment, it is clear that the rather remarkable early success of stock index futures is likely to be sustained.

INDEX